THE WAR ON ILLAHEE

THE
WAR ON
ILLAHEE

Genocide, Complicity, and Cover-Ups
in the Pioneer Northwest

MARC JAMES
CARPENTER

Yale
UNIVERSITY PRESS
New Haven and London

Published with assistance from the John R. Bockstoce Endowment Fund.

Yale University Press books may be purchased in quantity for
educational, business, or promotional use. For information, please
e-mail sales.press@yale.edu (U.S. office) or sales@yaleup.co.uk
(U.K. office).

Set in Janson type by IDS Infotech Ltd.
Printed in the United States of America.

Library of Congress Control Number: 2025938336
ISBN 978-0-300-27573-5 (hardcover)

A catalogue record for this book is available from the British
Library.

Authorized Representative in the EU: Easy Access System
Europe, Mustamäe tee 50, 10621 Tallinn, Estonia,
gpsr.requests@easproject.com

10 9 8 7 6 5 4 3 2 1

I dedicate this book to my family. To my parents, Will and Melissa, who raised me to value curiosity, embrace kindness, and chase my dreams. To my late birth father, Jim, who tried to pass the best parts of himself on to his children, including his love of history and food. To my aunt Sara, who showed me how to blaze another kind of path. And most of all to my wife, Alissa, who makes every part of my life and my self better. As we ride our metaphorical brontosaurus over the horizon together, I can't wait for the new adventures to come.

Contents

THE WAR ON ILLAHEE

Introduction and Apologia

ANY IN THE PACIFIC Northwest struggled in the hard times of the 1890s. One of the few avenues of government support was the Oregon Soldiers' Home, a network of care facilities meant for indigent veterans who had served in the Union Army during the U.S. Civil War, indigent veterans of the "war with Mexico," and "indigent soldiers and volunteers who served not less than thirty days in any of the Indian wars in Oregon, Washington Territory, or Idaho Territory." Hundreds of applications poured in.[1]

Required to describe which wars they had served in, many men simply wrote "Indian wars"—sometimes preceded by a location (such as Oregon), sometimes followed by a year or set of years. Most of these years fell between 1847 and 1858, when the wars of conquest waged by Euro-Americans in the Pacific Northwest were fought more by "volunteers" than by army regulars. The form asked veterans to list the specific wars they had been in. But the names since affixed to these wars—among others the Cayuse War, the Rogue River War, the Puget Sound War, the Walla Walla War, the Yakima War—were not the names used by most of the Americans who had fought in them. Alexander York remembered two terms of service in "Indian wars of 1855–1856." Jesse A. Applegate referred to an "Indian War" of 1853, Andrew J. Wiley to a "1856 Indian war." W. F. Tolmie referred to "Indian Disturbances in middle Oregon" in 1854, Elijah F. Whisler to "the outbreak of the Indians" in 1856. They were writing answers on a form that asked for the name of the war in which they had been involved—but specific names eluded most of them. They had fought against "the Indians," not in particular conflicts

I

with particular groups. As these White settlers remembered it, they had simply fought in the "Indian wars," wars of extermination against any and all Native polities and people in a given place and time.[2]

There is utility in considering the violent colonization of the Pacific Northwest from 1847 to 1858 (and in many places beyond) as a single period of "Indian wars," just as many of the perpetrators did, and just as they eventually convinced multiple government bodies to do. There were individual wars, supposedly with specific Native polities, within and beyond that period. Besides those listed above, one might, then or now, include the Coeur d'Alene War, the Fraser Canyon War, the "Snake" Wars, the Chilcotin War, and others; the Nez Perce, Modoc, and Bannock/Shoshone Wars of the 1870s, although more federal and perhaps more limited in their scope, were grouped into the same broad "Indian wars" by many.

But particularly in the middle of the 1800s, these wars were outgrowths of general invasion and attendant violence. Framing the Indian wars of the Pacific Northwest as many invading colonists saw them—as a continuous war on Indians generally—allows for a better understanding of the scope and reach of violence in the era. Separation and segmentation of particular wars can risk excluding critical context and underestimating the breadth of the killings and other devastation.

Indian wars, in the Pacific Northwest as in many other places, were an acceleration and consummation of existing threats and acts of violence, rather than a wholesale shift. As Washington volunteer Samuel Stewart wrote of the period, "We were fighting Indians before we joined the army just the same as we did in the army[;] a man did not ha[ve] to belong to the army in those days to fight Indians." Settlers committed innumerable acts of everyday violence before, during, and after the wars; indeed, the wars were often incited by just such acts. Viewing these wars as multiple manifestations of the same pursuit of conquest—as a structure rather than a series of events, one might say—better allows these everyday acts of violence to be legible as part of a greater whole. Many settlers dreamed of the day when they would be able to kill every Native person in the region. Nearly all shared a goal—or least an assumption—that Native polities and land rights would be extinguished, with or without the reluctant consent of Native communities. In the Pacific Northwest, settlers and the state embarked on a campaign of extermination from at least 1847 to 1858. The individual wars of this period were intensifications of that campaign.[3]

I refer to this campaign to destroy Native polities and people in the Pacific Northwest as the War on Illahee. The many Native communities struggling against settler conquest in this period used many different names in their own languages to describe their own lands. But most communities would at least have been familiar with *Illahee*, a term from Chinook Jargon (the simplified Chinuk *wawa* language used when trading with Europeans) that can be translated as "homeland." My hope is that this title might thus adequately describe a shared experience of war using a term both the defenders and the invaders would recognize.[4]

As a framing concept, the War on Illahee highlights the devotion to colonial conquest shared among different Euro-American settlers, governments, and military personnel. Disputes over the efficacy, feasibility, and (occasionally) morality of attempts to murder groups of Indigenous persons in the Pacific Northwest were common. But nearly all Euro-Americans supported movements to dismantle Indigenous peoples' power, control, and autonomy in their homelands. Historical Euro-American disputes over the best or cheapest means of dispossessing Native communities were typically disagreements about tactics, not goals. Some officials might have hoped to minimize the killings of Indigenous individuals. But they shared the goal of taking Native land and destroying Native sovereignty. Contemporary Euro-American disputes over how and when Native lands could best be seized, and how orderly the invasion could be rendered, should not be read casually as disagreements about the ultimate pursuit of Native land by the American empire. White conscientious objectors were the exception.

The War on Illahee was far from the first or last such general war on Native people in the history of the United States. In some ways it was a zenith of a movement that predated the formation of the country. Many participants in the Pacific Northwest wars had been in Indian wars they saw as analogous—wars against Creek polities in the 1810s and the 1830s; military and paramilitary attacks on the Cherokee Nation in the 1820s and 1830s; the Black Hawk War of 1832 and the brutal violence surrounding it; the wars on Seminole polities that stretched through the first half of the 1800s; and many, many others. Similarly, some of those who killed in the Pacific Northwest took part in other invasions in the years that followed. And many who took part in invasions of Illahee drew on experiences from the U.S.–Mexico War, similarly a brutal war for land justified through racialization.

The proposition of an overarching War on Illahee should not imply that individual conflicts in the Northwest were not important, or that each of the various wars does not deserve discrete analysis; indeed, many remain critically understudied. The sovereign governments of the United States and many Indigenous polities unquestionably dealt with the wars individually, with lasting effects on treaties and territory. Nor should the proposition that there was a War on Illahee between 1847 and 1858 exclude connections to later wars against Native polities and people in the region. The multiple attacks on Indigenous polities often grouped under the "Snake" War, in the 1860s especially, were in many ways a continuation of the War on Illahee. And the same White violence, thirst for land, and disregard for Native sovereignty drove the only somewhat more targeted Modoc War, Nez Perce War, and Bannock/Shoshone Wars the United States waged against Indigenous polities in the 1870s. There is utility in a more overarching frame, as historian Katrine Barber suggests, that takes in over three decades of "settler-perpetrated rape, murder, and alienation of territory [that] instigated retaliatory violence, drawing forth the killing capabilities of volunteer militias and the authority of the U.S. military" across the region.[5]

What sets the War on Illahee somewhat apart from the rest of the violent campaign to seize Native land in the Northwest is the extent to which it was fought by Euro-American volunteers outside the regular armed forces, *and* the breadth of the struggles over how it should be recorded and remembered. Because the seizure of Native land in the 1850s was a foundational part of the stories of Oregon and Washington, instigated and fought most often by local settlers, the wars of the era had to be addressed by early historians. There were sharp disagreements between Euro-Americans over the best means to take over Native land in the region; some government figures loudly complained about the inconveniently wanton violence inflicted by so many Pacific Northwest pioneers. The disagreements led to the creation of a record of contentions and crimes that had to be addressed, ignored, or silenced by those writing histories of the period.

Much of the violence dealt out in the War on Illahee was done by "volunteers," White settlers who were typically soldiers only in the loosest sense of the word. Men would organize into murderous bands of marauders at any hint of what settlers called "Indian perfidy," real or imagined, and attack any Native person they could find nearby. If these attacks led to full-scale war, then settler bands organized to do violence might be able to draw government pay. But the wanton violence volunteers inflicted was typically the same whether or not they were serving as soldiers when they killed. The only difference was when they might expect pay on top of the plunder they seized in their attacks. Money thus shaped disagreements over what counted as a war, and thereby which acts of violence might deserve remuneration from state and federal governments.[6]

The violence of the volunteers, often explicitly genocidal, presented a special problem for those who hoped to create a heroic history of the early Northwest in the decades that followed. The actions of volunteers were at the center of most nineteenth-century efforts to celebrate, censor, or calculatedly critique the worst aspects of colonial violence in the Pacific Northwest. But they were not alone. Almost all Northwest pioneers of the 1850s were complicit in genocide.

As norms shifted in the decades that followed, the first generations of heritage groups and Northwest historians warped historical evidence in contradictory ways. They were largely united in trying to render pioneers and most volunteer troops as blameless heroes. But there were significant disagreements concerning what kinds of violence should be celebrated, minimized, or silenced. Those writing the first drafts of pioneer history were often divided over which stories they should tell—and which stories they could sell.

This book is an interrogation of how Euro-American pioneers and the historians who first recorded their stories waged, remembered, commemorated, historicized, and covered up the wars and other violence they inflicted on Native people in the Pacific Northwest during the War on Illahee—and beyond. In my research, I dredged the records of the heritage organizations invested in pioneer narratives. I surveyed the published and unpublished writings of many of the early historians of the Pacific Northwest and delved into their correspondences and interviews. And I went through reams of pioneer reminiscences and letters, published and unpublished, famous and obscure, to find their stories of what they had done and what they thought should be said about it.

What emerged is a history of horrific violence and clashing cover-ups. Many historians and history-minded organizations deliberately and sometimes explicitly obscured truths about the pioneer conquest of the Pacific Northwest they deemed unsuitable for public consumption. Fortunately for my purposes, they seldom agreed on which acts of pioneer violence could or should be censured or censored. Certain acts of wanton violence, like the Lupton Massacre and the murder and mutilation of Walla Walla/Walúulapam leader Peo-Peo-Mox-Mox, were famous enough that early histories had to reckon with them. Other analogous events were celebrated, denied, or ignored—sometimes by the same author, in different settings. I was able to trace different and only somewhat successful strategies for silencing the most notorious acts, and a broader history of complicity in cover-ups.

The deeper I got into the sources, the more I found evidence of murder, mayhem, and acts of genocide that did not appear in most history books. This evidence led me back to more famous "official" sources from government figures with new eyes, seeing previously missed plans for attacks and dreams of extermination. Digging through the archives of pioneer historians sometimes led me to suppressed Indigenous sources from a century or more ago, ignored but retained by those who preferred heroic narratives to hard truths. The cover-ups I had planned to discuss, it turned out, were *still* helping to create silences and distortions in the historical record.

The War on Illahee is thus both a new history of pioneer violence within and beyond the wars on Native people in the mid-1800s American Pacific Northwest, *and* a new history of how the War on Illahee—along with the broader tides of colonial violence of which it was a part—was remembered, commemorated, and forgotten by Americans in the decades that followed. Pioneers and their hagiographers disagreed about which acts were heroic. Settlers clashed over when genocide was best celebrated, downplayed, denied, or ignored. These disagreements accidentally preserved archives of atrocity, from the mouths and pens of pioneers themselves.

Each Native polity, ethnie, and person had their own experiences and strategies in dealing with the invasions and ensuing erasures I discuss. Some Native people fighting to preserve their communities even selectively drew on pioneer nostalgia and distortion as a part of their survival strategies. I have done my best to amplify Indigenous voices past and present, and to underline Native dynamism and action in the stories I tell. But this is, primarily, a history of the American invaders whom the diverse Native peoples of the Pacific Northwest had to deal with.

Every choice of depth and breadth sacrifices something. Following the lead of my sources and interrogating the Pacific Northwest wars of the 1840s, 1850s, and 1860s as an interconnected story has turned up useful insights and continuities. Stories of Native persons killed while "trying to escape," for example, take on an even more sinister aspect when they pop up again and again and again across the region—occasionally with tacit admission that escape stories were only a convenient excuse for outright murder. A regional approach to the early writers of pioneer history has been similarly useful, particularly as the historians and heritage organizations I discuss coordinated, clashed, and conspired with one another across state lines. Zooming in on particular incidents and conflicts in even more detail than I do here would yield other insights; zooming out to connect the invasion of the American Pacific Northwest even more extensively to broader regional, national, and global narratives would, too. The stories herein deserve more space than they could be given. Some have already been well told. Many still need to be.

In chapter 1 I demonstrate that American pioneers brought settler colonial norms and genocidal ideations with them to the Pacific Northwest. I reexamine the Cayuse War of the late 1840s alongside other war acts, demonstrating the extent to which Euro-Americans pursued war on Native people generally, whatever the supposed casus belli. I argue that too much focus on inciting incidents as proclaimed by pioneers, and particularly on assumptions that any given Indian war stemmed from this or that act of supposed Native aggression, risks underestimating Euro-American dedication to colonial conquest. I examine threats and acts of extermination in early 1850s Oregon Territory, as they related to treaty making, land seizure, and war, pushing back against long-standing historiographical narratives that pit virtuous federal officials against wicked vigilantes. Genocide was often threatened and sometimes pursued in the 1850s, viewed as an unfortunate tool by some Euro-Americans and a long-term goal by many others. Nearly all, particularly among those in power, were complicit.

In chapter 2 I examine the most famous period of genocide in the history of the Pacific Northwest, amid the Rogue River Wars of southern Oregon in the mid-1850s. The wanton violence in southern Oregon is best known not because it was unusual, I demonstrate, but because military figures objected to more of the mayhem in that region than elsewhere in the Northwest—most often on practical grounds. I show the extent to which murderous pioneers expanded the war across the Northwest. I interrogate the often-abused pioneer identifier "friend of the Indians," showing how many who embraced that title perpetrated or at least supported violent conquest and even genocide. Murders and mass killings were not restricted to southern Oregon, nor were they necessarily limited by class, gender, or profession among the pioneers.

In chapter 3 I discuss the expansion of the War on Illahee in the Washington Territory in the mid-1850s, before and into what is typically labeled the Puget Sound War in northwestern Washington and the Yakima Wars in southeastern Washington. As in Oregon, Euro-American aggression incited these wars, and killings by pioneers and volunteers did not typically reach the official reports. I examine and deconstruct the pioneer presumptions of "Indian hostility" (including the fragile historical binaries that differentiated "friendly Indians" in settler imaginations). Devotion to empire and bloodlust was common among the invaders in Washington and Oregon alike. Dreams and threats of genocide came from military and territorial officials, as well as everyday pioneer men and women. Greater reliance on Native people for work and war than in Oregon modulated but did not negate Washington pioneer plans for mass murder.

In chapter 4 I examine the peak of the War on Illahee in 1855–56, when Euro-Americans strove to kill or capture almost every Native person they could in the Pacific Northwest. I discuss new details about mass killings, both the (comparatively) well known and the previously obscure, as war accelerated across the Northwest in this period. I reveal suppressed histories of torture and mutilation—and often, community celebrations of those acts—by volunteers and other pioneers. And I survey the understudied efforts, in Oregon and Washington alike, to force nearly every Native person in the region—"friendly" or not—into often-deadly internment camps amid genocidal warfare.

In chapter 5 I show how the War on Illahee continued into the supposed peace in Oregon and western Washington in the late 1850s, focusing especially on the Oregon Trails of Tears, the thievish tyranny that punctuated early reservation life, and the sharp limits of Euro-American law and allyship in the era. My overview of the Oregon Trails of Tears uses new lenses and new evidence to demonstrate travails even deadlier than has been typically asserted. I examine a few specific persons and places in the early reservation system to demonstrate broader norms of graft, theft, and quasi-judicial murder, implicating Indian agents and military officers alike. And I interrogate one of the more famous murders of a Native person in 1850s Oregon, both to probe the limits of White justice in the period and to unpack what stories of justice said and were meant to say in the era. Complicity in the murder of Native people, I argue, was nearly ubiquitous among pioneers. Even settlers who gently critiqued the worst excesses of pioneer violence and genocide typically sided with White supremacists over the neutral rule of law, during and after the War on Illahee.

In chapter 6 I discuss half-hidden histories of the lynchings of Native people in the pioneer Pacific Northwest, focusing especially but not exclusively on judicial and military lynchings during and after the wars in Washington Territory in the late 1850s. Lynching was a part of pioneer violence before, during, and after the War on Illahee—indeed, each of the previous chapters contains at least one account of a lynching. By removing the assumption that the involvement of a government or military official automatically makes a hanging just or lawful, I suggest, we can see the most famous hangings—in the aftermath of war in northwestern Washington and in the last steps of war in southeastern Washington—as akin to the same violence perpetrated by less official figures. Much as previous chapters draw on private pioneer accounts to show a genocidal war much more similar to many Indigenous memories of events than the official reports, in chapter 6 I use pioneer sources to show unjust killings in and beyond the courts extending before, through, and past the wars of the era—just as some Indigenous oral accounts remember it.

Chapter 7 connects the War on Illahee to the "Snake" War of the 1860s, perhaps the least known of the obscure wars of the Pacific Northwest. Although narratives of the war period often stop in the 1850s, I show that many of the same men fought the same war against Native people generally in the 1860s as they had in the previous decade. The term *Snake* was not a specific ethnic referent but an insult, widely understood as such by American and Indigenous communities alike. Americans deployed the term against the Yakama in the 1850s with the same venom as they did against Shoshone and Paiute groups in the 1860s—a slur that persists to the present in the standard naming of the Snake War. The targets and the terrain were sometimes different, as pioneer murder squads stalked eastern Oregon, Washington, and California, and ranged across the Rocky Mountains and the Great Basin—now often as regional regulars rather than local volunteers. The actions and rhetoric matched the War on Illahee, as ubiquitous calls for mass extermination were supported by the pioneer public. Perhaps because the obscurity of the Snake War made the work of erasure less urgent to pioneer historians, the disjunctures—deliberate and otherwise—between what certain military men on the ground wrote at the time and what they wanted their historical narratives to be are especially stark and provable.

In chapter 8 I examine one major method early histories of the pioneer Pacific Northwest used to deal with war crimes too recent and notorious to ignore or discount: historians blamed infamous acts on a violent fringe, and thus left the rest of the colonizers honorably innocent. By creating what I call "settler colonial sin-eaters," Northwest historians in the 1870s and 1880s were able to absolve those parts of the pioneer community with whom they identified from any inconvenient guilt. Here and in the following chapters, I underline some of the ways in which money shaped pioneer history and memory. Historians who were too accurate in their portrayals of pioneer violence, I demonstrate, struggled to find publication and profits—and this awareness of the history market shaped them and their successors.

In chapter 9 I show how pro-volunteer regional historians and heritage societies—especially the Indian War Veterans of the North Pacific Coast—significantly reshaped the ways in which the wars of the Northwest were remembered and honored, locally and nationally. Responding to narratives that made virtually all pioneers except them blameless, some Euro-American veterans of wars of the Pacific Northwest insisted instead that they deserved praise, pensions, and privileged posterity—all of which they eventually acquired. Historians and pioneers associated with the volunteer veterans embraced full-throated denials of pioneer war crimes in the face of overwhelming evidence, and they justified White violence with assertions of near-infinite Native perfidy. Their fight to distort the historical record in the 1880s and 1890s was largely successful, including the procurement of a federal imprimatur for acts that federal officials and generals had decried as illegitimate in the 1850s.

In chapter 10 I elucidate and analyze the "pioneer code": the broad understanding that all stories of Euro-American pioneers must be heroic, no matter the evidence. I examine the interaction between this code and changing opinions on which stories needed to be suppressed. Pioneer rape culture, for example, had always been framed as a subject unfit for print, whereas there were disagreements about where and when the killings of Native noncombatants should be covered up. Even as regional historians in the early 1900s strove for more rigorous scholarship, most still consciously avoided breaking the pioneer code as they saw it—and advised their fellow history writers to do the same. As American public tastes changed, historians of the Northwest diminished or excluded previously celebrated war acts, and even entire conflicts, that no longer matched what Americans wanted their story to be.

In chapter 11 I examine a clash between two public history narratives of the Northwest in the 1900s and 1910s. Monuments arose alongside more ephemeral acts of memory making, such as pageants and parades, that collectively crafted a gauzier version of the pioneer past in uneasy tension with continued celebrations of Indian killers. Inflected by a rise in questions about American empire and increased fascination with "authentic" Native life, the popular history imbued in these monuments typically continued and furthered the erasures and celebrations of the texts they drew from. But increasingly, old narratives of "good" and "bad" pioneers were replaced by new narratives of "good" and "bad" Indians. This chapter ends with a few instances in which Native people cooperated with pioneer historians, suggesting a view of early twentieth-century Native rights advocates that takes into account the decades of genocidal acts and policies they were struggling against. Native activists fighting for a future used the tools and allies that could get—which included, in some cases, playing along with nostalgic half-truths and pioneer puffery.

Putting pioneer crimes and cover-ups in the same narrative should shift conversations about credulity and complicity. There remains a tendency in most popular and some academic narratives of the pioneer Pacific Northwest to isolate violence to particular regions or particular actors. Colonial violence has sometimes been portrayed as a problem particular to southern Oregon, southern Washington, or just plain transplanted Southerners. This book demonstrates a continuity of violent intentions and genocidal dreams across the pioneer Pacific Northwest. Differences in the levels of support for colonial violence between different sections and Euro-American populations, though sometimes real, have been exaggerated. I demonstrate both the frequency of acts of wanton violence beyond official reports and the near ubiquity of pioneer acceptance of that violence. In the 1850s and 1860s, White invaders who stole from, assaulted, and murdered Native people would almost never face punishment from Euro-American law or society for their crimes. And they knew it.

Proving the untruths propagated by pioneers and their historians can also weigh on the balance of historical narratives about key events. When scholars are faced with vastly disparate stories from Euro-American and Native historical traditions, many have an instinct to report all stories with attempted neutrality. Others seek truth in the middle. Both stances might feel reasonable and are sometimes appropriate. But as I demonstrate, some of the differences between Euro-American and Native narratives of colonial violence are latter-day impositions by pioneers and those who loved them, or distortions—wrought of racism—that became canon. Most of the new stories of violence and dreams of genocide herein come from the perpetrators and their allies, writing before changing mores rendered their actions retroactively repugnant to some other Euro-Americans. Stripped of the veneer added for posterity, pioneer memories of what happened often mirror Indigenous histories of the same events. In many cases, there are *not* disparate narratives, but rather two sides of the same story—rendered obscure by the efforts of generations of history writers who preferred gauzy tales to hard truths.

Throughout this text, I predominantly and interchangeably use the terms *Native* and *Indigenous* to refer to the original peoples of the lands now claimed by the United States. I use the terms *Indian* and *Native American* historically but not pejoratively, typically indicating the language or perceptions of the persons or groups I am discussing. Occasionally, but not usually, I put quotation marks around these terms to highlight their constructed nature. When quoting historical figures who used particularly poisonous racial slurs, I have replaced some or all of the internal vowels with underscores. I recognize that norms regarding offensive language in historical texts vary and change; this approach seemed the best balance to me at the time of writing.

Where possible, I have used more exact designations for Indigenous persons and polities. First and foremost, I privilege self-identification for historical Native persons; I have attempted to explain in the notes when orthography or tribal identifiers in the text are unusual as a result. I have erred on the side of caution, for better or worse, in ascribing specific Native identities for the people described herein. Pioneer killers only sometimes knew the identities of those they murdered, and the ubiquity of displacements and deaths from colonialism has made tracing a challenge in many cases.

Nation is a particularly tricky term of multiple contexts. One sense of *nation* is a group of people with a mix of shared descent, history, or culture *and* sovereign rights and relationships to particular spaces, biota, and practices. In this sense there have been and are a multitude of Indigenous nations in the Pacific Northwest, since time immemorial, who passed their sovereignty and responsibilities on to their present and future heirs in recognized and unrecognized Native American nations. However, the web of reciprocal and personal relationships that characterized most Indigenous government structures in the Pacific Northwest before colonial invasion fits uneasily, at best, with discussions of *nation* as the term is typically used in history and theory. The nation-state chauvinism in American and international law might require a recourse to the broad use of the term *nation* to affirm the sovereign rights of Native peoples and governments. But I worry that reflexively projecting modern definitions of *nation* (in the narrow sense) into the past risks distorting history, hiding the pluralities present in many traditional forms of government, and erasing the work of nation building by members of Native nations past, present, and future. My uses of the term *Native nation* in this text thus refer specifically to Native nations perceived, projected, or built as such.[7]

In general, I instead use the word *polities* to refer to Indigenous governments or political units. In doing so I make no assertion that the group so described was or was not a nation at the point in history I am discussing; in other words, I leave the work of determining the precise parameters and historicity of any given Native nation's nationhood to other scholars and communities. I use the term *ethnie* to refer to groups with some mix of shared history, culture, or language, and with a shared identity therefrom. And of course, in the past as in the present, Indigenous polities *and* individuals often contained multiple ethnies.[8]

When discussing the invaders, I use the word *pioneer* in this book to refer to the mostly Euro-American migrants to the Pacific Northwest who styled themselves as such, largely during the 1840s to 1860s. Many Americans in the 1800s understood the term *pioneer* as a reference to foot soldiers of colonialism. I use it here with the original martial meaning of the word foregrounded. I use the term *settler* to refer more generally both to the pioneers and to the generations of migrants and descendants who have followed. Neither term is without flaws. To call the people who invaded the Pacific Northwest in this period pioneers risks conflating colonialism with innovation and discovery, the other valence of the term. To label them settlers might evoke stereotypes of Indigenous people as unsettled wanderers, and risks reifying the false notion that Indigenous peoples' and polities' rights to their land were somehow lesser. The term *settler* has been usefully problematized by scholars and theorists in recent decades; I herein attempt similar recontextualization with the term *pioneer*, as a way to signal the centrality of violence in the conquest of what became America.[9]

Euro-Americans unquestionably committed acts of genocide in the Pacific Northwest, as defined by the United Nations. My use of *genocide* and *genocidal* in this text is narrow, describing only the acts "committed with intent to destroy, in whole or in part, a national, ethnical, racial or religious group" that appear in United Nations Convention on the Prevention and Punishment of the Crime of Genocide. The U.N. Convention makes it a crime not only to commit genocide, but to conspire to commit it, attempt it, publicly incite it, or be complicit in it. The evidence exists to render a broad array of Euro-American leaders, government figures, newspaper editors, military personnel, and everyday men and women in the Northwest retroactively guilty under the convention. Even more pioneers and settlers could be found so under the section of the convention that makes the forcible transfer of children and "measures intended to prevent births," if committed with the intent to destroy, genocidal crimes. Although scholars disagree about some incidents, no reasonable and informed historian can argue against the basic fact that numerous acts of genocide, under these definitions, were committed as a part of many American invasions of Native lands.[10]

The U.N. Convention on Genocide offers a useful baseline definition because it puts forward parameters for a punishable crime that a great number of nations, including the United States, have agreed to. Adjectives might be one way to push past some of the definitional impasses that genocide studies and related fields are too often mired in. *Cultural genocide* (discussed briefly below) has been a useful means of discussing and differentiating certain acts of genocide that do not fall under the U.N. Convention. Government officials who enacted policies that they knew would result in genocide might be deemed guilty of "genocidal negligence" or what legal scholar Alexander Greenawalt has termed "knowledge-based genocide." The Holocaust and perhaps other modern acts of genocide that killed hundreds of thousands of people over a short time can, when suitable, be differentiated from others by means of language—political scientist Robert Melson suggests "modern genocide" as one possibility; "industrialized genocide" might be another.[11]

The worthwhile project of determining when, how, and whether nations or governments pursued or were complicit in genocide should not obscure genocidal acts by individuals. It makes sense, in many contexts, to weigh and assess the guilt of nations and governments. If nothing else, all of the American people who committed acts of genocide in the 1800s are dead, but many of the societal and governmental structures they were supported by and embedded in live on. Whether, when, and in what ways the "United States" (defined variously as the governments, citizenry, imagined communities, military forces, and so on that make up the whole) pursued genocide is an important scholarly question. But for better or worse, the law currently on the international books is primarily concerned with prosecuting "persons ... whether they are constitutionally responsible rulers, public officials or private individuals"; decisions related to the "responsibility of a State for genocide" are left to be determined by international courts. It is beyond question that persons in the United States—sometimes with official roles in government—committed acts of genocide and related crimes as defined in the U.N. Convention. I describe several such acts herein, along with an American pioneer culture that accepted them as normal and, in many circles, embraced them as admirable. Complicity in genocide (Article IIIe of the U.N. Convention) was so ubiquitous in the American Pacific Northwest of the 1850s and 1860s, from officials to everyday citizens, that the government and culture of the whole must be viewed as guilty.[12]

My use of the term *genocide* herein to describe only acts that count as such under the U.N. Convention should not be taken to imply that no other acts should be considered genocidal. In all likelihood, at least some of the many perpetrators of mass killings not specifically flagged as genocidal in this text had genocidal intent that has not yet been proven with historical evidence. And by and large, determining and applying extensions of parameters of the term *genocide* beyond what is explicitly stipulated in international law is not an ambition of this work.

I do make occasional reference to cultural genocide—acts attempting to destroy a people by destroying their culture. This grievous category of crime was abrogated from the original U.N. Convention on Genocide and remains uncodified as such in international law. I depart from some scholars in insisting on the utility of *cultural genocide* as a framework somewhat separable from physical genocide, particularly in discussions of resistance. *Every* act of physical genocide is also, of course, an act of cultural genocide, and the two often co-occur and intermingle. But the strategies used to resist coercive assimilation and other attacks on culture are sometimes different—and sometimes broader—than the strategies used to resist groups or governments bent on physical extermination. Critiques of the use of the term *cultural genocide* might more usefully be refigured as critiques of the *mis*use of the term. Differentiating acts of genocide does not make any of them *not* genocide. But aside from this stipulation, I have consciously avoided probing into or policing exactly what the edges of either concept should be.[13]

I also avoid the troubling term *attempted genocide*, which has some-times been applied to campaigns of extermination in the Far West. Nearly all genocides that receive historical attention were "attempted." Many Armenian people in the Ottoman Empire survived the Armenian Genocide, and many Indigenous communities in the Pacific Northwest and elsewhere persevered past the organized and disorganized attempts to eliminate them. Those who wish to append the term *attempted* to de-scriptions of genocidal killings must feel an onus to explain why *attempted* is appropriate for the killings in question. Overapplication of *attempted* risks diluting the heinous acts thereby described. I leave deter-minations about the boundaries of each of these terms to other scholars and eventually, perhaps, to the courts.[14]

The term *massacre*, indicating a brutal and unjust mass killing, has been used for centuries as a rhetorical and ideological weapon against In-digenous communities. In the Pacific Northwest, the most famous appli-cation of the term is in the so-called Whitman Massacre of 1847, a label I follow other scholars in rejecting. Different norms across cultures and times about what constitutes a valid act of war further complicate use of the term.[15]

In this text, I have used the word *massacre* only to describe mass kill-ings that *both* the perpetrators *and* their victims would recognize as be-yond the rules of law and war if inflicted on their own communities. I do not label as massacres mass killings that I might personally find abhor-rent, but which may have been acts of legitimate reciprocal violence ac-cording to the legal culture of at least one side. I have erred on the side of caution; it is likely that more mass killings were massacres, under this definition, than I describe as such here. But given the potency of the label, and the harms done by its promiscuous application to the actions of Native fighters, I have used it only when the evidence suggests a de-liberate act contravening the rules of warfare as understood by all the groups involved.

When naming massacres, I have tended toward naming them after the leader of the perpetrators. The other two standard ways of naming such actions—after the victims, or after the location—have been unsuit-able in some cases. Colonial killers did not always note or know whom they were murdering or where they were doing it.

I have attempted similar caution in my choice to use terms like *mur-derers*, *thieves*, or *lies* to describe people who kill unlawfully and unjustly, people who take what does not belong to them, and deliberate untruths.

This kind of direct language, when supported by the evidence, can be useful in demystifying, desanctifying, and denaturing killings and cover-ups like those at the core of this book. Historians often shy away from these words, especially when referring to individuals—which can lead to strange narratives of mass killings without mention of murderers, or of stolen lands without mention of thieves. Yet interpretive accuracy demands exact language. We need not omit the most fitting descriptors in pursuit of a false patina of neutrality.[16]

It is also worthwhile to discuss acts of colonialism or genocide using scholarly terms of art. Technical terms allow us to more precisely clarify motivations, draw lines of continuity between different events, and make clear commonalities of structural oppressions. But the use of technical terms can coincide with more everyday language to describe mass murders and other crimes against humanity. American "Indian fighters" weren't always just fighters and thieves—some among them, like other serial killers and mass murderers, found gratification in the killings they committed. The society in which they lived was typically willing to overlook or undercut the horrors of their actions. Overreliance on a specialized argot for describing historical violence risks doing the same. In his nearly three decades as an "Indian fighter," Oregon pioneer Loren L. Williams pursued necropolitical settler colonial transfers and embraced genocidal folk imperialism. He was also a serial killer, who would rather be killing Indians "than be in any other position [he] could name." Both kinds of descriptors are important.[17]

Although history is a field somewhat different from literature, I take seriously scholar Gerald Vizenor's call to pay heed to Native stories of survivance, including "renunciations of dominance, detractions, obtrusions, the unbearable sentiments of tragedy, and the legacy of victimry." But I echo theorist Scott Richard Lyons's gloss of Vizenor's "victimry" neologism: avoidance of victimry narratives does not and should not elide the acts of victimizers or diminish the harms they inflict. The use of the descriptor *victim* in this text should be taken not as a totalizing label for the people so described, but as an indicator of the crimes committed by the victimizers.[18]

Quantitative research on pioneer violence within and beyond the wars of the Pacific Northwest is beyond the scope of this study. Such research would need to reckon with both underreporting and overexaggerating. Pioneer violence was differently reported in different settings, and certain kinds of violence (especially rape and the murder of children) were only occasionally seen as part of a proud history, and they thus appear less often in the records. Some pioneer killers undoubtedly exaggerated the extent of those of their killings they believed were righteous. On the other hand, killings of noncombatants, women, and children often went unenumerated or unreported, especially in official records. I have attempted to mark in the text or notes the relative closeness of the evidence (whether a story is from the supposed participant, from a family member or friend, or part of broader community lore). I have tended to place somewhat more trust in stories of specific killings than in those of general mayhem, attempted to cast a skeptical eye on stories that smack of derring-do, and assumed most of the numbers given by those who bragged about killings were exaggerations.

But exaggeration is different from invention. The extent of violence in many of the reminiscences presented here exceeds that in most official reports, but it is not dissimilar from what was reported by Indigenous communities in the past (and often remembered to the present). Indeed, I demonstrate that local government figures were often motivated to downplay the killings of Indigenous noncombatants in the Pacific Northwest. Many of the killings described here were never marked in government records, persisting instead in less official recollections. But most pioneers did not leave reminiscences. There is little reason to think that those who died younger, or avoided the spotlight of history, were significantly less murderous than those who left a record of what they did. It is overwhelmingly likely that Pacific Northwest pioneers killed far more Native people than we can count.[19]

I have eschewed the terms *uprising* and *rebellion* when describing wars of the 1840s–1860s in the Pacific Northwest. Both terms imply an attack against an established government with previously recognized suzerainty. To claim (as many White people did in the period) that Native communities fighting against invasion were engaged in an uprising is to imply that they had previously accepted American governance. This descriptor might be appropriate for certain later wars, but for most American wars of the mid-1800s it is a problematic formulation. Independent polities fighting against invaders trying to conquer their lands are not rebels. To frame them as such risks naturalizing American assumptions of dominion over Native land, and even risks falsely transforming American wars of conquest into police actions.[20]

The language of "tragedy" often obtains in stories of the colonial conquest of the Pacific Northwest, as elsewhere. In the sense that tragedy indicates an enormity of suffering, destruction, and distress, this is apt. But the term *tragedy* can easily acquire a valence from its more theatrical uses—indicating destruction that stems from the fatal flaws of heroic actors. This is dangerous. Particularly, scholars must be cautious of framing the Indian wars of the region or murderous colonial conquest more generally as the result of tragic misunderstandings. As I will show, the thieves, rapists, and murderers who served as the vanguard of colonialism in the Pacific Northwest usually knew what they were doing.[21]

I attempt herein to prove pioneer norms of wanton and often horrific violence against Native people in the American Pacific Northwest, and to demonstrate some of the ways in which that violence was erased. To do so effectively, this text necessarily contains descriptions of numerous acts of violence, some of them graphic, and could thus be traumatic for some readers. I have attempted to be thorough and sensitive without being sensational, and to write in a way that is nuanced without being numbing. I expect there will be, perhaps inevitably, readers for whom I have not succeeded. A major goal of this work is to pierce through pioneer nostalgia and reveal the horrors it hides; I have thus erred on the side of demonstration rather than delicacy. There are reasons so many chose to cover up the crimes I discuss. The story I have to tell is an ugly one.

CHAPTER ONE

Settler-Soldiers and Folk Imperialism in the Pacific Northwest

I N 1884 JUDGE FRANCIS Henry, a former gold miner and soldier, gave a celebratory address to the gathered crowds of the Washington Pioneer Association. Indian wars in the Pacific Northwest, Henry proclaimed, were

> but the inevitable continuation of the old, old story of the coloni-
> zation and occupation of America by the whites, which has been
> enacted times without number from the shores of the Atlantic to
> the Pacific, during the last four hundred years—simply one of the
> three incidents of that inevitable destiny which has already sub-
> jected the whole continent to the use of civilized man, namely:
> First[,] the insidious invasion of the pioneer;
> second, a treaty by the government with the Indians;
> and third, their forcible expulsion from that territory to conven-
> ient reservations, to be taken from them by the same process at
> some future time.[1]

Henry's description was essentially correct, although different American colonizers attempted these steps in different orders in pursuit of their

"inevitable [manifest] destiny." Pivotally, Henry's gloss on colonialism included the settler pursuit of continuing seizures of Native land both before
and after initial treaties were signed, wars were fought, and reservations
were formed.

Much of the conquest of what became the United States was and is
settler colonial: that is, predicated on elimination more than exploitation
of Indigenous peoples and communities, and their replacement by presumptively Euro-"American settlers [who] came here to stay," as pioneer
historian Elwood Evans put it in 1869. Like Henry and Evans, many
American invaders in the 1800s were conscious of the structure and ideol-
ogy in which they took part. They came with a settler colonial script
honed by decades of American empire—and those not yet versed in colonialism were typically quick to adopt the violent norms of their fellow pioneers. Even before the War on Illahee began in earnest, Euro-Americans
were dreaming of, threatening, and sometimes pursuing genocide.[2]

If wars are defined by invasion, then the War on Illahee started before the
onset of the Cayuse War in 1847. Most Euro-American pioneers who
came to the region arrived without an invitation, often claiming Indigenous land without permission from the polities that stewarded it and,
initially, without the veneer of a treaty. A number of the early Euro-
American arrivistes into the Indigenous world of Illahee were treated civ-
illy, even welcomed. Some Native polities valued them as new trading
partners or allies, many Native polities tried to fold them into the existing
network of kinship and alliance that defined intergroup diplomacy in Illahee, and most Native polities treated newcomers with caution amid the
cataclysmic crises brought on by overlapping epidemics inflicted on Pacific Northwest residents, particularly in the 1830s and 1840s. But the fact
that Native communities sometimes welcomed or aided Euro-American
visitors should not erase the fact that many, eventually most, of the new
arrivals were bent on invasion. And that fact must color historical interpretations of violence between Euro-American and Native groups.[3]

Historian Gray Whaley has shown that settler musings about genocide were frequent in the fur trade era of the early 1800s Northwest, even
before the full onset of American empire, when Indigenous power was
still ascendant in the region. An itinerant trapper, Peter Skene Ogden, responded to economic setbacks along the Snake River in 1828 by dreaming
about mass extermination of "the whole Snake tribe" (a general slur that
in this case probably referred to Shoshone/Newe people). Responding

to the killing of two employees in 1832, John McLoughlin, who led fur trading for the British Hudson's Bay Company along the Columbia River, instructed his agent Michel LaFramboise to pursue retributive killings—standard practice among both Indigenous communities and communities of European descent in the area. But he also encouraged LaFramboise to threaten extermination, to say that while Hudson's Bay did "not wish to hurt the innocent," its representatives would "not spare one of the tribe" if those who had killed his employees were not given up. These were largely arguments for pursuing genocide against somewhat specific Indigenous polities, rather than universally against Indians. That would change with the American rush to Oregon in the 1840s and 1850s. Folk imperialism, as Whaley has termed the kind of on-the-ground ad hoc American colonization effort common in the Northwest, brought with it folk genocide: a popular, decentralized movement to murder Native people and take what was theirs.[4]

And long before the rush, plenty of newcomers were ideating genocide against Indians generally rather than against specific groups. Nathaniel Wyeth, a speculator and ice industry entrepreneur, traveled along the Columbia River looking for business opportunities in 1835. He established a base on "Wappatoo Island" (a few decades later renamed Sauvie's Island after a local settler of French descent), hoping to set up a salmon fishery and to recapture unfree Hawaiian laborers who had escaped the forced labor he inflicted on them. Wappatoo Island was not only centrally located along the river, but had recently been more or less emptied of people—first by the devastating epidemics of the early 1830s, then by sweeps of the island's remaining inhabitants by the Hudson's Bay Company a few years before Wyeth's arrival.[5]

Taking in the recent history of catastrophic epidemics as he understood it, and possibly mistaking a long-standing funerary ground on the island for a fresh ruin, Wyeth proclaimed that "providence has made room for me, and without doing [the Indians] more injury than I should if I had made room for myself[,] viz Killing them off." There is evidence that Wyeth took part in an attack on a Blackfeet polity in 1832; it is unclear whether he attacked any Native people along the Columbia River in 1834. But he evinced a readiness to kill to "make room for [himself]" if necessary. By necessity, many of his employees were Indigenous people. But this fact did not hinder Wyeth's daydreaming about the inconvenience and feasibility of genocide; as historian Susanah Shaw Romney has shown, there was already an enduring settler colonial tradition of traders dreaming about genocide before having the numbers or tools to pursue it.[6]

Missionaries arriving in the 1830s, whose minor role in the American conquests of the Pacific Northwest would be magnified again and again in the century that followed, saw genocide as inevitable. As one missionary, Samuel Parker, put it: "The aboriginal population claim [this country] as their own, and say, they merely permit white men to reside among them. ... But their claim is laboriously, extensively, and practically denied; for authorities, both of written law, and the opinion of living judges and expositors of law, sanction the principle that 'unsettled habitation is not true and legal possession, and that nations who inhabit fertile countries and disdain or refuse to cultivate them, deserve to be extirpated.'" *Extirpate* (to root out and destroy completely) had been a word of choice used to call for genocide in the 1700s, and it remained so in Parker's mournful prose.[7]

Samuel Parker professed regret (but not doubt) that pioneers would soon try to murder all the Native polities he had been visiting, much as he regretted legal denials of Native land rights. As he later wrote:

> I am not able to discover why the nations who have, from time immemorial, occupied this country, and who, like other nations, have their territorial limits tolerably well defined among themselves, should not still possess the domain which our common Creator and Benefactor has kindly given them. It is a subject of increasing regret to every true friend of humanity, that unless the rapacious and acquisitive spirit, which urges our nation to appropriate these western territories, shall be restrained by the providence of God, these Indian nations will be compelled to yield their lands, their rights, and their lives to the merciless invaders of their country. ... They are inevitably doomed to extinction by the hands of enlightened and powerful men[.] The history of the past, and the operation of present causes, show that as soon as the Indians shall be induced to sell and cede the best portions of their country, there being no farther west to which they can be removed, the Indian race must expire.[8]

Because Parker was not given the funds to create a mission, it remains unclear how this mixture of just philosophy and grim diagnosis would have shaped his actions as a missionary. Many of his American compatriots spent at least as much energy seizing land for agriculture and profit as they did on their supposed mission to save souls. Perhaps with funding Samuel Parker might have matched his words with actions, or perhaps he would have ended up like Jason Lee, whose mission in what became Salem, Oregon, was criticized for focusing more on land acquisition than on Native conversion. Lee wrote of hoping to save "a remnant" of the Native people of Oregon as "trophies" for Christianity, but he presumed the whole doomed to extinction—and managed to net a choice portion of Native land for himself and his institution.[9]

The missionary Marcus Whitman, who seized land in what became Walla Walla, Washington, came to see colonialism as central to his mission. As he wrote to his in-laws in 1844:

> It does not concern me so much what is to become of any particular set of Indians. . . . I have no doubt our greatest work is to be to aid the white settlement of this country and help to found its religious institutions. Providence has its full share in all these events. Although the Indians have made and are making rapid advance in religious knowledge and civilization, yet it cannot be hoped that time will be allowed to mature either . . . before the white settlers will demand the soil and seek the removal of both the Indians and the Mission. What Americans desire of this kind they always effect, and it is equally useless to oppose or desire it otherwise. . . . Indeed, I am fully convinced that when a people refuse or neglect to fill the designs of Providence, they ought not to complain at the results; and so it is equally useless for Christians to be anxious on their account.[10]

At most, Whitman, like Jason Lee, attempted a sort of "salvage theology"— which like the salvage anthropology of later years was a haphazard attempt to snatch a few Native souls as "trophies" before the pioneers forcibly removed them. Like Parker, Whitman saw Euro-American conquest of Indigenous land as inevitable. Unlike Parker, Whitman saw no point in desiring otherwise or feeling qualms about the impending attacks. Like many missionaries in the period, Whitman viewed ministering to the White invaders as more important than his attempts to proselytize to Indigenous communities, and he seems to have been ready to write off the latter as refusing and neglecting "the designs of Providence."[11]

And many of those invaders arrived ready to make war, at whatever scale. Elijah Bristow, a veteran of Andrew Jackson's wars on "Creek" (mostly Mvskoke) people, seized land in the southern Willamette Valley in 1846. He framed his conflicts with local and visiting Native communities as wars. When Bristow believed one of his oxen had been killed by a member of a local Klickitat/Qwû'lh-hwai-pûm band in 1849, "he declared war on the Klick[i]tat tribe generally," stealing from and assaulting any Klickitat/Qwû'lh-hwai-pûm who approached his homestead. Bristow had fatally wounded a visiting Klamath/Mukluk person a year earlier, and he made it known "that the Klamaths must not come over into that country for he would kill every one he saw." Many aspects of Bristow's story of himself were questionable, not least his assumption that his authority was being listened to by people who outnumbered him. One might venture that future Klamath/Mukluk or other Native visitors to the region might have simply steered clear of the bloodthirsty pioneer. But there is little reason to doubt Bristow's expressions of racial hatred or threats of White supremacist violence.[12]

Writing decades later, Joseph Henry Brown opened his pioneer narrative by invoking a family history of conquest. "I sprang from pioneer stock," he proclaimed, "both of my great-grandfathers being pioneers and participants in the war of 1812 and the Indian wars of the new country [Illinois] in which they had settled." Detailing his experiences on a pioneer wagon train in 1847—what he called part of "the advance guard of civilization to the western shore, to wrest a beautiful country from barbarism"—Brown wrote of pioneers ready for a fight with Indians at any moment.[13]

When Brown's pioneer party sighted "50 Indians on the top of the hill" as they were traveling along the Umatilla River, they had "no doubt but they intended to charge," and thus

> the men formed themselves between the enemy and wagons, and for a few minutes awaited attacks, but [the Indians] gave some insulting signs and rode away, and we did not see any more Indians until we camped on the banks of the Columbia River some eight days afterwards. Across the river at this place was a large Indian v[i]ll[a]ge, and as soon as we camped, Indians came over being well armed, bringing wood and commenced to build a fire in the center of our camp, stating that they had come to camp and trade with us. My grandfather immediately seized a gun and

ordered all the men to arms, which was promptly seconded by Bradshaw [the leader of the wagon train], who immediately placed himself at the head of the men, forming them in a line between the Indians and the families, and immediately advanced [on] the Indians who quickly d[i]vined the intentions of the whites and commenced stringing their bows, and bringing their guns to bear upon us. For a moment or so there was imminent danger of bloodshed. ... The Indians remained in sullen silence until the men c[a]me within a few feet of them, then slowly began to withdraw, they were pressed to the river bank and got into their canoes.[14]

Both these encounters took place before any known war between Native polities and White polities was under way in the region. Both incidents underscore the expectation of war and violence Brown's family—and countless others—brought to Illahee (including their grouping of all Indians into a single category, regardless of ethnie). The pioneer might have misread the first incident (presuming that the lookouts were planning an assault and assuming the signs given were intended as insults). The second incident was almost definitely a peaceful overture, an attempt to share a meal with newcomers as a welcome—until the pioneers assumed perfidy and escalated to drawing guns and making threats. The first Pacific Northwest "Indian war" considered as such by Euro-Americans would not start until December 1847, and Joseph Henry Brown only formally joined in attacks on local Native polities (as a courier) from 1855. But pioneers came ready to make war at the slightest provocation, real or imagined.[15]

Although there had already been pioneer violence, the War on Illahee arguably started with the advent of the so-called Cayuse War in December 1847, when Euro-American volunteers mustered to make war on Indians in the Oregon Territory and were soon followed by the deployment of federal troops. The Cayuse War (and the formal creation of the Oregon Territory) were precipitated by killings at the Whitman mission, built on Cayuse/Liksiyu land, in what is now the state of Washington. In an event variously known as the Whitman Incident, the Whitman Tragedy, the Whitman Massacre, or the Incident at Weyiiletpu, a band of Cayuse/Liksiyu people killed two missionaries, Marcus and Narcissa Whitman, and every adult male American ("Boston"—the Chinook Jargon word for an American) in their household that could be found—

probably thirteen people in all. The other survivors were held hostage, and stories circulated that some women were abused by their captors.[16]

The troubles that culminated in the Whitman killings had been brewing for years. The Whitmans were stingy squatters who had settled without permission or recompense on Cayuse/Liksiyu land, and who refused to participate in the gift giving that defined and solemnized intergroup relations in the region. Many sources suggested that Cayuse/Liksiyu bands had been told by one or another person of Indigenous descent from the East "how they have been treated by the *Whites* as soon [as the Whites] got strong + powerful[—]their country was taken away from them and they had to *submit*." The first ripples of the rising flood of pioneers that came through the mission from 1842 on would have confirmed these warnings as accurate. William D. Stillwell, a pioneer and volunteer, claimed privately that Narcissa Whitman had added to the trouble with her outbursts of physical violence on visiting Native children. Local people may also have resented her expressed wish that the diseases ravaging the area would kill even more Native people.[17]

And then there were the poisonings. A visitor to the mission hoping to deter "thefts" from the fields in which the squatting Whitmans were growing crops purportedly laced several melons with an emetic. He apparently joked later about the satisfaction of causing a few locals to fall ill, and those "jokes" made their way back to Cayuse/Liksiyu communities. Marcus Whitman pursued a standard Euro-American practice of killing wolves with strychnine-laced meat, and the warning he claimed to have given did not prevent a few locals from eating some poisoned meat and nearly dying. According to the pioneer who told this story, Whitman reacted to the news of these purportedly accidental poisonings with a laugh and thankfulness that perhaps now the local Native people would listen to him. There are unconfirmed accounts that local Cayuse/Liksiyu people had been told the Whitmans planned to poison them all. It is unclear whether these rumors were real or a later historical imagining, and whether or not the Whitmans *had* been murdering Native people with strychnine—as I discuss in later chapters, there were other pioneer poisoners who did just that. Local Indigenous people would have been primed to believe such a story, given the long history of poisonings at the mission.[18]

The Whitman killings were primarily an execution, carried out after Marcus Whitman was found guilty of medical and spiritual malpractice—a capital offense under Cayuse/Liksiyu law at the time. A measles epidemic that killed Native locals at a higher rate than Euro-Americans—while both groups were under the care of the Whitmans—was the final bit of proof for a critical mass of people. Legally responsible for the deaths of his patients, culpable for shuttling new invaders into the region, Marcus Whitman and his household were condemned. The killings were carried out according to Cayuse/Liksiyu common law but not necessarily committed with the consent of the many polities of Cayuse/Liksiyu people in the region. Tilou-kaikt, presumed to be the leader of the group that had attacked, seems to have framed the killings as getting "even" after years of abuse and murder by this specific group of "Bostons" who occupied his homeland. Euro-Americans responded by attacking Indians en masse, across much of the region they called Oregon.[19]

Despite the name Euro-Americans eventually gave it, the Cayuse War was a war on Indians generally. It was waged neither exclusively against the band that had killed at the Whitman mission, nor even exclusively against Cayuse/Liksiyu peoples. Upon receiving news of the killings and rumors of gory details real and imagined, the Oregon provisional legislature on December 9, 1847, authorized the raising and payment of a volunteer militia "for the purpose of punishing the Indians, to what tribe or tribes [what]soever they may belong, who may have aided or abetted in the massacre of Dr Marcus Whitman, his wife, and others." Many volunteers never got past the first clause. All Indians were seen as a threat until proven otherwise.[20]

The memorial sent to the U.S. Congress the next day, demanding federal support, was nearly as broad. It painted American settlers as under massive attack. As Jesse Applegate, the author of the memorial, put it: "Our relations with the proud and powerful tribes of Indians residing east of the Cascade Mountains, hitherto uniformly amicable and pacific, have recently assumed quite a different character. They have shouted the warwhoop and crimsoned their tomahawks in the blood of our citizens. . . . [They] have formed an alliance for the purpose of carrying on hostilities against our settlements. . . . To repel the attacks of so formidable a foe, and protect our families and property from violence and rapine, will require more strength than we possess." The small band of Cayuse/Liksiyu people who had made the attack was spun up into a vast and undifferentiated conspiracy of "Indians." And when the pioneers formed volunteer companies for counterattacks, they targeted all unfamiliar Native people.[21]

One of William Stillwell's favorite Indian war stories was about an arrow wound he sustained early in his first such war. Stillwell was one of many

Euro-Americans who joined volunteer soldier companies following the killings at the Whitman mission. But when Stillwell and his party started a battle with a Native group on January 28, 1848, they had no particular evidence that the group they fought were Cayuse/Liksiyu people—much less Cayuse/Liksiyu people connected to the events at the Whitman mission. As he and his party traveled south along the Deschutes River, Stillwell explained decades later, "we suddenly came on a band of Indians, as [we] rounded a sharp ridge, charging straight for us. . . . I remember I capped five guns before we had orders to charge. The Indians then changed their course and started south; we overtook them at the old emigrant road, and here the first Indian was killed in the Cayuse War, by Bill Chick [William C. Smith]." These Indians proved to be a band, with a load of salmon, returning to their camp.[22]

Stillwell and his party bumped into a group of Native people who were returning from a fishing trip. When Stillwell and his men began loading their weapons, the Native group swerved to avoid them. The Euro-American volunteers fired on a group of Native fishers who had made no obviously hostile act. It was only after one of the fishers was killed by a volunteer that this Native group fought back and defeated their attackers. Stillwell took the arrow to the hip, whose head he would carry for the rest of his life, as the White volunteers were retreating from a skirmish they had started and lost. A few days later a larger body of volunteers from the same force attacked, looted, and burned a Native village along the Deschutes River. In both cases the volunteers did not know or care that neither the fishing party nor the village was Cayuse/Liksiyu. They were there to fight Indians.[23]

The main body of 1848 Oregon volunteers, led by Black Hawk War and Seminole War veteran Cornelius Gilliam, blundered through Indian country for several months, opportunistically attacking and robbing Native people without any obvious effort to ascertain involvement in the war's supposed inciting incident. They attacked and robbed several Palouse/Palus bands, the volunteers only barely preventing their defeat in the one major battle they subsequently engaged in from turning into a rout. After Gilliam killed himself with his own gun, purportedly in an accident, a splinter force headed into Nez Perce/Nimiipuu territory— "arresting" any "suspicious" Indian, looting Native property, and shooting anyone who tried to stop them. The main body of volunteers never came close to finding those Cayuse/Liksiyu who had taken part in the Whitman killings. It is unclear how many Cayuse/Liksiyu people of any extraction were among those they attacked. But they claimed to have killed a lot of Native people.[24]

That was probably the point. In the Abiqua Creek region of the Willamette Valley (near present-day Silverton, Oregon), far from the initial locus of the conflict, a self-organized militia formed in 1848 and shot at any Indian its members could find. Their main target ended up being Koosta's band of Mollalas, who were not affiliated with any party in the war. The volunteer soldiers murdered at least ten people, although the vagueness and unreliability of the records mean it is possible they killed many more. It was later claimed by John Minto, one of the volunteers, that the militia believed Koosta's band was, by one tortuous feat of reasoning or another, in league with the Cayuse and up to no good. It is unclear if this unlikely claim, made thirty years after the fact, was an accurate recollection of volunteer motivations or a post hoc justification for murders. After the volunteers shot Mollala men, women, and children alike, as Minto decorously put it, "none of [the militiamen] were quite certain whether the Indians killed were of those that should have been killed." Minto was an active participant in movements to clean up the historical reputation of the volunteer soldiers; his modest equivocation should be read in that light. It is likely that the true story was worse. But how much murder and for what cause was, perhaps, beside the point. As Minto explained, "Killing the Indians was not the object, so much, as driving them off to their own country, which was done most effectively." In all probability, Minto and his fellows drove many of those they attacked far *from* their own country, as they intended.[25]

John Minto, like many other pioneers, came to Oregon with exterminatory instincts. He had been reared on a diet of Indian-killing literature from childhood that he embraced for the rest of his life; he thought of Native people as "fiendish" and beyond the pale of humanity. It is small wonder that Minto seems to have engaged without compunction in the expulsion and extermination of Native groups in Oregon, whom he saw as almost entirely beyond redemption. "Of course there was brave manhood and beautiful womanhood even among the degradation of the tribes," he wrote late in life, "but I saw to know none of the former and few of the latter."[26]

The Cayuse War formally ended in 1850, when five Cayuse/Liksiyu leaders agreed to surrender to Euro-American military authorities to stop the mayhem the Euro-Americans were inflicting and submitted to a show trial and execution. Despite a well-substantiated defense pointing out that the Whitman killings had been justified under Cayuse/Liksiyu law, and reasonable doubt that the five men tried for the killings had in fact been part of them, the outcome was a foregone conclusion. Indeed, as pioneer historian Frederick V. Holman proudly proclaimed in 1923, if the Cayuse Five had not been found guilty in court and killed by officers of the state, "Judge Lynch would have exercised jurisdiction and these murderers would have paid the penalty, for about five hundred Oregon pioneers came to Oregon City to see that these Indians did not escape justice for the Whitman massacre." Consciously letting themselves be martyred to bring peace to the Cayuse/Liksiyu—and many of the other Native groups in the region—the five were hanged by pioneers.[27]

In many ways, the Cayuse War was prototypical of the various individual wars that made up the War on Illahee. After a litany of Euro-American wrongs and crimes, a targeted counterattack by a specific Native group was used as a Euro-American casus belli for a broad-based war on Native people generally. The only unusual element was the lack of coercive land seizures at the end of the conflict—which would come soon after. Because although the sacrifice of the Cayuse Five ended one form of formal war, plenty of Indian killers and would-be Indian killers continued their assaults, with or without the backing of American governments.

War was not always necessary for mass murder. After volunteering in the Cayuse War in 1848, John E. Ross moved south and kept on killing. Leading a murder squad colloquially known as the "Oregon boys," Ross and his men ranged through northern California and southern Oregon between 1849 and 1853, killing Indigenous people as they found them. This they portrayed as revenge for crimes inflicted on Euro-American communities—though the records were often unclear on the perpetrators or even the existence of such crimes. Very clear in the records is public support for mass murder. As the August 7, 1853, extra edition of the *Yreka Herald* described events in Oregon: "Now that general hostilities against the Indians have commenced we hope that the Government will render such aid as will enable the citizens of the north to carry on a war of extermination until the last R_dsk_n of these tribes has been killed. Extermination is no longer even a question of time—the time has arrived, the work has been commenced, and let the first man that says treaty or peace be regarded as a traitor."[28]

During the Rogue River Wars of 1853 and 1855–56, Ross continued his attempts at mass killings as a military leader. He was not always successful; an attempt to kill men, women, and children at the Battle of Hungry Hill in 1855 went awry when Ross and the rest of the volunteer forces were decisively defeated by those they were targeting for genocide. Had he and his men won, Ross would have committed yet another massacre. For Ross and his "boys" killed Indians where and when they could, in California and Oregon alike, whether or not there was a formal war on.[29]

Jesse Applegate, a pioneer of 1843 who eventually became one of the few local White critics of genocidal wars in the Pacific Northwest, attempted to draw a distinction between the old, "virtuous" pioneers like himself who arrived before 1848 and the men (like Ross) who followed. In notes for a history of Oregon he never published, Applegate asserted:

> The Indian wars were the main historical incidents of the period [late 1840s to the late 1850s]—These . . . reflect no credit upon the whites. Since 1849 a new element, the gold hunters, was added to the population, having few if any of the virtues of the early pioneers. The prompt assumption of the Cayuse war debt by the Government being a precedent, suggested an easier mode of obtaining gold than digging it from the bowels of the earth. If new diggings were sometimes difficult to find, a new Indian war was easily provoked, which served their purpose equally well.[30]

There was an increase of Euro-American violence and war making from the late 1840s on, gold miners were often the most visible (and perhaps prolific) perpetrators, and many did hope to profit from the wars (by means of direct recompense, plunder, or land). But the sharp dividing line that Applegate drew is harder to support. Gold miners might press the issue, but war was always coming. Given the widespread agreement that Euro-American pioneers would, inevitably, attempt mass murder for land in the Pacific Northwest, the intensification of violence was a matter of numbers as much as anything. Men like Bristow, Stillwell, and Minto were ready for sweeping violence when the moment came. On at least a few occasions, so was Applegate.[31]

The Whitman killings that spurred the Cayuse War were not a necessary cause for the War on Illahee. The attacks on Indigenous lives, property, sovereignty, and rights in the decades of mayhem and murder that followed were first and foremost a product of Euro-American hunger for land and abhorrence of Indian-ness. If the Whitman killings had never happened, some other incident of violence as a response to settler pugnacity would have been used as an excuse for a similar broad war against Indians—whether real, rumored, or created after the fact.

William Thompson, a newspaper editor and volunteer, later described Indian fighting in pioneer Oregon as an entertainment as well as a duty. "For excitement, the frequent Indian uprisings, and more frequent Indian scares, afforded abundant material upon which the young enterprising and adventurous spirits of the day could work off their surplus energies," he wrote. "Hunting, too, afforded a pleasurable and profitable pastime to the young."[32]

The wanton pioneer violence of the 1850s was driven mostly by greed and racism—*and* for some people, killing was a pastime. Thompson, who wrote with pride of having shot a Native man he had been traveling with for no other reason than that his victim was "attempt[ing] to get away," killed for all three reasons. Shooting in the back this Native person trying only to leave, proudly watching him die "kicking the grass," and being praised for the murder by Euro-American companions who had watched him do it—this was the event that marked Thompson's teenage transition to adulthood in his memory. And there were many others like him.[33]

Joseph Lane, who took office as the first federal governor of Oregon Territory in 1849 and remained a central figure in Oregon politics until 1861, embodied the continuity between folk violence and officialdom. Like other U.S. officials, he counseled caution in treating with Native polities and voiced a preference for the bloodless seizure of land by treaty. Like other pioneer vigilantes, he condoned and engaged in sprees of rape and murder against Indigenous communities. Like other pioneers trying to shape history, he rewrote his own violent past into a more pleasing shape in later years, both celebrating assaults on Native men he deemed righteous *and* hiding the worst aspects of his violence from mainstream historical narratives for generations.

Before becoming a governor, Joseph Lane rose to national fame in the U.S.–Mexico War. One of several "mushroom generals" promoted by President Polk because of his Democratic bona fides, Lane earned fame for his ruthless "anti-guerrilla activity" along rural roads. Lane and his men took few prisoners and showed little mercy; as one local newspaper put it, the campaign was pursued "even to the termination of every last scoundrel of them." He was also responsible for the 1847 Sack of Huamantla (infamous in Mexican history, largely unknown in the United States)—in the words of the historian Malcolm Clark "an awesome orgy of rape, murder, desecration and drunkenness . . . the ultimate atrocity of a war made hideous by atrocities." Some reminiscences, like that of volunteer William D. Wilkins, claimed that Joseph Lane not only condoned but ordered the day and night of slaughter, mayhem, and theft Americans committed after the taking of the city. Another volunteer, Otto Zirckel, told his family that Lane continued this campaign of carnage, pillage, and rape into the settlements surrounding Huamantla. As one local witness reporting on Lane's "anti-guerilla activity" put it, "All sorts of atrocities were committed . . . an indiscriminate slaughter was made . . . women were forced, etc., etc." Given the evidence that he murdered and probably raped during his career in Oregon (see below), Lane may have not only tolerated but participated in these war crimes. It is not clear how Lane may have talked about the rapes and killings during and after the Sack of Huamantla in private. Publicly, he commended his men "for their gallant conduct"—the same approach, with identical language, he later took in Oregon.[34]

Arriving in the midst of the Cayuse War, in March 1849, Lane took pragmatic steps to limit its spread. Writing to Samuel Gilmore, the captain of a newly formed company of volunteers headed to southern Oregon, Lane laid out his official approach to Indian policy:

> While I will promptly protect the lives and property of the white inhabitants, I shall at the same time be equally ready and prompt in protecting the Indians in all the rights guaranteed to them by the laws of Congress, and from being forcibly ejected from their possessory rights in the Territory until the government of the United States shall have by treaty extinguished those rights. You will therefore carefully restrain your men from committing any act towards the Indians which would have a tendency to prejudice them against the white citizens. . . . If, by any cause, the Indians of Oregon should, in the present year, be aroused to hostility, the injury they might do to the settlements, in the absence of a greater part of the male population, would be incalculable.[35]

Lane counseled peace, even comity, but only because violence might pose a threat to White settlements. Like virtually all U.S. officials, he presumed the imminent extinguishment of Native title to the land by means of treaty. Like most, he was willing to threaten and employ violence in pursuit of expropriation. He might, in his official capacity, suggest that "the cause of humanity calls out loudly for [Indian] removal." But removal, not humanity, was his object.[36]

After his election as Oregon's first territorial delegate in June 1851, Lane resolved to spend the summer tying up loose ends, mining for gold, and hunting Indians in the Rogue River region. Although Lane described the conflicts he fought in as a "war [that] had commenced in good earnest," the main southern clashes he was involved in in 1851 were the result of one-sided aggression. In May 1851 a battalion of mixed regulars and volunteers led by Major Philip Kearny blazing a trail through southern Oregon saw a group of Native people running away from them, charged, and began the first of a series of pitched battles with any Native group they could find—a chain of failed surprise attacks, hasty retreats, and occasional victories. Kearny initiated these attacks at the requests of local White inhabitants. Though Kearny's campaign was quickly framed as a response to Native aggression, Kearny's own reports made clear that the Euro-American soldiers struck first.[37]

Joseph Lane proclaimed to the people of Oregon in letter to the *Oregon Statesman* of Salem that he (along with his friend Jesse Applegate) had joined in on the attacks as soon as he could. The battles that he was proud to have been a part of seem mostly to have been attacks of opportunity by Americans, rather than reactions to any supposed act of aggression by Indigenous people. As Lane described it: "We soon found an Indian trail leading up a large creek, and in a short time overtook and charged upon a party of Indians, killing one. The rest made their escape in a dense chaparral. We again pushed forward as rapidly as possible until late in the evening, when we gave battle to another party of Indians, few of whom escaped. Twelve women and children were taken prisoners; several of those who escaped were wounded."[38]

Lane did not name or care about particular tribal designations, nor did he make any indication that the Euro-American aggressors had attempted to connect the groups they attacked to any particular perceived wrongdoing—only a presumption that "the Indians had organized in great numbers for the purpose of killing and plundering our people passing to and from the mines." There had been some violence (the parameters of which remain unclear) between a party of gold miners and a Native group in early June 1851—a single encounter spun into a vast conspiracy by the Euro-American rumor mill. Whether the particular groups Kearny and Lane attacked had anything to do with any killings or plunderings was not seemingly considered. The people Lane, Applegate, and Kearny attacked were Indians, they were in the "wrong" place, and that was enough. And, Lane assumed, that would be enough for the readers of the *Oregon Statesman*.[39]

Just as he had praised as gallant the men under his command who had killed, pillaged, and raped in the U.S.–Mexico War, so did Lane praise as gallant the regular soldiers, volunteers, and vigilantes who killed in southern Oregon. And outside the newspapers, Lane indicated not only approval of but participation in acts of violence that were not fit to print. The important thing, Lane claimed, was that they had "done much to humble the Rogue River Indians, and taught them to know that they can be hunted down and destroyed." A short-lived treaty, never ratified by the U.S. Congress or respected by local Euro-Americans, followed the violence in 1851. There would be many more like it.[40]

Was Lane's violence, among a broader series of attacks on Native communities in south and southwest Oregon in 1851, part of a "war . . . commenced in good earnest," as Lane claimed? There were officers of the United States in charge of at least some of the Euro-American bands attacking Native people, and soldiers in the pay of the United States were in the vanguard. But Major Kearny's attacks on Native polities living along the Rogue River have typically been framed as prefatory "clashes" rather than as being a part of the Rogue River Wars (usually defined as either from 1853 to 1856, split into two separate conflicts in 1853 *and* 1855–56, or restricted to the part of the war with full federal backing, from 1855 to 1856). What sets the 1851 American attacks apart from those a few years after may be only that the 1851 treaty was even more thoroughly ignored by Euro-Americans than those that came later.[41]

Contemporaneous invasions of the Oregon coast in 1851, at what became Port Orford, are similarly seldom categorized as war. U.S.–Mexico War veteran and itinerant carpenter John M. Kirkpatrick landed with eight other men and a cannon on June 9, 1851, sent on a steamship by William Tichenor (a White merchant and mariner) to establish a port. A local Native community—most likely Kwatami Tunne, the Sixes River band of the Tututni peoples—initially welcomed them as traders. After the ship left and it became clear that the Euro-American adventurers planned to stay, however, local leaders (in the words of Kirkpatrick) "grew saucy and ordered us off." When a large group of local Native people came back—perhaps planning to evict the invaders, perhaps simply reopening negotiations—Kirkpatrick fired on them. After a battle in which the cannon played a decisive role, the two sides agreed to a fourteen-day peace, with the understanding that the steamship would return and remove Kirkpatrick and his men from Ma'-na'-xhay-Thet (or, as the invaders later called it, Battle Rock). Fifteen days later, with no ship in sight, a yet larger number of Native people—Kirkpatrick claimed over a hundred—encircled the Euro-American camp and shot arrows somewhat near it. Kirkpatrick perceived this as bad aim, or fear of the cannon, but these arrows may have been deliberate misses, warning shots reminding the invaders of their promise to leave. If so, the volley worked. The White "adventurers" were dislodged, and they made a long eight-day trek to Umpqua City—facing hunger and scares, but neither inflicting nor taking further casualties.[42]

Tichenor enlisted a second, larger group of volunteers to make a beachhead at the same point of the Oregon coast. According to Loren L. Williams, a volunteer who a few decades later wrote an extensive reminiscence of the invasion, men were enlisted in San Francisco with the offer of free passage to Oregon in exchange for three weeks of fort building and fighting. In the last days of the summer of 1851, the newspaperman, explorer, gold miner, and latter-day proslavery radical William T'Vault attempted to blaze a trail connecting Port Orford to the main Oregon-California route. Williams joined up.[43]

Williams remembered the expedition as a quasi-military adventure. T'Vault was a "mountaineer and experienced Indian fighter," and the men who joined him hoped to become the same, "looking forward to the time when they might immortalize themselves in some hand to hand conflict with the Indians we expected to encounter on the way." As usual, every group of Indians they encountered was assumed to be a threat. Most of the Euro-American trailblazers turned back as the food ran out, but a core group of ten continued, eventually coming into a conflict with a Coquille/Coquelle village, in which half of the adventurers were killed. The semiofficial story told by T'Vault at the time was of a sudden and inexplicable attack by previously friendly Indians. Williams, whose unpublished reminiscence contains significantly more details than T'Vault's record of events, proudly wove a story of theft, kidnapping, and lethal threats leading up to the supposed massacre.[44]

As the half-starved expedition made its way along the Coquille River in August, Williams spotted a Native man while hunting. After debating "whether to shoot him or not," without preamble Williams decided to seize the man as a prisoner, resolving "to kill him" if he "t[ook] affright and run away." Stripped of his belongings at gunpoint, the man was "persuaded" by T'Vault to pilot the expedition to Fort Umpqua using sign language (as the prisoner and his captors did not have any languages in common). The extent to which the man understood the demands of his heavily armed captors is unclear, but he signaled assent to their demands and led them first along the Coquille River and then in the direction the party thought they should go—northward.[45]

They came upon a small village whose inhabitants immediately ran away—one might conjecture, on the basis of their previous behavior, that T'Vault and his expeditioners leveled their guns at all and sundry. With an infant still wailing unheeded at the center of the village, the Euro-Americans set about eating all the food they could steal. Their captive took this chance to escape, and Williams, decades later, remained incensed that "our Indian guide [had] deserted us." Wandering northward, T'Vault and his company finally found a river and soon hailed a group of Native men in canoes—whom Williams described as "hostil[e] and very much to be dreaded," despite the fact that "no hostile demonstration was made." The volunteers hired the men in canoes for transportation, offering their shirts as payment (as they had little else besides their guns).[46]

After a few days' travel, they reached a large Indigenous community along the Coquille on September 14, 1851, and violently clashed with the residents. There was an altercation of uncertain origin during which Native attempts to either aid or disarm the Euro-Americans escalated into the five of the volunteers being killed, and the rest scattering and fleeing. Williams was first buffeted by clubs, and then took an arrow as he broke free and, he claimed, killed at least two of his pursuers. T'Vault escaped with the help of unnamed Indigenous boy. Neither was pursued past the initial melee, both blamed the other for getting the party into a trap, and both found succor in Native communities they stumbled into after the clash. The missionary Josiah Parrish, who visited the region shortly after the clash, was told that the local Coquille/Coquelle had simply been trying to help the adventurers with their canoes. All agreed that the Euro-American volunteers perceived hostility and started shooting; whether that hostility had actually existed before the firefight was quickly rendered moot.[47]

Fort Orford, established formally as military base on the same day as the clash, received news of the conflict a few days later and sent word south. Lieutenant Colonel Silas Casey "scraped together" another, even larger volunteer force in California and led a punitive expedition into the Coquille River region in November 1851. They claimed officially to have killed fifteen Indians. Yet no record indicates those killed had anything to do with the conflict, or that Casey and his company made any attempt to determine whether those killed had anything to do with it. Indeed, their preferred method was to kill before Native people realized the White invaders were attacking. Scuttlebutt among the soldiers farther north was that Casey's men had "come on the indians and without any hesitation began to slaughter them + killed every Indian on the ground," as many as four hundred slain. This number was almost definitely exaggerated, but it is entirely possible that Casey and his men killed more people than they let on in official reports, in addition to destroying the food supplies at every camp they raided. Loren L. Williams, however, was fairly certain the punitive expedition did not reach the village where he had attacked and taken an arrow in the gut. For him, vengeance came a few years later, in 1853, when "fractious miners, never merciful to Indians," killed twenty people in that community.[48]

None of the three bands of armed men who landed at Port Orford in 1851 were fighting in an officially declared war. All three were mustered in arms with the expectation of fighting Indians, the last under the command of a U.S. lieutenant colonel. All three expeditions killed people and suffered casualties. They were part of a decades-long war against Indians generally, and they could be counted as part of a long Rogue River War—even more than the Cayuse War, a war on all Native people in a region rather than a specific polity. Attempts to get treaties signed at the tail end of the conflict in the Coquille region faltered, in large part owing to language barriers; even if the negotiations had been successful, the U.S. Senate would probably have cast aside any treaties signed, as they did with other Oregon treaties negotiated at the time. Like Kearny and Lane's invasions and killings, the three 1851 campaigns on the coast are not typically included as part of the Rogue River Wars, or any other war.[49]

One reason could be that the 1851 attacks were not ordered from on high. Although they were led by military officers, they were framed as scouting and trailblazing expeditions rather than military campaigns. The distinction probably didn't mean much to the people being attacked by U.S. soldiers and vigilantes. But it is perhaps meaningful to distinguish these haphazard campaigns from organized, official warfare, as the U.S. federal government did from 1851 until 1901 (see chapter 9).

Or perhaps the lack of treaties explains the lack of designations as wars. Which killings of Indigenous people by soldiers count as acts of war has most often been defined by treaties, not by the nature of the acts themselves. When the 1853 Rogue River War is counted as such, accounts tend to focus on the treaty local Indigenous leaders negotiated with Joseph Lane at Table Rock. The period universally agreed to be part of the Rogue River Wars, from late 1855 to mid-1856, ended in a series of expropriative treaties. It is not unreasonable to suggest that if the treaty signed in 1851 had been ratified, Kearny's and Lane's attacks would be remembered as the first Rogue River War. Similarly, it seems plausible that if there had been a land-taking treaty negotiated at their conclusion, the 1851 invasions at Port Orford would have retroactively been labeled the Coquille War or another such title. This kind of work done by dating of wars was not restricted to southern Oregon, or to the broader Pacific Northwest. One advantage of framing the conflicts as part of a broader War on Illahee is that it breaks down artificial boundaries between war and peace erected by some historical government figures and (eventually) historians.[50]

For much of American history, the United States typically defined wars with Native nations through peace treaties. Violence between Indigenous and Euro-American groups that led to the signing of such treaties was more likely to be treated as war. Violence that did not was more likely to be seen as a "peacekeeping" or policing action. To the extent that Euro-Americans had a sense of what *war* meant in the 1850s, they saw it as organized conflict between nations.[51]

Seeing the many Native polities of the Pacific Northwest through the lens of settler colonialism, many Euro-Americans did not typify them as nations or view them as states, framing them instead as "the Indians" collectively. Or, perhaps, some chose not to see them as states. As the drafters of the Geneva Conventions a century later put it, "A State can always pretend, when it commits a hostile act against another State, that it is not making war, but merely engaging in a police action, or acting in legitimate self-defense."[52]

On the other hand, Euro-American treaty makers sometimes had to conjure suprapolitical Indigenous polities into being in order to have those Indigenous leaders who were willing to sign treaties stand for a multitude of sovereign communities. These Americans desired Native nations to exist only so long as they had the capacity to sign over their homelands, and no longer. This combination has meant that violence, even organized violence, that did not lead to treaties is often not considered war, and it was (and is) thus often diminished or disappeared in the record. If historians choose to define U.S. Indian wars by acts of war, in addition to the treaties that sometimes end them, there will be new periodizations if not new wars to consider.

The "insidious invasion of the pioneer" into Native lands in the Oregon Territory rapidly accelerated with the passage of the Donation Land Claim Act (DLCA) in 1850. With the DLCA, the federal government promised enormous grants of land in the Pacific Northwest to White settlers. It presumed a cession of Native land by Indigenous communities that had not yet occurred. Euro-Americans had already been seizing Native land without permission. With the federal government opening floodgates of legitimacy to the rising horde of Oregon colonists, negotiations for Native land, an afterthought for many, were a vital concern for federal forces hoping to forestall costly wars.[53]

Death was a pivotal tool in the arsenal of American invaders and negotiators throughout the War on Illahee. Death from a series of overlapping epidemics over generations had put many Native polities in a precarious position. The exact number or percentage of deaths from these epidemics remains highly speculative. Indeed, some historians have problematically presumed that deaths from causes other than disease (such as the wars, murders, and mass killings described herein) were essentially rounding errors—an oversight shaped, in turn, by the silences and deceptions described in later chapters of this book. But even without exact numbers, memory and history on all sides agree that the effects of epidemics were cataclysmic for most Indigenous communities.[54]

Death *threats* were also a potent tool for the Americans. Nearly all treaty negotiators used the long-standing Euro-American technique of threatening (or "warning") that genocide would follow unless Native people signed over their homelands. As Colonel Beverly Allen put it to a group of Santiam Kalapuya during an April 1851 treaty negotiation, "If you remain among the whites, it will inevitably end in your annihilation as a people." American treaty negotiators, as they had throughout the seizure of the continent, used the fact of White exterminators as a weapon against the Native peoples with whom they bargained. Whether the threatened exterminators were soldiers, pioneers, or both varied among persons and places—but the threat of murderous White violence was the constant.[55]

Nearly all Euro-Americans expected Native land to be seized, even those presented as sympathetic. John Pollard Gaines, Joseph Lane's successor as Oregon's territorial governor from 1850 to 1853, was sometimes pilloried by pioneers for being too soft on Indian issues. His preferred method of land seizure was "to treat with the Indians for the relinquishment of their right to the soil" rather than exterminatory war, and he expressed the hope that the U.S. Congress would pass acts "calculated to further the objects of justice and humanity towards this fading race." But Gaines was as steadfast as any in his pursuit of Native land. He urged generous land grants for all emigrants and "the immediate organization of the militia" to defend those lands. These grants could come only from as-yet unceded lands, and Gaines meant to have them.[56]

Gaines led a commission that signed treaties with a number of Native groups (including the failed 1851 Rogue River treaty discussed above) in the early 1850s, most famously associated with Indian superintendent, druggist, and land speculator Anson Dart. The team sometimes agreed to elements of some Native negotiators' demands, including assurances that Indigenous land rights in small tracts of the Willamette Valley would be preserved (while reassuring pioneers that "the reserve will [not] interfere with the convenience of the settle[rs]"). This proved to be too much for their fellow Euro-Americans, locally and in the national legislature, and these treaties were not ratified. But although apparently too generous for many Euro-Americans to stomach, Gaines and Dart's unratified treaties were nonetheless expropriative, seen as the best among bad options by the Native negotiators who acceded to them.[57]

Joel Palmer, a Cayuse War veteran, gold miner, and politician, took over treaty negotiations when he was appointed superintendent of Indian Affairs for the region in 1853. In his instructions to his recently hired friend and fellow Indian fighter Nathan Olney in 1854, Palmer made clear his goal was "to extinguish by treaty the Indian title to *all* the lands in Oregon" by 1856. And though he hoped that the "slaughter of women and children" could be avoided when possible, he also argued that Native communities "unfriendly" to the United States needed to be "disabused" of their "great confidence in their own ability to defend themselves" by "military o[p]erations." Palmer, like other negotiators, was ready to have people killed in his pursuit of Native land.[58]

"General" Joel Palmer, around 1870.
Courtesy of the Oregon Historical Society.

Like his predecessors, Palmer assured Native listeners that proximity to White people—Americans or otherwise—would lead to doom. As he told some Lower Chinook leaders in June 1853: "Experience has taught us the white and red men cannot always live together in peace. . . . When there are but few whites they can get along very well and not quarrel, but when there are a great many they will have difficulty. When they live together there will be difficulties; little difficulties will get to be great difficulties." Careful to specify White people generally rather than Americans when speaking to leaders with decades of experience dealing with people of European descent, Palmer warned them only somewhat obliquely that conflict with the arriving flood of pioneers was inevitable. As he framed the issue at an 1855 negotiation in eastern Washington, one could no more stop the flood of White pioneers than one could "prevent the wind from blowing" or "the rain from falling." Although Palmer was routinely criticized by those pioneers for not doing more to take Native land and lives, he nonetheless shared with them the goal of taking power over "all the lands in Oregon" as expeditiously as possible.[59]

Isaac I. Stevens was appointed governor of Washington Territory in 1853; like Joseph Lane before him, he was a U.S.–Mexico War veteran benefiting from the political patronage of a Democratic president. One of Stevens's early objectives, only partially realized, was to build up territorial armed forces. Frustrated in his initial attempts, he helped push through a law organizing the militia through the territorial legislature in February 1855—although he struggled to get enough funding for the force he imagined. As militia companies began to take shape in the spring and summer of 1855, Stevens and his allies conjured up visions of batteries along the coast, cavalry to "subdue" Native peoples in the east, and riflemen on snowshoes to "ferret out the Indians in the mountain fastnesses, and summarily punish them." His full dream of military force was frustrated by budget constraints; as usual, imperial appropriations fell short of colonial ambitions. But Stevens was preparing for war, dreaming of a force fierce and flexible enough to pursue and kill Indians throughout the territory.[60]

Preparations for war inflected treaty making in the region, which Stevens was in charge of from 1854 to 1857. Stevens (as lawyer and historian Charles F. Wilkinson put it) "had his script and he meant to keep to it." Stevens pushed for as much Native land as possible, and he only reluctantly accommodated his interlocutors when pressed.[61]

But like Dart and Gaines in Oregon, Stevens thought it "injudicious" to immediately attempt to uproot and deport all Native peoples across the territory—after all, funding for the artillery, cavalry, and snowshoed riflemen with which he hoped to "summarily" kill Native people had not coalesced. Stevens instead attempted the seizure of most Native land while affirming other sovereign rights, and in some cases affirming Indigenous control over land not then demanded by White settlers. Further diminution, he believed, could be worked toward in future years. Although Native negotiators were sometimes able to extract important

Isaac I. Stevens as he appeared in the 1850s.
Courtesy of the Oregon Historical Society.

concessions from him in writing, Stevens pursued expedient seizure of land above all else. And he would warn and threaten violence to achieve his ends.[62]

Some of Stevens's threats were more subtle than others. In preparations for the Treaty of Medicine Creek/She-nah-nam, in 1854, his representatives Michael Troutman Simmons and Benjamin Franklin Shaw laid the groundwork for a treaty by telling locals that treaty making was the only way to "solve their trouble with the whites"—troubles that included murders committed by local Euro-Americans, which had been (and remained after the treaties were signed) unpunished. By 1856, Simmons was masterminding a series of internment camps in western Washington, and Shaw undertook a series of killings in the east, culminating in the Shaw Massacre, a mass killing in the Grand Ronde Valley. Given their inclination toward such violence, both men may have earlier menaced local communities in ways beyond what records can currently show.[63]

Sometimes Isaac I. Stevens made threats of violence more directly. When Governor Stevens got fed up at the pace of negotiations with Yakama leaders in June 1855—by which time the organization of militia companies had nearly been completed—he let his mask slip. As negotiator Andrew Pambrun recalled it: "[The] Governor getting out of patience recapitulated all that had been said and offered and concluded by saying, if you do not accept the terms offered and sign this paper (held up paper) you will walk in blood knee deep." This threat, remembered by two different witnesses of partially Native descent who were part of the Euro-American treaty party, was not recorded in the generally voluminous official record of the treaty talks—one of multiple omissions that had a practical utility when Stevens was defending his conduct and denying his lies a few years later. Acknowledged or not, the threat of White violence was a weapon most Euro-American leaders brandished.[64]

Treaties are living and powerful documents. In the United States, many of the most important fights to have Indigenous rights respected by the settler colonial state have been predicated on compelling American governments to live up to the promises made in treaties signed by previous generations. The original Native negotiators were able to weave important confirmations of some of their communities' sovereign rights into a number of these treaties. Generations of Native communities and Native leaders since have turned treaties into cornerstones of protection for many Native American nations. But the efforts and successes of Native negotiators need not obscure the violence and coercion that went into the seizure of Native land by means of paper. The threat of White violence—by the soldiery, by the settlers, by the volunteers occupying a hazy status in between—haunted nearly every treaty negotiation, whether or not it was voiced.[65]

Except perhaps for a brief period in the mid-1850s, the War on Illahee did not stretch across the whole of the Pacific Northwest, nor was it ever uniform and continuous. There were areas at temporary peace, occasional ceasefires, and plenty of nonviolent interactions between Native and White people. But most pioneers shared an overarching goal and vision of conquest, ready (whether reluctantly or eagerly) to kill so they could seize Native land. Individual wars were a part of a campaign of racial conquest seen as inevitable even by those Euro-Americans, like Samuel Parker, who regretted it. The Whitman killings may have been the inciting incident for the Cayuse War and were referenced as such for the

War on Illahee more generally. But ultimately, the War on Illahee was driven by Euro-American land hunger, and it would have happened without the Whitmans, or any of the other inciting incidents mentioned in this and the following chapters. Any counterfactual that imagines a Pacific Northwest without the War on Illahee must imagine away a vast plurality of Euro-Americans, their land hunger, and their ready recourse to racist violence.[66]

There was no Native action that could have prevented the War on Illahee. Different Indigenous polities navigated Euro-American violence and land hunger in different ways; some were more successful than others, often for reasons beyond their immediate control. What is striking, when reading through the hateful reminiscences and letters of blood-thirsty Euro-American volunteers on the front lines of the War on Illahee, is how much Pacific Northwest Native communities were able to preserve of their peoples, their lands, and their cultures in the face of so many invaders intent on ending them. Incalculably vast harm was done by the legions of Euro-American invaders and the people and governments that backed them—through killings, through assaults, through thefts, through removals, through decade after decade after decade of genocides, physical and cultural. That so many Native people and polities have survived and, in some cases, thrived is a testament to the skill, grit, and perseverance of generations.

CHAPTER TWO

Everyday Violence and the
Embrace of Genocide in Oregon

ON OCTOBER 8, 1855, shortly after he was elected a territorial delegate, James Lupton undertook the killing spree he had been ideating for years. Just before dawn, self-appointed "Major" Lupton led his band of "Exterminators" in a surprise attack on a sleeping camp at the mouth of Little Butte Creek, in southern Oregon. They knew their target, an Indigenous polity known to Euro-Americans as "Jake's Band," could be caught unawares. In September, only a few weeks before, Lupton had met with local Native communities promising peace. Because of these lies, as he assured his men when recruiting in the local tavern a few days before the attack, it would be easy to "massacre them while off their guard." Lupton and his volunteers, acting without the authority or knowledge of federal or territorial governments, starting shooting from the trees while it was still dark, then moved in to close quarters to use swords and knives on any survivors.

The massacre was less complete than Lupton had hoped. Though caught unawares by this sneak attack from people who had promised peace, some members of Jake's Band were able to run, hide, or even fight back. Lupton and his men, seeing their targets flee, purportedly "compelled" the few Native women captured alive to call out to "their husbands, and sons, and brothers, that they might be shot." While he was threatening to murder his hostages, Lupton himself was fatally shot by one of the defenders. Faced with resistance, Lupton's men broke off their pursuit of the fleeing survivors, instead finishing their attack by killing the wounded and desecrating the dead.[1]

Though many aspects of the Lupton Massacre have been disputed over the years, Lupton's devotion to mass killing is an agreed-upon fact. It remains unclear how many Indigenous people were killed in the attack; estimates range from around thirty to one hundred or more. When U.S. soldiers were taken to the scene of the massacre by outraged survivors the next day, they counted twenty-eight bodies. But several more of the slain were presumed to have washed downstream, and some of the wounded who were able to escape later died of their injuries. It is difficult to determine whether the volunteer soldiers called themselves "Exterminators," or whether that was a widely accepted moniker after the attack—certainly calls for "extermination" were unremarkable at the time. The ethnic makeup of Jake's Band has been disputed: they may have been majority Takelma or majority Ka'Hosadi Shasta, or they might have embraced an admixture of local Indigenous cultures and beliefs. Lupton probably targeted them because they were nearby and vulnerable, on land he wished to make his own; suggestions by latter-day apologists that the attack was meant as some sort of proactive defense lack evidence and plausibility. And even they agreed on Lupton's race hatred.[2]

At the brink of war in 1853, the last time the constant thrum of Euro-American violence had reached a fever pitch in southern Oregon, Lupton had been only barely restrained from an attempt to shoot down a group of Native people who he felt had been insolent. Lupton and a few compatriots met a group of Indigenous fighters on the road, and each had interrogated the other about their intentions—a reasonable act in uncertain times. Lupton was livid, and he pressed his companions to circle back and shoot down all their interlocutors, "to teach them better than to interfere with white men." Had his group not been outnumbered at the time, his Euro-American companions would have been prepared to let him try.[3]

The Lupton Massacre was unusual but not extraordinary, the most publicly outrageous event in a vast wave of Euro-American violence perpetrated in the Pacific Northwest during the War on Illahee in the 1850s. It is most famous because of what followed: reciprocal killings of local Euro-American families by Indigenous fighters inaugurated the last and most lethal phase of the Rogue River Wars, which ended in the extermination or expulsion of most Indigenous communities in the region.

The Rogue River Wars, in turn, were early rumblings of the crescendo of colonial violence that engulfed much of the Pacific Northwest by 1856. Although the Lupton Massacre is not well known among Americans today, it was better known at the time and has drawn far more attention since than similar mass killings of noncombatant Indigenous peoples in the Pacific Northwest in the same period, discussed later in this book. Some of these killings, such as the Maxon Massacre on the Nisqually River and the Shaw Massacre at Grand Ronde Valley, were initially well-known but fell (or were pushed) into obscurity. Other mass murders, like Hicks Massacre near modern-day Tacoma and the Bates Massacre near modern-day Grants Pass, have attracted almost no notice at all.[4]

Although akin to less famous mass killings in the War on Illahee, and sometimes used as the only example of such killings, the Lupton Massacre was not typical. The aftermath was witnessed by uninvolved Euro-Americans with a vested interest in reporting the killings; soldiers and officers from the nearby Table Rock Reservation were brought to the site of the massacre by the survivors within hours of the killing. The recorded body count for the massacre was unusually though not uniquely high for the region; most accounts of Euro-American violence against Native people involved fewer victims for a single attack or less official documentation—or both. The success of the volunteers in perpetrating the killings was unusual; in many other conflicts with Native people in the area, Euro-American volunteers were less able to achieve the mass murders they desired. And, along with much of the rest of the violence in southern Oregon, there were unusual financial motivators for federal authorities to emphasize the atrocity of the Lupton Massacre as a means of drawing clear distinctions between licit warfare (which the federal government might be expected to bankroll) and illegitimate vigilante violence (which it would not).

But attempted extermination of Native people in the Pacific Northwest was *not* unusual; it was often threatened and sometimes pursued, throughout the War on Illahee and beyond. The Lupton Massacre was the crest of a particularly devastating wave of genocidal assault in the Pacific Northwest, but it was part of the ebb and flow of everyday violence against Indigenous people practiced by Euro-American colonizers. During and beyond the mid-1800s, settler acts of theft, rape, and murder perpetrated against Indigenous people were frequently unpunished, ignored, or even lauded by much of White society. Genocide in the region went beyond the incidents reported and was pursued beyond the most notorious areas of southern Oregon. Calls for mass murder came often and off-handedly; endorsements of genocide were an acceptable part of the Euro-American public sphere in the pioneer Northwest.

Most Euro-Americans who came to the Pacific Northwest, after all, came with a settler colonial script honed by decades of American empire—and those who didn't soon learned it. Many came already viewing "Indians" as an amorphous, violent Other, an existential threat until proven otherwise. In letters, newspaper articles, and speeches, settlers typically referred to "Indians" and occasionally "friendly Indians" rather than more specific tribal, cultural, or political designations. Most saw no need to append "hostile" to the former; for Euro-Americans of the time, Native people were presumed hostile until proven otherwise.[5]

Even those pioneers who did not directly commit wanton violence against Native people typically found it acceptable. White would-be perpetrators of crimes against Indigenous communities had little to fear from the Euro-American justice system once hegemony was established; only a few among the most outrageous acts of violence were ever meaningfully prosecuted and punished. Euro-Americans committing such acts had more to fear from Indigenous communities themselves, who would mete out their own justice when practicable. But those Euro-Americans who wanted to steal from, rape, or kill Indigenous persons could do so knowing that if a counterattack came, they could most likely count on the Euro-American community to rally around White supremacy rather than support justice for the victims.

Significantly more Indigenous people were killed by settlers in the Pacific Northwest than has typically been assumed in academic scholarship. Population figures and population losses in the Indigenous Pacific Northwest before and in the early stages of American conquest remain informed estimates. Thousands were killed through colonialism—but how many thousands, and how many of those thousands were killed directly at the hands of the invaders, remains inchoate. Settlers who feared Indian attacks routinely overestimated Indigenous populations, and stories of Indian wars often inflated the number of Native fighters killed by orders of magnitude. Scholars have already revised down early pioneer accounts of battles to more accurate and modest figures. I contend, however, that although the killings in battles were often inflated, killings outside the conventions of war often went unreported—particularly when there was no official war on. It is most likely that the cold-blooded executions, acts of opportunistic murder, and attacks on Indigenous civilians in the records I discuss only scratch the surface of these killings.

Even though American colonization in the 1840s and 1850s is among the best-studied periods in the history of the Pacific Northwest, much of the secondary literature has been shaped by decades of incomplete erasure. Pioneer acts of aggression deemed dishonorable were edited out of public memory early and often. Though events like the Lupton Massacre might be reported in the papers, letters from locals were substantially less likely to mention acts of wanton violence initiated by pioneers. Indigenous counterattacks and reciprocal violence were thus seldom differentiated from other forms of aggression, and they were used as proof for the righteousness of exterminatory violence already in progress.[6]

The shape of the cover-up would change significantly in later decades; public pride in exterminatory violence began to fade in the twentieth century. But obfuscation of the evidence was there from the beginning. Many pioneers and volunteer soldiers did not wish that their wanton violence against noncombatants, women, and children be reported. In the winter of 1855–56, probably not knowing his interlocutor, John Beeson, planned to publish his remarks, one volunteer described the murders he had committed in southern Oregon with pathos. "We found several sick and famished Indians, who begged hard for mercy and for food," he remembered. "It hurt my feelings, but the understanding was that all were to be killed. So we did the work."[7]

Whether or not this guilt was usual, the "understanding" was common. Often unspoken understandings of pioneer mayhem, mutilation, and murder were normal in local conceptions of the colonization of the Pacific Northwest and shaped most stories of it, through whatever mix of silence and celebration. Wanton violence and genocide were the foundation on which the heroic edifices of pioneer history were built.

U.S. Navy Lieutenant Neil Howison, reporting on an 1846 visit to Oregon, voiced his distaste for the attacks on Indigenous people he had seen committed. Writing about Columbia River peoples, he reflected:

> As if the proximity of the white man were not sufficiently baneful in its insidious destruction of these unhappy people, our countrymen killed two by sudden violence and wounded another in an uncalled for and wanton manner during the few months of

my sojourn in the country. The only penalty to which the perpetrators of these different acts were subjected was the payment of
a blanket or a beef to their surviving kindred. Public opinion,
however, sets very strongly against such intrusions upon the degraded red man, and perhaps a year hence it may be strong
enough to hang an offender of this kind.[8]

Howison's predictions were dead wrong. With very few exceptions,
Euro-American Indian killers in the Pacific Northwest from the 1840s
through at least the 1870s could expect little more than censure from
their fellow Americans—and they often received plaudits. Indigenous
communities might sometimes be able to exact more serious penalties
themselves (and the threat of Indigenous justice might have kept
some wanton Euro-American murderers in check), but any strike against
the killers by Native people risked devastating repercussions. Euro-
American killers of Indians might or might not face negative public
opinion, but they could assuredly count on their fellow Euro-Americans
to defend them.[9]

Indeed, many of those Euro-Americans arguing (and even acting)
against wanton murder drew on practicality and fear as much as or more
than morality. Howison may have been sympathetic to the people whose
murders he decried (and thought any "humane citizen" would feel likewise), but his more trenchant warning was that with bad treatment "the
consequence might in all time to come be most deplorable for the peace
and safety of this country; where, from the sparseness of the population,
a band of forty or fifty blood-thirsty savages might surprise and destroy
in rotation hundreds of inhabitants."[10]

Worries like Howison's occasionally spurred authorities into
action. George H. Ambrose, who worked as an Indian agent in southern
Oregon in the mid-1850s, pursued one of the few successful prosecu-
tions of a wanton Indian killer in the 1850s Pacific Northwest. His motive for doing so was clear—to protect the White community from
counterattacks.

In 1854 a pioneer named John H. Miller started and lost a fistfight
with a local man known to Euro-Americans as Indian Jim, who was part
of a Native community made up mostly of Illinois Athabaskan people.
Angry at the loss of face, Miller went back to his camp, grabbed a revolver, and shot Jim down. To stop the Illinois from "committing some
serious depredations," Ambrose pursued a criminal case.[11]

Matthew Deady, the presiding judge, took it upon himself to instruct the jury to remember that Indians technically counted as people in the eyes of the court:

By the laws of this Territory it is made a criminal offence for "any person armed with a dangerous weapon to assault another with intent to murder," that is to assault another *person*. An Indian without reference to the position he occupies in the intellectual or moral scale of humanity is within the meaning of the Statute "a person"—a human being. Although the loss to society resulting from the death of an Indian may be comparatively small, yet the guilt of the slayer, or one who attempts to slay is none the less complete, whatever may be the color of the victim.[12]

Unusually, John H. Miller was tried and convicted for the wanton murder he inflicted. The Euro-American view that the murder of an Indian was "comparatively small" may not have kept him from conviction, but it did influence Miller's punishment. Deady sentenced him to two years in prison for the murder he had committed. Miller may even have served some portion of that time. A Native person who had killed a White person in a similar manner would have been put to death.

But even this light criminal consequence for a Euro-American murderer of an Indian was unusual. Indeed, a different pioneer, also named John Miller, had escaped judicial punishment for a series of rapes and murders only a few months before. In the early 1850s, sentencing a killer of Native people to a few years in prison was as far as Euro-American justice could go in the Northwest. And in the pioneer period, it wouldn't go that far again.[13]

Although he might pursue limited justice to preserve peace, Ambrose was at heart sympathetic to genocide. Writing semi-anonymously about the Native people he claimed were in his charge, Ambrose proclaimed "I would not care how soon they were all dead, and I believe the country would be greatly benefited by it." His objection to genocide was practical, not moral—and it did not preclude the many deaths inflicted by the Trails of Tears he forced people through in 1856 (see chapter 5).[14]

General John E. Wool, the U.S. officer in charge of military operations on the Pacific Coast from 1854 to 1857, has sometimes had his distaste for wanton White violence mistaken for humanitarianism. His reputation

General John Ellis Wool, probably as he appeared in the 1850s.
Courtesy of the Oregon Historical Society.

as a "friend to the Indians" was made by his enemies in the Oregon and Washington territories, most of whom saw humanity toward Native people as execrable. In the aftermath of the 1855 Lupton Massacre, Wool refused to hand over federal arms to unsanctioned militias and explained that he didn't then have enough troops to assist in every volunteer effort across the region to deprive Native people of their land, liberty, and lives. Branded as a coward and a traitor by many—the *Oregon Argus* suggested that the general "deserve[d] to have his wool taken from the top of his cocoanut"—Wool was an "Indian sympathizer" only insomuch as he objected to killings without purpose, which might provoke counterattacks against White settlers. As historian Laurence M. Hauptman put it, "Wool was no humanitarian but a professional military officer," and his objections to vigilante violence against Native people stemmed from "cost efficiency" more than morality. He was perfectly willing to threaten genocide to compel compliance.[15]

General Wool expressed certainty about who was inciting the violence—"lawless whites," whose "lawless barbarity practices upon tribes of Indians of the most inoffensive nature [had] apparently no motive but wanton cruelty." He laced his letters with scorn for "the lawlessness and brutality of a certain class of white frontiersmen" and occasionally expressed sympathy for the Native people they attacked. But ultimately Wool believed his mission was to "give the best protection to the white inhabitants and restrain the Indians."[16]

Like other American officials, Wool was there for land, seized "voluntarily" or otherwise. His 1854 orders to his officers were to soften the ground for land taking through treaties and to be ready for the use of force:

> If you can use any influence with the Indians to induce them to comply voluntarily ... do so. You should be careful to make known to the Indians that the object in collecting them upon a Reserve is to locate them upon lands under control of the Government, and from which lawless whites who might wish to injure them, can by law be excluded. . . .
>
> The only circumstances under which you would be required to use your force in regard to the Indians, would be in case they were to commence hostilities upon the Settlers; or if the Superintendent should call upon you for military assistance in moving any tribe when it became a measure of necessity to preserve peace.[17]

These orders gave the officers serving under Wool relatively wide latitude to deploy force against Native people in the Northwest. Wool's framing suggests he expected Native compliance in their own removal from their homelands to be extracted sooner or later, voluntary or no. And the orders to use force if "the Indians ... commence[d] hostilities upon the Settlers" did not exempt Native reprisals for Euro-American violence. Indeed, even the perceived threat of retaliatory violence could be a pretext for removal to "preserve the peace."

In his letter preparing Army Inspector General J. Mansfield for his 1854 tour of the Pacific Coast, Wool was circumspect about the slaying of Native people but clear about national goals: "If we can get the Indians to settle on these Reserves and to cultivate the land, it will not only preserve these people [who] are fast disappearing by disease and other causes from the face of the land of their fathers, but relieve us of much trouble and a great expense maintaining [a] military post in the interior." Principal among the "other causes" were murderous bands of vigilantes, as Wool well knew. But ultimately those vigilantes were among the White inhabitants he was expected to protect.[18]

The volunteers, vigilantes, and criminals who attacked Native people and communities did so rightly suspecting that when push came to shove, they could count on the United States, sooner or later, to defend them from counterattacks. General Wool may have been denounced by locals because his willingness to pursue genocide lacked zeal, and he was blamed for providing insufficient federal resources to pursue war against Native people. Wool may have meant it when he declared the reservation system "to be the only mode of preventing frequent collisions with the whites and the ultimate extermination of the red men." But Wool's objections to the immoral actions and haphazard approaches of local settlers should not obscure that fact that he shared roughly the same dream of American empire. For Wool, killing in the service of empire was a last resort. For others, it was the first.[19]

William Henderson Packwood "contracted the western fever and decided [to] become a United States soldier" in 1848, at the age of sixteen, leaving his peripatetic midwestern slaveholding family and journeying west. Learning the ropes from a bunkmate who had been "a soldier in Florida in the Seminole Indian War," Packwood was deployed to Fort Vancouver, along the Columbia River. He first saw combat in 1852 in southwestern Oregon territory, attacking Indians in their homes. There was, as usual, no official war declared. After leaving the army in 1853, Packwood "decided to become a gold hunter," seeking treasure in the hills he had tromped over as a soldier.[20]

His career as an Indian killer continued. Packwood joined a "company of rangers" that formed to attack "bothersome" Coquille/Coquelle settlements in 1854, participating in the Nasomah Massacre/Abbott Massacre—a mass killing of Coquille/Coquelle people. Notably, the threadbare reasons for the massacre given in the official record (cutting the ferry rope used by the invaders, refusing to meet with a murderous mob) were not a part of Packwood's reminiscence; he recalled only that

*William Henderson Packwood around 1890, decades into
his political career. Courtesy of the Baker County Public Library,
Baker City, Oregon.*

"our camp and people in the surrounding country decided to beat [the
Indians] back." Packwood followed this unofficial vigilante violence with
an official government commission during the Rogue River Wars in
1855, and he rejoined the "volunteer militia" in Coos Bay, "running
down bad Indians" by, for example, attempting to imprison Native people whom pioneers saw as out of place, on pain of death. Then Packwood
returned to gold mining, always ready to take up what he called the
"rude laws" of mining country when necessary—whether against "man"
or "Indian," categories he differentiated in his account.[21]

After five years spent alternately killing Native people and mining
for gold on land seized from them, William Henderson Packwood was
given a job on the Siletz Reservation in 1857, occupied principally with

attempting to take away the weapons of those Native people placed there. His history of violence was an asset in his burgeoning political career, and it probably contributed to his election as a representative for Curry County to the Oregon Constitutional Convention in 1857; he eventually gained fame as the final living member of that body. Packwood continued his roundelay of wars, mining, and "Indian service" for much of the rest of the 1800s. Although Packwood consistently failed as a miner and speculator, he was able to gain success as a politician and public servant, leveraging his years of what newspapers lauded as "subjugat[ing] the turbulent r_dsk_ns" into a political dynasty that lasted generations.[22]

Violence against Native people as a volunteer was widely seen as a political asset in the 1850s. Distrust of regular army personnel was high—the first Oregon Constitution barred regular soldiers from voting. But citizen-soldiers were politically popular. In 1856 Judge Matthew Deady bemoaned how many had been "elevated so far above the earth ... [by] the mere *accident* of being at the head of a party of men who found and killed some Indians in an open country under none but ordinary circumstances." And support for Indian killing could be bipartisan— the Democrat-aligned *Oregon Statesman*, Whig-aligned *Oregon Argus*, and performatively neutral Democrat-aligned *Oregon Spectator* and *Oregonian* all printed editorials calling for mass killings in the 1850s.[23]

The political utility of volunteer violence was on display especially in the lead-up to the elections of 1855 (the same elections that got James Lupton his political office, shortly before he was killed perpetrating the massacre that bears his name). Joseph Lane and John P. Gaines were both running for the position of Oregon territorial delegate to Congress. Both were former territorial governors, both were U.S.–Mexico War veterans, and both claimed to have been participants in Oregon's undeclared Indian wars. Speaking before an appreciative audience in southern Oregon, each man bragged of having "taken 'a turn at the sq__ws' " in the wars of the early 1850s, a barely coded reference to rapes apparently approved of by the audience. This came as a moment of comity. The two men clashed over one another's war service in Mexico and argued about the Missouri Compromise. Lane accused Gaines of cowardice; Gaines archly accused Lane of being sexually attracted to smelly old men. The two men seem to have consistently agreed on three things when campaigning in southern Oregon in 1855: that Oregonians were "the wisest bravest handsomest ... most magnanimous most intelligent people on the face of the earth"; that although both men illegally enslaved people in Oregon, neither should bring up the other's involvement; and that bragging about sexually assaulting Native women was a good way to win some pioneer votes. This political posturing is indicative of a rough pioneer consensus on violence among many Oregonians in the early 1850s.[24]

The pervasiveness of Euro-American attacks on Indigenous communities in southern Oregon is a well-established part of the historical record. The infamy of incidents like the Lupton Massacre has waxed and waned, but the violence has always been part of the historical canon. Scholars have demonstrated beyond a reasonable doubt that bands of Euro-Americans pursued the mass extermination of Native communities in the region. Debate may continue regarding the culpability of regional officials, the extent of support (or success) the marauders enjoyed, and technical aspects of terminology. But as Gray Whaley, David G. Lewis, George B. Wasson, and many others have shown, it is established fact that there were multiple organized attempts at extermination in southern Oregon.[25]

And pioneers recognized that many of their attacks were, effectively, war crimes. As Charles S. Drew, a politician and eventual military officer, put it in a letter demanding pay for volunteers in 1854, Americans pursued "a mode of warfare, inconsistent perhaps in some instances, with the laws governing nations, yet altogether more effectual. The tactics of armies are but shackles and fetters in the prosecution of an Indian war. 'Fire must be fought with fire'; and the soldier, to be successful, must, in a great measure, adopt the mode of warfare pursued by the savage." As historian Karl Jacoby, among others, has demonstrated, Euro-American would-be exterminators often projected their genocidal intentions onto their foes. The money Drew demanded raised a scandal regionally, but the endorsement of war crimes did not.[26]

Plenty of pioneers killed without such a preamble. James Lupton was far from the only man waiting for his moment, and Loren L. Williams was far from the only volunteer who signed up for a chance at killing. As one volunteer, Charles Blair, wrote, "Every man [was] anxious to kill the first indian." And often, any would do. In 1851 a gang of Euro-Americans in southern Oregon, near Wolf Creek, "who had some grievance against the indians" decided they wanted to lynch a Native person and grabbed the first one they found. The incident became a local legend because one of the killers realized, as they began the lynching, that their chosen victim was not a stranger but an acquaintance—who owed him a dollar and fifty cents. So the men halted the proceedings long enough to collect "six bits," and for their victim to make arrangements for the rest of his money to be passed on to his family. And then they hanged him.[27]

Martin Angell (sometimes spelled Angel), a pioneer who took land near Jacksonville in 1852, stood out *even in southern Oregon* for having "an inveterate hatred of the [Indian] race." He was most infamous for urging the public lynching of a nine-year-old Native boy on the streets of Jacksonville in August 1853, shouting, "Hang him, hang him; he will make a murderer when he is grown," which convinced most of the last waverers in a lynch mob to stand aside as the citizens of Jacksonville finished strangling the child to death. Angell was also known for more spontaneous murder—it was remembered that "Angell, from his own door[,] shot a peaceable Indian who was passing." Angell's wife was described locally as "a half breed," but her supposed Indigenous heritage did not keep him from being an eager proponent of killing and genocide. After Angell was executed for his misdeeds by an unidentified presumed-to-be Native person in 1856, he was eulogized locally as "a kind husband and father and an influential citizen, but an implacable enemy to the whole Indian race." It is unclear whether there was evidence that Angell had been a kind husband, or if this descriptor was merely the standard pablum of pioneer eulogy. Whether or not he was kind to his partially Native wife, Angell was provably "an implacable enemy" to Native people generally. His marriage, whatever it was like, did not preclude a racism so violently vile that it attracted notice even in 1850s southern Oregon.[28]

Unlike local news and later legends, Euro-American letters home often ignored violence against Native people, even when the writer didn't have a stake in it. The letters of Clinton Schieffelin demonstrate this particularly well. Schieffelin and his brother Joseph bought a farm near Jacksonville in November 1853, a few months after the close of the first Rogue River conflict. Unusually for a Euro-American resident, and especially unusually for a would-be gold miner, Schieffelin initially appears to have hoped for coercive assimilation rather than mass extermination of his Indigenous neighbors. He wrote in 1854, "We never shal hav mor difficulty with th[e]m" now that local Indigenous persons were trying their hands at farming, one such farm sitting just across the Rogue River from his own.[29]

Clinton Schieffelin said that he nursed and fed "Old Jo" (most likely Chief Apserkahar) as the famed Indigenous leader was dying from tuberculosis in 1854—and later claimed that this act of kindness had saved the lives of himself and his brother. On October 9, 1855, the day following the Lupton Massacre, Joseph Schieffelin was stopped by "Ol[d] Sam the head Che[i]f" who "tol[d] him to go home." Indigenous fighters killed Euro-American families along the Rogue River in retaliation for the mass murder Lupton and his men had committed. Neighbors on both sides had their houses burned, and many were killed. But Clinton and Joseph Schieffelin (and their homestead) were "spar[ed] unhurt and unin[ju]r[e]d." Having previously shown a level of sympathy and humanity to local Indigenous communities and people, they were passed over during the measured reprisals that followed the Lupton Massacre. The Scheiffelins, however, sided unequivocally with their Euro-American compatriots. With his White neighbors dead and American supremacy in the Rogue River region threatened, Clinton Scheiffelin joined a volunteer company on October 20, 1855, and took part in the Battle of Hungry Hill (see below).[30]

Clinton Scheiffelin never mentioned Euro-American aggressions in his letters home. It is difficult to imagine that he was unaware of the Lupton Massacre or similar, smaller incidents. Clinton Scheiffelin tended bar in Jacksonville, where the attack at Little Butte Creek had been coordinated; his brother Joseph had traveled through Table Rock Reservation a few days after the attack; and Clinton probably served alongside men who had participated in it. It beggars belief that Clinton Scheiffelin did not acquire some sense of what had spurred his Indigenous acquaintances to respond with such violence. But the story of the Lupton Massacre he deemed irrelevant or unfit for consumption when composing his letters. Even to a comparatively sympathetic settler like Scheiffelin, the wanton killing of Native people was nothing to write home about.[31]

One of the few exceptions to the norms of complicity and silence was John Beeson, an Oregon Anglo-American settler horrified by the violence done to his Indigenous neighbors. The "mischief-making policy of Squatter Sovereignty," he declared after being forced out of Oregon in 1856, had allowed "violence and outrage ... to a dreadful degree." Beeson still wanted Native land for himself, and he hoped for a future where Native people rejected their culture and their past. But he was appalled that for so many of his fellow pioneers, Native people "came to be thought of as game to be shot, or vermin to be destroyed" and were "shot whenever it could be done with safety to the shooter."[32]

In his self-published *Plea for the Indians*—one of the most vital sources on Oregon pioneer violence in the era—Beeson suggested that many Euro-Americans in southern Oregon were (like him) dismayed by calls for mass extermination but were intimidated into keeping silent. But Beeson was one of the few such supposedly sympathetic settlers to make his objections public—and not without reason. Volunteers threatened to "kill him [as] an Indian just because he ha[d] spoken the truth out boldly against the rascality of this Indian War, or rather butchery of the Indians." Notably, the outcry reached a fever pitch only in May 1856, even though Beeson had been publicly against the killings since the 1855 Lupton Massacre. His plans to publish the truth, much more than the objections themselves, spurred the death threats he got from local volunteers. John Beeson was forced to flee Oregon in the dead of night, only hours ahead of a lynch mob. He spent the rest of his life campaigning for humanity toward Native people, but he was unable to return to his family until after the War on Illahee had concluded.[33]

Being a proclaimed "friend of the Indians" did not preclude participation in mass killings. Such claims may often have been latter-day fabrications or exaggerations. Joseph Lane trumpeted his friendship and honesty in dealing with Native people by the late 1870s, but he had run for office in the 1850s on his record as an Indian fighter, cracked jokes about sexually assaulting Native women, and commended mass killings of Indigenous people by other military officials. His sometime public focus on positive and honest relations with Native peoples in his old age was probably a reaction to the sordid reputation he had acquired during the Civil War as a Confederate sympathizer. But it may have been one-sidedly accurate. Perhaps, as his family remembered, Joe Lane *was* seen as a friend when he persuaded local leader Apserkahar to stand down at the close of the 1853 Rogue River War. Apserkahar did take the name "Chief Joe" in dealing with White people, possibly (as Lane family lore had it) intended to be a sign of esteem. And perhaps that perception of friendship survived among some of Apserkahar's followers after their leader died of disease, and after wanton violence from White settlers pushed them into an even more costly war, and after the Trails of Tears that followed. But that friendship, if real, was not reciprocated. Joseph Lane was a staunch supporter of Indian killing and Indian killers; he may have been a friend *of* the Indians, but he was not a friend *to* them. Rather, as he said in Congress and (perhaps) in church, Joseph Lane believed that "the Inj_ns should be skulped [*sic*]."[34]

And there were others like him. Late in life, James "Uncle Jimmy" Twogood wrote about his time as a miner and tavern keeper in southern Oregon in the early 1850s. He claimed unusual friendship with local Native people. "I made the Indians a special study," Twogood wrote in 1897, "learned some of their language. It pleased them; [they] were quite friendly; [they] seemed to like me and I do not think they would have killed me, from the fact that they had plenty of chance." This perception of friendship, he claimed, made him slow to realize "that the R_dsk_ns wer[e] on the War path" in 1855. If true, this required some mental dexterity on Twogood's part, for he knew of numerous instances of Euro-American violence in the period—and called for killings himself.[35]

Indeed, Twogood's transition from miner to tavern keeper was enabled by a massacre. In 1853, shortly after Joseph Lane negotiated a treaty that paused the Rogue River War, a group of Euro-American men led by a man named Bates lured a group of Indigenous people who lived along Grave Creek into Bates's tavern, promising a meal and conversation. Then the conspirators barred the door, murdered the whole group, and buried them in a mass grave. The number of dead was unknown—perhaps a few dozen. Bates decorated his tavern with the severed head of an Indigenous man; whether it was from this incident or another is unclear. When Bates left to seek his fortune in South America shortly after the killings, Twogood took over his tavern. It is not known why Bates left—perhaps he felt under threat by the few remaining relatives of those he had murdered, or he simply wanted to seek greener pastures. Whether he left up or took down Bates's grisly decorations, Twogood almost certainly knew about the Bates Massacre. But he made no mention of any of this in his reminiscences.[36]

James H. Twogood was a friend to the killers, not the Indians. Describing the 1855 Lupton Massacre as a counterattack responding to supposed depredations by Native people (which he said had been led by Chief Joe [Apserkahar], widely known in southern Oregon to have died in 1854), Twogood wrote that "a company of volunteers ... under command of my good friend, Major Lupton ... attacked the Indians Sunday morning, October 9. Quite a number of whites were wounded, and Major Lupton was shot through with an arrow that proved fatal." This account from Twogood was published in 1910, so perhaps his memory was distorted. But it is nonetheless striking that the Native deaths in the Lupton Massacre, the most famous event of its kind in Oregon, disappeared entirely from his narration.[37]

Twogood certainly remained cognizant of the exterminatory intent of his cohort. Writing about his experiences as a volunteer soldier, Twogood painted a vivid picture of his fellow pioneers on the eve of the Battle of Hungry Hill, which took place on October 31, 1855. They were hoping to pull off an attack similar to the Lupton Massacre along Grave Creek, to

> start down the creek as soon as it got dark in order to be near them and take them by surprise about daylight the next morning. Sq__ws and p_p[__]s_s [children] were with them, and they should shoot everything they came to, regardless; for nits bred lice etc. . . .
>
> Scalps were what they were bound to have. . . . I pitied every one of them, thinks I—if you had lived with those Inj_ns for four years, knew them as I know them, you'd not be quite so fierce, and what was the result? . . . Mr. Inj_n . . . ran the whole shooting match back to camp. . . . Not over 4 or 5 Indians killed; but s[o]me 30 Whites killed and wounded.
>
> And not a scalp brought into camp.[38]

Left: Joseph Lane after he was elected U.S. senator from Oregon in 1859. Courtesy of the National Portrait Gallery, Smithsonian Institution. Right: Joseph Lane in 1879, as he was trying to refurbish his place in history and politics. Courtesy of Willamette Falls & Landings Heritage Area Coalition and Old Oregon Photos.

As Twogood remembered (and as scholar Mark Axel Tveskov has proven), volunteers at the Battle of Hungry Hill had been intent on mass murder but were instead routed. Superior strategy and skill by the Native men and women defending their community from genocide outweighed the significant numerical advantage of the volunteers. The prevalence of racism and cowardice among the Euro-Americans also played a role—the former prompted a too hasty charge, the latter a quick retreat. But the rank incompetence of the volunteer forces should not obscure their deadly purpose. The volunteers attempted indiscriminate killing, and in this instance they failed. At other times and places they succeeded—usually at a smaller scale, when they possessed even greater disproportionate force than they had in the Battle of Hungry Hill. The site of the 1851 lynching at Wolf Creek was within a day's ride of the battle, Bates's tavern perhaps two days away. It is likely there were other murder grounds nearby, so far even less visible in the historical record.[39]

It is possible that some Native people did think of "Uncle Jimmy" Twogood as friendly (at least by comparison to other Euro-Americans), and that he fooled them into thinking that friendship was genuine. It is possible that Twogood did have knowledge of some Native language—or, more likely, a grasp of the simplified Chinook Jargon used to communicate with Americans. But familiarity with people or culture does not always breed sympathy. It is quite clear that Twogood's sympathies were with the exterminators, from his "good friend" Lupton on down. And Twogood, like most of his contemporaries, spoke of "Indians" rather than individual ethnies. Like Joseph Lane, he may have been a "friend of the Indians," but it is unlikely he was much of a friend *to* them—though he may have wanted to be remembered as one later in life. In a ranting letter sent to Joseph Lane in 1856, James Twogood expressed his abhorrence of so-called friendly Indians in a letter attacking those who critiqued southern Oregon generally or the Lupton Massacre specifically:

> Sir, I do believe in *nine cases out of ten* it is th[ese] *good Indians, these pets*, that have learned the manners and customs of the whites and have always been well treated, it is these *very pets*, sir, that are the ringleaders of these marauding parties. And then they have [a] peculiar way of expressing their thanks to their benefactors by shooting them down without a moment's warning. If the people in the States were really aware what *grateful*

beings our *good Indians* are I don't think they would be quite *so free* in expressing their sympathies in behalf of the *poor Indian*.⁴⁰

Around forty years later, "Uncle Jimmy" Twogood claimed he had always been a "friend of the Indians." He was lying to his interlocutors, deceiving himself, or possessed of a truly perverse definition of *friendship*. He stood with the killers.

Americans' belief in a vast race war could help create one. Decades after these events, John Hamblock reminisced about his role in bringing news of a general Indian war to Port Orford, Oregon, in February 1856. A careful reading of the evidence suggests Hamblock brought not just news but the war itself to the region, galvanizing pioneer race hatred to spur new attacks on local Native communities.

Even by late February 1856, Indigenous communities along the southwestern coast of Oregon did not necessarily think that the expanding War on Illahee would reach them. When Hamblock was riding hard for Port Orford to report volunteer military losses in the Rogue River region, he passed a large group of Native people (possibly Tolowa) coming home from a "shindig," in a jovial mood. Hamblock remembered having his gun at the ready, recalled being dismayed that the Native people who made way for his horse did not step back far enough, and imagined that he and his horse had shared a moment of solidaric racism as they were passing. He was sure that he had escaped death only because the Native people he had encountered did not yet know of "the outbreak"—a war that had been going on for at least three months at this point, and arguably for much longer than that. The notion that local Indigenous people would not necessarily have been interested in an all-out race war seems never to have occurred to Hamblock.⁴¹

A few nights after Hamblock brought his warning, a volunteer named Silvaster Long was guarding the beach south of Port Orford when he saw a person he perceived to be Indigenous approaching at the tideline. Long shouted at the person, and they began to move away from him. At this point Long opened fire, but he was unable to kill the fleeing figure before they got away. Hamblock's interpretation was that the person Silvaster Long had fired upon was a spy, sent to single-handedly "do us up before daylight." Hamblock thus presumed both that local Indigenous communities were initially unaware of a war that had been raging for months *and* that within two days of his arrival, they had sent some sort of commando ready to dispatch dozens in the dead of night—who then ran away at the first sign of trouble.⁴²

The sequence of events (and common sense) might suggest instead that Long brought local Native people into the broader race war Euro-Americans were waging by shooting at a neighbor without provocation. Local Indigenous communities had presumed, perhaps, that the war on the Rogue River need not touch them, that existing peaceful relationships would hold. Indeed, Hamblock's reminiscence included his distrust of a Euro-American man named Hinch, who had married a local Native woman, and who was prevented from warning his Indigenous in-laws to stay away from excitable volunteer forces. Hamblock assumed all Native people were simply waiting for their moment to attack the Whites, and people died. Such a presumption might have held water because of how many Euro-Americans were waiting (or *not* waiting) for their chance to attack Indians. The ragged volunteers who mustered in Port Orford initially inflicted more casualties on themselves in military accidents than on the peoples against whom they indiscriminately made war. But by March 1856, regular troops were murdering Native men and women alike in the region, with the advice and encouragement of local vigilantes.⁴³

There were innumerable killings beyond battles and famous events. Often only casual mentions persist in the historical record. When U.S. Army Captain Edward O. C. Ord marched through the Chetco River region of southwest Oregon in March 1856, he mentioned in passing in his diary that there had been "2 sq__ws killed here lately—on suspicion." These killings—without obvious specific cause or evidence—were treated as unremarkable and common. A few days later he killed some more Native women, either as participants or collateral damage in an attack, and gave no count of how many. Such killings would seldom make their way into a military report.⁴⁴

Caroline Stumbo, who moved to Oregon with her husband Hiram Niday in 1852, brought with her a hatred and perhaps a fear of Native people. She watched at least one execution performed by southern Oregon volunteers in 1854 with gusto, and she was ready for disaster or violence after her husband died (of natural causes) amid rising tensions in 1855. She fled her home expecting (not unreasonably) to be killed following the counterattacks responding to the Lupton Massacre in October 1855, and she and her children took refuge at Fort Leland, in the Grave Creek area, briefly the site of a battle that same night. As family lore had it: "With the volunteers was an Indian scout by the name of Hank Brown, who walked into the fort and said to his mother, 'Was you scared yesterday when the Indians was after you?' She said, 'Yes, Hank, I wish they were all dead.' Just then he threw seven long haired scalps into her lap saying, 'There are seven good Indians, my part of last night's fight.' " Caroline Stumbo Niday was directly involved in at least one later attempt to make the Indians "all dead," taking up a gun in a battle along Cow Creek in 1856. Making war on Indians was also how she met her second husband, David Sexton, who fought in the Indian wars from 1853 to 1857—the year of their marriage. Killing in the War on Illahee brought them together.[45]

Samuel R. Templeton, a volunteer who fought in the Rogue River region in 1855 and 1856, remembered four decades later that his company had shot at any Indian they saw. A few of Templeton's stories involved battles with well-armed groups. A few others involved shooting prisoners who were supposedly trying to escape (including "one of them we intended to hang if I had got him to the fort"). And occasionally, if the first volley missed, they might rob people without killing them first. A day after executing a prisoner, Templeton and his company shot at another Native man and woman, who immediately "fell down and said don't shoot." The company robbed him of "one hundred and ten dollars in gold dust a pistol and some am[m]unition," a detail that Templeton probably meant to be condemnatory—but which inadvertently showed that he and his men shot at and mugged the pair for no crime other than being Indian. Templeton left it unclear whether these victims had survived. The important part was the gold and guns he had looted.[46]

In December 1855, Oregon Territorial Governor George Law Curry answered questions about volunteer conduct with whataboutism rather than denial. As Curry put it in a letter to Judge William D. Kelley of Pennsylvania:

> You must not allow your benevolent feelings to prejudice your judgment in regard to our warfare with the Indians. You will read much in the papers about the War and the Conduct of the Volunteers which may seem barbarous and inhuman, but the truth is that the Indian on our frontiers who has so ruthlessly massacred our people, even little innocent children, does not possess any of the ennobling traits that marked the character of the aborigines who bordered the primitive settlement or colonies of the Eastern States. They are faithless and merciless, and the people of Oregon are as one man in sentiment.[47]

Notably, Curry did not deny the "barbarous and inhuman" conduct of the volunteers, instead implicitly arguing that it was justified by the supposed "faithless and merciless" nature of local people—and that volunteer violence should be excused by the broad support it had in the Oregon Euro-American community. Curry had attempted in vain to assert control over volunteer violence in the fall of 1855, and to disband autonomous units (such as William H. Packwood's, in the Coquille region) that were spreading the war in Oregon. But though they had ignored his orders and committed all manner of horrors, Curry still defended even those volunteers he had briefly tried to slow down. Politically, excusing genocide was the only move that made sense.[48]

Was it the genocide or the infamy that made southern Oregon unusual? The War on Illahee from 1847 to 1858 featured recurrent tensions between federal and local armed forces throughout the region, but those tensions were highest in southern Oregon. Bands of Euro-American murderers appear in the records to have been more numerous in southern Oregon (and northern California) than elsewhere. Euro-American reports of wanton violence were more common and more likely there. This infamy probably stems in part from there actually being comparatively more violence. But there were also unusually sharp distinctions between U.S. officials and local politicians in southern Oregon compared to elsewhere in the Pacific Northwest. Federal officials were motivated to weaponize the truth of local Euro-Americans' pursuit of genocide, in part to avoid being blamed for—or billed for—the expensive failures of the wars in southern Oregon.

Euro-Americans who objected to genocide in the far West often blamed it on low-class gold miners. But if, as men like Jesse Applegate averred, White gold miners were particularly prone to exterminatory violence, it bears remembering that gold miners notoriously did not stay in one place or profession. What they wreaked in southern Oregon they wreaked elsewhere. Where White miners went, they did violence—whether organized or not.[49]

Miners might become soldiers, and soldiers might become miners. Indeed, desertion to try one's luck in the mines was apparently a serious issue in the U.S. Army's Department of the Pacific in 1854; one officer suggested that it be widely put about "that there is probably more suffering among the miners than among any other class of people in this country." This problem was particularly acute among the volunteers.

Volunteer officers during longer campaigns of conquest in the Pacific Northwest expressed "strong doubts of their ability to prevent the desertion of the major part of their forces ... to the min[e]s[,] very many of them having been old miners in California." Many of the more notorious figures in the Pacific Northwest wars, including Joseph Lane, were also would-be gold miners.[50]

The notion that an onslaught of (presumptively White) miners meant violence against Native people was widely understood in the 1850s and 1860s. A "stampede" of White gold miners to the Colville region of northern Washington from 1855 to 1858 precipitated and continued wars there. Another stampede of White gold miners in the Fraser River area in 1857 and 1858 brought mayhem and murder farther north. As one man of the thousands pressing for the seizure of Nez Perce/Nimiipuu land near Clearwater River in 1861 put it, if "this portion of the reservation" was not purchased quickly, "we will have the Nez Perc[e] at war with us. Miners can not be kept from that country. Indeed the miners are the only hope of every body here." White gold miners were known to be prone to invasions and violence—which to many Euro-Americans was worth the prosperity they promised.[51]

One representative sample of the overlap between mining and soldiering would be the case of the appropriately named Andrew J. Miner. When Miner applied for military benefits in 1903, he wrote that when he arrived in Oregon, his only "regularly enlisted" service had been "in [the] Missouri militia in the Mormon Trouble 1844–5"—apparently indicating he was involved in the Illinois "Mormon War" of that period. But Miner, who worked as a miner, noted the several times when he had "served as a Volunteer in the Indians Wars." In the summer of 1854, when there was no declared war, he participated in a lethal surprise attack on a Coquille River camp that he claimed killed "sixty or seventy" Native people—possibly the Nasomah/Abbott Massacre, possibly a different mass killing. He fought as an irregular volunteer in a Jacksonville militia that mustered just after the Battle of Hungry Hill, in 1855. He teamed up with "about 15 Prospectors" at "Indian Creek, on the Klamath River, in 1856," and killed three Indians for unspecified reasons—notable because every other incident of violence he recalled was connected to a real or imagined murder. He claimed to have been involved in a killing of "about forty Indians" (probably Ka'hosadi Shasta) along the Scott River that same year. And he was later involved in the Idaho portion of the so-called Snake War in the 1860s.[52]

Miner's file was full of praise from witnesses who believed these kill-ings should earn him monetary support in his old age. As an accompany-ing affidavit put it, "Andrew J. Miner [was] engaged in frequent fights with the Indians. . . . [He] was a noted Character, and was well known among the Miners and frontier men at that time, and his reputation for and as an Indian fighter was well known among us mining men." It did not matter to the men who vouched for him when and whether Miner had been a soldier. They thought all his Indian killing counted toward his character.[53]

But many pioneer killings had nothing to do with mining. Sarah Lauer (née Freundlich, Anglicized to Friendly) regaled her grandchildren with the story of a killing she claimed to have committed as a pioneer in the city of Eugene in the 1850s. While she was visiting with a female friend from the household of the town's founder, Eugene F. Skinner, a Native man came to the house. As Sarah Lauer put it (according to her grand-son): "A drunken Indian came in, and they were scared to death, so they felt that the best thing they could do was to give him more to drink. So they sat him down in a big rocking chair in front of the fireplace and kept feeding him booze until he just about passed out, and then the two gals just took the rocking chair and pushed it into the fire. . . . He was pretty wild and they were scared to death and it was just a matter of sal-vation. So they 'done him in' as the saying is." The perceived drunken-ness and Indian-ness of their victim were apparently enough to justify murder in the name of fear; the only act of violence in the story was when the two "gals" burned a man alive.[54]

General fear and hatred of Native people were present in urban and rural spaces alike. Stories of so-called Indian depredations else where in the Pacific Northwest could spark mob violence in Portland. Captain John Commingers Ainsworth, who ran a sternwheel boat along the Columbia River in 1856, remembered that the "Indians as temporary help" that he had hired to unload the boat were unable to land safely in Portland because of "very intense" excitement about attacks hours to the east (with which the Native people on board, of course, had no obvious connection). Forced to continue with Ainsworth's boat after it had been repurposed for military support, these Native day laborers came within a hairsbreadth of being shot farther up in the Cascades by "sentinels [who] had been instructed to shoot any Indian they saw." Many Portlanders soon joined Hamilton Maxon's volunteer company, which committed a series of killings in northwestern Washington that year and attempted more in southeastern Washington.[55]

The Native men on Ainsworth's ship were lucky to escape with their lives. After a group of presumed Yakama and Klickitat/Qwû'lh-hwai-pûm fighters attacked the settlement known as "the Cascades," volunteers and regulars poured into the region, killing and scalping any presumed aggressor they could find. Their targets included local Native people as well as those who had traveled south for the attack. Philip Sheridan, later famous for his part in the Civil War, rounded up and imprisoned the locals. The volunteers threatened to shoot all the prisoners. Instead, a plurality were hanged by the military after a hasty set of courts-martial on the basis of evidence that ranged from flimsy to nonexistent. At least one was provably innocent at the time; none of the courts-martial were fully lawful.[56]

Would-be murderers in Oregon were sometimes open to waiting for the government to get rid of the Native people they refused to coexist with. Robert Hull, a settler in the Mollala area of the Willamette Valley, wrote to Commissioner of Indian Affairs Joel Palmer about a dispute with a Native Mollala neighbor. At first, Hull explained, "[I was] thinking to shoot him down, but I did not know whether I should be justified or not. I want to know of you whether I shall take the law into my own hands and shoot them down or shall I wait a little longer expecting to have them moved." Having recently seized land along the Mollala River, Hull saw no future with independent Mollala people as neighbors. Only two courses of action were acceptable to him: the government could compel the Mollala to leave, or Hull could murder the people he lived next door to—and he was willing to wait only "a little longer." It is worth considering how many people like Hull did not bother about legal clarification before they killed their Native neighbors, and how many people like Lauer did not have a grandchild who more permanently inscribed family stories of murder into the historical record.[57]

The worst of the attacks on Native communities may have been in southern Oregon, but in times of heightened tension, White violence was close to the surface everywhere. Violence against Native people in the Willamette Valley and along the Columbia in the 1850s may have been less pervasive and less organized than the violence farther south. But White recourse to violence was still very much a part of pioneer culture, and there are more wanton killings from the period lurking in Oregon and

Washington pioneer archives and reminiscences—and many more incidents about which no specific record survives. Nor were these pioneer norms necessarily exclusive to the Northwest—similar investigations of pioneer reminiscences will probably turn up similar ubiquity in other pioneer spaces.

The Lupton Massacre became the most infamous act of a violent time in the Northwest. Later historians of the region had to reckon with a few key stories of horror. And Native histories kept other stories alive. But the cupidity, fear, and hatred so many Euro-American pioneers brought with them to Oregon led them to innumerable smaller acts of murder and violence. Within and between the famous assaults on Native communities in the era, there were atrocities big and small that did not make their way into the history books, recounted (with pride, curiosity, or sorrow) only locally or privately.

CHAPTER THREE

Dreams of Genocide and the Roads to War in Washington Territory

ALMOST ANY STORY COULD be twisted into a tale of pioneer pride. Henry Van Asselt—a former Dutch Republic soldier, cabinet-maker, and early pioneer in the Puget Sound region—once accidentally shot himself. In variations on a reminiscence repeated by his family, he turned the story of a self-inflicted gunshot wound into a performance of racial superiority, revealing a presumption of Native aggression.

As Van Asselt was returning to his hunting camp in the Puget Sound region near Seattle in 1854, he spotted a group of Native people, assumed their hostile intent, and grabbed his gun to try and kill them. He missed, and instead shot himself in the arm. He remembered having been given the name "Sucway" (which he asserted without evidence translated to "a devil, bulletproof") among the Puget Sound Indigenous peoples and, he claimed, was avoided by most of them afterward. Van Asselt assumed this was because they were impressed by his hardiness after he had survived shooting himself; one might wonder if Van Asselt's habit of attempting to gun down Native people for no other reason than proximity might have played a role.[1]

Besides the self-inflicted gunshot wound he insisted was a sign of his heroic prowess, and another 1854 incident in which he gunned down Native people's dogs for howling near a calf, Van Asselt played a part in more formalized killings of people as a volunteer in the Puget Sound War in 1855–56. By December 1855 Van Asselt's land claim was a staging ground for volunteers under Captain C. C. Hewitt, "out to hunt Indians" in the region—Van Asselt being one of the hunters. In December 1855 and January 1856, according to pioneer Eli Bishop Mapel (sometimes spelled Maple), he and his brother Samuel were part of a volunteer company that "killed several Indians" who were trying to flee along Cedar River and at different times caught "a good many scouts, whom we settled with there and then." In other words, they captured Native people, presumed they were scouts for a hostile force, and then they killed them. It is unclear whether the killings stopped or continued when they went from Hewitt's company to longer service in the volunteer company of Arthur Denny.[2]

The killing of "scouts" and "spies," as Mapel put it, was common code in pioneer wars on Native people, indicating guilt by Indian-ness. Such assumptions of hostility are particularly striking in northwestern Washington, where White pioneers were especially reliant on Native allies and mercenaries to pursue their business *and* war aims in the 1850s. But this strategic necessity did not preclude broad-based hostility, nor did it prevent men like Van Asselt and the Mapels from trying to kill Indian strangers when and where they could. Volunteers and regulars alike killed "spies" on little evidence—sometimes with the semblance of a trial, often without one.[3]

By and large, these off-the-cuff killings did not make the history books. The 1862 marriage of Henry Van Asselt to Jane Mapel, attended by famed Suquamish/Duwamish leader Sealth/Siʔal ("Chief Seattle") and perhaps hundreds of his people, was legendary in the region. The arrival of both families before most other Euro-Americans, in 1851, is a staple of pioneer history. The killings members of both households attempted and committed in the 1850s have received much less attention. Indeed, some histories of the region omit the wars, mass killings, and internments of the period altogether.[4]

In the 1850s, there are commonly reckoned to have been around two to three wars between Native polities and Americans in Washington Territory, all purportedly stemming from unjust elements of the treaties pushed by Isaac I. Stevens. The Puget Sound War (ca. 1855–56) was waged against Native people living in the Puget Sound region of north-western Washington Territory. The wars against various Native polities in eastern Washington Territory are often grouped under the heading of one or more Yakima Wars (ca. 1855–56 or 1858 or later). As in Oregon, wars in Washington Territory were waged against any and all Native peoples not seen as under the control of Euro-Americans. As in Oregon, many early histories and reminiscences combined these conflicts into an overarching period of "Indian wars." And along with Oregon, they were fought as such: on both sides of the Cascade Mountains, the general War on Illahee accelerated into the individual wars named in history books when bellicose brigades of Euro-American soldiers pursued indiscrimi-nate attacks in Indian country. Misunderstandings of treaties just or un-just may have given the wars some of their shape and convinced some Native polities to cast their lot with one side or another. But ultimately, murderous White land hunger was the driving force behind wars in 1850s Washington, just as it was in Oregon.[5]

Some pioneer reminiscences and some historians propose a clear di-viding line between the period of wars and a purported period of comity that preceded it. Because Washington Territory had far more Native res-idents than White invaders, because Native people were already much more a part of the workforce in Euro-American spaces than elsewhere in the American Northwest, and because the percentage of White people who had married into Native communities was a higher proportion of the Euro-American community than elsewhere, there was less violence reported than in southern Oregon or California. But less did not mean none. In 1853 and 1854, there were at least three reported lynchings by settlers in the Puget Sound region—and there is no reason to think that the mob violence that made the papers represented the only killings in that span. As Seattle pioneer William Bell put it, in an unknown mix of reportage and bravado, "When an Indian would steal anything it was our custom to tie him up & lynch him." In the Washington Territory, the few American trials of White men who had killed Native people in the 1850s ended in acquittal. And many episodes of violence never made the papers or the courts. Fear of counterattacks from numerically superior Native communities seems to have kept many pioneers from acting as violently as they wished—but not all, and not completely.[6]

Many Euro-Americans in Washington Territory were already dream-ing of murder, and planning for extermination, before the formal wars of

1855 and 1856 were fully under way. Men and women wrote in their letters at the time and their reminiscences afterward of plans to kill Native people. Sometimes this was a reaction to a threat real or, often, imagined—Henry Van Asselt was but one of many hair-trigger pioneers who saw any group of Indians as a "standing menace." Sometimes Euro-Americans longed to kill (and acted accordingly) for no other reason than their perception that Native people were too "saucy" or insufficiently supplicant. Some wanted to kill any Native person they could get away with, much like some of those described by John Beeson, far to the south. Murderous racism and pioneer violence in Washington Territory was more like that in Oregon than has typically been acknowledged. Plenty of White people in both pushed for genocide, in a crescendo of violence and threats that expanded the War on Illahee across most of Washington Territory by 1856.

Jonathan McCarty, who settled on unceded Muckleshoot land in the Puyallup Valley in 1853, claimed to have fought as a volunteer in the Puget Sound region in 1856. In later years he would have little to say about his own actions in wartime, focusing instead on arguments for the righteousness of hanging the famed Chief Leschi "until he was dead, dead, dead" (see chapter 5). But McCarty did reflect on and relish individual violent encounters with Native people before the war. Particularly, he remembered an incident in 1854 when a Muckleshoot man had approached his farmstead, asking if McCarty would be willing to repair a gun. Incensed at the request, and feeling threatened by the existence of a Native person with a weapon, McCarty warned the man off and would have shot him in the back and made "a good Indian" out of him had McCarty's wife, Ruth, not intervened.[7]

Stories of near violence remained frequent for decades. The Gischer family of Bellingham told the story of the family patriarch, John Gischer, so worked up over "many tales of the wild Indians and their ferocious nature" when he first moved to the area from Germany that he reacted to Indigenous night fishers near his house by lying in wait with an axe in the dark. It was only because those fishers did not happen to come close to him that bloody murder was avoided. If they had, one might suspect that Gischer would have framed a story of axe murder for his descendants as one of righteous violence against an invading foe, adding family lore of violence against living Indians to the "humorous" stories the Gischers told of desecrating Indigenous graves to decorate their homestead with stolen goods and human remains.[8]

Indoctrination about the natural murderousness of Indians was endemic from childhood on in the pioneer Pacific Northwest. Roxa S. Shackleford (née Cock) remembered playing with Governor Isaac I. Stevens's daughters, from whom she was "inseparable," in the 1850s. They were given a "cedar bark 'poncho' trimmed with sea otter fur" by Michael Troutman Simmons, a lumber speculator, Indian agent, and eventually chief architect of the internment camps set up by Governor Stevens in the mid-1850s, whom *all* the Indians loathe[d]." "We children got a great deal of pleasure out of it when we 'played inj_n' + massacred each other," Shackleford wrote. Even at a very young age, pioneer children got the message.[9]

And as was the case elsewhere, Euro-Americans used racial violence for pecuniary purposes. As historian Corey Larson has shown, Euro-Americans brought a culture of legal impunity with them. In 1854 Euro-Americans James Burt and John Butler killed a Tsimshian leader named Tsus-sy-uch rather than pay him and the work party he led the originally agreed-upon wages. This killing made it into the history books because White people died in the reprisals that followed—murders to get out of payroll or other financial agreements would be much less likely to persist in pioneer memory when they didn't lead to known counterattacks.[10]

Pioneers and politicians were sometimes willing to distinguish between "Indians" and "friendly Indians." But the latter category was always provisional and subject to change. At any hint of tension between Native people and invaders, as Seattle cofounder Arthur A. Denny put it in his 1888 description of the buildup of war in the Puget Sound Region in the fall of 1855, pioneers would "declare most vehemently that all [Indians] were hostile, and must be treated as enemies."[11]

For many settlers, temporary friendliness toward Native people was predicated on assumptions of racial dominance. Jonathan McCarty narrated his move from an embrace of settler colonial genocide toward a preference for colonial exploitation as being enabled by the permission and force of the state. Sometime in the late 1850s, McCarty was walking through recently seized unceded land when he came upon a Native person grazing a horse, attacked him, and (purportedly) held off five of his friends. Told by a local Indian agent (probably Simmons) that "if the Indians trespassed on my rights to whip h___ out of them," McCarty then felt that his "trouble with Indians" was over, and he expressed "good satisfaction" with them as farmworkers. While the specifics of his violent encounter may be more racist parable than reality, the core of the story was that McCarty moved from threats of "making good Indian[s]" out of near every Indigenous person he met to accepting them as workers only after he had established his own imagined racial domination. And pioneer perceptions could go the other way: when fantasies of racial dominance frayed, support for genocide might increase. As in Oregon, newspapers across the political spectrum in Washington were quick to call for mass extermination—generally in the case of the Democratic *Pioneer and Democrat,* and against polities east of the Cascade Mountains in the case of the Whig *Puget Sound Courier.*[12]

The hardening of genocidal intent and the fragility of belief in "friendly Indians" is notable in the letters of the Malick family, who settled near Fort Vancouver, in what became southern Washington, in 1848. Various family members described local and regional events in a stream of letters to their relations back in Illinois until 1865. There were two especially frequent correspondents: Abigail Malick, the matriarch of the family, and John D. Biles, who married into the family in 1852 and managed many of their affairs through the 1850s. Both correspondents wrote of Indians on occasion, one of the only subjects beyond the immediate family and finances worthy of mention. Abigail Malick's assertions about Native people grew steadily darker over the years. Biles supported mass extermination from the beginning.

In her early letters to her daughter Mary in Illinois, Abigail Malick stressed the friendliness of local Native communities. In a January 1850 letter meant to convince her family to come west, Abigail Malick wrote: "We ... haves aplenty of Indians here, and aplenty of white people here of all sorts; and a very pleasant place to live, and a plenty of soldiers here to protect them too, from the States. The Indians are very good here, there is no more danger of them than of the people in Illinois." Abigail Malick, anticipating her daughter Mary's fears and objections, assured her of the goodness of local Indians and the proximity of soldiers. Her daughter Rachel was more direct a few years later, in 1852, urging Mary not to "get scar[ed] out of" the trip for fear that "there is too many and the country is 2 wild for any such thing." Their calls to emigrate tapered off after 1855, as local pioneers brought the War on Illahee near their doorstep.[13]

John Denormandy Biles was, like Abigail Malick, originally a resident of Pennsylvania and had been deployed to Fort Vancouver as a soldier in 1848. He began courting Rachel Malick in 1850 and married her

1852. This delay was in part because the family patriarch, George Malick, did not want his daughters marrying soldiers (still seen as a disreputable profession by many), and in part because Rachel Malick was
fourteen in 1850, and her family was skeptical about letting her marry
quite so young.[14]

Writing to his new in-laws, Biles seems to have taken for granted
that genocide was a reasonable response to any acts of violence against
White settlers by Native people. Describing three successive invasions at
Port Orford in 1851, discussed in chapter 1, Biles blamed the predominantly Tututni and Coquille/Coquelle Native defenders for all the violence, and he wrote approvingly that the army had responded by
attempting to "destroy all that tribe of savages." As far as Biles knew, they
had succeeded in that purpose. After a series of skirmishes, he told his
new family, the U.S. Dragoons "come on the indians and without any
hesitation began to slaughter them + killed every Indian on the ground
about four hundred in all +c." The numbers were almost certainly exaggerated, but the sentiment was not.[15]

For her part, Abigail Malick in 1853 still saw a distinction between
the Indigenous peoples near Fort Vancouver and those fighting the
Rogue River Wars a few hundred miles south: "The Indians [here] . . .
call us the Boston Teyes, which is interpreted Masters or grandees. They
like to work for us, both Indians [and] Indian Woman. The Indians are
very good and kind here and they would not do any thing to the Americans here, but the Rogue River Indians are at war with the Americans
and the miners there, but that is three hundred miles from here, and
General Lane went there to make a treaty with them or kill them all."
She differentiated local people by their friendliness and their perceived
subservience—typified by her nonstandard gloss of the Chinook Jargon
word *Tyee*, or leader. In a later letter Abigail Malick suggested that her
maidservant's "name was Mary; that is all. The Indians do not have two
names like white people have two names; they are like negroes—they
have but one name." This was ridiculous, of course. The maidservant
"Mary" undoubtedly had other names; indeed, it is within the realm of
possibility that the name "Mary" was bequeathed on her by Abigail, as
that name appears to have been her favorite moniker. The letters show
Abigail Malick's initial willingness to embrace exploitation colonialism
based on racially disparate labor—one might even interpret her comment about the local Native people being "like negroes" as stretching beyond the matter of names. Abigail Malick's domestic servant Mary left to

help her sister survive smallpox in 1853, and she appears to have avoided the Malicks for good thereafter.[16]

Abigail Malick's limited tolerance decayed in 1855. At first, she still differentiated between what she perceived as friendly Indians (the locals she interacted with) and unfriendly Indians (Indigenous peoples farther afield). In June 1855 Abigail Malick wrote to her daughter about the first Walla Walla treaty council: "The governor [Isaac I. Stevens] has gone to make a treaty with the Snake Indians. And if they will not treat with him, they will have war with them, and will kill them all off so that they cannot kill no more Americans as they travel to this country. And that would be the best way, to kill them all off. I recollect when we were among them that they were very saucy."[17]

Abigail Malick hoped that the government forces at Walla Walla would attempt extermination, and she thought genocide "the best way" to deal with a perceived threat to American lives. She followed with two examples of the "sauciness" she had experienced in 1848, which she saw as fair grounds for the genocide she wanted. One involved a Native man who asked Abigail Malick for a pipe as a gift, and who rode off upset when she refused to give him one. The other occurred when nearby Native people on horseback had kicked up dust near where Malick had been cooking. "They never tried to hurt us no more than to steal from us if they could get a chance," Abigail Malick told her daughter—while providing no evidence of intended theft. Yet the Indigenous polities along the east Columbia River having been "very saucy" seems to have been supporting evidence, for Malick, that is would be "best . . . to kill them all off." In the summer of 1855, though, she still wrote, "We are here in peace and all as one with [the local] Indian tribes."[18]

Her son-in-law Biles made few such distinctions in his letters. In November 1855, having just been elected first lieutenant of a volunteer company, he told his relations that "the Indians have declared war against the Americans and already much blood has been spilt. . . . Volunteers are being raised every day. Nothing less than a total extermination of the R_dsk_ns will appease the Americans."[19]

Biles counted himself among those unappeasable Americans. In a May 1856 letter, he transitioned from cursing his own continuing inability to capture any "Indian spies" to castigating the U.S. government for trying to make peace. Any peace, he warned, would last "in all probability only six or eight months. Then [the Indians] will again Commence Hostilities with ten fold more Vigor. The policy of our Gen. Gove[rnment] is to treat with the Vill[ai]ns, after they have murdered hundre[d]s of men, women + Children, and laid waste thousands of dollars worth of property. At the eleventh hour they come in And give them Blankets for the murder they have already Committed And give a clear Chance for them to commence again." Biles (now identifying as Captain Biles) believed that Native people were inherently treacherous. Moreover, he believed in the dream of White supremacy in the Northwest, bragging to his abolitionist in-laws in the same letter that there were "only about half doz. '*Kinky heads*' in this Territory. The atmosphere [here is] not healthy for them." Whether he was referring to the natural environment, the social environment, or both is unclear from the context of this particular anti-Black barb—but his dream of a White Northwest was obvious.[20]

Over time, Abigail Malick's attention to distinctions between Native peoples collapsed into a hatred more like Biles's. There were slippages in her sometimes sympathetic descriptions of local "friendly Indians" in December 1855:

> The people volunteered and went . . . and brought in all the friendly Indians. They were scared as bad as the white people. They said they were so glad that the white people came for them, that they did not know what to do. They said they did not think that white men cared about Indians. But it was not that they cared anything about them. [The volunteers] were afraid that [the Indians] would turn traitors and murder us all. For [the volunteers] all went war-like towards them, and if they had not come right along with them, they would have destroyed them all immediately. And now they have them at the Fort and keep a strong guard over them.[21]

Malick reported that the local Native community still sought alliance with local Euro-Americans, but she knew that volunteers had gone in ready to commit mass murder at any perceived sign of resistance. It is quite possible that those she labeled "friendly Indians" saw the specter of violence just as clearly. If they did, in truth, proclaim themselves "so glad that the white people came for them," such expressions were probably tactical, whether or not they were genuine.

Native communities in the immediate area had experienced White presumptions and violence before. One vivid example appears in the reminiscences of Judge William Strong, the commander of the volunteer cavalry rounding up Indians at Fort Vancouver. The events of 1855 were not the first time Strong had led heavily armed Euro-Americans into Native homes. Shortly after his arrival in 1850 and his assumption of a judgeship, he heard that the sheep the pioneers had brought to the Cathlamet region north of Fort Vancouver were being hounded by dogs (presumed to be the animals of a local Kathlamet community). Strong organized a vigilante group to execute Native peoples' dogs en masse, and he proudly repeated the story to his family over the years:

> [Strong and his fellow pioneer leader James Birnie] formed a protective association, and shot the dogs whenever they could catch them, until the dogs learned the trick of running into the lodges whenever they saw a white man around with a gun. This protected them for some time, until the sheep were nearly gone, when something had to be done, and Judge Strong, with a rifle in one hand for emergencies, and a Colt's revolver in the other for dogs, boldly went into the lodges and shot the dogs there. It was risky work. The inside of the lodge was all smoke and confusion, and the children and the Indians hid the dogs in the beds, but canine curiosity was too strong, and every now and then a dog would stick his head out and bark. Crack would go the revolver, half a dozen more dogs would break out simultaneously, and then it would be bow-wow, crack, crack, until the revolver was empty.[22]

When Strong and his men came to compel Native people to be interned at Fort Vancouver, some would already have known him of old—the man who had gone house to house, rifle readied at anyone he perceived as a threat, shooting into the beds of children to kill dog after dog after dog.[23]

The dog-killing story Strong was so proud of tends to be omitted from more recent popular memory. Instead, William Strong has sometimes garnered praise for not actively pursuing genocide in the region to the extent that other pioneers preferred. A group of Native people led by a man known as Chief Umtux/Umtuch (variously identified as Cowlitz, Kathlamet Chinook, Klickitat/Qwû'lh-hwai-pûm, or a mix of those ethnies) escaped their Euro-American jailers, fearing that the White men would act on their expressed wish to attempt extermination. Strong and his volunteers hunted down the escaped prisoners, who had been accused of no crime. There was a tense conversation, and someone murdered Umtux in the night. Strong claimed it was "some lawless rogue"; one suspect for the killing was Strong's second-in-command, Hamilton Maxon, given his murderousness elsewhere in Washington Territory in the months that followed. The murder was left unsolved; there is no record of any attempt by Euro-Americans to find, much less punish, the supposed perpetrator. With tensions running high, Strong agreed that the Native group could have a period of mourning, and they agreed to return to imprisonment at the fort afterward.[24]

Thomas N. Strong, Judge Strong's son, remembered that his father was only just able to enforce practical peace over reckless race hatred among the volunteers and the people of Vancouver:

> When the company came marching back in to the fort without any Indians either dead or alive and without a battle to report, excitement ran high and when it became known upon what terms they had allowed the Indians to remain, the excitement increased. There could be no talk of lynching, because the company contained practically all the fighting men of the settlement, so the women with busy tongues took the matter into their own hands, and when the company was assembled, appeared before it, and, in the presence of an excited crowd, presented to the Captain a woman's red petticoat as a banner for his soldiers. It was a deadly insult and the company quailed under it.[25]

Lynching was assumed as a likely option if feasible, and bloodthirstiness was shared among pioneers regardless of gender. Women were calling for vigilante killings as at least as much as the men—Abigail Malick wasn't alone. As Thomas Nelson Strong put it, pioneers' "boldness sometimes became temerity, their love of liberty license, and their justice revenge, and the wife of the pioneer was like unto him." Similar threats of having a petticoat inflicted as a brand of unmanly behavior had circled around Joseph Lane's bellicose peace negotiations in 1853, which were insufficiently murderous for some southern Oregonian White people.[26]

The situation was resolved, according to Strong, through his father's manly calm and masculine violence:

> For a moment matters looked serious, and there was every prospect of a general riot and a free fight, but the Captain was a man of parts and equal to the situation. With a white face he stepped forward and on behalf of his company accepted the gift [of the red petticoat]. In

a few manly words he told the women and the gaping crowd ... that
if it should be the good fortune of the company to be ordered to the
front that their flag would be carried into action, and if so carried
would be dyed a deeper red before it returned, and then turning to
his company gave a short military command. There was some hesitation in obeying it, and a tall, lanky fellow made some insolent re-
mark and drew a bowie knife. That was enough, and with joy in his
heart that his wrath could be unloosed and that he had somebody
besides women to expend his anger upon, in one bound the Captain
was up on him [and nearly choked him to death].[27]

As his son would portray it, only through this individual act of manly violence was William Strong able to keep the community at Fort Vancouver from turning forced imprisonment into mayhem and mass murder.[28]

Abigail Malick seems to have approved of the imprisonment of the
"friendly Indians"—a carceral policy being pursued throughout the
American Pacific Northwest at this time. In a March 1856 letter she
noted the economic benefits of the war along with her continuing predictions of genocide:

> The volunteers and soldiers are a-going to kill them all before
> they bring the war to a close. Congress are a-preparing and
> sending soldiers here all the time for the occasion, and Governor
> Stevens has ... told the volunteers that they shall have all that
> they take from the Indians where they are a-going besides pay
> from government, so I understand from all. And that will be
> great pay, for the Indians are very rich where they are, they have
> a great many cattle and horses, and [the volunteers] are a-going
> to take all as they go. ... The volunteers took the friendly Indi-
> ans and brought them to Fort Vancouver, and took their horses
> from them, and their guns, and their hatchets, and are as yet
> keeping them at the garrison.[29]

The perception that Isaac I. Stevens had promised volunteers plunder
was widespread, and many volunteers do appear to have helped themselves to Native livestock. As Susan Sleeper-Smith, Michael Witgen, Alexandra Harmon, and many other historians have shown, plunder was
frequently a prime motivation for Euro-American attacks on Indigenous
communities.[30]

Abigail Malick had a personal stake in the taking of Native riches; both her former son-in-law Biles and her new son-in-law-to-be Henry Pearson were volunteers who might hope to share in the plunder. Indeed, it was Pearson's success in the war that briefly brought Abigail Malick around on him as a suitor to her daughter Jane; she credited him with leading volunteer soldiers who had broken a siege at the Cascades of the Columbia in the spring of 1856: "There were a company [of] soldiers there called the Shanghais, and they came with Lieutenant Pearson in command and they sounded their bugle and the soldiers took after [the Indians], and they ran off in the woods, and soldiers killing [and] scalping them as they went."[31]

While assuring her family that Pearson was "no soldier, only appointed a Lieutenant" (since a regular soldier would be too disreputable a match), Abigail Malick used Pearson's position as the head of a company killing and scalping Native people as proof of his bona fides. Pearson, she wrote approvingly, was "very resolute, you may be sure, among the Indians." A few years later, in 1860, having come to despise him for perceived mistreatment of her daughter, she celebrated Pearson's death while he was on patrol in 1860, at the same time accusing him of the opposite, writing "Jane's husband was killed by the Indians. That was good for him, for he would rather be with the Indians than with white people." Abigail Malick even filtered her own bloodlust through a racial lens. After writing two detailed paragraphs about the creative tortures she would like to inflict on an accused child murderer, she summed up her fantasy of inflicting a slow, agonizing death by declaring that if she were the governor, she "would be a real Indian in such a case."[32]

Abigail Malick's last mention of Native people before her death in 1865 was an endorsement of the killing of Native men and women alike. Writing in September 1861, as the Snake War of the 1860s was picking up steam, Malick assured her relatives: "Three companies of Dragoons are a-coming soon. ... They are afraid of them, Indians and sq__ws are as afraid of the soldiers as death, and I am glad they are afraid of them. ... If [the Dragoons] get after them they will give them plenty of powder and lead for their supper or dinner." Abigail Malick's letter then transitioned smoothly to a discussion of her own dinner plans. Advocacy for mass murder was not extraordinary, and it needed no space from everyday concerns.[33]

The Euro-American habit of framing Native people as presumptively and broadly aggressive shapes periodization of wars. When writers of histories strive to put a start date on the Yakima War, they often choose the killing of Indian Sub-Agent Andrew Bolon by the Yakama and Klickitat/Qwû'lh-hwai-pûm leader Mishíil/Mo-Sheel on September 25, 1855, when the former was threatening, with his customary lack of tact, to bring more troops and death to Yakama country. Alternatively, some interpretations see as the inciting incident the actions that had brought Bolon into Yakama territory in the first place. Earlier in 1855, invading White gold miners had abducted and raped Yakama women (or attempted to) and were promptly captured and executed for their crimes by Yakama authorities. Bolon was sent to investigate. Early Euro-American rumors attributed the killing of Bolon to Yakama leaders in the ensuing war, Kamiakin/K'amáyakin and Qualchan/Kwálchin.[34]

A Native eyewitness recounted in the 1910s not only the identity but also the supposed motivations of the killer, who was remembered as taking revenge against "the man who hanged my uncles and cousins at Wallula"—thus acting against Bolon specifically, for his supposed role in killing the Cayuse Five, rather than Euro-Americans generally. Yakama Elder and scholar Virginia Beavert/Tuxámshish recalled traditional knowledge that "Mishíil was getting even for when the white people massacred his entire family." In all versions of the story, the inciting incident for the killing of Bolon reaches back to one or another instance of Euro-American violence. Yet the killing of Bolon, rather than the White violence that led to it, was often framed as the decisive moment among pioneers, in history books, and on monuments.[35]

Bolon's death was the start of a war only because Euro-Americans treated it as such. Despite attempts by some Yakama leaders to resolve the killing of Bolon diplomatically, a contingent of U.S. troops led by Granville O. Haller launched a broad-based punitive expedition into Yakama territory bent on retribution for Bolon. To the extent that the Yakima War is separable from the broader War on Illahee, it was this invasion—not individual acts of reprisal—that marked the shift to something more like full-scale war.[36]

Granville O. Haller was a lifelong military man. He took part in the long war of attrition that was the Second Seminole War in the early 1840s, went on missions into Indian Territory (later Oklahoma), then fought in the U.S.–Mexico War before his assignment in the Pacific Northwest. Long before Haller invaded Yakama country to get revenge for the death of Bolon, he had already conducted numerous discriminate and indiscriminate killings.[37]

In 1854, near what became Caldwell, Idaho, a member of a wagon train of Euro-Americans led by Alexander Ward killed a member of a band of Native people (presumed to be Eastern Shoshone/Newe), supposedly as the Native man was attempting to steal a horse. After both sides exchanged fire, the clash escalated into a lethal battle that left nineteen Euro-Americans and an unknown number of Native people dead. The event was dubbed the Ward Massacre by Euro-Americans, who tended to ignore the thorny inciting incidents and focus on the deaths of White noncombatants.[38]

Haller led two punitive expeditions from Oregon in response to this violence. The first, in 1854, was a comparatively measured affair. After soliciting the assistance of a few Umatilla/Imatalamłáma and Nez Perce/ Nimíipuu scouts, Haller and his men (in his words) "invaded the usual haunts of the murderers, killed a few, and recaptured the clothing and other effects taken from their victims." This was at least in theory a targeted response in keeping with norms of reprisal in the region— although it is entirely possible that some or all of the people they killed had nothing to do with the clash, and the "recaptured" items had been acquired by other means, such as trade.[39]

Haller's second attack in 1855, the "final punishment of the Snakes" (ordered by Major Gabriel Rains at the behest of General John Wool), was against perceived hostile Native communities in the region generally. Haller began, according to Wool, by working with local Native communities—identifying (by unknown means) four of "the murderers," and hanging them over the graves of Ward wagon train members. Then, on "patrol," Haller claimed to have led a rampage through the Mountain West. He ransacked fishing communities and "hung and killed" Native men in their own villages in the mountains—he estimated nineteen people in all. Haller's killing spree was not a part of any war recognized by the U.S. government, though he ended up listing it alongside the later campaigns of that year when recounting his military exploits. In a way, after all, the United States was always at war with "the Indians."[40]

When Haller acted on his orders to "invade the Yakima country" on October 1, 1855, he seems to have imagined a punitive expedition similar to the ones he had mounted earlier that same year. By Haller's own account, it was his invading force, not the Native defenders, who fired the first shots of the Battle of Toppenish Creek on October 5: "As we descended a hill to the bottom lands of Topinish [sic] Creek to encamp, we discovered the Indians taking position behind trees to fight. At the same time, a Chief on a distant bluff was making a harangue to his warriors, who replied to him with yells, and thus showed their positions and that they were not greatly superior in numbers. As soon as our mule train had come up and our rear was properly guarded, we attacked our adversaries and drove them off." As usual, Native defensiveness was read as Native aggression. The men Haller attacked were right to be defensive; he had come to kill them. He wouldn't succeed.[41]

After they attacked, Haller's force was surrounded by Yakama and Palus fighters, and he lost a series of pitched battles and retreats. The size of the Native force remains unclear. Haller insisted they numbered in the hundreds—he had a source claiming five hundred (which Haller glossed as "perhaps six hundred") in 1863. By the 1880s, Haller's guess had metastasized to "2200 fighting men." There may have been a few hundred.[42]

Retreating along unfamiliar territory while under fire, Haller and his men were only able to find a way through with the help of men of partially Native descent, Donald McKay and Archibald McIntosh. Haller faced significant pushback from his men for relying on the (accurate) advice of his scouts: "Donald McKay was Cayuse Indian on his mother's side and the men with Haller were afraid to trust him for he (McKay) said he must have time to reconnoitre their situation and get his bearings. Some of the command were bitterly opposed and discouraged Major Haller trusting him, and said, 'He was no better than any other damned Indian,' but after several hours deliberation it was decided the only way was to trust Donald McKay." Many volunteers were unwilling to put faith in any person of Native descent, no matter his or her bearing or background. In fact, some evidence suggests that the volunteers survived with only a handful of casualties not just through the skills of their mixed-race allies, but also because of the actions of Native forces they had attacked. Chief Moses, a Columbia/Sinkiuse leader who fought in the Battle of Toppenish Creek, implied later that the aim in attacking Haller's men had been more to "dr[i]ve them to the Dalles" than kill them, in keeping with limited warfare norms at a time when many were still hoping for a peaceful resolution.[43]

Haller and his men attacked the first Native group they found, then lost pitched battles over three days of retreat, leaving behind their supplies and spiking their howitzer as they fled. They failed badly, outnumbered and outfought, and with that failure they set off Euro-American fear across the region of an impending "invasion" by the people they had just attacked. The Battle of Toppenish Creek (sometimes known as

Haller's Defeat) is perhaps the best marker for the start of the—or at least a—Yakima War. And it was initiated by the American troops. But like most conflicts in the War on Illahee, the overarching cause was not a single event. The Yakima War, like the Cayuse War, was caused by continuing Euro-American devotion to settler colonial seizure.

Before they pillaged and burned the small Catholic mission built in Yakama country, the American retaliatory force sent out after Haller's retreat at Toppenish found a letter Kamiakin/K'amáyak̲in had dictated to a local Catholic missionary, Father Charles Pandosy. The letter, written as part of a broader community meeting, explained the actions of the coalition Kamiakin/K'amáyak̲in was leading, warned of all-out war, and signaled a desire for equitable peace. According to a copy of the letter that ended up in the archdiocesan records in Seattle, Kamiakin/K'amáyak̲in and the Yakama with him had instructed Pandosy to

> write to the soldiers, tell them we were peaceful, friends of the Americans; that we never thought at all about war; but the way that the governor [Isaac I. Stevens] spoke to us with the Cayuse [at the June 1855 treaty council] angered us and drove us to a general war that will not finish except by the complete disappearance of all of the Indians or of all of the Americans.
>
> If the governor had said to us: "My children, I ask of you a piece of land in each tribe for the Americans; but the land [of] your nation is forever yours," we would have willingly given him what he had asked of us and we would have lived with you others as brothers. But he grabbed us and threw us out of our native country, into a foreign land . . . in a place where good people do not even have something to eat.[44]

The community identified land taking and violence as core to the American approach to colonization, beyond Stevens: "Now we know the heart of the Americans perfectly. Since long ago, they hang us without knowing if we are wrong or right; but they have never killed or hanged a single American even though there is no place where the Americans did not kill Indians." Kamiakin/K'amáyak̲in and his allies recognized lynching as part of the American heart, and they knew it had little to do with justice. They recognized both the lack of fair trials for Native people and the lack of any consequences for American Indian killers.[45]

Indiscriminate lynching was a casus belli. But land taking and forced starvation were the foremost complaints:

> You want then, Americans, to make us die of hunger little by little. It is better for us to die all at once. It is you, governor, who wanted war with these words: "The country will be ours, of all tribes, of all the nations." . . . Our heart was torn apart when you pronounced these words. You fired the first shot. Our heart was broken, nothing was left of it but a sigh. We did not have the strength to respond. Thus we have made a Common Cause with our enemies to defend our nationality and our country all together.[46]

Kamiakin/K'amáyaḵin indicated an (aspirational) unity of purpose, noting the shared wrong planned against all Native nations, not just Yakama, and asserting a common cause among Indigenous peoples. "However, the war did not have to begin so soon, but the Americans who were going to the mines having fired on some Indians because [the Indians] did not want to hand over their women [to the Americans]. This gave us the right to defend ourselves. . . . It is not us, we can say, who started the war[;] we did nothing but defend ourselves."[47]

Kamiakin/K'amáyaḵin asserted that the inciting incident of the war had been American miners firing on Indians after being refused sex. This was, his people proclaimed, a defensive war. And the letter finished by indicating openness to peace:

> If the soldiers and Americans . . . want to withdraw and deal amicably, we consent to put down arms and to grant them a piece of land in the different tribes, as long as they do not force us to exile ourselves from our native country. . . .
>
> If they do not respond, this means they want war: we are in this moment one thousand and fifty men gathered here. Some only will go to Fight[,] but as soon as the war has started the news will spread among all of the nations and in a few days we will be more than ten thousand.[48]

There was diplomacy and perhaps bravado in this letter—certainly Kamiakin/ K'amáyaḵin's invocation of a united front of Indigenous polities against Euro-American aggression, and his estimation of his present and future troop counts, was more hopeful than descriptive. But the analysis of the American position was essentially accurate. Stevens did intend to take all the Native land he could, by force if necessary. And Americans did rely on wanton violence against Native people, in the near certainty that they would face no real penalty from their countrymen.

Major Gabriel J. Rains, who led the American retaliatory force, responded to Yakama diplomacy with threats of exterminatory violence. This was common practice, and unsurprising from Rains. He had been promoted, before coming to the Pacific Northwest, for killing Seminole people with explosive booby traps (something broadly considered to be a war crime when Rains did the same against U.S. soldiers after he committed treason and joined the Confederacy in 1861). Like many other army officers, Rains combined resolute willingness to kill on behalf of White supremacy with an occasional distaste for disorganized wanton White violence.[49]

Rains created a written message addressed to Kamiakin—although it was probably meant for his rambunctious men, and perhaps for the history books, at least as much as for the Native people he hoped to hunt down. He claimed to have left a copy at the burned remains of the mission, and he retained a copy for posterity. Whether or not the message he purportedly left was ever received and understood, it expressed his genocidal intent clearly. Rains's message read in part: "You know me and I know you. . . . You came in peace, we come in war, and why, because your land has drank the blood of the white man and the great spirit requires it at your hand. . . . You know you murdered white men going to the mines who had done you no injury, and you murder all Americans though no white man had trespassed upon your land."[50]

Rains's denial of Yakama accusations could not have been predicated on fact. It would be impossible for him to know whether the killed miners had done what they were accused of—that proclamation was based on his reflexive assumption of White innocence and Native guilt. Indeed, his statement was internally inconsistent, denying that White men had trespassed on Yakama land in the same breath that he castigated them for killing trespassers. Rains's denunciation eventually turned biblical:

Your foul deeds were seen by the eye of the Great Spirit who saw Cain when he killed his brother Abel and cursed him for it.

Kamiakin/K'amáyakịn as he appeared to the artist and
U.S. soldier Gustavus Sohon during negotiations with
Isaac I. Stevens in 1855. From A. J. Splawn,
Ka-mi-akin: The Last Hero of the Yakimas.

Fugitives and vagabonds shall you be, all that remain of you upon the face of the earth, as well as all who aid and assist you, until you are gone.

You say now, "if we will be quiet and make friendship, you will not war, but give a piece of land to all the tribes"—we will not be quiet but war forever until not a Yackima [*sic*] breathes in the land he calls his own. . . .

The country is ours already, as you must see from our assembled army, for we intend to occupy it, and make it too hot to hold you. . . . We are thirsty for your blood. . . .

Gabriel J. Rains some time before he committed treason by joining the Confederacy in 1861. Courtesy of the Library of Congress, Civil War Photographs, 1861–65.

The whites are as the stars in the Heavens, or leaves of the trees in the summer time. Our warriors in the field are many as you must see, but if not enough, a thousand for every one man will be sent to hunt you out, to kill you, and my kind advice to you, as you will see, is to scatter yourselves among the Indian tribes more peaceable and there forget you were ever Yackimas.[51]

In this letter Rains threatened genocide against Yakama people specifically rather than Native people generally—although there is little indication he made many such distinctions on the ground in the Northwest.

If Kamiakin/K'amáyakin did get Rains's message, it likely rang true. The Yakama had been warned by Pandosy in 1854 that White men more numerous than "grass on the hills" would "take your country as they have taken other countries from the Indians." Rains would fail in his quest to end the Yakama, but not for lack of trying.[52]

By 1856, the War on Illahee had escalated across most of what is now Washington and Oregon because of Euro-American invasions and attacks. The common pioneer view that there was a general Indian war at this time was, in this way, correct. Bands of Euro-American volunteer or regular soldiers made war on Native groups, who responded in kind— and who communicated with their kin and allies elsewhere. The broader context of pioneer invasions and White lies at treaty councils shaped and enabled these wars.

For generations, settler historians laid the impetus of war on Native defenders rather than White invaders; the Yakima War is only a particularly provable example of a general trend. This kind of colonial conceit continues to shape periodization, even as the racism that drove it is challenged. Those who would write more accurate histories of colonial invasion must take seriously the potentials and perils of periodization, particularly but not exclusively when it comes to wars. The important work of emphasizing Indigenous action, initiative, and agency should not lead historians to accept faulty presumptions about who was the aggressor in a given war, and under what circumstances. It matters who invaded whom.[53]

The wars of the 1850s were not, as one otherwise excellent historian puts it, "triggered" by Native "resistance" to "American authority." In Yakama country as elsewhere, it was the invaders who pulled the trigger, the invaders who started the wars, and the invaders who threatened to "war forever" until they had gotten what they wanted. American aggression, not Native resistance to that aggression, caused just about every escalation of the War on Illahee—and, arguably, just about every U.S. war for land fought across the North American continent.[54]

CHAPTER FOUR

Extermination, Incarceration, and the War on Illahee at Its Zenith

O N OCTOBER 22, 1855, Captain Charles Eaton led an expedition of mounted volunteers from Fort Steilacoom, south of Seattle, to detain or destroy "all the Indians [he could] find near the western base of the Cascades." News and rumors of Euro-American losses in the east played a role in this escalation. As a response to long-brewing White fears that the Native polities of western Washington would ally with those east of the mountains to wage an exterminatory war on Americans, the territorial government attempted to impose a carceral regime across the Native peoples of the region. Eaton had a free hand to inflict violence. "Should you meet any unusual or suspicious assemblage of Indians," his orders went, "you will disarm them, and should they resist, disperse them, and put any who resist or use violence to death, or send them to Fort Steilacoom in irons, or bound as you may deem best."[1]

Eaton and his volunteers planned for mass killing, not arrest. As U.S. Army Lieutenant John Nugen put it in his letter to Charles Mason, the acting governor of Washington Territory: "I am happy to inform you that Fort Steilacoom is once more a quiet place. . . . The Volunteer Company got off in fine order 2 1/2 P.M. yesterday—the men in fine spirits and apparently with a determination of taking the Scalp of every R_ dsk_n who may be so unfortunate as to fall in their way." Orders might have been to capture, but the government and the army knew that Eaton's men meant to kill.[2]

Longtime pioneer James McAllister was one of several who pushed for the company to ignore orders and try to hunt down Chief Leschi, a Nisqually leader widely seen as influential among those in local Native communities who thought war might be necessary to defend their rights and lands. Under the belief that Eaton was going in the wrong direction, McAllister took some men, struck out on his own, and exchanged fire with a Native group he bumped into. The fight was at best a draw; after the initial exchange (which killed McAllister and a few others, probably on both sides) the Euro-American force hunkered down in a defensive position, and the Native group they had battled eventually decided to leave. The expedition that was purportedly meant to collect Native people had embarked with the "determination" to kill (and scalp) every Native person they found; their ineffective attempts to do so had pushed the region into a war footing. This was even clearer the next day, when an unidentified group of people presumed to be Indians killed eight White settlers, mostly noncombatants, in the White River area fifteen miles north of the initial clash. It is unclear to what extent these killings were connected. It is unclear whether McAllister shot first. It is perfectly clear that Eaton's volunteers had sallied forth intending to massacre Indians.[3]

Some later reminiscences from pioneers asserted without any evidence that McAllister and Eaton had come in peace and been attacked without warning or provocation. Though numerous accounts recalled McAllister as a "friend of the Indians," the evidence seems to suggest only familiarity. And familiarity, famously, does not in itself indicate sympathy or support. Given that the most pervasive account framing McAllister and Eaton as peaceful came from territorial official Urban E. Hicks, who perpetrated the Hicks Massacre (see below) and other killings, contemporary evidence that Eaton and his men (including McAllister) intended extermination is far more convincing than latter-day protestations that they came in peace.[4]

Leschi has been central to most accounts of the Puget Sound War (sometimes known as the Treaty War or even the Leschi War) from the beginning. Many such accounts begin with Leschi's 1854 refusal to sign off on the terms of the first Treaty of Medicine Creek and end with his 1858 execution after the Puget Sound War was brought to a close. But although Leschi was a leader in the war, he did not start it. All reasonable candidates for an inciting incident come from the Euro-Americans who invaded his people's homelands—the most likely final straw being Eaton's kill squad. Generations of historians could frame this war, like the Yakima War to the east, as an act of Indigenous aggression only by conveniently ignoring numerous inciting incidents of Euro-American violence.[5]

The War on Illahee reached a crescendo from 1855 through 1856, as White invaders stoked counterattacks across much of the American Pacific Northwest. As discussed in chapter 2, the violence in southern Oregon was perhaps the most famous element of this war, followed by the violence in southern Washington. But the war was much more general than it has often been portrayed—both in the sense that the War on Illahee in this period was against "Indians" generally as much as specific groups, and in the sense that war reached nearly everywhere Euro-Americans could invade.

Records, especially from the volunteers themselves, reveal a broad-based war on Native life, as Euro-Americans tried to imprison those they did not kill outright. In Oregon and Washington alike, officials attempted to force nearly every Native person in regions they could reach—"friendly" or not—into often deadly internment camps in the mid-1850s. Unofficially, across much of the Northwest, there was toleration if not endorsement of genocide. Evidence from and about the volunteers in the Puget Sound War, particularly, suggests a sharp break from much previous scholarship, some of which has portrayed that conflict as nearly bloodless. New pioneer sources bring new and horrifying details to a few acts of terror in Washington Territory typically known to specialists, such as the murders in the Maxon Massacre and the brutality inflicted on Walla Walla/Walúulapam leader Peo-Peo-Mox-Mox. But this chapter also contains discussion of mass killings and massacres that have not yet made it into academic history, including some, like the Hicks Massacre, that left few survivors to tell the tale.

Anthropologist George B. Wasson theorized that his people, the Coquille/Coquelle, had to survive a cultural "black hole" inflicted by Americans in the 1850s and 1860s. Killings and other destruction in southwest Oregon were so pervasive that significant culture, records, and memory were lost. This was not isolated to the Oregon coast; the War on Illahee inflicted similar losses across much of the rest of the Northwest.[6]

The pioneer regime of violence, and the cover-ups that followed, means that official records for many of the killings, and even specific knowledge of some of the killings, may have disappeared into the black holes created by the violence of invaders. Some memories were kept alive by survivors, and some records were retained by killers proud of their part in the invasion. The evidence we do have suggests significantly more horrors beyond the horizon of the records than can be proven at present. But even a narrow reading of the sources on offer, from perpetrators and survivors, suggests a crescendo of killing and captivity in 1855 and 1856, wherever Euro-Americans in the Pacific Northwest thought they could get away with it.

As the War on Illahee reached a peak in 1855 and 1856, many Euro-Americans officials hoped to intern the Native people they did not kill. In some areas this meant imprisoning local people without cause or trial at forts, as Judge Strong had done at Vancouver. But in western Washington, without such means, Michael Troutman Simmons (acting on behalf of the territorial government) instead managed the creation of a series of internment camps among the islands of the Puget Sound. In October 1855 orders went out to round up Native residents of Seattle (excepting Native people working for the armed forces, a category that included both soldiers and workers at places like pioneer Henry Yesler's lumber mill). On November 12, 1855, those Native residents of the wider region not attached to military duties were instructed to report to these make-shift island camps, run by Euro-American citizen volunteers. The history of these internment camps across the western Pacific Northwest remains hazy and deserve further research. But existing details are harrowing.[7]

Isaac I. Stevens claimed to Commissioner of Indian Affairs George W. Manypenny that he had 4,000 Native people as "submissive and unconditional prisoners" just in the Puget Sound region, part of his broader attempt to get remuneration to feed "5,350 Indians." His numbers might have been overstated (as his presumption of submission certainly was), in order to extract the most possible money from the government. Or they might have been only the tip of the iceberg, as Stevens enumerated only those interned on the Puget Sound. His number omitted those imprisoned elsewhere in Washington Territory and those in Oregon (see below). The final toll of internment might reach very high indeed if the records can be found.[8]

Historians have sometimes been too credulous of colonial blandishments, describing the often lethal internment programs as "camps for non-combatants," or even "sanctuaries." It is clear there were thousands of Native people living in the camps, often under appalling conditions and always with the constant threat of an outbreak of White violence. It is also clear that many other Native people avoided the camps. And it is crystal clear that the typical internment camp was anything but a sanctuary. Cecilia Svinth Carpenter's landmark study of the camp on Fox Island suggested 720 Native people were interned there; Euro-American records show over 100 dying in 1856 alone (at a time and place where record keepers were motivated to keep such death counts low). One purported Snoqualmie source suggested 700 people were poisoned while interned at the Whidbey Island camp—through whatever mix of negligence or deliberate killings by the camp's administrator, Edmund Clare Fitzhugh, a murderous wife beater and latter-day Confederate who expressed support for the mass deaths of Native people. Estimates for populations and death rates for other internment camps, like the one on Squaxin Island, remain to be determined.⁹

There were killings, uncounted and perhaps uncountable, perpetrated in pursuit of internment. On October 28, two weeks before Simmons sent out his official internment order, a volunteer company under the command of C. C. Hewitt—the one that Van Asselt and the Mapels belonged to—went out on the first of several patrols of Native land outside Seattle. Although their orders were supposedly to assist in "removing Indians," they apparently expressed "the determination of exterminating all 'horse-style' Inj_ns" they found. Reminiscences suggest that the men of Hewitt's company were not even this discerning when they executed "scouts" without trial or shot Indians in the back as they fled the Americans along Cedar River.¹⁰

Samuel L. Stewart, in the same reminiscence wherein he recalled "fighting Indians before we joined the army just the same as we did in the army," wrote of his experiences as part of Hewitt's unit. He remembered the sort of fighting he had been involved in on Whidbey Island and in the Duwamish River area south of Seattle:

> We knew how to watch the trails our selves. . . . We knew how to locate an Indian camp and give them a round or two and if there were to[o] many of them to fight a retreat. The most of the fighting in that wood country was done by small squ[a]ds of men. . . .
>
> [The regular troops] wanted to beat their drums and toot their bug[le]s, but we could not stand that. I seen one fight at the

forks of D[u]wamish [R]iver where eight men took fifteen scalps[,] all warriors but one woman, without receiving a scratch.[11]

The official army reports from the Puget Sound War might be spare and sparse reading, but men like Stewart were engaged in violence that did not reach those reports. As usual, Stewart may have been exaggerating. But the devotion to killing he described aligns with other records of the period.

The killings Stewart related with gusto may have been the same ones Admiral Thomas Stowell Phelps would later decorously refer to in his 1902 *Reminiscences of Seattle* as the "unfortunate affair on the Duwam–sh River bottom; one of those cruel, senseless acts in cold blood, repeated wherever civilized races encroach upon the savage domain, and always productive of trouble, frequently of the indiscriminate slaughter of innocent people, and occasionally of war in its worst form—the wanton, deliberate, and unprovoked killing of unoffending Indians." Phelps did not elaborate. And notably, Phelps framed "unprovoked killing of unoffending Indians" as "productive of ... the indiscriminate slaughter of innocent people"—rather than being an act of such slaughter in and of itself. Even from a pose of sympathy, Phelps considered "unoffending Indians" and "innocent people" to be separate categories.[12]

There is little trace of which killing Phelps was referring to in extant historical records. The "unfortunate affair" may have been the mass killing and scalping Stewart wrote about, or it may have been an entirely separate incident of "wanton ... and unprovoked killing"; the framing and phrasing of Stewart's letter implies that this was not the first or last time Stewart or his fellow volunteers had been engaged in violence against their Native neighbors. And the mention of "but one" scalp taken by his fellows belonging to a woman is indicative of a broader norm of body mutilation (and woman killing). It is unclear whether these killings were perpetrated while Samuel Stewart was a part of C. C. Hewitt's volunteer company, or while he was killing with an even less official outfit. To Stewart, it didn't matter.[13]

Indian internments backed by lethal threats were already under way in Oregon, too. On October 13, 1855, Oregon Indian Superintendent Joel Palmer made official a policy to effectively incarcerate all Native men in the Oregon Territory, whether closely supervised on reservations, imprisoned, or worse:

The names of all adult males, and boys over 12 years of age shall be enrolled, and the roll called daily.

When any one shall be absent at roll-call, the fact shall be noted, and unless a satisfactory reason be rendered, the absentee shall be regarded as a person dangerous to the peace of the country, and dealt with accordingly.

Any Indian found outside of his designated temporary reservation, without being able to satisfactorily account therefor, shall be arrested and retained in custody so long as shall be deemed necessary; or should he be a stranger not belonging to any of the bands of this valley, he shall be placed for safe keeping in the county jail, or taken to Fort Vancouver. . . .

No Indian will be permitted to leave his assigned encampment unless by written permit from the local or special Agent.[14]

Native people, confined to reservations, were required to report daily (and Indian agents were encouraged to disarm them when feasible). Those unknown were to be imprisoned without charge or trial—at best, given the menacing tone of "dealt with accordingly."[15]

And although many of the details of Palmer's orders were guidance for his agents, they also contained a call for the White citizenry to temper—but continue—their vigilantism: "Any Citizens generally are requested . . . to exercise a due degree of forbearance in their dealings with Indians; but at the same time to keep a vigilant watch over them and report to acting Agents the presence of strange Indians among us, and render such aid in their apprehension, as may tend to protect our persons and property, and secure peace." Anyone deemed a "strange Indian" by any White citizens risked arrest or worse simply for existing, no matter their background. And that category could be broad, given how disinclined Euro-Americans were to reckon with diversity among Indigenous communities; as Palmer himself declared, "It is extremely difficult to distinguish among our Indian population." For White settlers and officials alike, any Indian was a threat until proven otherwise.[16]

Armed "citizen guards" who appeared in the records neither as regulars nor as volunteers stalked reservations and internment camps for Native people in the 1850s, enforcing incarceration. Alphonso D. Boone remembered being a "citizen g[u]ard" as a teenager in that decade, keeping armed watch over the "Grand Round [*sic*] Reservation" alongside Portland's future mayor David P. Thompson and others. Ezra Meeker recalled some pioneer women arming themselves to threaten with death Native people they saw as out of place. George Himes, in later decades a prominent historian of Oregon, was still an adolescent when he took up firearms as an unofficial "Home Guard" in the same region. As his friend and fellow historian John Watermelon Redington described it, "Mr. Himes was only a boy at the time of the war of '56, but he did a volunteer soldier's duty just the same." Euro-American teenagers "monkey[ing] with guns," as they later put it, helped to impose the carceral regime invaders demanded at the height of the War on Illahee.[17]

Joel Palmer, like General John Wool and many other government officials who negotiated with Native people, was scorned by many pioneers as soft on "the Indians." William Barnhart, a former volunteer and amateur historian who would go on to be a thieving and murderous Indian agent at the Umatilla Reservation, accused the man he referred to as "Hon. Palm-her" of "promiscuously ming[ling]" with "the aboriginal females [who] at that time infested the whole region of the Dalles." This (probably invented) association, he proclaimed, explained why the federal government had not backed the volunteers in the region sooner. The disgust was mutual. Palmer denounced the "the savage and brutal conduct of these miscreants who have provoked this war" (and the "corrupt and vicious demagogues" who encouraged them)—and, unlike Barnhart, Palmer had evidence. But he decried the violence in large part because it interfered with his department's efforts to "carry out the policy of the government in its effort to colonize these Indians upon the reservations designated." And Palmer followed his denunciation with a call for more regular troops "to enable us to commence active operations for the permanent location" of Native communities.[18]

Palmer, Wool, and many others shared the major overarching goal of the pioneer murder squads. They, too, insisted on the seizure of most if not all Native land for American empire. The difference was in tactics. What Palmer decried was less the end goal of the volunteers than their incompetence, bloodlust, and haste.

In the fall of 1855, few were more hasty and bloodthirsty than the Oregonian volunteer militias, who ignored or denied other military authorities and marauded through Washington and Oregon territories, attacking almost any Native communities they could find. Undersupplied and unfamiliar with the country, they couldn't find many. The disorganized troops would ride off in ragged pursuit of any Indians spotted, hoping to capture or kill them, and frequently would ride off in ragged retreat when confronted with any Native fighting force they did not vastly outnumber. Whatever their incompetence, these violent bands of volunteers were an existential threat to Native communities. Although people could sometimes avoid them, the volunteers pillaged and ransacked wherever they went, plundering Native food stores and "requisitioning" the livestock of Native people and (often) Euro-American settlers.[19]

On December 5, 1855, Walla Walla/Walúulapam leader and veteran diplomat Peo-Peo-Mox-Mox came under a flag of truce to negotiate with this new set of colonial invaders, hoping to forestall the rapidly accelerating war by negotiating reparations for the losses (real and perceived) of the pioneers. Ignoring the rules of parley, the volunteers instead attacked and imprisoned Peo-Peo-Mox-Mox and his party, touching off a series of running battles with Native forces. Between those battles, the volunteers killed most of their prisoners, including Peo-Peo-Mox-Mox, and then dismembered his body for trophies. Though not atypical of volunteer conduct during the War on Illahee, the murder and butchery of Peo-Peo-Mox-Mox would eventually become a lightning rod for critics—both in the sense that the story would be repeated and condemned in many circles, and in the sense that criticism of the killing of Peo-Peo-Mox-Mox *as extraordinary* drew attention away from other analogous acts of violence throughout the region. In the near term, the volunteers who killed Peo-Peo-Mox-Mox were condemned by General John Wool but commended by the territorial governments of Oregon and Washington alike.[20]

The commanding officer in charge of those who killed Peo-Peo-Mox-Mox and his associates, lawyer and politician James K. Kelly, relied on the standard excuse for the murder: Kelly claimed that his captive was killed while trying to escape. When publicizing his deeds, Kelly did not think the fact that Peo-Peo-Mox-Mox had been seized while trying to negotiate a peace was worth mentioning. As Kelly's report put it in the newspapers: "The loss of the Indians must be very great, as their killed alone, during the two days [of battle], cannot be less than fifty men. Among their killed yesterday was the noted chief of the Walla-Wallas the celebrated Pee-Peu-Mox-Mox [*sic*]. He was taken prisoner by my command . . . near his camp on the Touchet, and during the battle yesterday made an effort to escape. In doing so, he was killed, together with four others who were made prisoners at the same time, and who also attempted to get away." The killings had happened in between battles. By conflating them, Kelly could ward off any questions about justification and inflate the number of hostiles killed in a battle that was, at best, a draw.[21]

Native people were often killed while purportedly trying to escape. Indeed, even those who supposedly did escape may have, in fact, been murdered. The "scout and Indian trailer" Jeff Landers hinted in his memoir that he and his fellows had executed at least one Native person in the 1850s who had surrendered to his company and then "escaped." Other volunteers dropped the pretense. As Urban E. Hicks put it, "The volunteers got tired of the business and quietly resolved to take no more prisoners." He and his men murdered multiple Indians, some of them prisoners, as part of their reaving and raiding across western Washington in 1856.[22]

Newton Ward, part of the company that killed Peo-Peo-Mox-Mox, remembered that the question of whether to kill prisoners ended up answering itself:

> Asked what should be don[e] with the [prisoners,] some one said tie them or kill them. They under[s]tood that and they made a break to get [a]way, one of them had an old knife and he made a lung[e] at L[i]eutenant Miller[,] he threw up his arm and the knife struck it. Just at that time a man whose name I have forgotten struck the Indian over the head with his gun. He killed the Indian but he broke his gun all to pieces. There were five of the Prisoners killed and scalped, among the number was old Pe Pe Mox mox the head Chief. Every man wanted a scalp of his head, there was not enough to go around so [doctor] Mack Shaw cut his ears off.[23]

The extent of the bodily mutilation inflicted on Peo-Peo-Mox-Mox was extreme. James Sinclair, who had been present at the killing but claimed he did not take part, resignedly described it in a letter a friend a few months later: "The whole scalp was taken from his head, and cut up into 20 pieces, his skull was divided equally for buttons—his ears preserved in a bottle of spirits—and large strips of his skin cut off along his back to be made into Razor strops—such is Indian warfare."[24]

Scalping in and of itself was not unusual. Indeed, Newton Ward relished his claim that "there were 75 Indians killed and Scalped" in the battle the next day. This body count was almost certainly an exaggeration, probably a vast one. But the volunteers did commit further mutilations. Writing in his diary after the last battle, volunteer Plympton J. Kelly wrote, "Yesterday peu peu Mox Mox was taken up by Dr. Shaw and his ears cut of[f] and to day he has be[e]n taken out and subject to further in- dignities," including desecrations unrelated to trophy taking, like the de- struction of his eyes. Then the volunteers moved camp, Plympton J. Kelly noting that there was "enough beef entrails and dead Indians lying around the place to bre[e]d a pestilence if the weather was warm enough."[25]

Some of the volunteer soldiers who turned to history writing left lit- tle doubt where they stood on killings and mutilations. William H. Barn- hart, trying to sell his never-finished "History of the Yakima War" in 1856, while the war was still ongoing, joked to James W. Nesmith (shortly before Nesmith became Oregon's superintendent of Indian Af- fairs) that "the work will be bound in the hid[e] of PuPu-Mox=Mox tanned expressly for the purpose, so that everyone owning a copy of the work will always have 'really and truly' a part and parcel of the 'Yakima Indian War' in the House."[26]

Body parts taken from Peo-Peo-Mox-Mox were preserved and dis- played with pride by pioneers. Granville O. Haller remembered seeing "two ears, in alcohol, evidently an Indian's, and they were proudly shown to me at Fort Dalles, Oregon, as the ears of Pio-pio-mox-mox. I saw Razor strops of human skin, evidently an Indian's skin, and was assured they were taken off the body of Pio-pio-mox-mox. Those persons who exhibited these were highly respected citizens of Oregon, and seemed proud of their trophies." James K. Kelly was elected mayor of The Dalles shortly after this fort was decommissioned in 1857—whether or not he was one of the "highly respected citizens" Haller remembered, the butchery Kelly had overseen was an electoral asset.[27]

As it had for William Packwood, killing Indians helped launch James K. Kelly's political career—he eventually ascended to the national Sen- ate, then to chief justice of the Oregon Supreme Court. According to some later pioneer accounts, a portion of "the scalp of Pio-Pio Mox-a- Mox, greatest villain of all the Indian chiefs, became the hair on the head of a doll belonging to a little girl in St. Johns, Oregon" by the early 1900s. Given how many body parts were taken by volunteers eager for a share of the gory spoils, this may even have been true.[28]

As a volunteer soldier fighting in the eastern portions of the Washington Territory in 1855 and 1856, Waman C. Hembree appears to have assumed

Peo-Peo-Mox-Mox as he appeared to Gustavas Sohon in 1855. From A. J. Splawn,
Ka-mi-akin: The Last Hero of the Yakimas.

all Native people not under the command of White officers were enemy
combatants. A diary kept by one of his men (who was also his relative) records multiple instances of "Indian spies" being caught and killed. There
is little indication that these "spies" were anything other than Native people in the wrong place at the wrong time. Hembree wrote on March 1,
1856, of capturing two "Indian spies" of unknown names and ethnies who
were "tried by Court martial" in the Walla Walla valley and (in one case)
summarily executed. What offense had this supposed spy committed to
merit execution? There is no record. This execution was, in all likelihood,
a lynching under the thin veneer of military law.[29]

*James Kerr Kelly, shortly after he was elected U.S.
senator from Oregon in 1871. Courtesy of the Library
of Congress, Brady-Handy Photograph Collection.*

In April 1856, Captain Absalom Jefferson ("A. J.") Hembree bragged in a letter to his brother Joel that "we have run them all out. . . . We have drove the Indians from their country." And it was true that most Native communities kept their distance. Yet only a few days after writing this letter, A. J. Hembree was killed leading his men in a headlong charge against a group of six Native men he had claimed to have already driven away. When A. J. Hembree was shot off his horse, his fellows beat a quick retreat. The Hembrees' discussions of "the Indians" generally were typical, making no allowance for friendly or neutral forces in the area.[30]

William D. Stillwell, a volunteer in the Cayuse War and Yakima War portions of the War on Illahee, remembered that his compatriots tortured and mutilated as well as killed. Following A. J. Hembree's death, volunteer forces decided not to attack the main Native force in the hills, judging such an assault too hazardous. But they did kill isolated people where and when they could. Stillwell recalled:

> In the fight on the mountain ... Andy Wright shot one Indian through the hips at the rock-entrenchment on the highest point, where the Indians had barricaded themselves to do sharp shooting. Wright first scalped the Indian and then killed him with his butcherknife. Why didn't he kill him first? Oh he was mad because [A. J.] H[e]mbree had been killed. We were all neighbors at Yamhill.
>
> The next day we killed two Indians up the creek, above where the oaks set in. Col. ____ [omitted in original; probably Thomas R. Cornelius] looked ahead and called to me: 'Bill, Inj_ ns ahead.' I saw three Indian[s] with a pack horse. I deployed my men to right and left and we went after those Inj_ns. The Colonel killed one. I rode after one old fellow who made up a canyon overtook him and shot him. No! I did not scalp him, but some of the boys did scalp him. I never scalped an Indian in my life.[31]

As was typical for the reminiscences of men like Stillwell, foes were described throughout simply as Indians. The Native man Andy Wright wounded and then skinned alive before killing was not known to have had any role in the death of A. J. Hembree, and the Native people with pack horses killed the next day may not even have been involved in the conflict. They were Indians, and that was enough for the volunteers. Stillwell's insistence that he had "never scalped an Indian" was, in a way, also typical—many Euro-Americans who had committed violence that might be considered suspect were quick to point out acts even worse than theirs.

Euro-Americans attempted and sometimes succeeded in perpetrating wanton murders and mass killings in western Washington, too. Many of these killings, at least as much as those discussed above, are only a shadowy outline in the archival sources. In 1886 Urban E. Hicks, who had become a successful politician and newspaper editor, gleefully remembered murdering a small community in the South Prairie region east of modern-day Tacoma, Washington, most likely in the early weeks of 1856. He and his men snuck up on a large "ranch" dwelling and killed the people who lived there as they tried to get away:

As the savages came out of the one hole in front, they were shot down, big and little, sq__ws and all, except one b_ck and one sq__w, who ran, side by side, the full length of our fire and escaped. In the ranch was found numerous household trinkets, dresses, dishes, spoons, knives and forks, rings, and keepsakes, taken from the residences of the families massacred on White river. I also found the scalp of one of the white women who had been so cruelly murdered.[32]

If Hicks did, in fact, find Euro-American household goods and a scalp at the "ranch," he found them only *after* he and his men had murdered nearly every man, woman, and child who lived there. The Hicks Massacre occurred before any such evidence was conveniently found.[33]

The Maxon Massacre in the Nisqually area of Washington, perpetrated in March 1856, was similarly predicated on the notion that all Native people were to be considered hostile until proven otherwise. A volunteer force led by Captain Hamilton J. G. Maxon, who had previously volunteered in the Cayuse War, marauded through the lower Nisqually River region capturing or killing any Native person they found. It is likely that most if not all of their victims were Nisqually people, as it was predominantly Nisqually homeland Maxon rampaged through. But the killers did not distinguish. Even according to a flattering volunteer's account sent to a newspaper the next month, the men under Maxon had shot first and asked questions later. They compelled those who surrendered to give up the locations of others, and in at least one case forced a captive Indigenous woman to act as the bait for an ambush. Indigenous captives also served to identify those the volunteers had killed as culpable for previous killings of settlers. Whatever the suspect veracity of those identifications, they served the interests of all parties involved—the volunteers got to justify their killings; their Native captives got to try to forestall potential future executions of themselves or others.[34]

In the Maxon Massacre (sometimes called the Mashel Massacre) of 1856, the volunteers killed from seventeen to thirty or more people fleeing across the Nisqually River, mostly women, children, and unarmed men. Maxon and his men bragged in the newspaper of killing "Eight Hostiles" along the Nisqually River, although the higher death counts were widely known among Euro-Americans within a year. Even in the volunteers' own story of the events, all the Indigenous people they bragged of killing had been taken by surprise and had been trying to run away when they were shot (in the Maxon Massacre, and in the killings before it). Those killed were "hostile" only insofar as the volunteers presumed all Indians not under White control to be hostile. Maxon, like many other leaders of kill squads, routinely excluded killings of noncombatants from the counts. As Puyallup/Nisqually political leader and historian Henry Sicade later put it, "The old men and the women were shot down, the defenseless children were killed and later the babies were found crushed against the boulders by the river and in the river, not a life being spared." There were disputes over whether the Americans had waded in to murder the babies by hand, or whether they had simply watched them die in the current. But there was no question that the Americans had killed children.[35]

At least the outline of these deaths was known by local Euro-Americans, but they appeared neither in official reports nor in national news. Nisqually oral traditions have kept the memory of murders alive and have regularly reinserted them into Euro-American histories. But without willing contemporary Euro-American witnesses like those that wrote of the Lupton Massacre in southern Oregon or the horrors inflicted on Peo-Peo-Mox-Mox in southern Washington, the Maxon Massacre was obscured by historians hoping to minimize the misdeeds of pioneers—including Elwood Evans, a founder of the Washington State Historical Society. This omission, in turn, helped shape the work of even historians more willing to attempt to understand history with Native perspectives included. When teacher and amateur historian Oscar H. Jones wrote a glowing history of Henry Sicade's life in 1936, he chose the story of the trial and execution of Chief Leschi (see chapter 6), rather than Sicade's own history of the Maxon Massacre, as *the* example of pioneer iniquity.[36]

And there is evidence that more formal mass killings in western Washington Territory were contemplated at the highest levels, rejected only because they seemed too risky. Sidney S. Ford, a judge and a captain in the volunteer militia, mustered a group of mostly Cowlitz and Chehalis men to fight alongside the volunteer forces, after his government-mandated attempts to seize all of their firearms foundered in the face of carefully strategized Native resistance. He and Isaac I. Stevens hoped this muster would help dampen the likelihood of those groups joining a pan-Native alliance.[37]

But Ford and Stevens apparently also considered inflicting genocide on their allies. After hearing that a few Upper Chehalis people had met with a messenger presumed to be Yakama, Stevens and Ford contemplated "summarily dispos[ing] . . . [of] the men of the [Chehalis] tribe," as Stevens put it in a letter to Secretary of War Jefferson Davis. Stevens and Ford came to agree that if they attempted mass extermination, "the tribe would break out." Though they considered murdering all men among the Chehalis community they were allied with, Stevens and Ford decided that the genocide they were considering wouldn't be feasible—although there were some suspicious shootings.[38]

During the War on Illahee in Washington Territory, martial law against White people, not mass murder of Native people, gained the most infamy on the national stage. As the war was accelerating in 1855, suspicion fell not only on all Native people, but on many of the Euro-Americans who associated with them. In the fall of 1855, there were calls to lynch Catholic priests in Olympia, viewed as suspicious because of their perceived friendliness with Native communities. Similar calls were made to find and execute Father Pandosy after Rains's volunteers burned down the Yakama mission.[39]

Acting in close concert with Governor Stevens, James Tilton (a surveyor, enslaver, and adjutant general of the Washington militia) ordered soldiers to round up not only Native people, but their perceived allies. In March 1856, militia soldiers were instructed to seize

> French and other foreign born citizens, especially those who may have Indian wives. . . . You will notify these persons that the orders of the Commander in Chief are imperative that they shall immediately depart for the Post at Fort Nisqually, to be guarded. . . .
>
> Should you find any resistance from these settlers you are instructed to employ force, by tying the men and bringing them in as prisoners. . . .
>
> You are instructed to use every persuasion possible with these suspected persons before resorting to force, but should they resist, you are authorized to employ force, and coerce their immediate removal.[40]

Although focused especially on the "foreign born," and on men who had intermarried with Native people, the ambit of the troops was deliberately broad: "As they occupy that part of the country which is at present a part of the theatre of war, martial law of necessity exists there. Consequently you will have no hesitation in enforcing the order to secure all men whom you may find in a suspicious locality, or when the fact of their residence near the enemy, and within the range of the scouts of the hostile Indians seem to imply an understanding and which in itself is a doubtful and suspicious circumstance." In times of heightened colonial conquest, the invaders did not wish to suffer the ambiguity of a middle ground. As Isaac I. Stevens put it later that year, "There is no such thing in my humble judgment as neutrality in an Indian war, and whoever can remain on his claim unmolested, is an ally of the enemy, and must be dealt with as such." Martial law was made official in April 1856.[41]

Native people were hostile until proven otherwise, and non-Native people who did not agree were to be presumed complicit. Peaceful coexistence with Native people was to be treated as suspicious in itself—although such sweeping orders tended to be enforced primarily against those already deemed suspect, like the former Hudson's Bay men—or, some charged, Stevens's political opponents. This roundup, unlike the imprisonment of Native people, faced some political pushback. Hamilton J. G. Maxon imprisoned several White settlers on suspicion of treason—defined as "giving aid and comfort to hostile Indians"—and, with Benjamin Franklin Shaw, was part of a military commission that attempted unsuccessfully to try them for that capital offense. The Euro-American public was comfortable with perfunctory military trials and summary executions when it came to Native people, but these kinds of treason trials, when pursued against White persons, were seen by most Euro-Americans as too radical. Territorial and military authorities quickly quashed this attempt to treat suspect White men like Indians.[42]

While there was no organized roundup of White men living with Native women in Oregon to match the one ordered in Washington, there were calls for it. In April 1856 a volunteer named Peter Ruffner wrote to James W. Nesmith in his capacity as U.S. marshal, asking him to help the volunteers

> that went after ... the Pistol River + Chilco Indians ... [and] came upon them, some 60 men, women + children that all said they were willing to go to the reserve, so the party did not kill an Indian. ... These white men that lives with sq__ws found out that those sq__ws said that they would go there to the reserve. So rather than to lose their sq__ws, they told the Indians to take

to the mountain—that those men [the volunteers] was going to take them up the coast a ways to kill them all.[43]

The volunteers had, apparently, agreed not to murder this group of Native people so long as they agreed to be removed. Then this Native group fled into the mountains—some with White family members along. There are other records that confirm the insistence of some local Euro-Americans on banishing all Native people, even Native women married to White men, and the resistance of some of the latter's husbands. It is unclear whether the group of Native people that fled had, in fact, been warned by White family members of an impending plot to murder them all. It is likewise unclear whether the mass murder they avoided was a known plan or merely a predictable probability.[44]

Ruffner asked Nesmith for help paying for arms and provision to ensure that there would be "attention paid to those indians + some of the whites, if not we will be compelled to leave + give up to them." Nesmith, Ruffner hoped, would "do something in Some shape on [the] way to rid this portion of the Country of these Indians." And Ruffner wanted to use the guns on "some of whites" too—those who showed sympathy or family loyalty to the Native people whose homeland Ruffner was trying to finish taking. It is unclear whether Ruffner got any assistance from Nesmith or others to enact his dream of killing his neighbors. But the government did undertake the removal he and so many other pioneers asked for, sometimes including house-to-house searches to seize Native people for internment—or murder them outright.[45]

The Washington portions of the War on Illahee can be partially distinguished from those in Oregon by the much greater number of Native people known to have fought alongside Euro-American forces. But allies are not always friends, and many Native fighters were trusted even less by the Euro-Americans they fought alongside than Donald McKay. Many wished them ill. Edmund Clare Fitzhugh saw an opportunity in war to promote the deaths of potential Native allies as well as enemies, suggesting to one commander that he "make scouts of [the Northern Indians] & give them a *lively* chance for being killed."[46]

And sometimes volunteers, looking to kill any Indian they could find, attacked even those aiding the U.S. war effort. Upper Chehalis leader Koolah Yuanan was instructed to wear a white cloth on his hat, so that pioneers would know he was an ally and wouldn't take his Indian-ness as sufficient cause to kill him. As Koolah Yuanan told his descendant Silas Heck, wearing this mark of allyship was not always enough. Koolah Yuanan was nearly killed by volunteers near Olympia, Washington, who knew he was friendly but "were in favor of doing away with all of my people they could." The would-be murderers were stopped only because their fellows cautioned that "such an act would be annihilation for all the white settlers in this district"—the same pragmatism that had kept Isaac I. Stevens from acting on his desire to attempt a genocide of Koolah Yuanan's people (after Yuanan had helped make sure they remained armed). On other occasions, would-be murderers refused to be restrained by such reasoning.[47]

On May 21, 1856, a volunteer named James A. Lake murdered a "friendly Indian" just outside Fort Nisqually. Lake had lost family members in the killings along White River the previous year, and, as his commanding officer Urban E. Hicks put it, "of course he was bitter against all r_d-sk_ns, friend or foe." Squalli-absch Say-oh-sil, known to White locals as "Indian Bob," had been given special dispensation to leave the internment camp near Fort Steilacoom and work for the Euro-Americans. As Squalli-absch Say-oy-sil was chopping wood, James Lake gunned him down in cold blood.[48]

Urban E. Hicks, in a memoir of his war experiences published with George Himes in 1886, reminisced about how he and the men he commanded helped Lake get away with this murder of an Indian "friend":

> I scolded [Lake] for the act, but still could not help sympathizing with him, as, indeed, he had the sympathy of the entire company and camp. I cautioned him to keep quiet and promised that I would do what I could to shield him from further trouble. The next morning Dr. [William Fraser] Tolmie, accompanied by two or three sq__ws, appeared in camp, and immediately entered complaint before Colonel [Benjamin Franklin] Shaw that one of his friendly Indians had been killed the evening before, near the fort, by a volunteer. . . . The Colonel ordered all the companies to be drawn up in line. It then became generally known what had happened, and it required considerable effort on the part of the officers to keep the men in line while the roll was being called and they were being examined by Tolmie and his sq__ws. My company was the last to be examined, and although it was by that time pretty generally suspected who they were after, still it was hoped by the boys that by noise and confusion they would so frighten the sq__ws that they would fail to identify.[49]

Despite the "noise and confusion" meant to frighten them, the Native women identified the murderer. But this successful identification did not lead to justice:

> Scarcely had [Lake] been pointed out by the sq__ws, before the men, in spite of the efforts of their officers, broke ranks and with wild yells rushed for their guns, threatening dire vengeance upon Tolmie and his sq__ws if Lake was touched. It required the utmost exertion on the part of the officers to save them from assault. . . .
>
> Order was somewhat restored, when the Doctor agreed that if the men would permit him and his sq__ws to escape he would not molest Lake any further. A way was opened for them, through which they ran to their horses, quickly mounted, and galloped of[f], no doubt heartily glad to get away with their scalps, to the now infinite amusement of the men. No more was heard of the affair.[50]

After one volunteer killed a man in cold blood, his comrades were willing to kill several more people to keep him from any possibility of consequences. After all, he had "the sympathy of the entire company and camp."[51]

On May 26, 1856, James A. Lake was tried by a military commission—apparently for a different murder. While transporting a Native prisoner they called "Mowitch" (among other things, a Chinook Jargon term for "deer" used as a belittling generic descriptor for Native people) to Seattle to stand trial for supposedly taking part in the war, James A. Lake and his fellow volunteer Joseph Brannon murdered the man with two shots to the head. Facing the faint possibility of consequences, Lake claimed that he had been "firmly convinced that the Indian Mowitch was concerned in the depredations perpetrated [along White River] . . . [and] determined that no such savage monster should escape the fate he richly deserved."[52]

Both men were cleared by the military court. To what extent this was because the officers did not care about the killing, and to what extent because they thought Lake's justification righteous, is not recorded. If nothing else, the trial underlines the need for skepticism in other White killings claimed to have been specific acts of vengeance (like the murder of Nisqually leader Quiemuth, discussed in chapter 6). For the killing Lake told his friends about privately, his expressed motive was simply race hatred. When brought before a court for another killing, Lake identified his victim as a specific perpetrator. The few other pioneers brought before the courts of law (or public opinion) for Indian killing may well have done likewise. Some remembered "revenge killings" were probably more similar to Lake's murder of Squalli-absch Say-oh-sil/"Indian Bob"—capricious attacks of opportunity. Joseph Brannon went on to murder more Native people without legal consequence. There is similarly no indication that James A. Lake suffered any punishment for the wanton killings he committed—and there is no reason to think that the two murders for which he underwent brief legal inconveniences were the only murders he committed. What made Lake stand out in the memories of his fellow volunteers, such as the future newspaper editor and opponent of women's suffrage Harvey W. Scott, was less his murderousness than his lovely singing voice.[53]

The Puget Sound War has sometimes been portrayed as of a different character from that of the other wars in the Pacific Northwest. Euro-American wars on local communities have at times been subsumed within the narrative of Euro-American conflicts with Indigenous peoples and polities from British-claimed territory they deemed "Northern Indians," who sometimes attacked Euro-American and Native settlements alike, or within conflicts between Native polities in the broader Puget Sound region. There were relatively fewer conventional battles in the Puget Sound War than in other conflicts in the Northwest. The most famous clash, the 1856 Battle of Seattle, resulted in little loss of life on either side, and it may have been (as historian Mary Ellen Rowe has suggested) meant as "more demonstration than battle" by the Native forces who participated in the attack. But many pioneers were happy to attempt to murder Indigenous people, both locally and internationally. And that didn't stop when the wars began to wind down.[54]

On July 17, 1856, a force of mixed volunteers from across Oregon and Washington led by Benjamin Franklin Shaw attacked a large group of mostly Cayuse/Liksiyu Native people who were camped in Grand Ronde Valley, near what is now Elgin, Oregon. The Native people were harvesting camas, but they began to pack up and withdraw as soon as they realized White volunteers were nearby. Euro-Americans later claimed that the Native horsemen sent to speak with them were very rude—and they took this perceived "sauciness" and retreat as hostile acts worthy of mass killing. This was normal for volunteers; on June 30, 1856, when four Native men in canoes had seen Shaw's force and tried to paddle away, he had ordered his men to shoot them. As was also characteristic, the volunteers on July 17, 1856, were already forming lines to charge "the enemy village," even before the supposedly hostile retreat that was later claimed to have triggered the attack. After all, with the terms of many of the volunteers about to expire, this was (as Shaw put it) their last chance to "make a fight before going out of service." There was probably no action that could have been taken by the camas gatherers that would have held back pioneer bloodlust. In the Shaw Massacre, volunteers appear to have killed between forty and sixty or more people—mostly old men, women, and children. Then they looted and burned the encampment, seizing a wealth of horses and other goods—some of the plunder Governor Stevens had apparently promised at the outset of the war.[55]

Hamilton G. Maxon and those of his men who had not deserted were part of this attack, though only barely. After their massacres in Nisqually country, they had been sent to assist with the war effort in the east. Unwilling to take orders from Shaw and in trouble for having fired their weapons for practice without warning the rest of the volunteers, Maxon's company was at a sulky distance from the rest of the volunteers during the lead-up to the attack on Grand Ronde Valley. The fighting and looting were disorganized and chaotic, and Maxon and his men charged off and were lost for a few days—most likely in an attempt to continue the killing spree.[56]

The unprompted killing of dozens of Native people benefited the perpetrators. Benjamin Franklin Shaw used the mass killing perpetrated at the Grand Ronde Valley as a political asset; he won election to the Washington territorial legislature in 1857 and profited from occasional stints in the Indian Service for the next decade or so. Governor Isaac I. Stevens made the attack a centerpiece of a deceitful governor's address in 1856, transforming the impromptu killing and looting spree into a well-planned tactical masterstroke, "the hardest and most brilliant blow of the war." This false assertion largely stuck; the Shaw Massacre at Grand Ronde Valley did not attract the same censure as similarly wanton killing sprees by other volunteer companies elsewhere, such as those of Lupton and Maxon, and has sometimes been missed by historians since.[57]

This was not the only lie Isaac I. Stevens told in his 1856 address. He also proclaimed to his "fellow citizens": "You will find nothing to reproach the people of our beloved territory with, for their conduct either at home or in the field. During the first six months of this war, not an Indian was killed except in battle. Throughout the war, not an Indian has been killed in a volunteer camp. . . . We have waged war with humanity, with moderation, with honor to our country and honor to ourselves." These were lies that he repeated to the press, and that he repeated, somewhat more defensively, to the U.S. Congress a few years later.[58]

In May 1858 Stevens pressed Congress to pay six million dollars for expenses incurred in Oregon and Washington during the wars waged there (more than the infrastructure and public works budget for the entire federal government that year). In this speech, Stevens argued both that incidents of wanton violence by pioneers didn't matter *and* that there had been no such incidents of consequence:

> It has often been charged against us, that [the Washington and Oregon] war was brought on by outrages upon the rights of the Indians; that it was gotten up for the purpose of speculation; and that it was the treaties which caused the war. Well, sir, suppose the treaties did cause the war; suppose we did have vagobonds [*sic*] in that country who committed outrages upon the Indians; suppose some few citizens were operated upon by the motive of making a speculation out of the war; if these things be true, did they make it any less the duty of the people, and of the authorities of the Territories, a war having come upon them, to protect the settlements?[59]

He argued that even if all the allegations about Northwesterners were true—and Stevens went on to hotly deny them—they did not matter.

In this same speech, Isaac I. Stevens put forward deceits and distortions that would set the tone for many histories of the period to follow. He carefully separated those "few" pioneers who had committed outrages ("vagobonds") from those whom he termed "American citizens, the very choice and flower of your yeomanry." And he attempted to erase his own threat that Yakamas, and perhaps others, would "walk in blood knee deep" unless they signed the treaty he demanded they consent to. Responding to accurate charges that Native people had been compelled to sign under threat of violence, Stevens pointed to the "official record of its proceedings—a record which was taken verbatim by two secretaries separately. It is not a fixed up or patched up concern. . . . Pu-pu-mux-mux . . . every Indian chief, and every Indian there assembled . . . expressed joy and satisfaction."[60]

The deliberately incomplete record (as one of those two secretaries later attested) had been created for the treaty councils with political purpose, allowing Stevens to build documentary supports for his falsehoods.

He overshot even the half-truths of those documents in this memorial—although threats of violence during negotiations had been blotted out, a record of reticence remained. Stevens had lied to Native people and polities, he had lied to the citizens of Washington Territory, and now he baldly lied to Congress: "At no time during th[e] war was there any unauthorized killings by the volunteer forces. The Indians, whether friendly or hostile, were sacred in the camps of the volunteers during that war. Their conduct was throughout humane and meritorious." The deceptions, however flagrant, worked well enough. Stevens and Joseph Lane were able to push through legislation to pay for the war material and wages of the volunteer forces. After some back-and-forth and an audit of inflated expenses, recompense for some of the volunteers who had taken part in the War on Illahee flooded in during the Civil War, and more trickles of federal funding continued into the 1870s and beyond.[61]

Historian Kent D. Richards, whose 1979 biography of Stevens, *Young Man in a Hurry*, shaped historical interpretation for decades, extended credulity selectively to portray Stevens heroically. Richards then and since has denied that anyone in the territorial government had genocidal intent—at best a severe oversight. He rejected well-substantiated historical reports of White miners who attempted to rape Native women in 1855 as "pure fabrication"—without providing any evidence other than indirect reference to Stevens's denials. Isaac I. Stevens threaded enough untruths and omissions into his speeches and negotiations that generations of historians could, wittingly or unwittingly, cover up some hard truths. The lies Stevens spun about murder, rape, and colonial violence, repeated uncritically by people like Richards, are *still* misshaping the historical record.[62]

Organized violence by companies of volunteer soldiers sputtered to a stall in the fall of 1856, as undersupplied, underwhelmed, and (they felt) underpaid pioneers mustered out or deserted, and many Native communities negotiated the best peace they could. But killings by regular soldiers and by everyday Euro-American citizens continued, in the ongoing undeclared wars, in attacks by vigilante mobs, and in individual violent encounters. The conduct of the pioneers as a group was seldom "humane and meritorious" toward Native people, in wars or beyond them, not in the Northwest and not in similar spaces of settler invasion. The genocide Wasson labeled the "Oregon Holocaust" may have been the most intense in southern Oregon, but it was not limited to that region. Nor was it limited to times of war. Wasson's survey of the horrors of the 1850s along and beyond the Oregon coast took in not only official and unofficial acts of war, but also "the terrible years of concentration camps and virtual 'death camp' reservations" that continued through and after the wars. These, too, were a part of life far beyond southern Oregon. The War on Illahee continued in the peace.[63]

CHAPTER FIVE

Theft, Murder, Complicity, and the Oregon Trails of Tears

J OHN K. LAMERICK WAS sure the war wasn't over. He had fought and sometimes killed Native people in Oregon from at least 1852, related stories of his murders with gory gusto, and claimed the rank of (volunteer) brigadier general during the official portion of the Rogue River War in 1855–56, largely because of his reports of having recruited hundreds of men for the cause. In December 1855 he had been confident that "the quantity of men now in the field is quite suff[icient] to *kill* all of the Indians in this territory." He was wrong—many Native people survived and won battles even though they did not have the resources or numbers to continue the war. Peace seemed to have been made in western Oregon by June 1856. But Lamerick and pioneers like him were unconvinced. He wrote of "citizens . . . trying to get up a purse and offer a reward for [Native] scalps" to get rid of the last "few scattering Indians" in the region. And he assumed another exterminatory war would be under way in Oregon before long, to match the one still being fought in Washington Territory.[1]

In a few ways, he was right. The so-called Snake War on Native peoples in eastern Oregon and Washington (among other places) had been slowly picking up steam since 1854—although Lamerick chose to commit treason and join the Confederate army before recruitment for Snake War volunteers began in earnest, in 1862. More broadly, attacks

on Native people and communities continued, only somewhat attenuated, as formal wars across the region wound down.[2]

Nearly all early histories of the Pacific Northwest agreed there had
been an "Indian war" in 1855 and 1856. The War on Illahee was, perhaps, felt across the region more universally in that period than in any
other. Past those dates, the length of the wars depended in part on the
chroniclers. Those fighting for earlier volunteer claims extended the
wars backward. Those focused on eastern Washington Territory extended the wars forward. Some few even noted the continuing war with
Native groups in the eastern reaches of the Northwest that went into the
1860s, bridging the gap to the more famed conflicts of the 1870s, such as
the Modoc War and the Nez Perce War.

Within and beyond the wars of the period, there was a continuity of
settler violence, theft, rape, and murder. Attacks on Native sovereignty,
individual and collective, continued. Attempts by Euro-Americans to use
reservations as prisons and piggy banks continued. Lynchings, legal and
extralegal, within war and beyond it, continued. White theft of Native
land, individual and collective, continued. And Native resistance to colonial regimes, in ways big and small, continued.

The end of outright war in western Oregon and parts of Washington
did not end White depredations on Native communities. The Trails of
Tears that forced Native communities onto reservations traumatized,
tortured, and sometimes killed. Conditions on reservations could be just
as lethal as war, especially when aggravated by hatred and graft. And
those Native people beyond the reservation faced Euro-American legal
systems and social norms that would refuse to protect Native residents
from White violence. The War on Illahee did not suddenly end when
armies began to disband. Many pioneers, sometimes including those in
uniform, continued to rob and kill Native people into times of purported
peace.

From 1856 to 1858 and beyond, government authorities in Oregon Territory undertook a series of deadly removals to reservations—the Oregon
Trails of Tears. Both the journey and the destination could be lethal,
dogged by Euro-Americans with guns and murderous intent. The vision
of reservations as a carceral system that Joel Palmer had made official
during the war continued haphazardly in peacetime. Historian and anthropologist David G. Lewis has shown that reservations like Grand
Ronde were viewed—and at times administered—as "concentration

camps" by Euro-Americans in the 1850s. Native nations eventually made reservations into places of community and power, despite the intent of pioneers. But the initial years on the reservation were desperate for many Indigenous people.[3]

A full account of the Trails of Tears in the Pacific Northwest is beyond this study. The work already done makes clear that they could be lethal. Historian Stephen Dow Beckham's review of a removal from the Table Rock region of Oregon to the Grand Ronde Reservation, conducted in the dead of winter by George H. Ambrose in 1856, shows a ragged train besieged by pioneer murderers. Ambrose reported eight Native people dying on a thirty-three-day march, at least one of whom was killed by pioneer vigilantes prowling the edges of the train for just such an opportunity. As Ambrose knew, there were "some declaring that every Indian will be killed" in the removal. Whether or not the fund-raising for scalp bounties Lamerick described was successful, there were White killers eager to murder Native people, for a fee or for free. Nor were Euro-Americans necessarily innocent in those deaths Ambrose attributed to sickness; the forced march in the cold was a contributing factor for many who perished. The physical and psychological traumas brought on by pioneer violence were probably contributing factors for all.[4]

William Tichenor, who had spurred invasions of southwestern Oregon in 1851, masterminded an especially lethal set of removals of Chetco and Pistol River communities near Port Orford. As Gray Whaley has shown, Tichenor was given barely tacit approval for genocide by Indian Superintendent James W. Nesmith in 1857; he was informed that if settlers "hit upon some mode for [Chetco and Pistol River peoples'] extermination," it would "occasion no regrets at this office." Tichenor had at least seventeen Chetco people killed—supposedly while they were trying to escape—and he expressed willingness, even eagerness, to "kill the last one of them" to make Port Orford "quiet."[5]

Robert Metcalf, an Indian sub-agent who conducted a removal of Umpqua region Native people to Grand Ronde Reservation in the same period, encouraged the use of force even as he discouraged outright murder. His diary records both attempts to avoid *wanton* killings and attempts to rally more organized pioneer violence to force the movement of Native captives who "expressed a desire to die in their own country" rather than "leav[e] the land of their nativity where the bodies of their forefathers rest." Many Native people in the region were convinced they were being marched off to die in any case. Often, they were right. At least one person was murdered in the night during this particular forced removal. Metcalf assumed the murderer must have been an Indian, rather than one of the pioneers who had threatened and planned to kill Native people on the forced march. There is no record of how Metcalf came to his conclusion; he simply had an "understanding" that a Klickitat/Qwû'lh-hwai-pûm man had done the deed. And Ambrose, Metcalf, and perhaps even Tichenor might have been inclined to undercount the dead. Those listed as "deserted" may have escaped, but some may well have been murdered and left unfound.[6]

Indigenous accounts recalled brutal horrors beyond the partisans hoping to murder them. People died, and army personnel would not permit their families time to bury them. Soldiers "abused"—probably in multiple senses of the word—women on forced marches. These actions might not make the official reports—those in charge would have been motivated not to reveal them. But Native communities remembered.[7]

William Cribbs White, later a Euro-American farmer in Umatilla country, was haunted by his time working as a subcontractor (and perhaps a de facto guard) accompanying mass removals of Native people across the Northwest. His daughter Rosella White Hammer would

> recall many interesting stories of his adventures in this work. It was a pitiful sight to see them driven as sheep and cattle, different Tribes mixed together and fighting each other; Indians who had lived on lands on which their forefathers had spent all their lives. Those who lived on fish were placed inland, and those from the North, placed in the South. He told of difficulty the troops had in taking the dead babies and children from their mothers, as they would carry them for days, trying to hide them. There was nothing the Officers could do to stop the Indian women from wailing or chanting their death dirges; as soon as some tired, and quit, others would take up the mournful song. They were so homesick leaving their homes, that they could not eat.[8]

Official reports of the removals like those written by Ambrose and Metcalf tended to be sparse, stories of successes and challenges accompanied by terse counts of the dead. White's more jarring account was a family story, shared mostly in private among fellow Euro-American pioneer descendants. And it matched, much more closely, Indigenous histories of the removals.

Deaths due to Euro-American action and inaction continued on reservations. As one military report from the period put it: "The volunteers, without discipline, without order, and similar to the madmen of the revolution, menace us with death every day; they have already despoiled of their provisions the inhabitants of this country and the Indians who have so nobly followed the advice to remain faithful friends of the Americans. To-day these same volunteers are not yet satisfied with rapine and injustice, and wish to take away the small remnant of animals and provisions left." The report came from the Cayuse portion of the Umatilla Reservation, but one like it could have come from nearly anywhere.[9]

White fear often drove Euro-American misgivings—many of the calls to fulfill the basic promises the U.S. government had made were connected to a fear of renewed war more than a humanitarian cause. In an 1858 report on the Grand Ronde and Siletz reservations, Special Indian Commissioner Christopher H. Mott registered a worry about hunger:

> Since my first visit to Grand Ronde, at which time [James W. Nesmith m]ade an order for the reduction of rations to the Indians, there has been some complaints & threats from them. There is no fish or game within reach & the truth is that at this agency the department will have to feed the Indians, else starvation or the plunder of the whites will follow—then comes another Indian war. The latest intelligence from the Spokane Country is that our troops have met with some "brilliant" successes, and the war is ended *for the present.*[10]

The threat of starvation was not depicted as necessarily a concern in itself, but as a concern because it might lead to further war—perhaps reopening a war in western Oregon just as the campaign against Native peoples in eastern Washington was perceived to be winding down.[11]

Politically connected volunteer soldiers often ended up in positions of power on reservations. After all, as Matthew Deady had noted, Indian fighting was a political asset. And the men who killed and stole during the wars could continue to kill and steal beyond them—sometimes including those who ended up in high office.[12]

James W. Nesmith, a thin-skinned pioneer proud of his reputation for violence, claimed to have "commanded troops in every Indian war in Oregon since the year 1843 . . . to the commencement of the [1873]

Modoc campaign." He fought as a defiant volunteer, refusing to be placed under the command of regular U.S. forces. Indeed, he often refused any military authority other than his own—when leading a company in 1855, Nesmith ignored orders he did not care for both from military leaders and from Oregon Territorial Governor George Law Curry, and he ignored complaints that his men were committing "outrages"—typically code for rape, or murder, or both.[13]

Nesmith's political rise was boosted by his longtime ally Joseph Lane, who ensured Nesmith's appointments first as Oregon U.S. marshal in 1856, then as superintendent of Indian Affairs in 1857. Unlike Anson Dart or Joel Palmer, Indian Superintendent James Nesmith was popular among a critical mass of his fellow White Oregonians. With a proud history as a volunteer soldier and connections with the pioneer political powerbrokers known as the Salem Clique, he was elected by the new state legislature as U.S. senator from Oregon in 1860, taking over Joseph Lane's seat. He spent his time in the U.S. Congress fighting to preserve the Union, demanding more federal money be spent in Oregon and the Northwest, encouraging the people of Idaho Territory to take up arms and kill their Native neighbors, and fighting *against* citizenship and personhood rights for people of color.[14]

Nesmith railed in his letters against those who swindled Native people. This was not out of compassion; indeed, some evidence suggests he was not above a swindle himself (see below). Rather, Nesmith objected to the ways "the indians have been fooled and humbug[g]ed in th[e] Sale" of their lands largely because he viewed such tactics as ineffective. He thought Native people "would rather die than surrender their country," and thus would fight rather than acquiesce if tricked into sale; Nesmith preferred instead that cessions be compelled through force of arms. He occasionally pronounced that "the rights of the Indians as recognized by the law as well as the general usage and policy of the government should be protected." This may or may not have been an outright lie. But even if Nesmith meant it, this assertion was not sympathy for Native people, nor what Nesmith called "the farce of recognizing their national character," but a desire to avoid unnecessary deaths of White pioneers who did not yet have the numbers or arms for extermination. His support for genocide was not limited to his letters to Tichenor Indeed, as Nesmith was cutting food shipments to Oregon reservations in 1858 (thus worsening an already desperate situation), he was pushing for yet more killings in Washington Territory, calling on General Harney and Governor

*James Willis Nesmith, probably from his time as a U.S. senator
from Oregon, between 1861 and 1867. Courtesy of the Library of Congress,
Brady-Handy Photograph Collection.*

Isaac I. Stevens to order Colonel George Wright to continue his war of extermination by marching on Colville, Washington Territory, and "clean[ing] out 'the Vagabonds' of that valley."[15]

Nesmith had nothing but scorn for "Indian sympathizers," "exaggerated accounts of Indian consciences" by missionaries, and "hypocritical scoundrels who defend the savages [in] their histories." Nesmith hoped that such men would be murdered by Indians forthwith, so that others

> understand the proper policy to p[u]rsue towards these red devils
> who are bound by no honor and restricted by no law, whose only
> appetite is for blood and murder, and whose only instinct is to

steal and lie[;] the sooner the atrocious Red man ceases to be petted and spoiled by the penurious tribe of white cloaked ... Pecksniffs, and are remitted to the strong arm of the gov[er]nment to be enthralled by their fears, the sooner will the advance of civilization be quit of that course of blood and nest of scalps that has marked and marred its progress.[16]

This man was appointed to the newly combined position of superintendent of Indian Affairs for Oregon and Washington, officially charged with managing, controlling, and defending the Native people and polities of the region from 1857 to 1859.[17]

Visiting Special Indian Commissioner Mott initially perceived Nesmith as a "plain blunt man, of great force of character ... efficiency and integrity," and he hoped that Nesmith's "brusq[ue] and at times insubordinate" language indicated underlying honesty. But of course, neither bluntness nor brusqueness is necessarily a bar to the seeking of "pecuniary advantage," which Mott correctly feared was a recurrent goal of Indian agents. Nesmith's rudeness did not preclude corruption.[18]

In 1862 Timothy W. Davenport, about to start work as an Indian agent at Umatilla, seems to have asked Nesmith for advice, knowing that Nesmith would be "likely to voice the prevalent knowledge and sentiments of those engaged in Government employ." As Nesmith apparently put it:

> The Indian, like the negro, is the product of a long succession of ages, with an environment favorable to barbarism. ... On the outside the appearance is, that the Government is trying to civilize the Indians, when in fact there is no such intention. They are put upon reservations, where goods and rations are occasionally doled out to them, for the reason that it is cheaper to do that than to fight them. The agriculture and mechanics supposed to be taught on the agencies is all a pretense. ...
>
> Dr. Marcus Whitman ... sacrificed his life mainly in their interest and I shall assume there is nothing to show for it. My advice is, not to spend your time experimenting where others, after long trying, have failed. Go and do something for yourself.[19]

For some, the purpose of Indian Affairs was to suppress violent resistance to colonialism—reservations were cheaper than war. And the advice included a call for corruption, recommending that Davenport "do something for [him]self" while in the service.[20]

Assertions that Native agricultural learning was "all a pretense" notwithstanding, James Nesmith's daughter Harriet remembered from her childhood on the family farm that men from Grand Ronde and Siletz were "allowed out on passes" in the late 1850s to do "good work in the harvest fields binding grain by hand." Like his fellow pioneer Jonathon McCarty, Nesmith did not let his disgust for Native people or his support for genocide preclude the exploitation of Native labor. It remains unclear whether or how these laborers were coerced; whether or how they were paid; and whether or how James Nesmith managed to profit from the labor.[21]

William Barnhart, the former volunteer and historian who in 1856 had joked about binding his scatological "history" of the Yakima War in the skin of Peo-Peo-Mox-Mox, became an Indian agent at the Umatilla Reservation in December 1861. Despite the murders Barnhart committed and commissioned there, he was unable to enact the reign of terror he sought. But he excelled at embezzlement. He purportedly informed his successor, Davenport, that the use of "paper fiction" had been the key to his success, bragging that he had earned $4,000 in his position despite a salary of only $1,500. Among his purported "paper fictions" were relatives hired for inflated paychecks, friends with salaries as "clerks" without clear duties or school-less "schoolteachers," and falsified bills of sale created with the help of the sutler. Similar corruption, as historian Robert E. Ficken has demonstrated, was pervasive in the Northwest—and, as historians Ryan Hall and Michael Witgen have shown, across the United States.[22]

Besides self-enrichment, Barnhart saw intimidation and control as among his main duties. One of his first acts was to call in troops from Fort Walla Walla in an attempt to seize and imprison "a small band of renegade Indians who have never lived on the reservation, but whose tribes are parties to the treaty." Too many Native people, Barnhart opined, still believed they were "their own master much as they were before the white man was first sent among them. In my intercourse with them thus far, I believe I have to some extent disabused their minds of that hallucination, and have convinced most of them that the glorious Union was as powerful to-day as ever it was, and unless they observed the laws they would be made to feel its strength." This was not an idle threat. At some point during his first summer as an Indian agent, Barnhart believed that a "prominent young Cayuse" man had spoken rudely to him. After the young Cayuse/Liksiyu man turned to leave, Barnhart shot him in the back, killing him. Barnhart then requisitioned a unit of cavalry led by Captain E. J. Harding for his protection, in June 1862, who used the threat of mass violence to prevent the local community from holding Barnhart responsible for the murder he had committed. These men were soon supplemented by a contingent of "California volunteers on detached duty."[23]

A few months later, in August, Barnhart called in the cavalry again. Captain George B. Currey, at Barnhart's instigation, tracked down and killed four Native people in the Grand Ronde Valley, principal among them Tenounis, a prominent figure in the Indigenous "Dreamer" religious movement. Colonel Justus Steinberger wrote in his official report:

> Efforts to carry out [the arrest] was met by resistance, and re-sulted in the killing of four Indians among whom was their leader, Tenounis, or the Dreamer, as he is called. This Indian, I have learned, has been for a long time disaffected. He has always denied and opposed the authority of the Government and their right to the lands now occupied by white settlers. . . .
>
> To have arrested a few of the leaders engaged in these hostile movements [denying the authority of the Government] it was supposed would have broken up the band. The more summary punishment resulting from their resistance has, I have no doubt, accomplished the same end, and more effectually. . . . The imme-diate punishment served has, I think, produced a salutary effect for [the Indians'] future good conduct.[24]

Barnhart hoped to rule by fear. He had people killed. Steinberger and his fellow military men though it "salutary." And multiple military historians since, incautious about their own evidence, have glossed these murders as righteous police actions against "attackers" (despite the fact that Tenou-nis and his men engaged in self-defense only after they were assailed), or even against "true terrorist[s]."[25]

Although he did plenty of damage, Barnhart's racist presumptions of acknowledged supremacy seem to have been wrong. There is no evi-dence that the Native people he oppressed, stole from, and attacked were "disabused" of the truth of their sovereignty over their land and their persons. For all Barnhart's claims of rounding up Native people and forcing them onto the reservation, his successor, Davenport, found that "very few of the three tribes were there. . . . They were away, fishing along the Columbia, hunting in the Blue Mountains, digging camas in the Grand Ronde Valley, picking berries along the water courses, or hanging around the towns where they bartered their 'ictas' [in this context, probably 'stuff'']."²⁶

But this continuance of lifeways and sovereignty existed uneasily with continuing vulnerability to murderous pioneers and soldiers, pillaging opportunists, and government officials that typically either abetted or ignored the attackers. Though many people were able to avoid confinement (in part because some Euro-Americans, such as Indian agent General Robert H. Milroy, recognized that forced internment of "peaceable Indians" where "they would starve" was "a sure way to start an Indian war"), the threat of imprisonment or death always loomed. Even if Barnhart's lethal dream of White supremacy was a mirage in the minutiae, collectively racists like him inflicted continuing harms. They would always have their fantasies of unquestioned supremacy frustrated. But they could still murder people, sometimes under the thin veil of military justice.²⁷

In the last months of 1862, a nearby White miner was shot in the dead of night by a person or persons unknown. All Euro-American parties immediately assumed the wounded man must have been shot by Indians, and they charged Timothy W. Davenport, then the new Indian agent, with finding the people responsible. Davenport was led by interpreters to a village of Native "renegades" across the Columbia River, and the locals handed over two men to be held responsible for the shooting. The men had a show trial early in 1863, before a military commission. According to one soldier (who later claimed to have deserted in disgust because of what he saw), the trial was concluded without any evidence, witnesses, or deliberation. Captain E. J. Harding, a member of the commission, proclaimed, "Damn the Indians, hang them." The other two commissioners (Colonel Reuben F. Maury and Colonel Justus Steinberger) quickly acquiesced. There was some dispute among those who knew the story over whether this accession resulted from a desire to bring the matter to a close, a wish to support Harding, or a hunger for murder—Harding claimed Steinberger "want[ed] to kill an Indian [and] ha[d] never." Steinberger killed two by hanging the day after the show trial. This was normal; George Wright, from 1861 to 1864 the commander of the Department of the Pacific, encouraged "summary execution" by "hanging a few of the worst Indians" whenever "peace and quiet" was disturbed.²⁸

It is unclear to what extent the two condemned men understood the charges against them. Davenport remembered no sign that they spoke any English, and they were never given an interpreter. A soldier who had been a part of the execution claimed to remember one of the condemned giving a speech "in which he denied committing any crime which would confine a white man," but not whether the speech had been in English, Chinook Jargon, or some other tongue—and the soldier may well have conflated this execution with another.[29]

Whether or not they spoke English, the two Native men probably *did* have a sense why these Americans in uniform were planning to kill them. The men were Indians. And people in the region had known for years that White soldiers didn't need much of a reason beyond race. There were at least two more hangings over the winter, possibly more. The disheartened Davenport was discharged nine months into his job— and was replaced by the man who had tried to show him the ropes of embezzlement. Barnhart and his "paper fictions" were back by 1863, able to profit from Umatilla annuities until the end of the decade. As a historian, Barnhart was a flighty failure. But he was a resilient grafter.[30]

Many Pacific Northwest Native people in the 1850s and beyond avoided both the bands of ravaging Euro-Americans and attempts to intern all Native people on reservations. Individuals and even whole communities managed to persevere beyond the gaze and the reach of the Euro-American state. But White depredations in the Northwest continued to be a threat off reservations, at least as much as on—as the story of Dick Johnson, perhaps most famously, demonstrates.[31]

Dick Johnson was a very careful settler. He moved to the Yoncalla area of southern Oregon around 1850 to do farm labor and soon after started a farm of his own. Johnson married a local Umpqua woman, and by the mid-1850s he, his wife, two children, and other relatives were living on his homestead in a large farmhouse built by their own hands, surrounded by close to three hundred acres they had cleared themselves, in an out-of-the-way portion of Rice Valley.[32]

Dick Johnson was Klickitat/Qwû'lh-hwai-pûm, and as a Native person he was mindful of the prejudices of his Euro-American neighbors from the beginning. When he first decided to create a farm of his own, according to his neighbor Jesse Applegate, "by the advice of his white friends he settled upon an isolated [portion of] the valley some distance removed from the new settlements." They counseled him that a far-off location would help forestall would-be land thieves. Despite this distance, it is likely that he and his family felt the pressures of colonialism even from their supposed "many warm friends among ... white neighbors." Applegate, who claimed to be one of the warmest, lauded Johnson's "efforts to throw off the savage, and conform to the usages of civilized life." Meant no doubt as a compliment, this comment reveals the level of scrutiny and prejudice the Johnsons faced. Their "friends," like the Applegates, saw Indigenous peoples of their background as what Jesse Applegate framed as naturally "treacherous and rapacious[,] if not so warlike as those East of the mountains," gaining virtue only if "taught" otherwise.[33]

And many of their neighbors meant them harm. From at least 1852, Euro-American settlers tried to seize the Johnson farm for themselves. Although he had been encouraged in his pursuit of farming by some White neighbors, Dick Johnson had no European descent and was thus forbidden from filing a claim on his land under the Donation Land Claim Act. And although he had made his farm in a ravine, off the beaten track, there were few places in Oregon where Euro-Americans wouldn't deal out violence to grab good farmland. In 1852 a pioneer named Bean (or Beane) seized about half of the land Dick Johnson had cleared and physically attacked the Klickitat/Qwû'lh-hwai-pûm farmer when he complained. In 1854 a newly arrived pioneer named Henry Canaday filed a land claim for the rest of Dick Johnson's property, encompassing the remainder of his family's farm and their houses.[34]

When Dick Johnson refused to leave his farm, members of the Canaday family broke his fences, killed his livestock, and eventually physically assaulted both Johnson and his stepfather (known to Euro-Americans as Old Mummy). It is unclear from the records just how many assaults they suffered, and how many beatings were related to the attempts to seize their land, as opposed to racial violence for its own sake. Sallie Applegate Long, a young girl at the time, remembered Old Mummy being viciously attacked by a pioneer named John Marshal at a Christian religious service, with no stated reason other than "because he was an 'Inj_n.' " But she did not indicate whether this was targeted violence or hate-fueled opportunistic mayhem.[35]

Dick Johnson and Old Mummy did not fight back physically when assaulted. They took the advice of White neighbors like Jesse Applegate, who wrote later that "in view of the prevailing prejudice among the people against Indians, they were strictly enjoined under no circumstances to resist or use arms against a white man." Jesse Applegate and others might have thought of themselves as Johnson's "white friends," but they were unwilling (or thought themselves unable) to protect their "friend" if he defended himself from fellow pioneers who beat and robbed him. According to a suspect account by his political enemy Indian Sub-Agent William J. Martin, Applegate and his ilk briefly considered running off Henry Canaday themselves. Instead, they wrote a sternly worded letter to the federal government. Canaday and Bean's assaults of Dick Johnson were illegal under the law but not by Euro-American custom. Johnson's White "friends" were unwilling to risk reprisals.[36]

Federal authorities wouldn't help Dick Johnson either. Martin colluded with Bean and Canaday to help them steal Johnson's land in 1853–54, probably acting on his belief that (as he wrote to Joseph Lane) the "red devils" should be "turn[ed] out" wherever possible. Rumor had it that none other than Joseph Lane himself had assured Canaday that he viewed Dick Johnson's property claims "with neglect and contempt." Indian Superintendent Joel Palmer saw no clear way for Johnson to remain without an act of Congress, and he encouraged him to leave his farm behind. Palmer, "very anxious to set[t]le [Johnson] on the Reserve, as an example to the other Indians," offered to pay Johnson for his improvements if he would move—an offer Johnson refused, wanting instead to keep his land. All Johnson got from Palmer was a reference letter, asking any readers to "refrain from disturbing" Johnson or his rapidly diminishing homestead. The pioneers seeking to seize Johnson's land by force were not deterred by this polite request.[37]

Johnson's fortunes did not improve when James W. Nesmith, the former volunteer and lifelong Indian hater, replaced Palmer as Indian superintendent in 1857. Jesse Applegate sent letters explaining the situation to Nesmith, and Dick Johnson (on Applegate's advice) met with the new Indian superintendent in person. Nesmith was unsympathetic— which is not surprising, as he was generally unsympathetic toward those he labeled "atrocious . . . red devils." Dick Johnson wouldn't even get a polite letter from him. Instead, Nesmith suggested that Johnson should leave his farm for his own safety and proclaimed that the federal government would neither help him keep his land nor even help him be remunerated for the improvements he had made on it. Nesmith closed by offering Johnson a "cheap calico dress" for his wife; when Johnson refused this "paltry present," Nesmith was incensed and had to be talked down from unspecified rash action.[38]

The Canaday family eventually turned to murder in their drive to steal Johnson's farm. At first, they attempted to get the pioneer community as a whole to kill Dick Johnson. As Applegate put it, the Canadays had "attempted either by Traducing [Dick Johnson's] character, or surprising his prudence into some resentment of injury[,] to deprive him of his powerful protectors. In the hope he would fall a victim to the popular fury when most excited by Indian atrocities in the late war, he was charged with murder it was impossible he should have committed, to provoke him into resentment his fen[c]es were broken his stock killed and both his father and himself most inhumanly beaten with clubs, and lastly a criminal prosecution commenced against him in the courts [for arson, of which he was acquitted]."[39]

Accusations of crimes real or invented have long been a way for Euro-Americans to rally their fellows to murder and rob people of color they find inconvenient, in the Pacific Northwest as elsewhere. Canaday's action may have been unusual only in its failure: foiled, and thus visible in the historical record, because Dick Johnson was well-known and the attempts to frame him were sloppy. But Canaday faced little more than limp censure for his actions. When practiced against Native people, theft, destruction of property, and assault were not, apparently, chargeable offenses. Almost no crime committed against a Native person was.[40]

The Canadays murdered Dick Johnson and Old Mummy at sunset on November 28, 1858. Jesse Applegate had the most detailed contemporary version of the story, taken from the testimony of the survivors. Eight men—Canaday's sons, future sons-in-law, and a few toughs from California—approached the Johnson homestead by subterfuge. One member of the group pretended to be Indian Superintendent James Nesmith and ordered Dick Johnson to divest himself of weapons and come along. Dick Johnson replied that

> "he knew that this was not Nesmith" but if [the spokesman] wished to shoot him to do so, he would not resist. Upon this, the spokesman deliberately discharged his rifle into Dick's bosom, the ball a large one, tearing away the right nipple and coming out under the shoulder blade near the back bone, doubtless causing instant death as no other wounds were inflicted. Upon the fate of Dick, Mummy seems to have attempted to go to him but was prevented by two rifle balls[—]one taking effect in the breast, another in the abdomen. His death may not have been

immediate as there were several ball holes through his clothes and one revolver ball penetrated his back, just where the spine joins the hips.[41]

As Dick Johnson's wife ran to where Johnson and Old Mummy had been murdered, the shooter, now out of ammunition, knocked her unconscious with the butt of his pistol. Dick Johnson's brother-in-law Jim, just returning home, had his horse shot from under him but managed to sprint into his house with only a grazing bullet wound. Fearing that Jim might have a rifle in the house, and unwilling to risk a confrontation with a lone armed man in the midst of their murder spree, the eight assailants fled into the darkness. Binding his wound with a piece of saddle, Jim stood guard over his family, living and dead, until morning.[42]

Euro-Americans did briefly investigate the murders of Dick Johnson and Old Mummy. This was rare, whether or not it was (as Jesse Applegate asserted) "the first time an Indian's life or property ha[d] received so much attention." The crime was particularly overt, the victims having given "no provocation . . . either by word or act"; this was seen as clear evidence that "the motive to commit this bloody deed [was] pecuniary, only and purely." There were worries that further stories of atrocity by Oregon pioneers might make it even harder for volunteers to extract money for the wars they had already fought against Native people from a balky Congress. And there were multiple Native eyewitnesses, who could identify exactly who the murderers had been.[43]

According to Applegate family lore, the Johnsons' friends and neighbors initially considered forming a vigilante party to avenge the murders outside the law, and only Jesse Applegate's intercession calmed them down. The inquest found that Dick Johnson and Old Mummy had maintained a nonviolent stance to the end. It was surmised that as "the nonresisting policy of the Indians" was widely known, the killers had seized "their share of the spoils" "upon the extermination of the Indians" "without risk."[44]

The killers were swiftly identified. Another piece of Applegate family lore had it that "Old Lemyei" (Dick Johnson's mother and Old Mummy's wife) "stripped the shirt from 'old Mummy's' back and sitting down beside the body placed one finger on the bullet hole then pointed it straight at the face of an old man present [John Allen] and said in plain jargon 'Your son did this.'" But despite numerous witnesses, outraged neighbors, and the attention of both the press and the government, the murderers lost little more than face. Eight men were arrested, but they were bailed out almost immediately (with the help of local government functionaries). Dick Johnson's family were eyewitnesses to the crimes, but they were also Indians, barred from testifying in Oregon courts. Formal charges were never brought against the murderers. Johnson's White "friends" sold off his movable property, purportedly to set aside money for his widow and children. The farm itself was seized by the Canadays, with the help of the federal land office receiver—who, it was rumored, had encouraged them to commit the murders in the first place. No one could find the means—or the will—to stop any of them.[45]

Applegate family lore recorded and rerecorded the "attempt to bring the murderers to justice" represented by the inquest and the brief arrests. Jesse Applegate was correct that such an attempt was unusual. But it was also hesitant, diffident, and quickly abandoned. In the first years of the 1850s, when it seemed that particularly wanton murders by Euro-Americans might spur reprisals from Native groups, Indian agents and other Euro-American officials found ways to prosecute at least a few White murderers. By 1858 such fears had waned, along with the semblance of justice they could motivate. The criminal investigation of the Johnson murders, if one actually occurred after the inquest, was perfunctory. The crimes leading up to the killings had sometimes been committed in public—one of the assaults of Old Mummy had been at a camp meeting, with White witnesses galore. But nothing was ever done. Even Jesse Applegate, meanwhile, seemed ready to endorse or at least accept grim penalties for any Indian who tried to "resist or use arms against a white man," even in self-defense.[46]

Dick Johnson's supposed White friends valued White lives—arguably even the lives of his murderers—more than they valued his. Jesse Applegate, one of the louder voices in the pioneer Pacific Northwest decrying mass murder, still despised Indian-ness. He professed to "hold the doctrine that [what others called] 'inferior races' are human and entitled to live if they behave themselves," but his very formation of that doctrine presumed White supremacy, and with it the right to kill "inferior races" that did *not* "behave themselves." Toward the end of his private report to Nesmith, Jesse Applegate mused that "it would perhaps have been better" if the murderers had succeeded in killing all of Johnson's family, as there was "little hope, if they are suffered to live, that they can long prevent themselves from falling back into the degraded condition from which . . . [Dick Johnson] had retrieved them." Less than a week after his supposed friend Dick Johnson was murdered, Jesse Applegate was speculating— with an unknown mix of earnestness and whimsy—that Johnson's surviving family would be better dead than Indian.[47]

It would be unfair to say that all Jesse Applegate did to pursue justice for Dick Johnson was write a strongly worded letter. In fact, he wrote at least six strongly worded letters, to Nesmith and to his successor. And, if family lore is to be believed, he stopped his neighbors from avenging Dick Johnson outside the boundaries of the law—ensuring, whether Applegate suspected it or not, that no justice would be found. His yen for an orderly society precluded vigilante justice on behalf of Native people, but not against them. Indeed, he was widely credited for urging miners to join in the organized killings of Rogue River Native peoples in 1851. Perhaps Applegate viewed those attacks in a different light, as official and legitimate violence. Perhaps he had changed over time. Or perhaps he viewed White comity as more important than Native lives.[48]

Though Jesse Applegate continued into the 1860s to press fruitlessly for something to be done about the murders, he did not in the 1850s seem to want to risk his public standing to that end. Much of the surviving historical information on the killings of Dick Johnson and Old Mummy comes from two letters Jesse Applegate sent to Indian Superintendent Nesmith on December 3, 1858. One, a short letter meant for public and government consumption, succinctly stated that the killings had occurred and warrants had been issued for eight persons. The other, much longer letter related the details and background for the slayings, including input from Johnson's family.[49]

As the investigation fizzled out over the next few weeks, Applegate pestered Nesmith to "keep from the public eye any communication I may make the publicity of which would mortify the writer, favor the escape of the guilty, or cast suspicions upon the innocent." A few weeks later Applegate made clear that his correspondence on Dick Johnson had been meant to be private, "merely for your amusement, for you not your successor." This may all have been characteristic Applegate sarcasm Jesse Applegate explained in the same missive that he had "aimed to give [the letter meant for the record] that vague indefinite and pointless character in which official letters are usually couched." But in the end Applegate did let the matter drop. And his belief that Joseph Lane had encouraged the killings did not prevent Applegate from supporting Lane for political office several years later. Maybe he changed his mind and no longer believed Lane was supportive of these murders (or the many,

many others Lane had called for and committed). Maybe he let bygones be bygones. Or maybe Jesse Applegate didn't believe killing a few Indians should come between friends.[50]

Not all pioneers were murderers. Many probably never killed anyone. But almost every pioneer in the Pacific Northwest was complicit in the killings. Though he was no John Beeson, Jesse Applegate was unusual among Euro-Americans in the extent of the measures he took to support his Indigenous neighbors. In the case of Dick Johnson, these measures were woefully inadequate. But they were more than most other Euro-American invaders seem to have attempted.

The murder of Dick Johnson has floated visibly at the edges of Euro-American historical memory since it was perpetrated, largely because of the unusual extent of the records generated by it. Jesse Applegate kept the (sharply attenuated) case alive, and his descendants kept the story alive. It is worth thinking about how many other Dick Johnsons were quietly killed for their wealth without people like the Applegates bringing their stories regional and historical attention. By Jesse Applegate's own reckoning, it was not the killing but the outcry that was unusual. And that outcry wasn't enough to save lives or punish murderers.

Henry Canaday, James Lupton, Joseph Lane, James Lake, Loren L. Williams, Bates the tavern keeper, and many, many other pioneers, named and unnamed, discussed in the previous chapters and the following ones, sought out opportunities to kill Native people and take what they had, secure in the knowledge that their White supremacist settler society would defend them. Many Euro-Americans deplored particularly wanton acts of violence, or at least claimed to have done so when appropriate. The understanding that all Indians were to be killed was common but not absolute. Much more universal among White settlers was the understanding that Euro-Americans must be defended from Native violence at all costs, no matter what those Euro-Americans had done. And "defense" might well include preemptive attack.

Joseph Lane once wrote, "I am in favor of the war . . . and for paying *all* who serve in war, and never stop to ask whether the war was right or wrong." Some other pioneers, like Jesse Applegate, *did* ask. But they didn't stop to do so. Once there was a threat of Native reprisal, whether in a war or in an individual dispute, White "friends of the Indian" tended to close ranks with White belligerents. They might seek peace instead of extermination, but even sympathetic Euro-American pioneers were unlikely to allow any real consequences to affect White people who did harm to Indians.[51]

The War on Illahee broadly was provably full of genocidal killings, but many individual killings are more difficult to affirmatively label as such under a narrow legal definition of the term. Thieving racists like William Barnhart and Henry Canaday may have murdered mostly for money; it is unclear from the records the extent to which genocidal intent animated their actions by the late 1850s. Some thrill killers, like Loren L. Williams and (purportedly) Justus Steinberger, may in some circumstances have wanted to murder only some Indians, rather than destroy the entirety of a given community. Scholars could debate, perhaps, whether Williams's broad support for extermination in eastern Oregon means that we can interpret his wanton murders of Indigenous persons elsewhere as presumptively genocidal. Whether a plurality of killings were genocidal can matter—such distinctions can help illuminate choices and changes in the survival strategies of Indigenous communities or the tactics of the invaders. But the potential usefulness of theoretical distinctions should not distract from the ubiquity of racists getting away with murder. Whether or not a given race-based killing should be counted as genocidal under a given scholar's schema would matter at most a little to the survivors of the slain. Murder is murder.[52]

Hundreds of Euro-American pioneers in the Pacific Northwest wantonly attacked Native people—for profit, for political power, for pleasure. They knew they had the support of thousands of other Euro-Americans. And they knew that in almost every case, they would be defended from reprisal by the power of the United States, and the White citizenry thereof. For all but a very few Euro-American pioneers, in the Pacific Northwest as elsewhere, White supremacy trumped justice.

CHAPTER SIX

Lynchings Legal and Extralegal
in the Pacific Northwest

IKE MANY PACIFIC NORTHWEST pioneers, John E. Smith in his old
age wanted recognition for his roles in the invasions. In one
way or another, Smith had been part of the War on Illahee for
much of the 1850s. He joined volunteers in the Rogue River
region in 1854, worked on the Siletz Reservation during the height of internment and disarmament in 1857, and marched along with Colonel
George Wright's forces in their campaign in eastern Washington in 1858
(see below). But John E. Smith was a packer, tasked with freighting
rather than fighting, and thus had never taken part in direct combat with
any Native people.[1]

Instead, he stressed his role in the hangings. In 1858 Colonel
George Wright had his men lynch a Palus man named Jo-Hout for unspecified and unproven thievery. And, as Smith wrote with pride decades
later, "They used my lasso rope to do it." Along with accomplishments
like the size of his family and the creation of a local school, John E.
Smith wanted it known that he too had killed Native people in pursuit of
a White Northwest—even if only through the loan of a rope.[2]

This chapter examines connections between lynchings and the War on
Illahee, including most famously the execution of Chief Leschi in western Washington Territory and the hanging spree undertaken by George

Wright in eastern Washington Territory. None of the hangings connected to either are typically counted as lynchings, presumably because all were performed by representatives of the state. But it is worth considering both what part due process should play in definitions of lynching, and whose law should be considered operable in so defining. Native people executed under alien laws and procedures to which they did not accede might well be counted as lynchings; so, too, might hangings that lacked due process, or sometimes even the semblance of it, even if they were technically carried out by a military or civilian court.[3]

Michael J. Pfeifer, a leading historian of lynching in the Pacific Northwest, counted just six lynchings of Oregon and Washington Native people in his 2011 monograph *The Roots of Rough Justice*. This is, as he has said, almost certainly an undercount. Even by the narrow definition Pfeifer uses (excluding executions with even a whiff of legal authority, and including only vigilantes who kill by means of hanging), there were more. The problem is one of sourcing as well as of definition. Pfeifer's counts of lynchings, and the scholarship shaped by them, rely mostly on newspaper sources. And in many times and places in the Pacific Northwest, especially in the major papers of record, Indian killing wasn't news. Either it wasn't meant to be talked about, or it wasn't anomalous enough to be mentioned. Most of the lynchings reported in late 1800s Northwest newspapers involved crowds storming jails to seize their victims; accused or suspected Native people often never made it to jail. Accounts that suggest most lynchings in Oregon or Washington "tended to be white, with a few Indians" should instead read that most lynchings *reported on as such* in Oregon and Washington "tended to be white."[4]

Besides adding new cases of lynching under traditional narrow definitions of the term, this chapter argues that "legal lynching" needs to be included in the frame. As many civil rights activists and thinkers have argued since the early 1900s, the distinction between hanging by civil courts and by civil mobs is not always so vast that the difference needs to be defined categorically. And the "summary justice" employed by the military often varied not at all from the approach taken by more conventional lynch mobs. Talk of fair trials was, in many though by no means all cases, a colonial fiction, meant to inhere legitimacy. As Yakama leader Kamiakin/K'amáyakin put it in 1855, "They hang us without knowing if we are wrong or right." Killings without proof of guilt or due process were not much different from one another, even when the person holding the rope had a uniform on.[5]

One of the most infamous acts in the War on Illahee was the judicial execution of Leschi, a Nisqually leader seized after the Puget Sound War in 1856 and hanged in 1858. As the Puget Sound portion of the War on Illahee ground to a halt, Isaac I. Stevens pursued the capture and prosecution of Leschi. He intended to make executionary displays as way to establish (or perhaps reestablish) what he called "the prestige of the white race in the mind of the Indian." In truth, part of the peace in the Puget Sound region came from Stevens renegotiating the terms of the Treaty of Medicine Creek to make them more acceptable to many Nisqually and Puyallup in August 1856—a longtime goal of Leschi's and an unusual achievement in the annals of Native American treaty negotiation.[6]

But publicly, Stevens falsely presented himself as unwilling to negotiate. As he put it at a November 1856 dinner honoring Benjamin Franklin Shaw for the massacre he perpetrated at Grand Ronde Valley, "The only terms that should be allowed hostile Indians is unconditional submission. Mercy ought then to be extended to the great body, but murderers should be hung. Such are the conditions of a permanent peace." Stevens had already acceded to terms other than unconditional surrender a few months before. But the occasion called for bravado, not truth.[7]

The purported "murderer" he (and the newspapers) had named most often was Leschi, in part because he was "familiarly known to most of our citizens." As Stevens wrote in a June 18, 1856, letter to Colonel George Wright, the man then in charge of troop operations in eastern Washington Territory: "I presume your views and my own do not differ as to terms which should be allowed the Indians, viz; unconditional submission, and the rendering up [of] the murderers and instigators of the war for punishment. I will, however, respectfully put you on guard in reference to Leschi, Nelson, Kitsap and Quiemuth from the [Puget] sound, and to suggest that no arrangement be made which shall save their necks from the Executioner." When Wright argued that seizure of the men named should be "suspended for the present" to keep the war from becoming more general again, Stevens persevered: "If this demand is not inflexibly insisted upon, and peace is made under milder terms, it will be, it seems to me, a criminal abandonment of the great duty of protecting our citizens [which] will depreciate our standing with the Indians and pave the way for wars hereafter."[8]

As in similar frictions across the Northwest, the disagreement between Wright and Stevens was over strategy, not morality. Wright wanted to suspend—not necessarily forever—attempts to execute Leschi, as he thought that milder policies would in this case better enable American supremacy at a lower cost. Stevens thought harsh treatment would be a better path to the same goal.

Stevens had a target list, and Leschi was the first name on it—with a bounty on his head. In 1857 Stevens went to Washington, D.C., to take up his new position as territorial delegate, presenting a false and potentially lucrative history of the volunteers in wartime to the National Congress. The push to execute Leschi went on.[9]

Leschi was seized and brought in for trial; his brother and fellow leader Quiemuth turned himself in shortly after. Vigilante mobs assembled to murder them both. Leschi was successfully whisked into secret imprisonment, so that territorial authorities could attempt to kill him through more socially acceptable avenues. Quiemuth was cached in Stevens's office, where he was assassinated—shot and stabbed to death—while under arrest and before any trial could commence. Although stories conflict, the killer (or one of the killers) seems to have been the volunteer Joseph Bunting, backed by a mob of other pioneers. Isaac I. Stevens stated a desire to find and punish the principal perpetrator—according to one self-proclaimed participant, Joel Theodore Ticknor, "[Stevens] said it didn't matter so much that the Indian was killed, but he didn't like it to be done right in his office." After all, another vigilante murder did not mesh well with Stevens's public assurances that law and order prevailed in the territory. Yet the brief inquest into Quiemuth's murder, by lawyer, historian, and future volunteer apologist Elwood Evans, yielded no formal charges.[10]

Leschi was tried for murder twice, officially because he had killed volunteer Abraham Benton Moses early in the war. The first jury hung. The presiding judge had instructed that killings by soldiers in wartime were not a civil matter, and a few jurors were persuaded by the argument that the killing of Moses while on a military expedition had been an act of war. The second jury, convened in a city more hostile to Leschi and with a judge less concerned with such distinctions, convicted. Subsequent appeals delayed but did not stop the execution.[11]

The outcome of the case was seldom in doubt. Even if Leschi had weathered the second murder trial and the vigilantes had been foiled, there were reportedly other indictments for other killings to which he had been tendentiously tethered being drawn up in other counties. But for a trial of a Native person accused of murder in the 1850s, the trial of

Leschi looked faintly like due process. Leschi had two competent law-yers, and both sides were able to call witnesses. The first jury actually de-liberated, for five hours, before being declared hung. And the second jury at least slept on it. The trial was unjust, and the evidence thin. But at a time when courts might engage in little more deliberation than a "Damn the Indians," many Euro-Americans called it fair.[12]

The killing of Leschi may have been, as historian Lisa Blee suggests, "the [Washington] territory's first official execution and the only Puget Sound war trial to end in punishment." And, indeed, some of the leaders who were targets on Stevens's list, such as Kitsap, avoided the mobs and were acquitted in the courts. But the killing of Leschi followed and was followed by legions of military, quasi-judicial, and extrajudicial executions. Blee discusses the extralegal execution of Leschi's brother Quiemuth in some depth. Reporting from the period also discussed the killing of Quie-muth, as one of several purportedly avenging James McAllister's death. On April 22, 1859, the *Puget Sound Herald* ran a scathing story about the indictment and execution of "Too-a-pi-ti," supposedly suspected of having gunned down James McAllister at the opening of the Puget Sound War. The posse that formed to serve the warrant (which included McAllister's son George) fatally shot Too-a-pi-ti; drawing on a long volunteer tradi-tion, they claimed to have killed him while he was trying to escape.[13]

The *Puget Sound Herald* correspondent archly suggested that maybe pioneers had gotten enough revenge—pointing especially to the Maxon Massacre. And they argued that further attempts at extralegal revenge might endanger federal recompense and aid: "By letting the law take its course ... our vengeance will certainly be ample. We certainly had more completely subdued the Indians, before the troops were withdrawn from the field, than was ever the case before or since; for, after having whipped and driven them, and after the last hostile shot was fired by them, on the 10th of March '56, more than thirty Indians, counting men, women and children, were killed by our people. This in itself is more than we have lost by the Indians, during the whole war on this side of the mountains."[14]

Notably, the editorialist assumed his readership would already know about the Maxon Massacre—it was treated in the text not as a revelation, but as general knowledge.

Quiemuth was killed in the Governor's office by relatives of McAllister ... and the Indians say that George McAllister killed one-armed John on the Reservation, and now the law comes in and claims Too-a-pi-ti, all for the same offence. We thus get three or four Indians for every white man. . . .

We only fear that Congress will discover how well we can take care of ourselves, and withdraw the troops, and delay the payment of the war debt, or send it back for settlement here.

We hope our new Governor will take the subject into consideration.[15]

They did not hope in vain. Wa He Lute/Yelm Jim, one of the last Nisqually veterans of the Puget Sound War to face murder charges, was found guilty by a Euro-American jury but was eventually pardoned by Territorial Governor Richard Gholson in 1860. Native memory had it that he only just escaped a mob, with foreknowledge and the help of friends, or "they would have shot him as he was leaving the jail."[16]

As historian Brad Asher has shown, Native people charged formally in a civilian court of law in Washington Territory could expect at least the semblance of a fair trial. Conviction rates for crimes committed against White victims were similar for Native and non-Native defendants. However, White residents of Washington Territory could expect much lighter punishments and to be acquitted for crimes against Native people. Many of those who killed Native people in this era were never charged with a crime. The few who did get charged were released, sometimes after being acquitted. In the Washington Territory, Asher found just one conviction for a White man accused of murdering a Native person before the 1880s. The defendant in that case was sentenced to fifteen months in prison, which he may have served. An Indian would probably have been put to death.[17]

Cases pursued in civilian courts were only a small fraction of the legal and extralegal wrangling of the era. Many Americans meted out violence against Indians generally at the presumption of a crime, and many courts (like those following the Whitman killings) did not much bother to establish individual guilt when it came to Native defendants. The judicial murder of Leschi is an imperfect if sometimes powerful and useful metonym for Euro-American attacks on Native communities in the Pacific Northwest. Most Euro-Americans who killed Native people did so with less pretense. As Blee has written, "Leschi's case was extraordinary while Quiemuth's was all too common." Indeed, most killings got even less Euro-American attention and due process than Quiemuth's assassination. As Nisqually leader Cynthia Iyall remembered her elders putting it, "Lots of Indian men went through the same thing." And so too did many other Native people—Indian men were especially but not exclusively targeted by murderous Euro-Americans.[18]

There was already a sense by the end of 1856 that too much wanton murder—or talk about it—might harm the reputation of Washington Territory settlers, and perhaps even harm efforts to get federal funding for the war. The Olympia *Pioneer and Democrat*, which had been calling for killings the previous year, urged at least a temporary halt in the wake of Leschi's conviction: "We have had no news this week of fresh Indian disturbances in any quarter. . . . For the sake of preserving the good name our citizens have so justly earned since this Indian war commenced, it is to be hoped that no provocation (unless in self-defence), will induce any person to undertake the killing of any of the Indians. Under present circumstances, nothing but evil could result therefrom. Gen. Wool and his pensioned scribblers would like nothing better than to learn that a score of Indians had been murdered every week." Killing would be a problem only if Wool, and officials like him, heard about it.[19]

If one takes George Wright's letters as honest, there is reason to believe that if the U.S. Army, rather than the civil government of Washington Territory, had been in charge of the case against Leschi, he would have justly walked free—at least in the short term. But this outcome would have been a pragmatic and possibly limited exception, made for the purposes of peace. In general, army leaders in the Pacific Northwest were willing to execute Native people with only the flimsiest of trials. There were legal proceedings civil and military against Native people, even during the wars, that resulted in "not guilty" verdicts. But many, many Native people were "legally" killed, during the wars and beyond them, in circumstances even more unjust than those that Leschi faced.[20]

The appeals court that denied Leschi relief in 1857 suggested that it would have been preferable under the law for Leschi to be given a "summary mode of trial" by the army in the field. They may have been referring to the hasty military tribunals that condemned people to death within hours of capture, or they may have been alluding to the even hastier execution of those deemed a danger—or described as "trying to escape." As U.S. Army troops attacked Native communities in eastern Washington Territory in the 1850s, they performed many of each kind of summary trial—and many summary executions.[21]

It is likely that George Wright committed more lynchings in the Pacific Northwest than anyone else. As he took responsibility for most acts of war the U.S. Army pursued in eastern Washington Territory from 1856 to 1858, he executed several people, typically with little to no trial beforehand. After the quasi war turned to a quasi peace, and Wright eventually ascended to commander of the Department of the Pacific in 1861, he continued a policy of "summary justice," encouraging his men to "hang a few of the worst Indians" any time there was friction between White and Native communities. He was a ruthless killer of people of color he perceived as enemies, "whether battling with the savage foes in the far West, or deadly hummocks of Florida, or contending with the hosts of Mexico," as he put it. Like General John Wool, Wright believed that "most difficulties with the Indians have been brought on by the wanton aggressions of [the Whites]." To Wright, perhaps even more than Wool, this didn't matter. He pursued White supremacy in the Pacific Northwest with violent vigor. Wright may have believed that wanton White aggression was what brought on "difficulties with the Indians." But like the military figures he replaced and those he preceded, Wright chose *deliberate* White aggression as the default response to those difficulties.[22]

The "trial[s] by military commission" that Wright conducted were not trials in the conventional sense. He would interrogate prisoners, and then, most of the time, he would kill them. Evidence seldom played any role in the proceedings. This was normal for U.S. military officers attacking Indians in the 1800s, although (as Wright's biographer Donald L. Cutler has shown) Wright was purportedly even less likely to accept exculpatory evidence than some of his contemporaries.[23]

Wright's most intense period of violence was in the summer and fall of 1858. The war in eastern Washington had not so much ended as petered out in 1856. Invasions by volunteers had ebbed, as their commissions ended and they went home. Invasions by pioneers had temporarily slowed, as fear and bad weather discouraged many would-be thieves. Violence done by or against Euro-Americans had receded, but did not disappear.

In May 1858, in response to reports of a few more gold miners being killed, Colonel Edward Steptoe took 160 armed men on an ill-prepared expedition into northern Washington Territory. According to a Coeur d'Alene/Schitsu'umsh oral tradition, Steptoe's men shot at and caused the drowning of a young Palus women as they wended their way northeast. Under still-contested circumstances, Steptoe and his men blundered into a battle with a force made up mostly of Palus and Coeur d'Alene/Schitsu'umsh fighters. The battle quickly turned into a fighting retreat, then a full-scale rout, as Steptoe's command spiked their howitzers and escaped—with the help of Nez Perce/Nimiipuu allies, and probably with the permission of the opposing army. Known to Americans officially as the Battle of Te-hots-nim-me, and regionally as Steptoe's Defeat, a Native victory and rout of U.S. soldiers once again shocked and appalled Euro-Americans in the region.[24]

The U.S. Army sent out troops to "punish the Indians who had defeated Steptoe." As usual, this command was taken broadly. One contingent, led by Lieutenant Jesse K. Allen, "ascertained [through means unknown] that there were some of the murderers in the camp of friendly Indians not far off." A skeptic might wonder if proximity rather than proof shaped his ascertainment. His cavalry commenced a surprise attack at dawn, purportedly mistook Allen himself for an Indian—and then shot him. The village surrendered without exchanging fire. The American soldiers executed three captives, without obvious evidence, and seized all the wealth of the village they could find. Local people may have been "friendly," but the soldiers were still going to take their food, livestock, and household goods—and at least three lives. Shot by his own men while prosecuting an unprovoked attack, Allen was recorded, in army documents and then in early histories, as a "gallant [who] lost his life" when he "surprised a camp of hostile Indians."[25]

George Crook, who had already been a part of attacks in California and Oregon and would continue fighting Indian wars into the 1880s, wrote in a later memoir of choosing what he saw as a gentler path, negotiating with a local village to turn over five "murderers" for execution. Because Crook "could not tell who the murderers were," he coerced a local leader (named Skimarwaw in the official report) and his son to identify the "murderers" and turn them over to the military. Crook warned that if they did not, "many" would be killed and "they would lose all their stock and many of their families, camp equipage, etc. etc." They acquiesced and turned over five men for execution—who supposedly confessed, after they were informed that Crook "intended shooting them before [he] left" in any case. Perhaps they did confess, and perhaps they had attacked White people in the past. Or perhaps they were a sacrifice to preserve the rest of the community—after all, there was no choice that would preserve the lives of all from the American invaders. Crook at this point in his life found execution distasteful, so he had his man, Second Lieutenant Turner, who "rather enjoyed that kind of thing," arrange for a firing squad. The five "murderers" were killed, without trial as usual. Turner presumably enjoyed himself.[26]

As squads of Euro-American soldiers raided "friendly" villages and committed vengeance killings, George Wright assembled the largest U.S. armed force to take part in the War on Illahee—about 900 men strong, including 680 Euro-American regulars, 33 Nez Perce/Nimiipuu soldiers, and 200 packers and herders. Compared to Steptoe's sortie and most volunteer attacks, Wright's expedition was meticulously planned and logistically disciplined. They might not know where they were going or whom they were fighting, but Wright and his men would wander with crisp military precision.[27]

War-making technology played a key role in the Battle of Four Lakes, fought on September 1, 1858, between the U.S. Army under Wright and fighters from (among others) Spokane, Yakama, Palus, Kalispel, and Columbia River Salish/Sinkiuse communities. Many of Wright's men were armed with new long-range Sharps carbines (nicknamed "Minies" after the ammunition they used), which forced an early retreat by the other side. In most conflicts of the War on Illahee, technological disparities had been either nonexistent or noncritical. In Steptoe's and Haller's ill-considered forays, howitzers had been at best useless. This time, long-range rifles made a decisive difference.[28]

There are several disputes about the events of the Battle of Four Lakes. The number of fighters on the Native side was initially estimated to be between 400 and 500, about half the size of the Euro-American force. Over time, as Euro-American historical memory veered away from lived experience, estimations of the size of the Native force doubled, quadrupled, and eventually decupled—rising to "5,000 Indians" by the time a monument to the battle was erected in 1926.[29]

The Battle of Four Lakes was followed by a running skirmish on September 5, typically called the Battle of Spokane Plains. Native forces on this occasion shifted strategy, attempting to use fire, smoke, and hit-and-run tactics to neutralize the Euro-American advantage in munitions. But it wasn't enough, and the Native forces broke off without having inflicted significant casualties. The Euro-American soldiers murdered everyone who surrendered and anyone wounded they could catch—although many of the wounded were evacuated from the battle before they could be executed, a particular traditional focus of the women fighters in Spokane and Coeur d'Alene/Schitsu'umsh armies.[30]

Along with these two major battles, Wright made war on Native livelihood, deploying the starvation tactics long standard in American wars on Native peoples. His men pillaged or burned foodstuffs necessary to make it through the upcoming winter, shot ponies and cattle, and, most infamously, methodically slaughtered around seven hundred horses over the course of two days. Wright and many of his men had significant qualms about the execution of horses, unlike their feelings toward the killing of Native people—as Cutler puts it, some "attribute[ed] more of a human quality to the animals than . . . [they] ascribed to the Indians." Others "appeared to exult" in all of the killing.[31]

Throughout his campaign, George Wright tortured people to death to make his points. In lieu of a conventional hanging, where the executioner combines the noose with a sudden drop that severs the spinal cord, Wright had his victims strangled. There were generally no trials for the men Wright killed, although the executions were sometimes labeled as such in records and histories. Sometimes he would ask a few questions of the condemned before having them tortured to death, as in the case of the Palus man named Jo-Hout mentioned at the beginning of this chapter, accused of murder without evidence and strangled until dead with John E. Smith's lasso on September 8, 1858. A Spokane peace negotiator named Amtoola was comparatively lucky—he was fatally shot earlier that same day by Wright's soldiers, while holding a white flag, and at least died quickly. There were many other killings and executions committed by Wright and his men over the first weeks of September—for most, neither the names nor the alleged crimes of the victims appear in Euro-American records. Some of these killings may have left no record at all.[32]

Wright's most famous execution was of Qualchan/Kwáłchin, a Yakama leader well-known for his part in the war effort. By September 23, 1858, Wright had begun talking surrender terms with a number of Native leaders. One of the leaders who came to talk peace was the Yakama leader Owhi/Áwxay, Qualchan/Kwáłchin's father. Wright seized him, put him in chains, and sent word to Qualchan/Kwáłchin that his father would be executed unless Qualchan/Kwáłchin showed himself. When Wright was among his Euro-American compatriots, he vowed to "hang [Qualchan/Kwáłchin] in fifteen minutes after I catch him." But rather than being caught, Qualchan/Kwáłchin came in willingly, possibly before the message reached him. And it turned out to be only ten minutes.[33]

Qualchan/Kwáłchin, accompanied by his wife, Whist-alks, and a younger relative, rode in to talk, apparently before Wright was ready for him. Thomas J. Beall, a packer and Wright's chosen hangman, described Wright asking a nearby packer of partially Native descent to stall for time:

"Can you talk to this indian and make him understand[?] If so do it, tell him anything, lie if necessary."

While talking, The Col had some soldiers to surround Qal-chen, and take him off his horse and make a prisoner of him. . . .

[The Col] gave orders to take him out and hang him, so Qa-lchen was not ten minutes in camp 'til he was hung and the rope was good and did not break. Another incident connected with Qalchen[']s death. After he was buried it was reported to the Col that Qalchen had considerable money on him in a belt. He was ex[h]umed but nothing in the shape of mon[e]y was found on him.[34]

The hanging, as was typical for Wright, was of the slow, torturous kind. Assisted by U.S. soldiers, Beall used a noose to slowly strangle Qualchan/Kwálchin to death. Before the hanging, Whist-alks was able to drive a beaded lance into the ground in defiance and ride away. After the failed grave robbing by Euro-American soldiers, the story goes, Qualchan/Kwálchin's body was reclaimed by his sisters and given a funeral with full honors. His father, Owhi/Áwx̱ay, was lethally shot ten days later, on October 3, 1858—supposedly while trying to escape.[35]

Wright finished his campaign with more hostage takings and hang-ings. In one illustrative incident on September 30, 1858, Wright gath-ered around a hundred Palus people who had assembled for peace talks. He declared them captives in their own country, forbade them from con-sorting with other Native groups he deemed hostile, and threatened, "If I come here again to war, I will hang them all, men, women, and children." He demanded that the assembled Palus produce the person or persons who had killed Euro-American miners in the region earlier in the year—though he had little evidence that would lead him to think that the killer or killers were present or even Palus. His audience talked among them-selves, and one of them came forward—quite possibly a man innocent of the purported crime, but willing to die to save his people. To drive the point home, Wright decided to lynch three men alongside the Palus vol-unteer. The three were identified only as "notorious marauders"; they may well have been chosen at random. All four men were slowly choked to death hanging from a nearby tree. Wright and his men marched on. The night after torturing four more men to death, Wright and his men dined on "grass-fed beef and a basket of champagne" to celebrate their success.[36]

*The Yakama leader Owhi/Áwxay as he appeared to Lieutenant Johnson
Kelly Dunston, a military leader, in 1853. Courtesy of the Ellensburg
Public Library, Ellensburg, Washington.*

To those he targeted, Wright's brutal campaign was little different
from those of the volunteers. Wright and his men possessed better guns
and more discipline, but they had the same goals and many of the same
tactics as earlier bands of Euro-American marauders. The volunteers
under Kelly had killed Peo-Peo-Mox-Mox while he was under a flag of
truce; the regulars under Wright killed Amloops in similar circumstances, though no evidence has been found of similar postmortem
butchery. Volunteers and regulars alike killed capriciously, although the
volunteers may have been more wide-ranging in their capriciousness.
There was less violence against noncombatants reported regarding the
regulars than the volunteers—but given that many of the surviving reports on the wanton violence of the volunteers *came* from those in charge
of the regulars, the reasons for this disparity are open to interpretation.
The difference between Wright's campaign and the murderous ravages
of volunteers was mostly a matter of effectiveness. If the campaigns of
the regulars involved fewer acts of wanton violence, it was only because
Wright and men like him believed the goals of White supremacy were
better served by somewhat more targeted attacks.

In eastern Washington, many Euro-American historians put the end of the
Indian wars somewhere in the late 1850s, after Wright's campaign or after

the treaties that followed it. The War on Illahee as defined by pioneer historians came to a close in 1858 or 1859. But the war on Native independence did not. Lynchings and murders continued within and beyond the law, perpetrated by soldiers, sheriffs, and civilians. Outright war continued, too, in the so-called Snake War against plateau and mountain peoples in the 1860s and in the more famous Northwest wars of the 1870s. In his papers, Joseph Henry Brown, a would-be historian, volunteer, and Snake War veteran, included reports of lynchings as "material on Oregon volunteers." Killings after the wars seem to have been, to Brown, part of volunteer service. They were certainly a part of pioneer life.[37]

Andrew Jackson Splawn—a pioneer cattleman, sometime sheriff, and eventual Washington state senator who claimed in his memoirs to have "always treated [Indians] right"—wrote nonchalantly about helping his fellow pioneers get away with murdering Native people over dinner. Sandwiched between his prideful boasts of taking food from the mouths of Chinese-descended miners and cheating the leader of a local Entiat Indigenous community, Splawn told a story of coming upon the frozen body of a dead Native man near present-day Rock Island, Washington, in the winter of 1865. Without context, and hoping local Native communities wouldn't discover the death, Splawn threw the body into the Columbia River. Later that night he was thanked by local trading post proprietor Jack Ingraham who "said that the fellow had given him much trouble and, to get ride [sic] of him for all time . . . had given him strychnine." Splawn, who was remembered as a "friend of" Indians, had covered up the murder on instinct, without knowing the perpetrator, and without regret. It was simply one more pioneer anecdote. And it wasn't even the only story of a pioneer murdering a Native person with strychnine in his book.[38]

Nicholas McCoy, an Austrian American gold miner, cattleman, and (probably) former slave trader, was remembered in pioneer histories as having been "in all the Indian troubles" between 1858 and the 1880s. It is unclear how many people McCoy killed when participating in gold rushes in the 1850s, or as part of wars of the 1870s. But Splawn related one confirmed murder by McCoy, in Yakima County, Washington, in the early 1870s—a murder that went unmentioned in most published pioneer biographies: " 'Old Nick' . . . never cared for companionship and would rather be among Indians than with whites. One day an Indian slapped him for bothering his wife. Nick came to Yakima City a few days later and bought some strychnine and a dollar's worth of sugar. When

Andrew Jackson Splawn, probably as he appeared in the late 1800s.
From A. J. Splawn, Ka-mi-akin: The Last Hero of the Yakimas.

the Indian went to his cabin next time, Nick invited him to dinner and when the Indian wanted sugar in his coffee, Nick shoved him what he desired. The next day the Indian was dead. . . . Nick was an eccentric character with many good qualities."[39] Feeling demeaned after being slapped for "bothering" another man's wife, "Old Nick" McCoy murdered the man over dinner, in cold blood. Splawn regarded McCoy as a friend, and he bought out his cattle business a few years later.

And the sangfroid with which Splawn described this pioneer poisoning might even weigh on the balance of evidence in other instances wherein pioneers were accused of attempting to murder inconvenient

Native people with poison. Splawn's reminiscence treats such murders as unremarkable. Settler poisonings are known to have been a significant part of land takings and mass killings in Australia; reminiscences like Splawn's, and similar evidence, suggest they may have played a similar role in North America.[40]

Andrew Jackson Splawn did, in the last decade before he died in 1917, express support for at least a few Native people he considered friends, particularly the Yakama leader Charlie Saluskin. He had in early eras relied on them for his economic success: buying horses cheap from Native communities to sell dear to miners in the 1860s and hiring Native cowboys in the 1870s and 1880s. But whatever his possible or perceived support for Native rights by the twilight of his life, Splawn saw no need to act on the murder McCoy committed in the 1870s; nor did he show any regret when he and his wife, Margaret, were composing his memoirs in the 1910s. Splawn had been a deputy sheriff for portions of the late 1800s, and he had investigated McCoy for suspected cattle theft—but never for the first-degree murder he knew McCoy had committed. Splawn denounced Ingraham for selling liquor to Native people—but not for the first-degree murder Splawn had helped him conceal from his Native neighbors. Splawn might have played the part of a "friend of the Indians," but his friendship with White killers trumped that support.[41]

The pioneer William H. Osterman lynched Native people, but it remains unclear just how many. The records point to lynchings in northwestern Washington in the 1880s, but there may have been others. There was one vigilante murder for which he was regionally infamous: the 1884 lynching of "Louie Sam," a Stó:lō man framed for the murder of a White shopkeeper named James Bell, pursued by a horde of about a hundred settlers across the border, arrested in Canada, then dragged from a Canadian jail and murdered by the American mob. This lynching created an international incident, and a subsequent investigation by the Canadian government found that Osterman had probably committed the murder of Bell and been part of the lynching of Sam.[42]

Osterman's family remembered a different lynching story. As his daughter Susan Osterman Alverson put it: "Father came on to Washington where he got employment with the Postal Telegraph Co. He had many thrilling experiences, especially with Indians and, one time, was about to be lynched for murder which he knew nothing about and was only saved by the timely arrival of a mail carrier who had noticed the

Indians around his home; and they were traced into British Columbia where (there being two of them) they were hanged in trees." This could be the same story through a distorted lens. It could also be a separate murderous incursion to lynch those seeking refuge with First Nations people in Canada.[43]

Or it could be that the many lynchings Osterman seems to have been involved in blended together in family memory. Captain John Kilcup of northwestern Washington, a murderous vigilante and boat operator, remembered that Osterman had been part of his "bunch," a gang of White men known for lynching Indians (and possibly others). As one member put it, "I would kill a Chinaman as quick as I would an Indian, and I would kill an Indian as quick as I would a dog." Another, Peter Harkness, took historian Percival R. Jeffcott on a tour of some of the trees around the region that he and the "bunch" had hanged people from.[44]

In the extant records, Osterman and the vigilante group (or possibly groups) to which he belonged acted with relative impunity. In one case, after torturing an Indian boy who they falsely believed had information on a crime, the vigilantes were briefly detained—but the event did not seem to cause them any legal or social harm, according to Kilcup: "Captain Ro[e]der had the bunch ar[r]ested for being so rough with the young Indian. The bunch consisted of Moultry, Osterman, Bud Walker, Sam Harkness, Birt Hopkins [who] was leader. When the trial was over at Whatcom we all went to a dance, and the floor man[a]ger jokingly war[ned] the ladies that it would be a disgrace for any of them to dance with the Convicts, but his advi[c]e was not he[e]ded, and the boys were shown a very pleasant evening." Murder and torture of Indigenous persons did not, it seems, bring much legal or social censure. Released from a courthouse where they faced no consequence for the assault on a child they had just committed, the lynching "bunch" found plenty of willing dance partners among the ladies of Whatcom County; from the tone of the reminiscence, many found the racial violence practiced by the bunch compelling.[45]

Because lynching Indians in the Pacific Northwest was often the handiwork of small bands of men rather than a spectacle for the entire White community, the kinds of evidence ubiquitous in the Jim Crow South are less common in the region. The killings in northwestern Washington have slipped through historians' accounts; not one appears in Michael J. Pfeifer's landmark works on lynching in the territory.[46]

Some lynchings and other vigilante violence may have passed beneath historical notice because they were not seen as vigilantism by

White people in much of the nineteenth-century Pacific Northwest. In southern Oregon in August 1852, newspapers of the time reported, a Native man known to Euro-Americans as "Warty" was accused of stealing bread in a threatening way, whereupon local White men, "hearing the alarm, and knowing the Indian character, arrested him, summoned the neighborhood, tried, condemned and hung him on the same day." In eastern Oregon, Elizabeth Laughlin Lord remembered the community hanging of a "handsome and saucy" Native man accused of attempted sexual assault in the 1850s as a righteous and lawful act—unlike her recollections of "vigilance committees" targeting White people. In 1878 Elijah L. Bristow Jr. discussed with historians his father's casual acts of vigilante murder inflicted on Indigenous persons in the 1840s, and he remembered even more intense mob violence against Native people in the gold mining regions of southern Oregon. But he proclaimed, in the same interview, that he had "never heard of any vigilance committee" in the region. For both Bristows, killing Indians was not vigilante violence—it was just part of pioneer life.[47]

Some lynchings can be inferred, if not proven. In 1893 the controversial Puyallup leader Peter Stanup was embroiled with Indian Agent Edwin Eells in a fight over the allotment of Puyallup land. Both agreed allotment was inevitable, but Eells wanted continued wardship for the Puyallup and for land sales to go to Euro-Americans; Stanup wanted all the profits to go to the Puyallup, and for most of the land to be retained individually. As events reached a crescendo seemingly in Stanup's favor in May 1893, Eells called in the military. By the end of the month, Stanup was found dead in a river, with a broken neck. Puyallup witnesses also saw defensive wounds on Stanup's arms, although the White coroner either didn't see or didn't record them. A brief perfunctory investigation was dropped without progress, despite a Puyallup petition declaring Eells's involvement. Land speculators seized Puyallup lands without permission or remuneration. Puyallup Nation investigators noted at least six more Puyallup deaths under suspicious circumstances in years before and after Stanup's mysteriously broken neck—each one resulting in yet more land transfers out of Native hands.[48]

Familiarity and friendliness did not necessarily halt vigilante violence. Mattie Gallaway, who grew up in eastern Washington in the late 1800s, remembered that "the Indians were friendly but the family always kept a gun in case of emergency and never lost a sense of fear." Julius Charles, a Lummi/Xw'lemi nation member, remembered that in the 1890s and 1900s (and perhaps later), he had been warned by "friendly whites" whenever there appeared to have been a murder in the region, so he would know to "keep away from certain neighborhoods where ill will existed against the Indians." The assumption that all Native people were responsible for any suspicious act of violence persisted for decades in some quarters.[49]

The lynching of Native people, during wars and after them, through show trials and no trials, needs much more attention from scholars, in the Pacific Northwest and elsewhere. The judicial murder of Leschi is now better known regionally than it has been in generations. The federal hanging of thirty-eight Dakota prisoners of war in 1862 is rightly growing more infamous nationally, even if the broader context of genocide within which those executions were situated remains less well known. But there were legions of other hangings, by the military and civilians alike, with even less due process than those unjust events—often with little more than "Damn the Indians." And there were many more lynchings, by other means, continuing long past the pioneer period. Vigilante killings and opportunistic murder predated and continued after those few legal lynchings that garnered widespread Euro-American attention—attacks that in some cases were still constrained only by fear of Native reprisal. There are many, many more histories of lynchings targeting Indigenous people than current academic history has yet examined or acknowledged.[50]

As Louie Wapato of the Moses Band Colville put it during an interview in 1973:

> There was many killings of Whites and Indians, see, they fought. You don't find that in the history but they did. There was several, several murders that was in the history, but a lot of them aren't, see. Just a dead Indian, or a dead White man found, and that, nobody knows what happened. . . . I don't expect you [historians] to put those in, but I want you to know, have an understanding, have a history of the people before. Before the state of Washington, in the early history, there was a lot of Indians. And a lot of Whites coming, and they were taking advantage of the Indians, see. In some ways, the government would not protect the Indian, they would not prosecute, they would not try to find the murderer of an Indian. A dead Indian was just a dead Indian, you see? That was the idea.[51]

CHAPTER SEVEN

The Snake War as a Continuation
of the War on Illahee

IN OCTOBER 1861, ELISHA "Lish" Applegate sent a letter to James W. Nesmith, by that time a U.S. senator, demanding that the federal government establish a new military post in southern Oregon to continue the conquest of Native lands. The presence of numerous Native people was, he argued, reason enough:

> On the Eastern frontier of Jackson County there are numerous bands of savages. Persons that have passed through that Klamath Lake Country report *thousands* of them. It is a grea[t] country for Indians—those grea[t] lakes affording an abundant supply of fish, and the rich vall[eys] abounding with roots, which they dig—so much so that those tribes are distinguished far and wide as the *diggers*. These savages are not in open war as yet with our settlements; but what of that? Nor are they friendly with them; and what if they will? We know they cannot live in close proximity with the whites without difficulty and war. They have murdered and robbed our people im[m]igrating through our their country. This they have practiced as we all know for years and years.[1]

The fact that the varied Native polities that Lish Applegate lumped together were not "in open war" was immaterial to him. They were not "in open war as yet," and Lish Applegate saw war as inevitable. Applegate originally referred to Native land as "our" country before correcting himself to write "their" country, a perhaps half-conscious assumption of future Euro-American conquest. His brother Jesse Applegate had been eyeing the Klamath Lake region as a business opportunity for years (although Jesse was not nearly so comfortable with conquest). And Lish Applegate knew his audience—James Nesmith could be counted on to despise Native people.[2]

Klamath/Mukluk, Modoc, and other Native peoples had been to Jacksonville to trade for much of the 1850s, risking the notoriously brutal tempers of the White residents there to exchange goods and renew relationships. But because Native people were sometimes buying guns (which could be used for attacks or self-defense as well as hunting), Lish Applegate declared that these mutually agreed-on trades had

> become an almost [unbe]arable nuisance. If something is not done, and that pretty shortly[,] war must inevitably follow.
>
> There ought to be a military post established near the Klamath Lake as soon as possible next Spring. A reservation and agency should also be established there at an early day.
>
> It is positively necessary that these things be done at the present session of Congress—necessary to the saf[e]ty and satisfaction of the people. And if promptly attended to, even if the effort should prove unsuccessful, it will disarm our political enemies, and increase the confidence of the people in their Friend at Washington.[3]

The threat of political repercussions was serious. Southern Oregon, perceived to be a hotbed of Confederate sentiment, was also a core part of Nesmith's base in a swing state. Perhaps more important, being seen as an "Indian sympathizer" was a potent insult across party lines.[4]

Lish Applegate's letter demanding military action concluded with a petition signed by a number of Oregonians—including at least a few who would join in the killing of some of the Native people being discussed only a few years later. This petition made clear that the core drivers of these settlers' demands were land hunger and White supremacy. It began:

> This Klamath Lake Country, so called, embraces a large area of arable land, well adapted to granging and agricultural purposes,

containing a population of several hundred Indians, who gain a precarious living in the summer by fishing and hunting, and in winter depend ch[ie]fly for their subsistence on the generosity of the contiguous white settlements, to whom it is exceedingly annoying, and which must ultimately and inevitably lead to a war between the races; as all past experience goes to prove that to have peace between the white man and the Indian[,] a free and multilined intercourse must not be tolerated.[5]

A "war between the races," Applegate and his few dozen signatories proclaimed, was inevitable (even as their assertions about dependence were doubtful). First and foremost, they wanted the "large area of arable land." Fort Klamath was eventually established, in 1863, by Charles S. Drew—the same man who had suggested during the Rogue River Wars that acts of violence that would be considered war crimes under normal circumstances should be standard procedure when attacking Native communities.

Drew's embrace of murder as policy had not dimmed. In keeping with the standing orders of George Wright, Drew would react to whispers of trouble by executing Native people without trial. Just before treaty negotiations with Klamath peoples began in 1864, Drew seized and killed two Native men with only vague justifications—and while noting that both men were against accommodation with the Whites. The 1864 treaty was pushed through shortly afterward. The involved Applegates profited off it for years.[6]

The threat of force—and of being "given up to the soldiers for punishment"—hung over treaty negotiations in southeastern Oregon in the 1860s, just as it had in the 1850s. And there was, as usual, an undeclared and ill-defined war, not only in southeastern Oregon but across the Pacific Northwest. As Charles S. Drew put it when describing one 1864 encounter with a Native group he identified as "Piute": "He and his comrades do not wish to be considered belligerents, and treated accordingly. . . . Though appearing every way friendly with our whole force present[ly]. . . . They are doubtless assassins by nature, but are too cowardly to attack any party of armed white men unless by surprise." Drew and many, many other White pioneers would always be suspicious of Native people, no matter the circumstance. They were "assassins by nature" to him, untrustworthy even if they "appeared in every way friendly." Drew still objected to what he perceived as unnecessarily risky racist violence, when it might spur counterattacks. Rasher men than Drew would shoot first and ask questions later.[7]

The killings Drew committed, and the broader invasions of (among other places) southern and eastern Oregon in the 1860s, were arguably part of the broader Snake War—one of the least-known, least-discussed, and least-researched U.S. wars against Native communities. In the Pacific Northwest, it also might be considered an extension of or sequel to the War on Illahee. The invasions of the early 1860s were fought for similar reasons, with similar goals, and in many cases by the same volunteers as the more famous conflicts of the 1850s. It was similarly prosecuted but differently remembered. To an even greater extent than the wars of the 1850s, the Snake War in the 1860s was waged against an amorphously defined enemy—essentially, any and all Native polities in the Great Basin and Plateau regions (and possibly beyond) that Americans perceived as independent. Even its standard title refers to a general insult rather than a particular polity or ethnie—*snake* is a slur indicating an inherent enemy, probably borrowed from Indigenous communities, rather than a specific referent. Some pioneers used the slur to refer to any Native group coded as especially hostile. In the 1850s, it might have been used in reference to Cayuse/Liksiyu, Palus, or Walla Walla/Walúu-lapam peoples. In the 1850s *and* 1860s, Euro-Americans in the far West applied it to Northern Paiute/Numu peoples, various Shoshone/Newe peoples, many Bannock/Nimi peoples, Modoc communities, and (seemingly) almost any other Native polity or ethnie they found threatening in the Great Basin and Plateau regions.

Perhaps because the United States embarked on it as an unusually amorphous war against Native people generally, there has not been an agreed-upon periodization for the Snake War. In pioneer Oregon, nineteenth-century historians Frances Fuller Victor and Hubert Howe Bancroft did not date the Snake Wars (and mentioned the term only in a footnote in their *History of Oregon*), but they seemed to frame it as lasting from 1862 to around 1868. In Idaho, a periodization beginning in 1866, when volunteer troops were mustered across Idaho Territory, is not uncommon—but there had been violent attacks by bands of volunteers and soldiers in the region for years, since before the Idaho Territory was created in 1863. Some on the Warm Springs Reservation in Oregon have argued that a war—or something close to it—inhered in lethal clashes between some reservation residents and some Northern Paiute/Numu communities in 1859. Oregon's Governor George Lemuel Woods, who took office in 1866, opined that the Snake War had effectively been under way since the so-called Ward Massacre of 1854, using the (presumed) role of Eastern Shoshone/Newe women in that incident to justify his public and repeated calls for genocide against *all* Snake Indians, regardless of age or gender.[8]

The Snake War is typically periodized as happening from 1864 to 1868 in modern historical texts—but there has been little to no discussion of what distinguishes the 1864 military expeditions of the volunteer infantry across eastern Oregon from earlier military operations by volunteer cavalry drawn from the same pool. Some authors have treated the Snake War as a war on specific Native groups—in Oregon, as a war on the Northern Paiute/Numu. But though Northern Paiute/Numu people were certainly targeted, American soldiers and other killers were seldom concerned with which ethnies the Native people they were attacking belonged to. Even many modern histories avoid the question of when and what the Snake War was. Historian James Robbins Jewell describes cavalry engaging in "violent encounters" to "brutally subdue" Northern Paiutes/Numu and others so "whites could colonize their lands," *without* labeling that violence as part of a war—framing it instead as part of the "vital role" volunteers played "in opening the interior Pacific Northwest."[9]

This fuzziness has meant that the most infamous act that was arguably a part of the Snake War has not typically been included under its mantle. The Bear River Massacre, perpetrated in a portion of Washington Territory about to become Idaho Territory on January 29, 1863, was one of the largest known single mass killings of Native people by the U.S. Army in the mainland United States. Colonel Patrick Edward Connor, who had been a part of genocidal attacks against Native communities across the West throughout the 1850s, led a regiment from California to massacre hundreds of mostly Northwestern Shoshone/Newe people. At least 280 people were killed; recent historians have suggested the death toll might be over 500 people. Many more were raped and otherwise wounded.[10]

The Bear River Massacre was singular in its horror and scale. But the pursuit of mass killings of those labeled Snake—in Idaho Territory, Washington Territory, Oregon, and elsewhere—was not. Arbitrary periodization of the Snake War has caused what would be the most infamous war crime of the conflict to be discussed instead as a separate, perhaps isolated event. Gregory Michno's 2007 book *Deadliest Indian War in the*

West, one of the few monographs on the Snake War, not only severs the Bear River Massacre from the broader Snake War but largely omits the mass killing and raping—and lauds the massacre as a U.S. battle victory. An embrace of the odious racism of sources from the 1860s and the studied ignorance of historians of the later 1800s remains far too common among the handful of modern military historians who discuss the Snake War, even as new studies of the Bear River Massacre (and other war crimes in the region during the 1860s) make the extent of the horror clearer and clearer.[11]

Most of the fighters on the Euro-American side of the Snake War were short-term volunteers, even those mustered as regulars. With professional troops marching off to fight in the U.S. Civil War, locals (often with experience in the wars of the 1850s) were recruited into U.S. Army regiments in the Pacific Northwest to inflict violence on Native communities. Lieutenant John W. Hopkins of the First Oregon Cavalry was sure that with "extra arms and plenty of clothing," one could "raise a good many men among the Emigrators and disgusted miners" to have a "bully fight" with what he called "the *Bloody Snakes*"—any and all independent Native people the army could find. Recruitment was slow and incomplete; some officers complained, yet again, of soldiers leaving to try their hand at mining, and conscription was seemingly off the table. Enlisted men wrote to newspapers, under pseudonyms, of how they pined to kill Indians. As a soldier who called himself "Snake Hunter" put it, "If the boys had a chance there would be a fine slaughter of Snakes, and that too in a short time." As was the case in the 1850s, Euro-Americans' desires for mass killings exceeded their capacity. If they had been able, a number of Euro-American soldiers in the early 1860s would have committed many more Bear River Massacres.[12]

And as in the wars of the 1850s, many of the killers in the 1860s were neither regulars nor volunteers. In a reminiscence of her 1862 migration through the Great Basin, pioneer Susan Gregg Walton recalled a Mr. Young, whose brother had been wounded in an ambush during a previous sojourn through the same region. Although he had not seen his brother's attackers, Young was apparently sure he knew where his brother had been attacked and rallied men to "get up before daylight and go kill every Indian they could find" at a nearby village once they were in the general area. There were no pioneer objections over issues of identity, equivalence, or morality. The notion that these particular Native communities might not be those responsible for an attack only vaguely in the same region was not raised. The idea that a nonfatal wounding should be answered with mass killing was not challenged. And the planned murder of combatants and noncombatants alike was not addressed as such.[13]

Rather, Walton's father argued against Mr. Young on the grounds that there might be a counterattack:

> There were a number just "raring to go." This raised trouble among the men, of course. Some could see how Young felt but thought he should have more concern for the [White emigrant] women and children than to run such risks simply for a matter of getting a little revenge. One word brought another until the whole crowd was angry. My father told them they would be responsible for more trouble if they carried on like this[,] for the Indians would likely raise in mass and massacre the whole train; for them to act like men and just go to bed, forget all this foolishness and in the morning they would be glad. But this did not have the desired effect.[14]

Young and a number of other men of the train left in the night to "kill every Indian they could find," and returned

> carrying fish poles, fish baskets, moccasins, beads, and in fact, everything they could find, and telling how they had made those Indians run—all that they did not leave dead. . . . I heard my father scolding Tom Potts for hanging a fish-basket in top of his wagon bows right over his head and strapping a fish pole on the outside of his wagon cover and [my father] told him there was not an Indian in fifty miles from there who would not recognize that basket and fish pole, adding that we were sure to be overtaken and would have more trouble. Now, I disliked to have father talk that way to him for he was such a nice boy and a friend to us.[15]

Again, the objections were not to the looting or the killing but to the potential danger that violence and theft brought. And Susan Walton, writing decades later, still seemingly had no sympathy for the Indigenous people who had been killed for the stated reason that some White person had been wounded by some Indian some months earlier. Her sympathy was for the killers. Looking back, Walton expressed regret that Potts had lost face when her father scolded him for the murders—and no regret that Potts had committed them. He was, in her memory, "such a nice boy"—the killings he committed did not matter.

The train split, and those whom Walton's family left behind seem to have died in an apparent counterattack a few days later. Walton's breakaway train, which did not contain those who had killed and looted, was stopped by Native fighters. They inspected the wagons, presumably for plundered Native possessions. Finding none, they let the emigrant pioneers go on without consequence. The plunderers, Walton heard later, were attacked—she presumed by the same force that had stopped her family—and ten of them were killed. The killing of some of the pioneers who had raided and pillaged a (probably Western Shoshone/Newe) Native village in the night was folded into the half-fictitious narrative of what settlers called "Massacre Rocks," a site in Idaho (now a state park) dedicated to Euro-American pioneers killed in 1862. That these killings appear to have been a limited reciprocal response to immediate and specific wanton violence by White emigrants does not yet appear to have been made part of the narrative of Massacre Rocks. Alternatively, it is possible that Walton had mistakenly connected the actions of her train to a more notorious incident of violence, and that the men of her train who murdered and pillaged never faced any consequence at all.[16]

"Big" George L. Freeman claimed to have fought in the Snake War from 1861 to 1866. Speaking to a Baker City, Oregon, interviewer in 1913, he remembered "several encounters with the Indians" wherein he and his fellow soldiers ensured that "several r_dsk_ns were made to bit[e] the dust and left unburied." Their Indian-ness, in his memory, was enough to prove hostile intent, and the livestock pillaged from them was assumed to have "been stolen from emigrant wagon trains"—part of a broader pioneer norm of framing Native livestock as always already stolen, and thus justifiably plunderable.[17]

Many of Freeman's anecdotes are hard to track onto other historical and contemporary narratives. He free-associated about killings and hardships without providing much contextual information. However, he was wounded in one of the encounters he described—and the historical records for that battle differed significantly from Freeman's memory. As Freeman told the journalist W. W. Stevens: "[We] started out to locate the rascals. About 200 of them. . . . A charge was made and a hot fight ensued for a time, but the renegades beat a hasty retreat and scattered back into the hills. Seventeen dead Indians were left behind and 200 head of stock recaptured that had been stolen from emigrant trains. Five government soldiers were killed and six wounded."[18]

The casualty counts for U.S. forces are the only portions of this memory that match other records of the time. Freeman's commanding officer, John M. Drake, estimated a little under seventy fighters he presumed to be Paiute, who had suffered perhaps three casualties before making an orderly retreat. This encounter was at best a draw between Euro-American and Northern Paiute/Numu forces. The "stock recaptured" was about fifty "Indian horses" seized as plunder by the Euro-American soldiers. Whether through distortions in the interview, the transmogrifying effects of memory, or outright lies, W. W. Stevens and George Freeman transformed the inconclusive clash into a victory against raiders. "Indian horses" were turned into "stock ... stolen from emigrant trains," and Northern Paiute/Numu fighters were turned into "renegades." The size of the party the Americans had attacked was roughly tripled, and their casualties quintupled. Freeman wanted to be remembered for even more racist killings than he had actually committed, whether or not he was aware of how tall his tales were.[19]

John M. Drake's papers suggest that this kind of manipulation of memory was common. Drake, a gold miner and pioneer in California and southern Oregon, was most famous for leading "an Indian campaign in Eastern Oregon in the year 1864," where he kept a diary of his experiences and actions. When he and his daughter Ruth Drake were preparing this diary for publication (unsuccessfully) forty years later, they edited out or altered a few key passages to soften Drake's image in history. Both the original and the altered version were retained and eventually donated by Ruth Drake—allowing for an unusual view of what material the Drakes had attempted to alter.[20]

Notably, the Drakes did not soften John M. Drake's scorn for the volunteers and pioneers who critiqued the regular armed forces in that period, or his assumptions about the genocidal intent of Native people generally. As he opined in 1864:

> The Web-foot nation ... have persistently heaped reproach on their own troops while in the protection and defense of their own frontiers; sneering at brass buttons at sight of an officer of the Cavalry on the street. Were it not for the helpless women and children I would rejoice to see the Indians wipe out the

Columbia River country one of these days, just to let the people of Portland and Dalles know what slippery ground they stand on. The thing will be done as surely as the troops are withdrawn from this upper country. The different tribes of Indians would confederate under the leadership of some Pi-li-ni [Paulina, a Northern Paiute/Numu leader], and the white settlement from the head of the Columbia to the Dall[e]s would be swept out of existence. Three thousand men and ten millions of dollars would become necessary to subdue the revolt.[21]

It is unclear whether Drake's vitriol toward pioneers ("the Web-foot nation") played a role in the difficulties in finding a publisher in 1905. There might be reason to believe that Drake's repeated assertions that "the citizen volunteers that went out . . . behaved badly" might not have been the sort of copy that sells books (see chapters 8 and 10). His opinion of the "different tribes of Indians" is very clear. With or without the perceived leader of the moment, Drake believed they would sooner or later attempt to sweep White settlements out of existence. Notably, he also characterized such violence as a "revolt"—a renunciation of subjection rather than a war waged against a foreign power. Drake viewed the independent Indigenous polities he attacked as always both subjugated and hungry for violence. Like John Minto, Drake had from childhood learned that a Native person was a "savage" and a "wol[f]," dedicated only to "his hunt in the abode of his forefathers" and to his "barbarous orgies."[22]

Unlike Loren L. Williams (see below), Drake welcomed Indigenous persons he saw as under Euro-American control to his side of the war. A detachment of fighters from the Warm Springs Reservation fought other Indigenous groups and suffered casualties alongside the Euro-American troops (many of whom were Wasco people, and some of whom may have identified as Wascos to Euro-Americans since Indigenous people thought to be of that ethnie were less likely to be arbitrarily murdered). Just as Native fighters allied with Euro-American forces in the Puget Sound War had worn white swashes on their hats, Drake's Warm Springs auxiliaries were given special cloth in an attempt to keep his Euro-American troops from shooting at them—"bright red scarfs to be worn by the friendly Indians to distinguish them from the hostiles." Edmund Clare Fitzhugh had advocated sending hired Native fighters into the more dangerous situations in the Puget Sound in 1856. In the 1860s, Orlando Humason

John M. Drake as he probably appeared in the 1860s, during his part in the Snake War. Courtesy of the Oregon Historical Society.

(a race-baiting politician, gold speculator, and volunteer since 1856) similarly suggested "the substitution of Indian risk for white risk." Beyond immediate harms, this clash heightened tensions between different Indigenous ethnies in the region, sometimes long after the war.[23]

And there may have been other Native people with Drake's force. Drake wrote that the Warm Springs Indian Agent William Logan "brought me an Indian boy for a servant," a boy who was not mentioned again in his journal. Was this "servant" kept for the duration of the campaign, or only for the evening at Warm Springs proper? Was this boy unfree, like the Native boys enslaved by Joseph Lane in southern Oregon and Edward Steptoe in southern Washington a decade earlier? The record is thus far unclear.[24]

Although John M. Drake's 1860s racism survived the 1905 edit, the Drakes blotted out many of his assumptions of Native cowardice, presumptions of incompatibility, and original fears about his Native allies. The people he had been attacking were changed from "the Indians" (in 1864) to "the hostile Indians" (in 1905), at least at the beginning of certain passages. Descriptions of his allies as "likely to become unmanageable" remained, but he deleted his original descriptions of them as "uncontrollable." Originally, Drake proclaimed that "Snake Indians are entirely incompatible, so far as white men are concerned"; in the 1905 version, Drake's rejection of assimilation as impossible was entirely removed.[25]

The Drakes also attempted to soften the section of the journal dealing with the capture and likely assault of an unnamed Native woman and her child. Both versions mentioned (without exact explanation) that her captors "didn't show her much leniency, handling her pretty roughly and taking her child away from her." They also stripped her of at least some of her clothing; Drake himself took possession of "a fine robe made of the skins of the long-tailed deer." And with only minor variations, both the 1864 and 1905 versions argued that ripping their captive's child from her was necessary for the purposes of interrogation. The updated version, however, added details (remembered or invented) to attenuate the story. The 1905 account describes interrogation by means of providing "the stimulus of a chunk of meat and some bread," a detail absent from the original. "Her child" in 1864 was changed to "the child" in 1905, subtly neutralizing the woman's right to her baby. And the child was changed from a "little thing" to a "little creature," shifting from a term of endearment used for children among Euro-Americans to language more commonly used for animals and Indians in the early 1900s.[26]

The woman managed to escape two days after being captured, fleeing with her child into the night in the midst of a surprising June snowstorm. In both versions, Drake claimed to have been on the verge of releasing her anyway. But he added even more cost-free grace in the 1905 version, claiming that he had "meant to give back the robe that was taken from her"—which might have kept this woman and her child warm as she fled from the "pretty rough" treatment of his company into the frozen night. Northern Paiute/Numu oral histories recall bands of settlers and soldiers reaving and raping in the 1860s. It is unclear if this is what Drake meant by "rough" treatment. But even if his company didn't, others did.[27]

Drake and other career military officials complained about the volunteers—what they called "the enterprising part of [their] command"—both for their inconstancy and their incompetence. "[Nathan] Olney," Drake moaned in a letter about volunteer commanders, "pays no attention to and will not obey his orders." Another regular officer, Reuben F.

Maury, warned that in the countryside "the citizens behaved badly. . . . Independent bodies are always dangerous to the success of military movements." And as in the 1850s, the objections to the "bad behavior" of the volunteers were predicated on pragmatism. Maury was perfectly willing to lynch Native people without noticeable evidence of wrongdoing, but he strove for domination rather than destruction. Like John E. Wool in the 1850s, Maury argued in 1864 for interning all the remaining free Native people in the Northwest in order "to remedy both evils—ext[ermination] and the cost of fitting out expeditions every summer."[28]

Military figures stressing economic concerns as much as human ones, and presuming the inevitability of exterminatory attacks, remained common in the 1860s. In 1863 Captain John Mullan included very similar advice for the government in his report on the military road he had just finished between Fort Walla Walla in Washington Territory and Fort Benton in what was about to be Montana Territory:

> Swarms of miners and emigrants . . . must pass here year after year. . . .
>
> This . . . is to be regretted; but I can only regard it as the inevitable result of opening and settling the country. I have seen enough of Indians to convince me of this fact, that they can never exist in contact with the whites. . . . But they have been removed so often that there seems now no place left for their further migration. . . . And now that we propose to invade the[ir] mountain solitudes, to wrest from them their hidden wealth, where under heavens can the Indians go? And may we not expect to see these people make one desperate struggle in the fastnesses of the Rocky Mountains for the maintenance of their last homes and the preservation of their lives[?] . . .
>
> The Indian is destined to disappear before the white man, and the only question is, how it may be best done, and his disappearance from our midst tempered with those elements calculated to produce to himself the least amount of suffering, and to us the least amount of cost.[29]

Maury's and Mullan's stance, and John E. Wool's before them, can be considered humane only when compared to that of many of the volunteers and civilians. According to pioneer Ralph Fisk, Euro-Americans mining in eastern Oregon in the 1860s would call out, "Indians or White

Men?" if they heard someone in the dark of night. The former could expect gunfire without any further questions. Recent arrivals acclimated quickly to this murderous norm. Small wonder that Maury saw the pursuit of extermination as unstoppable, and Mullan predicted it would reach into every corner of the mountains. Both men took the fact of pioneer killings as a given. They sought largely to control the costs and seldom tried to stop the murderers.[30]

For many participants, the Snake War was simply another chapter in the continuing battle for White supremacy in the Pacific Northwest. This was certainly the case for Nathan Olney, a longtime trader and Indian agent celebrated as an "Indian fighter" by his Euro-American contemporaries and their immediate descendants. He fought as a volunteer officer in the Cayuse War in 1848. He was part of Granville O. Haller's killing spree through what would become the Idaho Territory following the attack on the Ward wagon train in 1854, at one point taking an arrow to the head. He played a role in the expansion of the Yakima War in October 1855, using his role as an Indian agent and his supposed expertise on Native issues to help convince Governor George Curry of Oregon that there was already a wide alliance of Native people who had "either commenced open hostilities upon the whites, or are concentrating their forces for that purpose":

> I am doing all in my power to check the gathering storm, but I fear nothing but a large military force will do any good towards keeping them in check. The regular force now in this country, I do not consider sufficient for the protection of the settlers, and the chastisement of the Indians.
>
> One thousand volunteers should be raised immediately and sent into this part of Oregon and Washington Territories. Delay is ruinous. Decisive steps must immediately be taken. They must be humbled, and in all conscience send a force that can do it effectively and without delay. These Indians must be taught our power.[31]

Pushing for "chastisement" as well as protection, Nathan Olney was one of several voices pushing for war on "the Indians" in general in 1855. He was also one of many to take part in the murder and dismemberment of Peo-Peo-Mox-Mox.[32]

Nathan Olney was thus celebrated with a parade when he raised a unit of volunteers in The Dalles to join in the Snake War. One keynote speaker praised Olney and his men and proclaimed that the regimental flag could not and would not be soiled, for "the more the flag was drenched in the blood of the foe, the cleaner and the *whiter* it would be." Olney's expedition failed to be the bloodbath his fellow White Oregonians had called for. This campaign, as was typical for Snake War campaigns, was left off later plaques honoring Olney's military career. But the speaker was right; Nathan Olney fought for White supremacy in the Pacific Northwest until his death in 1866. And there were others like him, volunteer veterans of the 1850s who during the Civil War rose again to attack Native polities.[33]

Loren L. Williams's career as a serial killer of Native people spanned a quarter century, from at least 1851 (see chapter 1) to the mid-1870s. On October 5, 1865, Williams was serving as a lieutenant in the U.S. 1st Oregon Infantry, a federal force made up of local volunteers raised the year before. Camped in southeastern Oregon a few days northwest of Malheur Lake, Williams wrote out what he considered to be one of the most noteworthy official orders of his military career. He read the order to his men, then saved a copy for posterity, eventually attaching it to the six-volume journal-cum-autobiography he would produce about a decade later. As he proclaimed to his troops:

No friendly Indians exist within the jurisdiction of this command. . . . They will therefore wherever found be pursued and punished as [hostile], regardless of any profession of friendship they may make, or any certificates of good character they may hold from Indian Agents, or other persons. . . .

The experience of the last four years, has taught us that paper treaties are productive of no permanent good, they are only made to be broken by the Indians the first opportunity. . . . A more permanent treaty than a paper one is required to be made for the better protection of our frontiers, and this expedition is expected to make the desired treaty within its jurisdiction and it is not to be made by Agents, Missionaries and Indian sympathizers, on paper and parchment, with pen, ink and pencil, but is to be made by soldiers and made on the mountains and plains and in the Valley of Harney Lake, Malheur and Silvies River, and with the musket and Bayonet and Carbine and Saber.[34]

Williams told his men to attempt broad-based genocide. He rejected the very notion of Native allies or neutrals, and he called for killing any and all Indians his men found. Mass murder, he proclaimed, was the "more permanent treaty than a paper one" required. And he ordered his officers to pursue genocide to the end, even ordering, presumably with grotesque whimsy, that they should commit cannibalism, if necessary, to do so. Each officer, he proclaimed, must "exhaus[t] every means in his power [to] overtake and punish [the Indians] as they deserve, even subsisting themselves and their men upon wild game, horseflesh, and *dead Indians*. . . . Depredations and cruelties must cease and treaties be respected, or the more permanent treaty will soon be closed by the extermination of their entire warlike tribes." This was not a one-off; Williams had long believed in a policy of exterminatory warfare. Accepting the surrender of Native men, he wrote elsewhere, was part of a "mistaken policy of extending too much leniency to a barbarous digger Indian."[35]

Williams killed Native people for at least twenty-five years, but he never achieved the scale of massacre that he hoped for (and ordered his men to pursue). The confirmed killings he wrote about were individual, typically surprise attacks on unaware or outnumbered Native men. Sometimes Williams killed as an officer in the U.S. Army. A few weeks before Williams ordered his men to commit genocide, they ambushed a Native fisherman in southern Oregon, gunning him down in cold blood and then eating his fish (a kind of murder and theft common in the Snake War in Oregon). Sometimes Williams killed as a civilian. One of the last primary sources he stuck into his autobiography was a letter describing his trip through the Great Plains in 1875, where he "met no Indians who were at open war with the whites. Yet had the satisfaction of killing [a] couple"—one man for chasing a bison too near Williams's campsite, the other man "on suspicion" because Williams thought the man looked like he might be thinking about stealing Williams's horse. And sometimes Williams killed as a volunteer, shooting down an unknown number of Native people during the invasions of the Port Orford region in 1851 and 1852.[36]

Williams was bald in his call for mass extermination, and in his contempt for laws and treaties. But his genocide order hid as well as revealed. Williams was writing from a position of weakness, not strength: he was resting his men after losing a pitched battle that had begun with a failed attempt at killing an adolescent boy and his caretaker (see below). Williams's declaration that there were "no friendly Indians" nearby was based

Loren Lyman Williams posed as an "Indian fighter," probably in the mid-1870s. Courtesy of the Douglas County Museum, Roseburg, Oregon.

in an abhorrent moral philosophy, not objective experience—if nothing else, there were other, more successful army contingents in southern and eastern Oregon, including John M. Drake's, that relied on Native fighters as scouts and auxiliaries. As for the "treaties [that must] be respected," most of the Northern Paiute/Numu polities Williams and his men were trying and failing to exterminate had not signed any treaties—not that Williams distinguished much between different Indian peoples.

Loren L. Williams's most famous act looked very different in his reports than it did in his journal. The story of the Silvies River Battle has remained more or less unchanged in most histories, from the second volume of Victor and Bancroft's *History of Oregon* in 1888 to Michno's *Deadliest Indian War in the West* in 2007. The official story, in brief, was that Williams and his troops were patrolling on foot for "Snake Indians" in southeast Oregon near Malheur Lake, spotted two Native men, and pursued them. Before Williams and his troops could catch the two, however, other Native people with horses and guns arrived. Williams and his men ended up conducting a slow, hours-long retreat under fire, killing fifteen of their pursuers while suffering only two casualties and no fatalities of their own—what Victor and Bancroft called "the best fighting of the season under the greatest difficulties." The story of this retreat was taken uncritically from Williams's letter to his commanding officer and repeated and repeated since.[37]

In the more detailed account in Williams's journal, certain troubling aspects of the story are clearer. The "two Indian men" were, in fact, a man and a boy, probably Northern Paiute/Numu people. Williams recalled: "The men were eager for [a] chase as this was the first sight we had had of a hostile Snake Indian, the most dreaded of all the Western Tribes. . . . We soon found ourselves gaining upon the Indians, and not long afterwards observed that one of them was a boy who appeared to be unable to make as fast progress as his larger companion. This was encouraging to the men and a greater effort on our part was made!"[38]

Before Williams and his men could run down and attack the boy and his caretaker, "two Indian horsemen came out of the swamp" to the rescue, pulling the man and boy onto horseback and whisking them away. Assuming that was the end of the matter, Williams called for a short rest, only to find more Native cavalry riding up on his position and harrying his forces—first (by his estimation) fourteen horsemen, then forty. Williams and his men were encircled and driven off.[39]

The presumably Northern Paiute/Numu fighters never closed for battle, instead taking potshots from the edge of firing range while keeping up a steady war cry. Williams assumed that this was because of the doughty resilience of his men, and there might have been some truth in his assertion that the Native fighters preferred to shoot only when they could dodge return fire, and then "glide away to . . . watch for another or more favorable opportunity." The Native fighters may well have valued their own lives more than the deaths of hapless Euro-American volunteers. Or they may have simply been achieving their goal of driving the U.S. Army away for the present, without needing to inflict lethal casualties.[40]

Williams's counts of the number of casualties his men inflicted appear to be a series of exaggerations. To historians after the fact, he claimed they had killed fifteen Native fighters. This was an inflation of his estimate in his journal—of ten casualties. But both numbers were probably incorrect—the guesses of men whose pride and persons had been wounded in an hours-long retreat. Unlike most other clashes recorded in his journal, Williams gave no account of how or by what means the casualties he claimed had been inflicted. His men had fired three hundred shots, and they felt sure they had killed at least ten people and wounded many more. But they had no proof. And Williams throughout his journal had a habit of presuming himself particularly effective at killing when there had been no Euro-Americans around to check his facts or his math.[41]

Beyond Williams, Euro-Americans in the Pacific Northwest often claimed to be especially deadly in retreat. While fleeing from the band of Native fishers his men had attacked in January 1848, William Stillwell claimed to have killed an uncountable several of his pursuers, each shot being lethal. "My gun was to be respected," he wrote, "and whenever it spoke, there was another good Indian in the land of 'The Happy Hunting Ground.'" Euro-American volunteers in the Rogue River War were nearly always "certain they killed some" whenever they retreated. Edward Steptoe, reporting on his famed and disorganized 1858 retreat, declared that that where the two seniormost officers were killed, "twelve dead Indians were counted" and "many others were seen to fall." Who did the counting was unclear—after all, the Euro-American soldiers had fled. Williams's claims to a heroic and deadly retreat were part of a long tradition of military fantasy, probably imagined lethality as a salve for punctured pride. Skepticism of these kinds of claims is necessary—and not just in the Pacific Northwest.[42]

Noting the difficulties he and other companies fighting the Snake War had in finding the Native people they were hunting—and carefully omitting his recent experience finding and running away from a Native force—Loren L. Williams late in 1865 suggested that the recent end of the Civil War should enable the import of technologies of racial violence from the South: "To relieve the Troops in the field from *great embarrassment,* and to *insure* the *extermination* or *capture* of the last *remnant* of the hostile tribes of Oregon during the summer of 1866, I would most *earnestly recommend* that *Bloodhounds* from the Southern States, be brought to the Country, and employed to search out the Savages in their mountain fastnesses." Williams's suggestion was in a way an evolution of Isaac Stevens's 1854 hopes for riflemen in snowshoes—a yearning for some tool to overcome Native fighters' superior knowledge of the terrain and environment.[43]

There is no record that Williams's suggestion was widely acted on— that the dogs trained to hunt escaping enslaved persons were redeployed to the Northwest to hunt Native people. But the end of the Civil War did shift the responsibilities for the ongoing Snake War back onto regular troops, rather than just those recruited locally. By most accounts, they too pursued exterminatory violence. As in Wright's campaigns of the 1850s, the regulars were occasionally more effective than the volunteers, but about as brutal—still taking scalps, still killing children, and still shooting Native leaders when they "tried to escape."[44]

Williams and his men murdered when they had the opportunity, but they mostly failed in their attempts at genocide—outwitted or outfought by the Native peoples they were trying to kill, like the volunteers at Hungry Hill a decade before. They would have committed genocidal war crimes like those perpetrated during the Bear River Massacre if they could have. Historians should not mistake incompetence for morality.

The Snake War attracted less attention—and far less controversy—than the Pacific Northwest wars of the 1840s and 1850s that made up the War on Illahee. The Snake War in the early 1860s was fought mostly by local volunteers hired as regulars on the federal payroll. The killings attempted and sometimes perpetrated by soldiers enlisted as part of the Snake War did not attract the same clashes over compensation as the volunteer forays of the 1850s, since most of the killers were counted as Civil War veterans. Although there were occasional frictions about violence seen as unhelpfully wanton by some military figures, these disagreements did not endanger anyone's pay or place in posterity significantly. Coming after the wars that were seen by pioneer historians as essential to the origins of Oregon and Washington, the Snake War did not need the same level of attention, veneration, or equivocation from those invested in forging a mythic past. Euro-American media did not durably latch onto any singular narratives from the general war the way they did in covering the Modoc or Nez Perce Wars of the 1870s. Perhaps most critically, the U.S. Civil War of 1861–65 loomed (and looms) so large in the American historical imagination that the Snake War is even more invisible in its shadow than the wars of the 1850s.[45]

Although American conquest of Native land and war on Native independence continued for decades in the Pacific Northwest (and much of the rest of the country), pioneer history writers in the region tended to focus on the "Indian wars" of the 1850s. In large part, this was because those wars punctuated the origin stories of Oregon and Washington, including how residents of both would distinguish "pioneers" from later settlers. Posterity and profit for volunteers were still at stake for the wars of the 1850s. And the infamies of those wars—particularly a few famous signature acts of horror—presented a stumbling block for simplistic heroic histories, which different would-be historians reckoned with in disparate ways. The war crimes of the Snake War were more easily ignored.

CHAPTER EIGHT

Settler Colonial Sin-Eaters and
the Isolation of Atrocity

THOMAS JEFFERSON CRAM, A talented engineer and mediocre
mapmaker, became a surveyor in more ways than he bargained for. After years spent mapping the Pacific coastline of
lands claimed by the United States, in June 1855 Cram was
sent to complete a topographical memoir of the far West. By the time he
submitted it, in March 1858, his report had also become an ad hoc investigation into the origins of the wars in the Pacific Northwest over those
years. Drawing from interviews with other army officers (and perhaps
guided by his patron, General John E. Wool), Cram found credible ways
to pin the errors and expenses of the War on Illahee on political leaders
like Isaac I. Stevens and the "self-constituted volunteer service," thereby
rendering the U.S. Army blameless. He disparaged volunteers and had a
particular scorn for gold miners—among whom there were "some well-
disposed persons," but "many of the most unprincipled and ungovernable
white men from all countries."[1]

Cram blamed miners particularly in his discussion of the onset of the
Yakima War:

Hundreds of whites went flocking to the auriferous district
[near Fort Colville] . . . and as the whites passed, some of them
committed excess and outrages of the grossest kinds upon the

hitherto unoffending Indians of the very tribes the proceedings of the council [led by I. I. Stevens] had so much and so recently disturbed. The bare recital of some of the crimes committed by these Anglo-Saxon devils, in human shape, is sufficient to cause the blood of every virtuous man, whether of red or white skin, to boil with deep indignation. They were not satisfied with stealing the horses and cattle of the Indians, but they claimed the privilege of taking and ravishing Indian women and maidens *ad libitum* [at their pleasure]. What wonder, then, that the Indians who had been so grossly outraged should have retaliated, as they did, by killing some half dozen of these miscreants?[2]

Accurate summations like these were present only in Cram's discussions of the more roguish elements among volunteers and miners. Those he perceived as part of the regular armed forces were not subject to the same scorn. The southern Oregon exploratory killings by Silas Casey in 1851 he framed as a "smart successful conflict"; Joseph Lane in 1853 was a "gallant general" of "sound judgement." But Cram denounced the "notorious Ben Wright" for having engaged in "infernal acts of cruelty"—that is, his well-known acts of rape and murder in southern Oregon—and suggested his violent death at the hands of one of the women he had probably abused was "just retribution for his own treachery." Cram similarly disparaged Lamerick, Lupton, and others for having started the wars of Oregon, accusations accurate in their essentials if perhaps debatable in their specifics. And he blamed the spread of war in Washington not only on the wanton violence of miners but on the pecuniary pursuits of volunteers attacking erstwhile "friendly Indians." When Stevens, Cram reported, "sends an armed force of volunteer[s] into a fertile valley in which the Indians are known to have fine, fat beeves and excellent horses in herds of great abundance ... it would be a very easy matter, upon the smallest pretext, to draw or provoke the Indians into a fight, and afterwards justify the act, particularly as in such cases there is only one side whose story is seldom, if ever, told to the world."[3]

Cram, like his patron John E. Wool, was not a humanitarian, nor did he have much sympathy for Native people as such. He predicted but did not necessarily mourn that "another less fortunate race will be crushed—blotted out of existence—to make the way clear for the 'Bostons.'" He echoed claims of grotesque Indigenous Otherness, including accusations of cannibalism. In a later text he wrote eagerly that military funding to beat back the "cupidity and hostility of the red men" was imperative for the "Northwest to be filled up" with "at least twenty millions of civilized [C]hristian people." Native people, he declared, should be colonized on reservations, where "the practice should be to have a sufficient [military] force at all times immediately on the spot to prevent encroachment and to enforce obedience." The problem, for Cram, was not with the conquest but with a particular subset of the would-be conquerors—"bad citizens" who fomented unnecessary war and lacked respect for the military, rather than "orderly" settlers who would be "civilized [C]hristian people."[4]

Some early histories of the Pacific Northwest reckoned with the infamous thefts, rapes, murders, and other wanton violence of the 1850s more or less as Cram did. Written to valorize and venerate, these histories resigned whatever violent or avaricious Euro-American acts they had to discuss to the actions of a blemished few. Cram's official report was not necessarily a part of these discussions—it was prefaced upon publication in 1859 by a denunciation from Secretary of War John B. Floyd (a Virginia patrician famous mostly for incompetence, treason, and possibly malfeasance in the 1860s). Floyd deemed Cram's report "irrelevant," decried the author for his "animadversions toward public functionaries," and declared that the whole was "in no sense sanctioned or endorsed" by the War Department. But although these attacks helped drive Cram's report into obscurity, other military and national critiques of notorious volunteer incidents nonetheless had to be dealt with by early historians.[5]

For some settlers and historians, criticism of the worst excesses of pioneer violence could be a means of absolving settler society as a whole. Euro-American writers in the 1800s often bemoaned the more infamous atrocities committed by those at the fringe of settler society while nonetheless reaffirming the divine righteousness of manifest destiny. They were thus able to reap the fruits of settler colonialism while blaming a small subset for its moral costs. This instrumentality does not necessarily indicate duplicity; no doubt many Euro-Americans were earnestly horrified by reports of pioneer rape, murder, and mutilation. But condemnation of the violent fringe also served to absolve America as a whole. The volunteers who committed the worst of the atrocities were turned into what I call "settler colonial sin-eaters"—the violent few, typically framed as poor outsiders, whose condemnation could rhetorically render blameless the Euro-American majority that had profited from that violence.

Religious overtones were famously a part of justifying settler colo-nialism, from the calls to manifest destiny to what Elwood Evans in 1893 called "the American ... 1st great commandment, to subdue the Soil." Religion, of course, has a long history of being used to justify all sorts of violence, including genocide. In the American Pacific Northwest, reli-gion was only sometimes invoked in the 1850s by the people perpetrat-ing the direct violence of settler colonialism (who often preferred racial, patriotic, or simply pecuniary justifications). Religion appeared much more in later legitimations of the land taking. And religious language went well beyond specific evocations—pioneer histories took on tropes, iconography, and zeal similar to more explicitly religious writings. Pio-neers had to be paragons, which meant that any unworthy acts had to be someone else's fault.[6]

I thus borrow the term *sin-eater* from traditions of folk Christianity, wherein families would hire someone—often someone poor and margin-alized—to ritually consume and take into themselves the sins of a dead loved one. As scholar Jane Levi has shown, northern European sin-eating practices (sometimes imported to rural early America) were inflected and sometimes inflicted by class—the sin-eaters were internal outsiders, at least sometimes exploited for their spiritual labor by local economic elites. The metaphorical line I am drawing to the subset of settlers blamed for the sins of the whole was similarly shaped by class.[7]

Only a few of the colonial killers in the Pacific Northwest accepted a metaphorical role as settler colonial sin-eaters; as I will discuss in chapter 9, former volunteers led largely successful campaigns against histories that accurately described the wantonness of their violence. But with or without the willing participation of those being blamed, for generations boosters and many historians of the pioneer Pacific Northwest have sought to transfer the sins of settlers to the actions of an especially murderous (and often impoverished) fringe. Those wishing to valorize pioneers as a whole, and ignore their broad complicity in murderous invasions, can always blame the violence they cannot ignore on a few worst offenders and avert their eyes from broadly supported horrific norms.[8]

In 1856 George Ambrose, the southern Oregon Indian agent, used just this tactic in his official response to (accurate) reports of widespread wanton murders of Native people: "While I am forced to admit some acts of violence have been perpetrated by some bad, irresponsible and reckless white men upon the Indians, our population as a general thing are composed of good men. . . . It is a foul slander upon the settlers of

Oregon to thus accuse them. The people in this valley deserved peace and sought to maintain it by every means in their power until forbearance ceased to be a virtue any longer with them. I am speaking of the mass of the people, not of the acts of a few transient individuals."[9]

A broad-based project of genocide could be rhetorically contorted into the "acts of a few transient individuals." As the Pacific Northwest lawyer and newspaper editor William Lair Hill put it in 1883, "Leaving out the small element of gold-hunters and the smaller one of reckless adventurers—classes inconsiderable in number in comparison to the true Oregonian of the earlier days ... the pioneers were strong and brave." History makers unwilling to baldly lie or face the full truth could simply "leave out" those whose actions they disagreed with—leaving the "true Oregonians" untouched by their sins.[10]

One of the earliest major histories of Oregon, Herbert O. Lang's *History of the Willamette Valley* (1885), used the perfidy of volunteers and vigilantes to differentiate them from "the Pioneers of Oregon" whom the author exalted. Building his book from primary sources, pioneer informants, and personal reminiscences, Lang hoped to commemorate and celebrate the "Discovery and Settlement by White Men" of the Pacific Northwest. Lang wanted to redeem the "virtuous" settlers from the violent reputation Oregonians had acquired on the national stage. Lang had hinted at this in his ghostwritten *History of Southern Oregon* (1884), bemoaning famous episodes of wanton violence, including the Lupton Massacre. But here he was unusual in the reach and extent of his narrative and source base, and in his often ham-handed efforts to grasp at Native peoples' motivations. *History of the Willamette Valley* was Lang's attempt to square a heroic pioneer history with the torrid violence in some of his sources.[11]

Like most White intellectuals of his day, Lang believed that "Indians" were an inferior race rapidly headed to extinction in an unavoidable Darwinian struggle with Euro-Americans. Native people were, in his view, "so warlike, so brave, so intelligent, and so numerous" but were fatally undermined by "treachery ... the predominating trait of the Indian character." Although Lang assumed and supported an inevitable Caucasian triumph, he recognized that Native resisters were fighting to defend their homelands. Lang proclaimed that the wars in southern Oregon, and by inference across the Pacific Northwest, "sprang from the one great fountain head of all our Indian wars—the aggressiveness of the higher civilization and the natural resistance of a warlike people to the

encroachments of a superior race. It was an effort ... to expel white in-
truders from the home of their ancestors, superinduced by special acts of
ill-treatment by the invaders [in some cases]; and [in others] an attempt
to ward off the same evils [Native people] saw had befallen the tribes of
other regions." Lang's appalling beliefs about race did not prevent him
from determining that often Native causes for war were largely defensive, predicated on present outrages or accurate visions of the future—or
both.[12]

Lang divided White settlers in the early Northwest into "two classes
of persons, rogues and honest men"—or, as he put it elsewhere, "invaders"
and "pioneers." His heroes were White missionaries and administrators,
gentlemen whom he saw as fair dealers—whether British fur trade factors
or American governors and generals. He also praised Native peacemakers
and negotiators—at least those who, like Peo-Peo-Mox-Mox ("killed
while unjustly a prisoner of the ... white[s]"), were tragically dead rather
than inconveniently alive. The archetypal buckskin-clad frontiersmen, and
the rough-and-ready volunteer soldiers more generally, were far from heroic in Lang's telling. They were "a class of wild, reckless and brutal men"
for whom "Indian fighting was one of their chief accomplishments." Setting gentlemen like himself apart from the violent conquest of Oregon
territory, Lang condemned trappers and frontiersmen as "the lowest stra-
tum of American society ... guilty of many acts of injustice."[13]

Lang's assessment of "rogues and honest men" shaped how he narrated racial conflict. Where missionaries such as the Whitmans had
"fallen before the treacherous blows of ungrateful savages," the Rogue
River War, Yakima War, and most other "trouble with Indians" were
caused by "wanton murder" inflicted by violent racists. He framed such
violence as inevitable and regrettable,

> but a continuation of that fierce race conflict which began with
> the first advent of settlers into the valley, and ended only with
> the extermination or removal of the native proprietors of the
> soil. [In the Rogue River valley], more than at any other place,
> had race prejudice been developed to its extreme pitch by four
> successive years of conflict. Indians were both despised and
> hated. The least "insolence" on their part met with swift retribu-
> tion, while on the other hand, indignities put upon them, even,
> in instances, to the taking of life, went uncondemned by the bet-
> ter portion of the community, and by the more irresponsible and

less morally developed, were approved as being "good enough for them."[14]

Lang's perception of who counted as "brave pioneers" shaped the extent to which he was willing to face foul deeds from settlers. In contrast to his discussion of southern Oregon, Lang's story of the Maxon Massacre aligned with the false narratives put forward in the late 1850s: "Governor Stevens . . . was fearful that if something was not done at once to humble the hostiles, they would corrupt the Nez Perces, Spokanes, Colvilles, and Coeur d'Alenes, and a most powerful combination be formed against the whites. Quiet had been restored to the Sound, the last sign of war being a brief battle on the N[i]squally early in April, between Indians and Captain Maxon's company." The wanton killing of noncombatant Nisqually people was tendentiously portrayed as a battle—though it is unclear if Lang, unlike some of his contemporaries, knew he was writing a falsehood.[15]

By contrast, Lang was particularly sharp about the Lupton Massacre. He framed the perpetrators as intemperately violent and lacking in class as well as decorum:

> On the seventh of October, 1855, a party of men, principally miners and men-about-town, in Jacksonville organized them-selves. . . . Major James A. Lupton . . . was a man of no experi-ence in bush fighting, but was rash and headstrong. It is the prevailing opinion that he was led into the affair through a wish to court popularity, which is almost the only incentive that could have occurred to him. Certainly, it could not have been plunder; and the mere love of fighting Indians, which drew the greater part of the force together, was, perhaps, absent in his case. The reason why the particular band at Butte Creek was selected as victims also appears a mystery, although the circumstances of their location being accessible and their numbers small, possibly were the ruling considerations. This band of Indians appear to have behaved themselves tolerably.[16]

John Beeson had written dolefully of broad community involvement in the killings; some of the most notorious murderers, like Martin Angell, had been farmers. Lang recorded the Lupton party as "principally miners and men-about-town," and thus falsely separated them from the broader pioneer community. But Lang was unblinking when it came to the massacre itself:

Lupton and his party fired a volley into the crowded encampment, following up the sudden and totally unexpected attack by a close encounter ... and the Indians were driven away or killed without making much resistance. These facts are matters of evidence, as are also the killing of several sq__ws, one or more old decrepit men, and a number, probably small, of children....

Accounts vary so widely that by some it has been termed a heroic attack, and others have called it an indiscriminate butchery of defenseless and peaceful natives. To temporize with such occurrences does not become those who seek the truth only, and the world would be better could such deeds meet at once the proper penalty and be known by their proper name.[17]

Lang suggested Lupton's men should not have been allowed to get away with murder. And like many Euro-Americans, he mourned the counterattack most of all:

As usual, the storm of barbaric vengeance fell upon the heads of the innocent and defenseless. Swift and cruel was the revenge of the Indians for this great and unexpected outrage which had been committed upon them, and the massacre of defenseless settlers, unwarned of their danger, is one of the saddest pages of Oregon's pioneer history. Language can not too strongly condemn the act which precipitated such a bloody scene, and much of the time and breath spent in abuse of General Wool and execration of the Indians should have been devoted to the denunciation of this brutal and unwarranted act.[18]

Lang's condemnation of the Lupton Affair was unusually unsparing, though even Lang conformed to the custom that only the killings of White people would be labeled *massacres*—even "indiscriminate butchery" of Native children he would not call a massacre. Most of the rest of the chapter was standard fare, a distorted depiction of pioneer heroes triumphing in the face of numerically superior "red devils." The book as a whole focused on stories of White heroism, faith, and agricultural production, and it included several hundred pages of thumbnail pioneer biographies. But passages like the excoriation of Lupton may have been what so badly tanked Lang's sales.[19]

Herbert Lang and his publisher, George Himes, had bet big that a large pioneer audience would want to buy a thoroughgoing history of the region—especially one in which they themselves would be listed in a place of honor. But the book provoked immediate outcry, among both those Lang classed as "rogues" and the "better portion" that had refused to restrain them. *History of the Willamette Valley* helped spur the creation of a regional group for volunteer veterans of the War on Illahee: the Indian War Veterans of the North Pacific Coast, who made it their first order of business to condemn the book and its author (see chapter 9). With a high page count and low sales, *History of the Willamette Valley* flopped, hard enough to sink Himes's first publishing business entirely.[20]

Hubert Howe Bancroft's mammoth *History of Oregon* (1888), ghostwritten largely by the local historian Frances Fuller Victor and ghost-edited by Judge Matthew Deady, also used the famous incidents of Euro-American volunteer depredations to separate the violent fringe from pioneer posterity. Bancroft and Victor balanced moderate respect for the historical record with a heady mix of Darwinian scientific racism and manifest destiny. "The fate of the savages was fixed beforehand; and that not by volunteers, white or black," they wrote, "but by almighty providence, ages before their appearing, just as we of the present dominant race must fade before a stronger, whenever such a one is sent." As Victor had publicly put it in 1871, "Decidedly, I am not . . . sympathetic on the Indian question." To Victor, average settlers (men and women alike) were heroes "whose brave deeds during these savage wars of southern Oregon must forever remain unrecorded"—and Bancroft argued for the same. Most settler violence they either downplayed or framed as justified retribution for Native aggression.[21]

Victor and Bancroft blamed the more famous episodes of unprovoked killings by settlers on a small subset who alone acted "with the avowed purpose of waging a war of extermination against the Indians without respect to age or sex." The "mangled bodies . . . [of] mostly old men, women, and children" found in the aftermath of the Lupton Massacre of 1855, Victor and Bancroft wrote, "incited great indignation among the better class of white men." The "better class" could include almost anyone and almost everyone. Where Lang had decried broad swathes of the territory and the people of the Pacific Northwest when writing of atrocity, Victor and Bancroft portrayed such violence as anonymous and anomalous, the work of a few bad men to which the "better class" was unattached.[22]

The historian Frances Fuller Victor as she appeared in the
author photo she used multiple times in the late 1800s.
Courtesy of the Oregon Historical Society.

Bancroft, after all, was in the book *business*—and pioneers were potential customers. As historian Richard White has flintily noted, Bancroft
"was a man who quite literally made history pay, and history that pays is
often not a particularly critical history." In pursuit of making history pay,
Bancroft sent door-to-door salesmen to the Pacific Northwest, offering
books of pioneer posterity as one major class of offerings. Records from
Homer Jenne, a Northwest book peddler who worked in the "subscription
part of the business," show that salability to everyday pioneers was a key
part of Bancroft's profitable strategy—and probably a key influence on the
writing of history in the era more generally.[23]

According to John C. Ainsworth, the Oregon steamboat captain and
pioneer, Bancroft tried to make money in production as well as sales. In a

semiprivate autobiography written for his descendants, Ainsworth claimed that Bancroft had interviewed him for both *The History of Oregon* and a planned book to be titled "The Chronicles of the Kings." Bancroft, Ainsworth alleged, had insisted on a "large sum" of money from him in both cases—possibly for preorders, possibly as an out-and-out bribe. Ainsworth claimed that after he refused to pay, he was excised from both volumes. He nursed a "determination not to have anything to do with Mr. Bancroft" into old age. Bancroft was infamous for scheming to get pioneers across the West Coast to pay for prominence in his attempted opus, "The Chronicles of the Kings"; Ainsworth's claims suggest there may have been pay-to-play dynamics in Bancroft's other historical works, too. This was common at the time; in 1867 Oregon state legislator Isaac Cox apparently attempted to solicit pioneers to pay for pride of place in his own never-published Oregon history, shortly before he was voted out of office.[24]

The distrust between Bancroft and Pacific Northwest pioneers was mutual. The scuttlebutt in 1903 was that the Bancroft Library would "remain closed to all North West investigators so long as Bancroft [was] living. There are too many stolen Mss. to invite North West Coast people there." Whether or not these accusations were true, Bancroft seems to have stolen at least some materials from "North West Coast people." The library's response to requests to return documents that had been loaned by Northwest historian Clarence B. Bagley was a proclamation that said materials would remain " 'as safe as possible' in the Bancroft collection," rather than being returned. But whatever the extent of mistrust or corruption behind the scenes, in their writing on the Northwest Bancroft and Victor were effusive in their praise, prolific in their name-dropping, and driven to make their history pay.[25]

Lang had carefully criticized a few among the "better sort"; in *History of Oregon*, Bancroft and Victor instead depicted the "better classes" as entirely blameless. Both books, however, declared the wanton violence against Native people that had been broadly supported during the 1850s and beyond to be inevitable *and* isolated to volunteers, leaving the rest of settler society innocent. Victor and Bancroft framed what they called a "history of aboriginal extermination" as a regretful inevitability, which the "better classes" (usually cordoned off from the "Indians wars" chapters) had little hand in.[26]

There were those, even among the southern Oregon volunteers, who embraced a version of the sort of distinctions that Lang, Bancroft, and

Benjamin Franklin Dowell, probably in the 1860s or 1870s.
Courtesy of the Oregon Historical Society.

Victor proposed. Benjamin Franklin Dowell was a packer, newspaperman, and former slaveholder who in the 1850s sold supplies to various
volunteer companies—first in southern Oregon, then in eastern Washington. Like Charles S. Drew, he attracted opprobrium at the time for
what many believed was some mix of usury and embezzlement. Dowell
spent much of the 1860s and 1870s as a lawyer trying to extract money
for the volunteers (and himself) from various government bodies. But although professionally Dowell pushed hard for volunteer claims and pay,
he still tried to differentiate honest men from rogues in some of his historical accounts.[27]

　　When he was interviewed for posterity by Bancroft and company,
Dowell framed himself as having been an honorable man among villains
in 1853 southern Oregon. Dowell claimed he had pushed against the
calls to "exterminate the Indian!" Particularly, he recounted his fruitless

efforts trying to keep a Jacksonville mob from lynching a nine-year-old. He fixed the blame for the murder of this child on the notorious Martin Angell, who had pushed hardest for child murder. As proof of the difference between him and men like Angell, Dowell claimed that he had been able to carry the mails throughout the period because the local Native leaders "wouldn't hurt a paper man and one who had tried to save a 'tenas tillicum,' little p_p__se." Martin Angell was the rogue, Dowell one of the honest men. In this context, Dowell's part in the brutality inflicted on Peo-Peo-Mox-Mox and other Native people went unmentioned.[28]

In later life, Dowell argued that all Americans should have suffrage and equal rights "without regard for race, color, or sex"—the only way to be "not only free in name but in fact." This unusually enlightened position may have shaped his interviews—his memories of his younger self filtered through his later curve toward justice. Or he may have been responding to his audience (especially since Dowell followed his call for universal suffrage regardless of race or gender with an appeal to stereotypes about "savages [who] compel their women to do all the menial labor, and still give them no voice in the affairs of the nation"). When speaking to those looking for gentlemen among rogues, Dowell told a story of gentle manliness. When speaking to Elwood Evans, a historian hoping for stories of martial glory, Dowell would sing a different tune.[29]

Celebrations seem to have found more fertile ground than critique. Jesse Applegate's most famous work, his 1876 paper "A Day with the Cow Column in 1843," embraced the tropes of triumphant manifest destiny. Pioneers like him, he wrote, were "singular people": "No other race of men with the means at their command would undertake so great a journey [as the overland trail across the continent]. The way lies over trackless wastes, wide and deep rivers, ragged and lofty mountains, and is beset with hostile savages. Yet . . . they are always found ready and equal to the occasion, and always conquerors. May we not call them men of destiny?"[30]

But Jesse Applegate's unfinished and unpublished attempts at Oregon history were more critical. As he got older, particularly after setbacks and betrayals by friends, he came to critique not only individual atrocities but the broader one-sidedness of Euro-American history. Applegate's description of the Lupton Massacre was unsparing—but, notably, turned James Lupton from a newly elected territorial delegate into "a packer," and thus (from Applegate's perspective) more of a low-class outsider:

"Some 30 or more, ruffians under the lead of a packer, came out of Jacksonville in the evening, sent spies to the Indian camp to ascertain its position and that there was no *dangerous* Indians in it. And at daylight next morning rushed upon it slaughtering indiscriminately male and female old age and helpless infancy. . . . A small boy who escaped from the Massacre found his way to the hunters in the Mountains and told them the whites had killed all that were dear to them. These infuriated Indians did what of course it was expected them to do[—]rushed upon the defen[s]eless settlements and committed a long list of savage atrocities. None of them exceeding in cold-blooded fiendishness the provocation.

But in this like the thousand other cases[:] The Indian atrocities were largely commented on and wide spread[,] his provocation not even hinted at.[31]

At least when it came to violence against Native people neither he nor his friends had taken part in, Jesse Applegate was unusually willing to see the wrongs in wanton violence. Labeling Lupton's killings a "Massacre" and equal in "cold-blooded fiendishness" to the revenge killings they provoked, Applegate even began to plumb the vernacular structures and silences that kept such stories one-sided.

Jesse Applegate's planned critical history of Oregon was never completed or published. This may have been a deliberate choice, out of a sense of decorum—"the pioneer code"—or because he was sick of the whole enterprise. As Applegate put it to a friend, "Oregon . . . has no history at present worth a student[']s five minutes attention, it has produced no new idea, or any man much out of the common to give it a history in the future." Applegate's "Notes upon Oregon History," with its sharp critique of pioneering in the Pacific Northwest, ended up hidden in archival collections. "A Day with the Cow Column in 1843," his celebration of manifest destiny, became one of the most famous records of the Oregon Trail.[32]

Granville O. Haller's history, "The Indian War of 1855–6, in Washington and Oregon," similarly does not seem to have found a publisher or an audience in his lifetime. The book was in some ways a spiritual successor to Haller's more successful work, *The Dismissal of Major Granville O. Haller*, his account of how he came to be dismissed from the army for disloyalty during the Civil War that was part of his successful campaign to have his name cleared and rank restored. Like *Dismissal*, Haller's history of the "Indian War of 1855–6" was meant to exonerate as well as educate—after some success as a politician and a long military career, he remained stung by his most famous act in the state of Washington being nicknamed "Haller's Defeat." Haller's approach departed from Lang's, Victor's, or Bancroft's, who washed their hands of wanton White violence, and from Isaac I. Stevens's, Charles Drew's, or Elwood Evans's, who denied its very existence.[33]

The eventual historical narrative Haller created was unusually honest about the horror of pioneer violence, but it was nonetheless supportive of exterminatory warfare, especially in what he called a "war of races":

> War is simply savage or civilized Barbarism! Humanity and moral law are out of joint in War times. They cut no figure in a war of races. In a War between the Red and the Pale Faces, there will be no peace until the One or the other Race has been effectually crippled and subdued. . . .
>
> Until paralyzed by fire and sword, accompanied necessarily with the devastation and [horrors] of war; until their means for carrying on war are exhausted or destroyed; until their unyielding spirits are broken and subdued; in brief, until absolute submission to the will of the stronger Race is affected, forbearance and generous conditions are premature and only procrastinate the final result. Wars in Asia and Africa, as well as our own experience with the Natives in the Americas, confirm and illustrate this subject. . . .
>
> Think of it! Our Pilgrim Fathers without warning fell upon the Aborigin[es] of Massachusetts, and reveled in blood and carnage until tired, when such as escaped their fury were seized as Prisoners of War and sold at Public Auctions for servants or slaves for life.[34]

Haller voiced a position that had been common during the wars he discussed—certainly Isaac I. Stevens and George Wright had said as much in their official letters to one another. And Haller connected the wanton violence he had taken part in with the broad sweep of global colonialism and American history, using the killings and enslavements inflicted by the "Pilgrim Fathers" as a perhaps exculpatory comparison.

Like Jesse Applegate, Haller noted the hypocrisy of treating violence against Native people as righteous while treating violence by Native people as treacherous: "We read of the contemptable Indians,—the deceitful! the treacherous!! the blood thirsty Indians!!! Ad nauseum. But notwithstanding these historical stereotyped phrases, the Writer's observations and experience in active Indian Wars, lead him to regard such obnoxious expressions equally applicable to White individuals, whose fancied wrongs or, perhaps whose experience, have embittered them against the Indians. Recall, for a moment, Peo-mox-mox [*sic*] Dead! "They that have done the deed are honourable." Neverth[e]less, such deeds, by our fellow citizens, cannot fail to rouse the flush of shame."[35]

Even within his justification of war as "civilized Barbarism," Granville O. Haller still condemned acts that he considered beyond the pale—like the unjust killing of Peo-Peo-Mox-Mox. In contrast with his Shakespearean denunciation of "White individuals" who had killed prisoners, Haller framed his erstwhile Native adversaries as patriots defending their homelands:

> It is not love for war that induces [the Indians] to take the war path, but their love for their homes, and their independent habits. It is the conflict of civilization with savage life that worries them, and drives them to arms—the code of last resort. . . .
>
> And, if we are candid, we must admit that the Indians of Washington and Oregon are entitled to some commendation for their patriotic spirit in resisting the tyranny of civilization— if our Revolutionary Fathers were in resisting the tyranny of Royalty—for we find they were loyal to their Indian customs, and rights, [and] fought for them.[36]

Here and elsewhere, Haller was unusually clear-eyed about the motivations of many of the Native people he had spent his life fighting, depicting at least a few figures villainized elsewhere for their war on Euro-American invaders as "mak[ing] a last desperate effort to save [their] Country and people from the baneful presence of the whites." Haller saw race war as inevitable but horrible, and he was far less willing than almost any other Euro-American historian of the period to gloss over the violence of the War on Illahee.[37]

Haller never got his Indian wars book published. His Civil War book was a success, and his book of unfounded conspiracy theories surrounding the 1859 "Pig War" between American and British settlers at least found a printer. But not so his critical take on the wars of 1855–56. Though cordial in letters with other pioneer historians, he expressed disappointment at those who "yielded up the vital part of Indian history, by curtailing the truths."[38]

Too many books, Haller complained, were "*ex-parte* and a plea to excuse, if not justify, the horrible facts of History." He warned historical novelist Eva Emery Dye that books of Oregon history had to be "read with many grains of allowance. . . . It is needless for us to deny—history testifies to the fact—that our Pioneers were not Saints. As soon as they believed themselves strong enough to overpower the Natives, they treated them like the Hebrews in their migration treated the Heathen inhabitants Wherever they located. Of course, such facts are not the most agreeable for the Descendants of Pioneers of the XIX Century—such statements will not be popular with them, will even be, as they have often been denied, but are nevertheless *True!*" Such assertions were especially unacceptable to supporters of the more notorious volunteers, those who had been blamed by Lang, Bancroft, Victor, and other historians for the few "horrible facts" of pioneering that could not be avoided.[39]

Historians of colonialism, and indeed historians broadly, must be mindful of the ways markets shaped how and whether histories were written and published. Truths about the War on Illahee didn't sell in the nineteenth-century Pacific Northwest. But there were some frictions over how much and what kind of deception was warranted in pursuit of a heroic history. Applegate and Haller were too honest for print. Lang, Victor, and especially Bancroft attempted to meet hagiographic standards for pioneer history by containing the unseemly Euro-American violence to a marginal few—often picking the volunteers who had been the most publicly and wantonly murderous. But those volunteers wanted special honors, not accurate critiques, for the roles they had played in the conquest of the Pacific Northwest. They refused to be sin-eaters. There was money, fame, and honor at stake. And the volunteers and their allies organized to get all three.

CHAPTER NINE

Indian War Veterans and the
Battle for Northwest History

T HE WASHINGTON PIONEER ASSOCIATION was initially unblushing
in its support for genocide. In the first recorded speech inau-
gurating the organization in 1884, Judge Francis Henry reflected on the history of the region. Since 1846, Henry
proclaimed, "great and wonderful changes have been wrought by the
hand of man." Among the pioneer achievements he listed: "*The savages
have been exterminated,* the wilderness subjugated, three States and seven
Territories, with a present population of some two millions, have been
organized from this domain as parts of the American Union, whose dominion is here undisputed. ... This is the argument of our Association.
We have organized ourselves into a society for the reason that we have
witnessed, participated in, and in some measure contributed towards reclaiming a portion of the earth from nature and opening it up to the use
and enjoyment of civilized men from our own race."[1]

Elwood Evans gave the keynote address the following year. As was
typical for such an address, Evans lavished praise on the pioneers
and celebrated the changes they had unleashed. A major purpose of pioneer meetings was to gather (as Francis Henry had put it) "for the purpose of exchanging mutual congratulations." On this occasion, Evans
praised himself and the gathered throng as "pioneers in the real sense of
the word—'Soldiers who have cleared the way for the advance of an

army.' . . . Dedicated to the Americanization of the wilderness." The notion that "the Native race . . . had proprietary rights to its lands or rivers or seas" was mere "sentimentalism [to be] repudiated. Practical experience," Evans proclaimed, "teaches that American supremacy . . . can only be extended by Americans, utilizing the whole continent as the homes of American men, women and children." In only slightly cagier terms than Henry, Evans expressed the same support for a murderously White Northwest.[2]

Evans's attention to the martial roots of the term *pioneer,* when applied to those who arrived in the Pacific Northwest before 1860, matched the predilections of many who attempted to craft the history of Euro-American settlement in the area. There were several former volunteers among the founders of the Washington Pioneer Association. C. C. Hewitt, who had led lethal raids and executed men without trial in the Puget Sound region, was the first vice president. Benjamin Franklin Shaw, who had commanded mass killings of Cayuse/Liksiyu and other Native people at Grand Ronde Valley, was the second vice president and one of the authors of the organization's constitution. They had a stake in the martial prowess of pioneering, and in defending local volunteers like themselves as righteous.[3]

In some of the early transactions of the Washington Pioneer Association, there was an edge of defensiveness, as in an 1888 speech from Judge Orange Jacobs:

> It must be remembered that from the same wild valley or dark woods in which ascended the smoke from the humble cabin of the pioneer, there also ascended the smoke from the wigwam and the council fire of the savage. . . . The Indian never chose an open fight. Ambush was his rule. The poisoned arrow or the deadly bullet came from the covert of a thicket, the shade of a tree or the protection of a rock. He was ever ready to start up, like a felon wolf, at midnight in a war of extermination. When he was apparently the most friendly, and his seeming friendship the most demonstrative, there was the greatest danger.[4]

By insisting Native people rather than Euro-Americans were inherently duplicitous and always ready to commit genocide, Jacobs could justify whatever act of pioneer violence might come up. "The pioneer," he proclaimed, "was in constant danger from savage beasts and still more savage men. . . . You say he was cruel; we say he was but obeying the law of self-preservation." In general, the early speakers at the Washington Pioneer Society wanted pioneers to have the credit but not the blame for their conquest of Native lands and peoples.[5]

Like Elwood Evans, many members of the Oregon Pioneer Association connected *pioneering* to its martial roots. Prominent Indian war volunteers like James Nesmith and John Minto took up leadership positions. In 1876 Nesmith, too, underlined the martial roots of the term *pioneer*, speaking of his emigrant wagon train as a "gallant battalion" ready to do battle "against the ruthless savages." As was typical for early pioneer speakers, he attempted a list of all "persons" present in Oregon when he arrived—and excluded all Native people from personhood when he did so.[6]

The lawyer and historian Frederick Van Voorhies Holman made explicit the comparison of pioneer honors to war glories: "You cannot call a man a member of the G.A.R. [Grand Army of the Republic] who might have gone to war and did not, or the man who might have come here in 1842, 1843 and 1845 and did not, a pioneer. [To be called a pioneer is a] privilege that is distinctively sacred and honorable, that is due to the hard service, the hard toil, the privations, the fighting, the cutting of the way through the wilderness that was endured by these pioneers." Just as only those who had fought for the Union in the Civil War could join the G.A.R., Holman argued, only those who had taken part in the toil, privations, and *fighting* that had wrested the Pacific Northwest into American control should be able to join the Oregon Pioneer Association. Indeed, as historian Lindsey Peterson has shown, G.A.R. chapters across the West framed settler colonial invasion as a continuation of the righteous violence of the Civil War.[7]

And when efforts were made to count Euro-Americans who arrived in the 1850s as pioneers, they were initially justified by connection to the wars. As William Lair Hill put it in an 1883 address, "The circumstances connected with the Indian wars of 1855–6 do themselves constitute a just claim of all who were residents of the territory at that time to the same position as pioneers." The War on Illahee could be used as a dividing line, separating pioneers from latecomers. The real pioneers, many argued implicitly or explicitly, were those who killed for a White Northwest.[8]

During the late nineteenth century, historians local and national, pioneer associations, veterans' groups, and others with a stake in history and public memory usually recognized that violence against Native people had been a constituent part of the Euro-American seizure of the region. Almost all wanted to honor the portion of that violence they considered righteous. But although most Euro-Americans celebrated the expansion of the United States into the Northwest, struggles over the causes, frequency, and righteousness of the violence that enabled that expansion drove interpretive divisions over the past.

Many former volunteers pushed for histories that glorified race war and excused or erased any war crimes by exalting those who had taken up arms against Native people as especially worthy of pioneer praise. Pioneer organizations and veteran's groups formed for the "purposes of mutual congratulation" were one means of promulgating this narrative. Historians supported by the perpetrators of those acts mounted a campaign to simultaneously justify and deny the wanton violence of the pioneer era. Their efforts were in some cases successful enough to falsely contest well-known mass killings. By the turn of the twentieth century, the atrocities acknowledged by many among the first generation of Northwest historians had been disappeared from most Euro-American history books. Even the federal government shifted. The original stance of the United States had been that Northwest pioneer violence outside the bounds of war in the early 1850s was illegitimate. By 1902, federal legislation supported the pioneer view that there had been a single, multifront war against Indigenous people generally throughout the era, worthy of remuneration. Decades after the killings, the War on Illahee was given a federal imprimatur.[9]

Attempts to deflect blame from the volunteers had been persistent throughout the War on Illahee and continued after it. Would-be volunteer hagiographers often drew on a centuries-old tactic of justifying settler violence by emphasizing and generalizing Native perfidy. Charles S. Drew, who had endorsed war crimes and been credibly accused of graft in 1854, did just this in a memorial to the U.S. Congress in 1860. Drew denounced the reports of John Wool, Thomas Cram, and others like them, submitting instead a fantasy of unremitting and unmotivated Native aggression in the Northwest. He posited an "Indian War in Oregon" across Oregon and Washington territories lasting from 1847 to 1857, composed almost entirely of wanton murder by "the Indians." Listing the non-Native dead (real and speculated), Drew wrote over and over variations of "all these murders were entirely unprovoked." Assertions to the contrary, Drew proclaimed, were instances of "the Indians . . . falsely

Charles S. Drew posed in uniform and speckled with flies. This image may have been created when Drew was in military service in the 1860s, or it may have been taken in the 1870s after he was no longer an officer, meant to commemorate that earlier period. Courtesy of the Southern Oregon Historical Society.

accusing the whites of being 'the first aggressors.' " He argued that "the Indians" were throughout the 1850s plotting a general war of extermination against White people—though the mere rumor of White volunteers once again taking the field, Drew insisted with his typical lack of evidence, was enough to "thwart their purposes" until government weakness once again encouraged them. In private in 1854, Drew had argued that war crimes against Native communities were a necessary part of Indian war. In public in 1860, he ignored accusations that volunteers had caused conflicts with their war crimes and argued instead for limitless Indian perfidy—and thus for latter-day government payments to support volunteer actions.[10]

Drew omitted almost every act of volunteer violence that couldn't be easily framed as a heroic battle. The Lupton Massacre, alone among the more infamous incidents, appears to have been unavoidable. Drew threw a number of arguments at the wall in his attempts to downplay the Lupton Massacre: he claimed the volunteers had not known there were women in the camp; he suggested the fact that Lupton had died in the attack indicated that there were plenty of "warriors" present too; he proclaimed Lupton was "not even a private of the volunteer corps," so even if he had committed wrongs, he "had nothing whatever to do with its organization." Although Drew begrudgingly admitted the existence of Lupton's killings, this did not stop him from claiming that there had been "no provocation given" for the killings inflicted by Native people in the counterattacks following the massacre. Drew framed the Lupton Massacre as an isolated event, disconnecting it from the violence it had culminated from and unleashed.[11]

Other killings Drew denied—using a lack of prosecution as evidence for a lack of wrongdoing. Responding to one of Palmer's reports on non-combatants being murdered by miners, Drew wrote: "With regard to the killing of the 'seven sq__ws' &c., it is probably that Mr. Palmer derived his information from the Indians themselves who hoped by such a story to elicit his sympathy and thus obtain a larger amount of presents . . . for, though it was sufficient to incorporate in his report, he did not consider it of sufficient account to cause the arrest of the alleged offenders." Of course, Palmer would have had great difficulty making such an arrest. Beyond his lack of authority, manpower, or will, Native testimony was forbidden.[12]

Drew ended his letter to the U.S. Congress with a transcription of an 1856 resolution from the Oregon Conference of Missionary Bishops:

Whereas, our Territories have been the theater of a disastrous Indian war during the past year; and whereas an impression has, by some means, been made abroad that the people of Oregon and Washington have acted an unworthy part in bringing it on: Therefore,

Resolved, That though there may have been occasional individual instances of ill-treatment of the Indians by irresponsible whites, it is the conviction of this body of ministers whose fields of labor have been in all parts of the Territories, at the beginning and during the continuance of the war, that the war has not been wantonly or wickedly provoked by our fellow-citizens, but that it has been emphatically a war of defense, and that that defense was deferred as long as Christian forbearance would warrant.[13]

Even God, Drew argued, was on the side of the volunteers. The actions of "individual . . . irresponsible whites," according to Drew, the Methodist Episcopal ministers whom he cited, and legions of other pioneers, should not reflect on the wars or any other aspects of settler life. Acts of genocide were transformed into acts of defense. And Congress should pay up.

The Indian War Veterans of the North Pacific Coast (IWV-NPC) was created in 1885 to pursue pensions and a place in posterity for volunteer soldiers who had fought in the wars of the region during the 1840s and 1850s. The purpose of the organization, according to its constitution, was the building of brotherhood among former soldiers, the transmission of patriotism to future generations, and the creation and propagation of a "true history of the Indian wars of the North Pacific Coast"—one that painted the volunteers as unrivaled heroes rather than the useful villains they became in parts of Lang's or Bancroft's works. Over the next four decades, the volunteer veterans largely achieved their goals. They helped bring into being new history books that minimized the wantonness of the violence they had inflicted during and beyond the wars they had fought. By the early 1900s, the volunteer veterans had gained eligibility for pensions from the federal government, along with additional payments from the states of Oregon and Washington, and they were feted as heroes by local newspapers and the cheering crowds at pioneer events.[14]

The IWV-NPC was one among a welter of heritage groups and fraternal orders attempting to craft a heroic history for the Pacific

Northwest during the late nineteenth and early twentieth centuries. The IWV-NPC began as an especially rarefied offshoot of the Oregon Pioneer Association, and it shared significant goals and personnel with the Washington Pioneer Association. Members framed themselves as pioneer paragons, a "vanguard of civilization" especially worthy of honor because of their leading role in the conquest of the Northwest. In parades, which were frequent in the late 1800s and early 1900s, a standard pioneer procession marched by year, with an earlier date of arrival indicating especial honors. But the IWV-NPC marched separately; its members saw their role in the "Indian wars" as marking them out for special praise over and above their seniority as settlers.[15]

The dues-paying membership of the IWV-NPC was probably small but potent, led by men of influence and serving a constituency much larger than the core members who could afford to join. The first leader ("grand commander") elected, T. B. Wait, was the former mayor of Salem as well as a prosperous merchant. Two later long-serving grand commanders, T. A. Wood and Cyrus Walker, were similarly successful, and the organization counted among its ranks politicians—and killers— like James K. Kelly, John Minto, and LaFayette Mosher. Professional history makers also played major roles, including Elwood Evans, the *Oregonian's* editor Harvey W. Scott, and the longtime Oregon Historical Society curator George Himes. While initially conceived as a sprawling fraternal order across the Northwest, the IWV-NPC drew most of its dues-paying members from Oregon's Willamette Valley, particularly from Portland, Salem, and (farther south) Roseburg. Incomplete records and inconsistent rolls make it difficult to estimate the exact membership during the early decades, particularly because the leadership had good reason to exaggerate numbers—but even at the group's peak it is likely that they had fewer than two hundred paying members. The few surviving letters from grand commanders suggest, however, that the organization enjoyed support and engagement from many more volunteer veterans, perhaps hundreds or even thousands, unable or unwilling to travel to meetings or pay dues. This support was reciprocated; grand commanders helped several indigent nonmember "Indian war" veterans get coveted spaces in Soldiers' Homes across the Northwest. Moreover, the IWV-NPC achieved political power beyond its size. By the early twentieth century, the remaining volunteer veterans could reasonably expect not only mayors but also local candidates for national office to attend their meetings and heap praise on them.[16]

When the general membership of the IWV-NPC had its inaugural meeting in Oregon City in 1886, the first order of business (after parades, celebratory welcoming speeches, and a barbecue lunch) was to proclaim that the organization "[did] not approve of the extreme statements of cruelty by white people toward the Indians" in Lang's *History of the Willamette Valley* (see chapter 8). In 1887 they expanded this statement and accused Lang of being "wantonly malicious" toward them and "flagrantly inaccurate, incorrect and unjust to the early settlers of Oregon and Washington" more generally. The volunteers responded to Lang's descriptions of the "wanton murder" committed by some among their membership by accusing the historian, in turn, of "wanton malice."[17]

The IWV-NPC's attacks on unflattering histories were not limited to Lang's. They loudly disdained the "loose and incorrect ways of nearly all 'so called histories of Oregon,' " including those by Victor, Bancroft, and every other not among their ranks. The volunteer veterans believed themselves entitled to be the sole arbiters of the truth about the Indian wars, and demanded "true history . . . that neither the veterans, nor their descendants would be ashamed of." Particularly, they pushed against histories that documented the many, many acts of wanton violence their members had performed.[18]

Supporters of the IWV-NPC tended to respond to accusations of war crimes with counterattacks rather than direct denial. Their attempts to sanctify their service rested on the creation of a legion of enemies. They painted the national government as inept and out of touch, the regular troops as high-handed and wrong-footed, and historians who relied on the records of either rather than the reminiscences of pioneers as arrogant and unscholarly. Above all, the IWV-NPC evoked an image of Native people as "dreaded red men" who were more "demons of another world" than human beings. It is difficult not to read at least some deliberate duplicity in the IWV-NPC's objection to "extreme statements of cruelty by white people toward the Indians." Not only did the membership include famous killers like James K. Kelly, the leader of the men who had murdered and butchered Peo-Peo-Mox-Mox (and built a successful political career on that war record), but some members, such as Urban E. Hicks, left behind significant records of at least some of the wanton murders they and their friends had perpetrated.[19]

In truth, celebrations of brutal violence were common among the IWV-NPC, even as they publicly denied any acts of cruelty. Speeches reveling in the mutilation of Peo-Peo-Mox-Mox became a recurrent theme in private meetings of the organization. Justificatory statements about killing Native people were common, and calls for future killings of Indigenous persons (abroad and perhaps at home) were implied at various times. Grand Commander Wait initially proposed as the organization's motto "Ick Close Tillicum," Chinook Jargon typically translated as "One Good Indian"—a reference to the adage "the only good Indian is a dead Indian"—with a matching badge featuring a volunteer shooting down a Native man about to scalp a White woman. This plan to celebrate genocide using Indigenous language was rejected in favor of *Omne solum forti patria est*, Latin for "Every land is a homeland for a brave man"—in part because many members, including Mosher, initially found the use of Chinook Jargon to be distasteful.[20]

Though IWV-NPC members celebrated wanton Indian killing when swapping stories among themselves, and they wanted their part in the Indian wars glorified by the public, the "true history" they demanded would falsify the details of volunteer violence. The IWV-NPC's clearest voice in this pursuit was Elwood Evans's 1889 book, *The History of the Pacific Northwest*. Evans was himself a former volunteer, and he shared writing duties for the section on the Rogue River Wars with Mosher, who was elected grand commander of the IWV-NPC in 1888. The two men financed publication of the book in part by having the membership solicit preorders. Taking aim at "certain publications called histories," Evans and Mosher attempted to redeem "the good name and fame" of the volunteers by highlighting supposed Native atrocities and remaining silent on settler violence. The "mangled bodies . . . [of] mostly old men, women, and children" at the aftermath of the Little Butte Creek Massacre that Victor and Bancroft's *History of Oregon* had decried were neither mentioned nor specifically denied in Evans and Mosher's history. Instead, the book described the incident as a "murderous band" getting "the punishment they deserved" in an "attack which resulted in the killing of most of the warriors." This silence regarding the deaths of Native women and children is palpable throughout much of the book; although mentions of the *capture* of Indian women were relatively frequent, virtually all descriptions of settler violence falsely implied that it was meted out only against Native men.[21]

Evans proclaimed in print that Native violence against Euro-Americans always had the same cause: "not because of any personal outrages committed by Whites, not because of any injustice sought to be inflicted . . . but solely because it was the Indian purpose to exterminate

*Elwood Evans, probably from some time between the
1860s and the 1880s. The "fraternally yours" signature
reflects Evans's involvement in fraternal societies like
the Freemasons. Courtesy of the Oregon Historical Society.*

the white settlements." Most Euro-American historians of the Northwest
at the time agreed with Herbert Lang's assertion in *History of the Willamette Valley* that "treachery . . . [was] the predominating trait of the Indian character." But Evans, unlike these historians, made few distinctions
between "good" and "bad" Indians, and Mosher, who had been an active
participant in the pogroms and wars of the Rogue River region, made
none. Treaties and declarations of peace were tricks designed "to allure
the white race into a belief of their security." Indian "perfidy"—Evans's
favorite descriptor—justified and sanctified any white violence. Any Indian group could be considered "a standing menace to the Whites," and
thus could be attacked in an act of proactive defense. The murders of
Native leaders during peace negotiations Evans and Mosher excused as
"the taking of adequate revenge" on "implacable savages" by White "men
who had lately buried the mutilated bodies of women and children."

That the volunteers also had created plenty of mutilated bodies passed without mention.[22]

Victor and Bancroft's condemnation of the more outrageous actions of the volunteers had allowed them to separate the volunteers' violence from American civilization. Evans's assertion of overriding Indian perfidy elevated those volunteers as necessary shock troops of American empire and excused them from culpability: "However much it is to be regretted ... Indian wars are but the essential concomitants of American settlement, the necessary evil from which untold good emanates. It measurably, however, removes the asperity of such cruel fact by the remembrance that the Indian himself invariably selected ... the place and time for the commencement of hostile operations."[23]

In Evans's work, the "perfidious cruelty" of Indians was absolute, and Indian wars sprang solely from "repeated and unprovoked outrages which were committed by savages upon unoffending and defenseless white men, women, and children." "In no respect," he insisted in a speech in 1877, "were [pioneers] the aggressors ... they were innocent of every justifying incentive for [war] being forced upon them, save their lawful presence in the country." He discounted any of the voluminous evidence to the contrary as partisan backbiting, or the ignorance of those too far removed from events to know.[24]

Many of Evans's informants followed his lead. When Benjamin Franklin Dowell had spoken to Bancroft's team, his story about trying to defend an innocent Native child from the mob came to the fore. In the second volume of Evans's *History of the Pacific Northwest* (even more closely aligned with the IWV-NPC than the first), this story from Dowell disappeared along with the rest of the child murders Evans ignored. Dowell instead provided a distorted narrative of the killing of Peo-Peo-Mox-Mox that Elwood Evans described as "perhaps the most accurate and full description ... that ever has been or ever will be written." This "description" insisted that Peo-Peo-Mox-Mox had been planning treachery from the first (justifying the volunteers forcibly detaining him) and insisted that the slain prisoners had been the aggressors—stabbing volunteers, refusing orders to surrender, grabbing for guns. There was no mention of the volunteers discussing the upcoming murders of the prisoners, of the executions, or even of the famous mutilation for body trophies that followed.[25]

In his private correspondence, Evans was more honest. Writing to his fellow historian Granville O. Haller about the cause behind the Indian wars in Washington, Evans laid out his archetypically settler-colonial outlook—which was not, in fact, so different from Haller's own: "My own view is that the whole history of American settlement and colonization is a struggle of two civilizations or the conflict between two races for occupation of the country. American settlement means, necessitate[s,] absor[p]tion, appropriation of the country itself—to the exclusion of the aboriginal race. Hence the passage of the Donation Act, and the non observance of treaties[,] were illustrations of the American thought[.] 'The continent is ours' [is] the American theory[.] Our construction of the 1st great commandment, to subdue the S[oil] and replenish it."[26]

Communicating privately with Haller, who had taken direct part in the invasions, Evans admitted unabashedly that Euro-Americans had been the ones to ignore treaties. And he was willing to grant that Native people were resisting American land taking, rather than acting out pure "perfidy" (as Evans claimed publicly): "[The Yakama leader] Kamiakin appreciated what American advancement and occupancy meant. The acts and treaties were not the great underlying cause—nor did they not[e] the initiation of the conflict. They were moments which would be referred to, that the conflict was on—and meant what it always had meant, that the inferior race must yield."[27]

The lobbied-for DLCA, Evans proclaimed, was a knowing federal endorsement for mass expropriation: "[Senators] Linn and Benton ... ratified their support by American Governmental action in Oregon, and by the Federal Government the strongest character of evidence to support the Statement that the American settlers were expected to appropriate the soil, exclude the Indian therefrom, and that the United States were *pledged* in advance to uphold the act." Evans publicly insisted that Native people were always the aggressors in Indian wars. When corresponding privately, he agreed with Haller that Native people like Kamiakin/K'amáyakin were simply defending their land, and that the American plan had always been exclusionary conquest. Like his former employer Governor Isaac I. Stevens, Evans lied to craft a more beneficial story. For both men, honor was more important than truth.[28]

In his capacity as president and cofounder of the Washington State Historical Society, Evans was a key figure in obscuring the Maxon Massacre, the mass killing of Nisqually people along the Nisqually River, from the historical record. These killings had been well-known (and sometimes lauded) by Euro-American residents of Washington Territory in the 1850s, but they had not been as nationally famous as the Lupton

Massacre. When the matter was first brought before the Washington Historical Society in 1893, Evans proclaimed that the notorious killings had not happened because there was no evidence from contemporary military reports—the same reports he urged historians to ignore in the case of Oregon. This denial was effective enough to cast doubt on the reality of the killings for decades, despite numerous Nisqually attempts to correct the Euro-American historical record. Evans was a history enthusiast and a diligent collector of records, but his yen for a history of heroic White supremacy trumped any attempt at objective practice. This was not a matter of sloppiness; Evans, known as "the terror of the old time printers," was punctilious to a fault about his prose. Yet in spite of the evidence he'd seen, in spite of the stories he must have heard at IWV-NPC meetings, against all evidence, Elwood Evans insisted to the end of his life that "the *people* of Washington and Oregon did not commit *personal* outrages against Indians."[29]

Lobbied by the IWV-NPC in 1890, the state of Oregon sponsored a new history of the early Indian wars of Oregon along similar lines, hiring Frances Fuller Victor to compile and compose it. One purpose of this work was to craft a record of who had volunteered in which conflicts; official paperwork was often lacking, and some proof would be needed if the volunteer veterans were ever cleared for pensions. Notably, the Oregon Legislature passed a bill in 1891 giving the IWV-NPC grand commander plenary power to certify the service of Indian wars veterans, with no further evidence required (according to the letter of the law). Drawing from interviews and records, Victor, a diligent historian, re-created Indian wars rolls, preserving evidence that remains a critical resource for proving participation in the Indian wars of the Northwest.[30]

The new history the volunteer veterans had pushed the state to commission also supported their version of historical events. In a departure from her previous work with Bancroft, Victor absolved the volunteers of nearly all blame. While not going as far as Evans, Victor no longer discussed the "mangled bodies" and "butchery" of the Lupton Massacre, as she had while ghostwriting for Bancroft. And she repeated the unlikely volunteer claim that none had known women and children were present—while tartly noting that the U.S. regulars who reported the massacre "went out to view the field after the slaughter, instead of preventing it." Denying the well-established historical truth that the Lupton Massacre had provoked the counterattacks that followed (because, as she put it, "savages do not move with such celerity"), Victor instead embraced the volunteer fantasy of a vast Native conspiracy to make war that had somehow paradoxically been encouraged by the presence of federal forts and reservations. A number of scholars have reported Victor's occasional critiques of individual pioneer excesses in her earlier works, but they have minimized the racist embrace of White American empire triumphant that was a much more frequent throughline of her historical writing—perhaps a part of what historian Margaret Jacobs has discussed as the persistence of "triumphalist interpretation[s] of white women in the West." With Victor's help, the volunteers' assertions of their own blamelessness and of the foolishness of the regular troops were now a part of official Oregon history.[31]

The IWV-NPC achieved pensions on the heels of its victories over the historical record. Pensions and land grants had been a means for the federal government to recruit and reward Euro-American settlers who had soldiered against Native people since the foundation of the United States. A major goal for the IWV-NPC was getting the irregular volunteer forces of Oregon's Indian wars counted and included in the expanding pension regime the federal government was building in the late 1800s, primarily for veterans of the Civil War. They succeeded. Congress extended eligibility for benefits to veterans of some earlier Indian wars in 1892, and to the Pacific Northwest volunteers of the IWV-NPC in 1902. Rather than listing all specific conflicts, the 1902 law provided pensions for veterans of the "Cayouse war" and "the Oregon and Washington Indian wars from eighteen hundred and fifty-one to eighteen hundred and fifty-six, inclusive." U.S. policy now embraced the volunteer veteran historical narrative of a general period of Northwest Indian wars" rather than a narrative of specific inglorious or valorous conflicts. During the 1850s, U.S. federal officials such as General John E. Wool differentiated attacks such as the Lupton Massacre from formal war. By 1902, federal policy no longer made such a distinction.[32]

While they framed themselves as excluded underdogs, the volunteer veterans of the IWV-NPC, with its well-connected membership and popular cause, always enjoyed political support regionally. Convincing Oregon and Washington politicians to request national funds for local veterans was relatively straightforward; the pursuit of federal recompense for the costs of Oregon's Indian wars had been a state-level campaign issue since the successful runs of Joseph Lane and Isaac I. Stevens in the 1850s. The expectation of federal funding was thought by some to have helped spur some of the attacks on Native communities. And even

*Stories and pictures celebrating the Indian War Veterans of the North Pacific
Coast (like this one from June 21, 1911) regularly appeared in the* Oregonian
*newspaper, run by Harvey W. Scott, an IWV-NPC member. William Stillwell,
who wrote of pioneers who tortured as well as killed, is on the far right.
Courtesy of the Oregon Historical Society.*

before their triumph over the historical record, the largely Oregon-based
IWV-NPC was able to get their constituents included in Oregon soldiers' home legislation.[33]

But in the late 1800s, convincing state governments to set aside
funds for veterans' claims was more difficult. William Paine Lord,
elected governor of Oregon in 1895, probably echoed many previous
governors when he politely rejected the volunteer veterans' entreaties
and declared pensions a national rather than state issue. By the twentieth
century, however, the volunteer veterans' cause was popular enough, and
their ranks thin enough, that the State of Oregon could be convinced to
pick up the some of the costs federal pensions would not cover. In 1903
the Oregon state legislature set aside up to $100,000 for outstanding In-
dian war claims from 1855 and 1856. After the 1912 election, during
which representatives from both parties promised to do more, a bill set-

ting aside an additional $50,000 for Indian war claims related to horses passed the Oregon state legislature, and the Pacific Coast delegation in the national Congress got federal pensions for Indian war veterans raised from eight to twenty dollars a month. By 1920, Oregon had extended Indian war benefits to the whole of the War on Illahee, at that point by law a period from 1847 to 1858. Men who had perpetrated the worst violence of the colonial conquest of Oregon and Washington, men who had previously been used as a foil to excuse other settlers, were officially now recognized as the heroes they believed themselves to be.[34]

And financial realities continued to shape which history was told. As Oregon Historical Society President Frederick V. Holman warned the rising historian Clarence B. Bagley in 1908, "There is not the great interest in books of historical interest on the Northwest Pacific Coast to make it profitable to publish" on a sales rather than a subscription model, especially when a book "takes the unpopular side of most of the questions involved." And much of the pioneer purchasing public preferred prideful pablum to critical candor.[35]

Many of the voices seeking to invert or bowdlerize the truth of volunteer and pioneer violence relied on volume and detail to create the impression of accuracy. Victor's *Early Indian Wars of Oregon* was carefully sourced in both senses, appearing replete with evidence yet leaving aside some of the contemporary primary sources she had relied on when working with Bancroft in favor of those that painted Oregonians in a more flattering light. This seemingly thorough use of sources in the creation of pointedly incomplete narratives gave authority to the careful erasure of violence and inequity. Victor's book was scrupulously footnoted compared to Herbert O. Lang's *History of the Willamette Valley*; a reader might well assume that Victor's story was truer, even though Lang more accurately described the violence of Oregon's creation. Elwood Evans's framing of his objections to actually accurate histories of pioneer violence as issues with evidence did similar work. Individual critiques of evidence from Evans could read as plausible—but collectively they were internally inconsistent, driven by political goals rather than historical facts.

Scholars must be on the lookout for the use of facsimiles of facticity to prop up fictitious histories. Much as Isaac I. Stevens had created incomplete but voluminous records that he then used to back up the lies he told Congress, Elwood Evans was especially effective in his efforts to further frontier fictions when he did so while pantomiming objectivity. Other deceivers, including Victor, may or may not have been as aware of

the extent to which they were engraving untruths into the historical record. The appearance of rigor was—and is—a powerful tool.[36]

Increased professionalization of history in the 1900s did not end the
distortion of the Pacific Northwest's history of violence. Many of the
omissions and lies of the pioneer generation were by then engraved in
the historical record. And often omission rather than outright fabrication
was the tool of choice; as Haller and others had argued, pioneer societies
distorted (and distort) historical narratives when they ignored violence
by settlers while condemning retributive violence by Native people.
Many professional historians, too, would choose a variation of what became known as the "pioneer code," pursuing histories free from outright
fabrications but filled with gaping silences and willful blindness.

CHAPTER TEN

Settlers, Scholars, and the
Silencing of Pioneer Violence

I N 1883 WILLIAM LAIR HILL caused a hubbub among the members
of the Oregon Pioneer Association. In his annual address, Hill had
as usual praised the pioneers for their strength, their "patriotic intel-
ligence," their virtue, and their part in "securing to [their] country
dominion over a vast empire." But then Hill had the temerity to suggest
that the early Euro-American arrivals "were not mere missionaries of
civil liberty, nor patriots voluntarily sacrificing themselves in unselfish
devotion to the extension and aggrandizement of their mother land," but
had come primarily to seek individual liberty and, he hinted, free land.[1]

To many pioneers, this was outrageous. Responding to an angry letter regarding the speech from John Minto, Jesse Applegate gave his own
opinion with his characteristic and increasingly embittered wit.

> I read the address of Mr. Hill soon after it was delivered. I thought
> it in bad taste, [n]ot because it was untrue, but [because it was] not
> suited to the occasion or the audience. I regard the Pioneer Associ-
> ations as a kind of Mutual Admiration Society which assembled
> annual[l]y to praise and be praised by each other. As these assem-
> blages were not a public nuisance, and seemed to afford those con-
> cerned great pleasure, those not in sympathy with them have no
> . . . right in any way to defeat the objects of their meetings.[2]

Applegate was making acerbic reference to the "pioneer code," an unofficial understanding that stories destructive to heroic images of pioneers should not be made public—the same code, he privately decried, that afflicted "books improperly called histories" by the likes of Elwood Evans and Frances Fuller Victor.[3]

As D. J. Holmes put it in at the beginning of his laudatory address to a Polk County Oregon pioneers' reunion in 1901: "The history of mankind comes down to us frequently written in blood through honor or disgrace. The good, we emulate and point to with pride. From the evil and wrong, we blush and shrink and turn it back into the eternal darkness of our memories[,] never to be referred to save in sorrowful recollection."[4]

Although only occasionally spelled out, and most often noticeable in the breach, the widespread belief that Euro-American pioneers had to be heroes shaped history for generations—in both what was said and what was shared. John Minto, in conversations with multiple historians in the 1890s, screened access to his trove of letters carefully. As he wrote to Eva Emery Dye regarding requested letters from William Tolmie, a fur trader and politician, "I shall not let any of them go out of my hands without a very definite understanding as to the manner of their use." Only those who obeyed the pioneer code and told the right kind of stories, Minto believed, could be permitted to see the letters in his possession. Similar beliefs shaped primary source availability for decades; in 1937 amateur historian J. Orin Oliphant denied others access to his pioneer primary sources unless they agreed in advance to omit "language . . . too undignified for quotation."[5]

But which stories needed to be altered or suppressed for the sake of pioneer posterity varied a great deal among organizations, people, and time periods. At the same meeting where Hill had raised hell by suggesting early pioneers were motivated by anything other than selfless patriotism, Matthew Deady related the history of Bates, the southern Oregon man who had lured almost an entire Native community into his tavern and murdered them. Deady told this history as one of evolution; Deady's own arrival in 1853 marked the point at which "the word of the law superseded the edge of the sword" in southern Oregon (cf. chapter 2). With this framing, Deady's isolated stories of Euro-American butchery and horror did not attract the same opprobrium as Hill's seemingly mild suggestion of widespread self-interest. Hubert Howe Bancroft was kicked out of the Society of California Pioneers in 1893 largely because he voiced distaste for the violent pioneer fringe, epitomized by rough gold miners—his fellow pioneers took issue with his tone, as much as or more than his flirtations with accuracy. Increasingly by the end of the 1800s, anything other than celebration was suspect.[6]

Pervasive, ephemeral, and sometimes uneven, the unofficial "pioneer code" deeply influenced which histories were told or suppressed. But because this code was neither stable nor static, stories were not suppressed evenly—indeed, much of the evidence throughout this book comes from those who subscribed to a version of the "pioneer code" that permitted braggadocio about wanton violence. This chapter begins with a discussion of one of the more enduring erasures—the sexual violence and partner abuse that was almost never seen as appropriate for pioneer annals. It then moves to the new norms of erasure that emerged in the first two decades of the twentieth century, as historians blotted out even more of the historical record of violence. For some, like Eva Emery Dye, violence could be changed to create a more romantic narrative of the past. For others, like academic historian Clarence B. Bagley, omission seemed to be the appropriate middle ground between a responsibility for historical accuracy and a desire to make history heroic. For nearly all, the "pioneer code" demanded decorous silence over fealty to the facts.

Pioneer rape culture appears to have been a vast and shadowy phenomenon. As discussed in the previous chapters, Native communities complained of and struck back against Euro-American rapists across the American Pacific Northwest, from the southern reaches of Oregon to the northern expanses of Washington (and farther north, in what became Canada). These accounts were affirmed by Euro-American administrators charged with keeping the peace. George Ambrose, who spent the mid-1850s trying to seize Indigenous lands in southern Oregon while minimizing the costs of colonialism, complained of a "transient, reckless, irresponsible se[t] of m[e]n, whose only occupation would seem to be to create disturbances and difficulties with the Indians, who are constantly tampering with the sq__ws." Similar complaints came from army officers in eastern Washington, particularly after Colville-bound gold seekers who attempted rape were executed under Yakama law—a key inciting incident for the Yakima War (see chapter 3).[7]

The pan-Native alliance that gathered to fight the Yakima War in late October 1855 included mention of rape in their discussion of war and peace terms. According to the missionary Father Charles Pandosy:

"They would consent to a peace if the Americans wished a peace and would grant a reserve on their own lands, and not exile them from their native country. But in case that their conditions were not accepted, they were resolved to fight to the last extremity, determined, even if they succumbed (these are their literal expressions) they would sooner destroy their wives and their children, than to have them fall into the hands of the Americans, who would gratify with them their infamous passions."[8]

The "infamous passions" of Americans were well-known by 1855, enough to stiffen the resolve of those calling for war. Kamiakin/K'amáyak̲in and those allied with him knew that if Native women and children fell "into the hands of the Americans to become their plaything[s]," rapes like those already attempted by the invading gold miners would follow. And they were aware that "the heart of the Americans" meant the invaders would typically refuse to prosecute or perhaps even recognize such crimes. As historian Rosemary Stremlau has suggested, Anglo-American rape culture, like settler colonialism generally, was (and is) structural— "sexual violence [experienced] as a process and a persistent threat instead of a single event." And across the Pacific Northwest, Native communities knew it.[9]

Gold miners in the Northwest, like gold miners elsewhere, were especially associated with rape. This no doubt reflected a truth. Scholars have long noted (and often avoided discussing) the frequency of rapists in American gold mining camp cultures—where White rapists were typically tolerated as long as they targeted non-White women. But it remains unclear to what extent the notorious connection between those who raped and those who mined is a function of rapists being more prevalent in mining camps than in other Euro-American social circles, rather than a function of what kinds of sexual violence Euro-American authorities were willing to see, and whom they were willing to blame. Much as gold miners especially but by no means exclusively pursued genocide, the evidence shows that rape was part of a broader pioneer culture, beyond the mines.[10]

Accounts from Native people make clear such horrors were, and remain, frequent. But among Euro-American records, there are only whispers of evidence. Even pioneers proud of their part in genocide knew that stories of rape were not fit to print. Many mass killers would avoid even a cursory mention of it; Loren L. Williams prattled gleefully in his journal about bloody murder but never expressed a whiff of sexual impropriety. Prosecuting rape in court was difficult for anyone in mid-

1800s America; for Native women in the Pacific Northwest, it was close to impossible. But there are signs and shadows.[11]

One of the clearest comes from Matthew Deady, a prominent Oregon political figure and judge, whose private account of the 1855 race for Oregon territorial representative described Joseph Lane and John Gaines each bragging of having "taken 'a turn at the sq__ws' " in the wars of the early 1850s. Deady included this description in a letter to James Nesmith, probably knowing that Nesmith liked scuttlebutt generally and sexual stories specifically. As discussed in chapter 2, both Lane and Gaines knew that bragging about implied sexual violence would be a hit with a southern Oregon audience. No word of this part of the political speeches they gave seems to have reached the papers. But men knew.[12]

Among Euro-Americans writing for a public audience, the subject could be nearly unspeakable. Reticence extended even to those Euro-Americans who wanted to present themselves as sympathetic to Native people. J. G. Rowton, a "citizen volunteer" in the Nez Perce War, was open about the causes of that conflict. Contrary to pioneer claims that Native people had started the war, he told historian Lucullus Virgil McWhorter in 1930, "all the shooting was done by the [White] citizens who was excited. There was no cause for shooting and when the shooting started the indians run to the woods and hid."[13]

Although willing to see his condemnation of killings by White "citizens" put into print, Rowton did not want implications of rape to appear. Apparently Rowton had mentioned sexual violence in an earlier conversation with McWhorter, and he was worried that McWhorter might publish his memories on the subject. After a reminiscence written in long, flowing paragraphs, Rowton added a set of staccato sentences in the postscript:

I mentioned the las[s]oing of the sq__ws as a conversation I
heard between two fellows
They were talking to each other
I do not believe the story worth consideration
They were telling each other of their experience with the
sq__ws
Each for all I know might have been trying to out do the
other
I do not believe the story is worth tak[i]ng notice of

I tell it merely to indicate what the indians had to induce from some of the white men when the indians [were] even peaceable and friendly.[14]

With his scattered sentences and repetitions that the story was not worth writing about, Rowton expressed an almost visceral concern that Mc-Whorter might publish a story breaking perhaps the greatest taboo of the pioneer code. It is clear that Rowton believed something illicit and unmentionable—worse than the casual killings he described freely—had occurred, despite his prevarications about hearsay. There are multiple accounts of White settlers and soldiers lassoing and raping Native women. But Rowton repeatedly asserted that the story was not "worth tak[i]ng notice of." Whatever the two men had bragged about doing to Indigenous women, whatever they had done, Rowton did not want it in the history books.[15]

What other correspondents preferred is more ambiguous. Christina McDonald McKenzie Williams, who identified as being of White, "Iroquois," and Nez Perce/Nimiipuu descent, wrote about the rapes invading soldiers perpetrated in eastern Washington to Eva Emery Dye. Nellie Garry, the daughter of the famous Spokane leader Spokane Garry/Slough-Keetcha, told Williams stories of sexual assaults: "She said it was only too true + shameful what the soldiers did. . . . [They] abuse[d] her, this lame woman [name redacted]'s daughter. This Nellie G[a]rry's eyes filled with tears when relating the affair to me. . . . The soldiers were + officers were a little too familiar with the Indian women when they could overtake them or found them with tired horses[.] [O]f course this naturally made the men more desperate towards the whites. [T]ogether with taking their country +c." Williams identified sexual violence, both specific and general, perpetrated against Native people by Euro-American soldiers in eastern Washington. In the 1850s sexual violence against Native people was sometimes reported—but usually as something gold miners or other low-class people did. The testimony of Nellie Garry and Christina Williams accused the soldiers *and* officers of the same crimes.[16]

Dye, who had been reaching out to Williams about a different topic, never breathed a word of this sexual violence in her writing (see below). Dye ignored the testimonies of Nellie Gerry and Christina Williams. In 1915 Williams gave a public-facing interview about Native life in pioneer Washington to the *Washington Historical Quarterly*, conducted by the generally sympathetic historian William S. Lewis. No acts of violence against women were mentioned, and there are no records that they were even discussed. It is unclear on whose wishes rapes committed by pioneers were omitted from this history. But it is highly unlikely anyone involved in the publication of the *Washington Historical Quarterly*, from its editor Edmond S. Meany on down, would have printed such a story, and their readership probably wouldn't have wanted to hear about it. The pioneer code, in perhaps all its variations, demanded that histories like that should be suppressed.[17]

In 1996 historian of violence David T. Courtwright associated rape in the West and across America with single men, culminating in a troubling proposal that Americans should marry off young men early to minimize how much raping (and other violence) they would commit. Beyond the other problems with this formulation, any scholar of women's studies or the nineteenth-century American South could have informed Courtwright that marriage has not historically barred American men from committing sexual assault—particularly against women of color. Both Lane and Gaines were married, as were many of the gold miners, volunteers, officers, and others who raped in the West. Married men might be even less likely to have their atrocities recorded, but plenty of them committed rapes, in and beyond their marriages.[18]

Spousal rape and other intimate abuse that was legal in the nineteenth century is especially difficult to trace—even more so in those marriages and marriage-adjacent relationships that did not leave a paper trail through the courts. Excellent work has been done in recent decades examining Indigenous survivance, persistence, and resilience through the traditional tool of exogamous marriages. But this historical fact can lead to oversimplification.[19]

Marriages—or perceptions of marriages—between Native people and Euro-Americans should not be read as unassailable proof of loving relationships. Nor should they be assumed to be hostile, violent, or exploitative, without proof. As the previous chapters show, marriage to women of Native descent should not alone be taken as a signifier of friendliness toward or allyship with Native people. Being "married" to someone of Native descent did not keep the notorious Indian hater Martin Angell from murdering multiple Native people, including at least one child, in early 1850s southern Oregon. Nathan Olney, the volunteer who spent much of the 1850s and 1860s fighting Native communities in pursuit of White American supremacy, was married to a woman of Wasco descent named Twa-Wy "Annette" Hallicola—according to custom by 1853, made official in Euro-American law in 1859. Unlike some mixed marriages of the period, the union was public and widely acknowledged; Olney seems to have at least sometimes acknowledged and provided for his Native family members, and his descendants became valued and proud community leaders. But Nathan Olney himself was nonetheless a lethal crusader for White supremacy in several wars.[20]

One of the rare detailed accounts of typically invisible spousal abuse perpetrated by pioneer men against Native women in the archival records comes from the Snohomish/Samish leader (and sometime chairwoman of the Tulalip Tribes) Harriette Shelton Dover/Hi-ahl-tsa, along with her mother, Ruth Sehome Shelton/Sh-yas-tenoe. Percival Jeffcott reached out to the two in the 1950s for help with historical names. Over time, the Sheltons also informed Jeffcott of some of the wrongs done to their family by a man he had been planning to write about—Edmund Clare Fitzhugh.[21]

Fitzhugh, a Virginia patrician who gained money and influence in the region as variously a would-be coal baron and political operator, seized Native land in northwestern Washington from 1854 on. Drawing on his status (and perceived threat) as an agent of the U.S. government, Fitzhugh demanded of local Native leaders that he be provided with a "Chief's daughter." Ruth Shelton/Sh-yas-tenoe's adolescent sister Julia/ E-yam-alth (S'Klallam/Samish) was eventually procured and coerced into "marriage" with Fitzhugh against her will. Soon Fitzhugh inveigled Julia/E-yam-alth's aunt Whelas/Xwelas into the household as well, under murky circumstances. As Ruth Shelton/Sh-yas-tenoe put it, "E-yam-alth . . . first was the consort of Mr. Fitzhugh. . . . My sister Julia didn't want to be his wife; she cried and cried." Although Julia/E-yam-alth's descendants and relatives had different stories about the exact sequence of events that led up to the Indigenous teenager "marrying" the middle-aged Euro-American, there was agreement that she had not wanted to marry Fitzhugh and had been unhappy in the marriage. As historian David Peterson del Mar has found, murky evidence of both such coerced marriages and "more episodic forms of rape" occasionally persists at the margins of the records of soldiers, officers, miners, and other settlers.[22]

Edmund Clare Fitzhugh has always had the reputation of a violent killer. He participated in a duel in San Francisco. He was indicted and then released in Washington for killing a man named Wilson in a gambling dispute; oral histories claimed he had more or less served as the judge on his own murder case. And there were stories and rumors of additional killings even less present in the records.[23]

Like Isaac I. Stevens, Fitzhugh privately argued for brutal violence against Native people, even when they were seeking peace. "The Indians of course, are willing to play quits, save all their people and stop the war," Fitzhugh wrote in an 1856 letter urging Stevens to pursue instead a broad-based war of extermination. "If they succeed in doing that, as soon as they are well prepared to carry on the war with any prospects of success, the government will have the same expense and trouble over again." It is, as usual, difficult to tell how expansive Fitzhugh's conception of "the Indians" against whom he urged genocide was. He sometimes wrote of "Our Indians" (those he viewed as provisionally friendly and tractable) and "the Indians" (whose entreaties for peace could not be trusted). Both, of course, were Other.[24]

Fitzhugh, known for capricious violence, abused both of his Native wives, who left him. Ruth Shelton/Sh-yas-tenoe remembered that the breaking point had been when Fitzhugh kidnapped their children: "Fitzhugh took his two children to Seattle, and placed them in an all-white family. . . . When he took the two children, my sister Julie and our Aunt Whelas walked out of his home, and never returned. And although they tried to locate the children, they never really knew what happened to them until years later, when Mason Fitzhugh returned to Bellingham; looking for his mother; and he was about seventeen years old when he returned. They had had some years of hardship."[25]

Both of Fitzhugh's children eventually made it back home, despite being taken from their mother and left in California by a White father who did not acknowledge them as legitimate. Mason Fitzhugh, as Harriette Shelton Dover/Hi-ahl-tsa remembered decades later, suffered abuse at the hands of the White family he had been "given" to, but he did find his way back to his people as a teenager—and "told his father to go to 'you know where.' " Julianne, the other kidnapped child, made it home many years later, eventually choosing to emphasize her Euro-American heritage and "pass" amid the racist hostility of early 1900s Washington.[26]

Harriette Shelton Dover/Hi-ahl-tsa remembered a different version of how the family parted from Fitzhugh. According to an account from her aunt Julia/E-yam-alth, sometime after taking the children away, Fitzhugh attempted to beat both of his wives. After the first hit, as the story went, Julia/E-yam-alth struck back, pummeling him half to death with a length of firewood—badly enough that he was still walking with a limp when he left Washington Territory on his way back to Virginia (where he reneged on his oath and fought for the Confederacy in the Civil War). Fitzhugh's other wife from the period, Julia/E-yam-alth's aunt Whelas/Xwelas, responded similarly to later acts of intimate violence—in 1878 shooting down another abusive White husband, in a case that became locally famous.[27]

Percival R. Jeffcott, who in the 1930s began exploring the history of interracial marriages in northwestern Washington, saw such dynamics as common. In his account of a spousal abuser named Billy Clark, he intimated that Euro-American men's ill treatment of the Native women to whom they were married was considered normal:

> Billy Clark [was] not overly ambitious himself, yet with the help of his Indian "woman" and the assistance of his two daughters he managed to make a fair and easy living [in the 1870s]. It is said that he was overbearing to his wife but *that was the lot of most Indian women*, and he and his stepson, George Kinley, did not get along well together. ... Trouble with the boy probably led to trouble with his mother and she finally rebelled against Billy's harsh treatment and left him. ... Trouble seldom visits its victims singly, and so it was with Billy.[28]

Strikingly, Jeffcott framed Billy Clark as the victim of this story, even though Clark was clearly abusive—and it is not unreasonable to read a history of physical violence into descriptors like "overbearing" and "harsh." Oral histories collected (but not published) by other historians of the region found similar patterns.[29]

As Peterson del Mar has shown, spousal abuse was common across the Pacific Northwest in the late nineteenth and early twentieth centuries. And as historian Katrina Jagodinsky has suggested, Native women in northwestern Washington may have been both more societally vulnerable to abuse by Euro-American men because of colonial circumstances *and* more prepared to fight against that abuse through Indigenous mores and support systems. Many marriages between Euro-Americans and Native people were loving and supportive—including, according to her family, Julia/E-yam-alth's third marriage, to a Euro-American man named Henry C. Barkhousen—who, perhaps coincidentally, had helped publicize Fitzhugh's acts of voter intimidation in 1859. But the presence of marriage, sex, or commerce relationships between Native and White persons does not in itself necessarily mean an absence of racial violence, White supremacist thought, or genocidal dreams.[30]

Though they were silent about sexual violence, many pioneer accounts were open about killing Native women, children, and other perceived noncombatants. According to James Twogood, the genocidal axiom "Nits breed lice" was common currency among volunteers—similar to the famous phrase "the only good Indian is a dead Indian," but even more specific in its targeting of children. There seems to have been some dissension over how appropriate it was to pursue (or at least discuss) the killings of noncombatant Native women. Gabriel Rains, in his public-facing missive promising to wipe the Yakama from the face of the earth, risibly claimed that Euro-Americans did not kill women and children. Loren L. Williams, in his genocidal order meant for the record, suggested that his troops should try not to deliberately kill any Native women—although he allowed such killings might happen when "mercilessly" attacking Native settlements. Others, like Abigail Malick and Oregon's Governor George Lemuel Woods, proudly endorsed the killing of men and women alike.[31]

It was common to omit the killings of Native women from military reports, but the motives of those who so omitted are often opaque. Benjamin Shaw reported only six official casualties for the forty to sixty (or more) people killed in the 1856 Shaw Massacre in Grand Ronde Valley. But it is not clear whether shame, an eye on posterity, or a perceived need to report only those casualties considered fighters shaped his response. Edward O. C. Ord, when he was killing in his campaign along the southwestern Oregon coast, wrote in his diary on March 26, 1856, that his unit had killed "8 Indians, besides sq__ws and wounded at least as many more" in a battle the day before. This implies not shame but indifference to killings of Native women. Ord omitted them not out of guilt but because he though they didn't matter—perhaps he perceived them as noncombatants. The same logic may have shaped Hamilton Maxon's undercount of "Eight Hostiles Killed" in the massacre that bears his name—it is possible he listed only the men not because of shame, but because he did not view the Native women, children, and infants he and his fellow volunteers had murdered as worth counting.[32]

Early pioneer histories tended to be mournful or silent about the killing of Native women and children. Herbert Lang found the deaths of Native women to be proof positive of the ungentlemanly nature of many southern Oregon White men. Hubert Howe Bancroft mentioned such deaths only occasionally (and Frances Fuller Victor even less), but he typically portrayed them as unfortunate or accidental. Elwood Evans, characteristically, ignored the deaths of Native women almost entirely and amplified every story of purported Native perfidy he could find.

In the early twentieth century, historians and heritage groups followed the lead of those like Evans and omitted wanton violence by settlers. Though most edited out pioneer violence they viewed as iniquitous—rapes, attacks on the unarmed, some of the mutilations, mass murders—they embraced American imperialism as a virtue. They celebrated "pioneers" as the vanguard of an American army conquering a new land. Indeed, although illicit violence was written out, they depicted purportedly righteous violence against Native people as part of the legacy of *all* pioneers, not just the volunteers. Early twentieth-century histories were even more likely to cordon off complication and tell limited stories of righteous violence against "bad Indians" alongside stories of "good Indians" who had aided explorers, welcomed settlers, and then mythopoetically faded into the background.[33]

This emerging metanarrative is perhaps best demonstrated in the works of Eva Emery Dye, which celebrated righteous violence *and* peacemaking in the service of race and empire. She based her creations on extensive historical research, filling gaps in the historical record and details in the historical fabric with her own imagination. The fictions she created thus sometimes had more evidence behind them than conventional histories of the time, while also containing clear departures from the provable historical record. Dye leaned variously into her reputations as a historian and as a novelist, depending on the situation. This mix did not always sit well with other Northwest historians. As Frances Fuller Victor put it in a book review that cooled the friendship between herself and Dye, "The necessity of . . . melodrama does not excuse the perversion of history. . . . When, either by assertion or implication, it leads the reader to believe that which is essentially erroneous[,] it becomes mischievous." Omission, a routine part of Victor's work, was one thing. Dye's inventions, however, Victor perceived as "perversion."[34]

Dye's most successful work, *The Conquest* (1902), brought popular attention to the Lewis and Clark Expedition, and to Sacagawea's role within it. It was, as the title implies, a celebration of conquest, putting Lewis and Clark *and* Sacagawea within a broader story of righteous American violence for empire that ran for generations. The conquest of Oregon had followed on the conquest of Missouri had followed on the conquest of Illinois; the "conquest" of a "weaker race" by a stronger one was inevitable to Dye, as it had been to Victor and Bancroft. But in place of the long Indian wars Elwood Evans had praised as a necessity, Dye framed the invasions as short and successful—brief, violent clashes won by White supremacy and immediately followed by peace. Dye ended her mammoth book with praise for those "fighting new battles, planning new conquests ... of the Poles and Tropics," celebrating the seizure of the Philippines and pointing to further imperial expansion as the natural corollary of Anglo-Americans' manifest destiny. And indeed, volunteer veterans of the War on Illahee (and other Northwest Indian wars) were known to pass on war relics to children shipping out for colonial wars in the Pacific.[35]

Dye was not the first to explicitly connect the pioneer invasion of the Pacific Northwest with new imperial seizures abroad. When the Reverend Plutarch Stewart Knight gave a keynote address at the Oregon Pioneer Association in 1898, he linked the ongoing Spanish-American War to the actions of pioneers like himself back in the 1850s—and connected this to a call for bellicose colonialism in the name of civilization overseas: "While statesmanship debated, hesitated and protested, [the pioneer] with his ox whip and his rifle went forward and settled the issue. While statesmanship would have confined our young life to the eastern rim of the continent and made our national interest narrow and provincial, the pioneer led it across plains and mountains[,] spreading it from ocean to ocean and making it continental."[36]

Knight drew a direct line between the pioneering of the West Coast and the American overseas invasions: "What means this sound of battle from the distant Phi[l]ippines, this sailing of thousands of our best young men, a goodly number of them sons of the pioneers, across the western seas? Does all this imply that our march is ended, our mission closed? Or does it imply, rather, that our last Chinese wall has crumbled before its foundations were half laid?"[37]

Knight, Dye, and other Northwesterners saw American colonial conquests overseas as an extension of pioneer and volunteer heroics in the past. A 1903 fund-raiser for a memorial to "veterans of the four wars—Civil, Mexican, Indian and Spanish-American" at Portland's Lone Fir Cemetery (one of the few to prominently commemorate the IWV-NPC) featured a "sham battle" with Euro-Americans in brownface playing "wicked Filipinos." Many federal and military officers saw the new imperial conquests in the same way.[38]

*Eva Emery Dye early in her writing career. Dye preferred
to look away from the horrific violence of colonial invasion.
Courtesy of the Oregon Historical Society.*

While praising righteous violence, Dye deliberately ignored misdeeds she knew from her research had occurred. Dye knew that historically Toussaint Charbonneau, who had bought the adolescent Sacagawea
as a "wife" and claimed her wages for the expedition, assaulted her
viciously enough to attract rebuke from William Clark. But Dye had her
character "Sacajawea" praise her fortune at being married to a White
man. Dye knew from Christina Williams that Euro-American volunteers
and officers had sexually assaulted Native women during the wars of the
1850s—but soldiers across her works are almost unfailingly gallant. Dye
knew from every facet of her research that many trappers had been
"loose and lawless in almost every particular," but she broke from historians like Lang and Bancroft to make them into rustic champions of her

novels. Dye wrote heroic historical fiction, and such stories had no place in it. As one of her major informants, John Minto, approvingly put it, the focus was on "the Sentiment more than the Story." Dye prided herself on being "as impartial as any one" in the creation of what she called her "living histories," but her impartiality went in only one direction. She might mint new heroes, but any sense of settler crimes was generally scrubbed from her narratives. Dye's "living histories," anticipating popular memory to follow, typically framed Indian wars as short outbursts of violence spurred by a few treacherous Native people amid a sea of honorable men and women on both sides, after which Native communities would obligingly fade into the background.[39]

In the early 1900s, Dye's books, particularly *The Conquest*, significantly shaped popular narratives of Oregon pioneering. Her stories of Oregon were read across the country and locally, admired by some historians and adopted by Pacific Northwest universities and Indian schools alike. Native people at the Salem Chemawa Indian School from at least 1902 were encouraged to read Dye's *Stories of Oregon*. Perhaps administrators there found her mix of praise for "good Indians," pioneers, and the westward course of American empire instructive. Or perhaps it was the stories of honorable submission. Joseph Lane was presented in this work as a stern patriarch; James Lupton was absent, as was wanton White violence more generally. But for settlers, "massacre followed massacre." White invaders were presented as the victims, not the aggressors. And inevitably in Dye's *Stories of Oregon*, the Indian characters all learn they "must give up the vast areas over which [they were] wont to roam, and come under the laws of civilized life."[40]

Dye was not the only writer to place the invaders of the Pacific Northwest in the long sweep of imperial America. John Minto, a volunteer who took a decades-long interest in shaping regional history, argued that early "Oregon pioneers" in the 1840s "were largely of the same blood as those who took permanent possession of the 'Dark and Bloody ground' " in the 1700s—in other words, of those pioneers who had made war to seize land from the Indigenous nations of what is now Kentucky. At the very least, Minto asserted, there was a "spiritual . . . connection." Minto, like Dye, framed pioneers as part of a longer story of invasion.[41]

Minto and other volunteer veterans saw the wars they had fought in the Northwest as part of a multigenerational war against "the native race." Minto remained proud of these conquests, and he saw no contradiction in celebrating both the wars and his claim that "the race prejudice against Indian or negro blood the American homebuilder brought with him from Missouri to Oregon" had been "well nigh conquered" by 1903. Minto's own reflections about the "diverse tribes" of "savage men" "whose general mode of attack was that of the wolf" as they pursued "massacre, rapine and death" in Oregon was somehow not, in his estimation, a function of Minto's own "race prejudice." After all, he had Indian friends.[42]

Yet some Northwest historians in the early 1900s celebrated invasion while omitting wars entirely. As the engineer and pioneer historian Hiram Chittenden put it in his essay on what he called the Pioneer Way: "The ceaseless, steady flow of colonization from the Atlantic to the Pacific ... was throughout a spontaneous, individual movement by a liberty-loving people—not organized by military force nor compelled by a thirst for armed conquest. It was a process of pathfinding and up-building all the way, distinguished by heroic toil, by battle with savage foes and with unfriendly Nature, yet withal by an indomitable spirit and steadfastness of purpose that do high honor to human nature." Rather than celebrating or condemning the wars of conquest in the 1850s, Chittenden ignored their existence as such—the wars had presumably been a part of battling "with savage foes and with unfriendly Nature"—but they did not need separate mention, nor did he count them as "armed conquest."[43]

Later, in 1917, Chittenden did refer to mass killings and Native people, in a condemnation of genocide against Armenian people. But in his comparison he placed Native people in the role of the aggressors rather than the aggrieved: "We have stood by, in this Twentieth Century of Christian civilization idle spectators of the most atrocious barbarism which human history records. Nothing which we can recall from the bloodiest annals of the race even approaches in infamy the recent Armenian persecutions. Something like a million human beings have been swept out of existence under circumstances of barbarity which even the untamed American savage could not surpass."[44]

Chittenden, like so many of his fellows, was a fervent believer in White supremacy. He saw the 1910s Armenian Genocide for what it was (and argued that "Virile Americanism" was needed to stop it), but he portrayed the genocides perpetrated against Native people by Americans only as "that evolutionary process by which a weaker race disappears before a superior." He ignored Indian wars as wars but maintained the attitude that Native people were always the aggressors. He celebrated racial violence, even as he disavowed conquest.[45]

Clarence B. Bagley, a grafting government functionary and Northwest pioneer, has sometimes been labeled Washington state's "first and preeminent historian." Though he did not touch upon the subject often, Bagley's approach to the War on Illahee and its sequels was an evolution of Elwood Evans's and Charles Drew's. Bagley omitted pioneer misdeeds while acknowledging that they existed in the abstract, yet he separated the crimes of pioneers entirely from Native reactions to them.[46]

Bagley in the 1906 inaugural issue of the *Washington Historical Quarterly* heaped praise on

> volunteers, who left their homes and family to go to the Indian country in defense of the outlying settlers or to avenge the unprovoked and brutal crimes against them. . . .
>
> It has been the fashion among a class of persons, absolutely ignorant of conditions on the frontier, to prate loudly of the wrongs visited upon the poor Indian. No one, with any knowledge of the facts, will deny that the Indians were oftimes wrongfully treated by the whites, but as General Sheridan wrote in 1870, "So far as the wild Indians are concerned the problem to be decided is, 'Who shall be killed, the whites or the Indians?' "[47]

On the same page, Bagley both noted that Native people were "oftimes" mistreated *and* insisted that attacks on White people or communities were "unprovoked." Like Charles Drew, Bagley seems to have reflexively described Native aggression as unprovoked when discussing the volunteers, even though he acknowledged later in the essay that "the 'land greed' of the Americans . . . has caused most of the disturbances and wars between them and the Indians." Taking a less duplicitous version of the position assumed by Isaac I. Stevens (whom Bagley framed as a hero), Bagley argued that bad treatment by Whites did not ultimately matter, quoting General Philip Sheridan's justifications for genocide generally and the notorious Marias Massacre of 1870 specifically. To Bagley, "Indian fighting" had been a self-evident good, and "the mixture of races . . . ha[d] been unalloyed evil." Bagley was intellectually and financially interested in Native people and stories, collecting "legends" for publication. *And* he was in favor of seizing Native land, segregating Native people, and killing any Indian who got in the way.[48]

Clarence B. Bagley in 1920. Courtesy of the Seattle Public Library.

Bagley counted two Northwest pioneer wars with the Indians: the Cayuse War following the Whitman killings, and a "general" Indian war from 1855 to 1858. This focus on the Cayuse War—a war with a seemingly clear inciting incident and a comfortable narrative of Euro-American victimhood—was normal. Survivors of the Whitman killings were much prized on the pioneer circuit. Nancy Jacobs was perhaps the most prolific of the multiple Euro-American child survivors of the 1847 Whitman killings who toured the Pacific Northwest in the early 1900s, an honored guest at pioneer and volunteer association gatherings across the region. The slain were at least as cherished; hairs supposedly belonging to Narcissa Whitman took on the status of relics, passed between pioneers and historians as sacred objects. When future historian Edmond Meany was first embarking on his "life work" of history writing in 1895, he proved his interest and bona fides to Elwood Evans by lending the elder historian a supposed "lock of Mrs. Whitman's hair." Although there were disagreements about Marcus Whitman's purported pioneer heroism (see below), the war that followed his death appeared to Euro-Americans to be righteous. Regarding later conflicts in the War on Illahee, however, there were murmurs of dissension that broke through the pioneer code.[49]

Ezra Meeker was warned. An old Washington pioneer who had made and lost a fortune running a hops empire, Meeker in the 1900s launched a new career as a history entrepreneur. His first history book was a set of reminiscences about his time in the Puget Sound region in the 1850s, and particularly the conduct of the trial of Chief Leschi there. But before Meeker's book went to print, he was warned that it had content that would wreck his reputation and sink his potential sales. Clarence Bagley and amateur historian Edward Huggins both advised Meeker that "there was too much '*Leschi*' " in his book, and too much "*venom* and *bitterness*" toward Governor Isaac I. Stevens. Meeker edited out an unknown but significant amount of the Leschi and Stevens content. But some venom remained. Meeker's 1905 autobiography-cum-history, *Pioneer Reminiscences of Puget Sound: The Tragedy of Leschi*, broke from the pioneer code enough to get the author in trouble.[50]

In his autobiography, Ezra Meeker set himself out as an exception on issues of race. When he and his family had first come to the Pacific Northwest in 1852, he remembered, "[we had] guns by our sides if not in our hands for nearly half the time. . . . We took it for granted that Indians were our enemies and watched them suspiciously." It was only after learning how to bake clams and communicate in Chinook Jargon from a Native woman that their attitudes shifted. Native people, in Meeker's eyes, changed from "enemies" to "little children"—but more "short lived."[51]

Meeker's opinion of Native people shifted more permanently when he came to view them as an exploitable labor force. Meeker, like his fellow pioneer Jonathan McCarty, seized land in Puyallup country in the early 1850s. Unlike Meeker, McCarty had been an avid pursuer of genocide. And Meeker found far more success in his hop-growing empire than McCarty did in anything. But both attributed the change in their attitudes toward Native people to the wealth each man hoped to glean from Native labor, and both embraced pernicious assumptions of Indian subordination. McCarty believed he ruled by fear over his Native laborers. Meeker believed Native people lacked "mental capacity" and "the power to discriminate in the abstract as to right or wrong," but could be compelled to work industriously (and cheaply) if treated honestly and firmly by White employers like Meeker. Native people who worked for Meeker made the best of it despite low wages, and they managed to extract small concessions, including maternity pay. Evidence of Indigenous pickers in Meeker's fields striking for higher wages in 1882 might be a sign of his stinginess. Or it might be a sign that workers believed themselves able to survive going on strike with Meeker rather than some more lethal racist as their employer. Or both. Whether or not Meeker was the kind boss he claimed himself to be, he was still a White supremacist trying to turn a profit, blithe in his belief that he and the land he had taken belonged to a biologically "superior race."[52]

Meeker's version of Social Darwinism specified the "superior[ity] of pioneer stock," over and above his belief in broader White supremacy: "The pioneers had lost a large number of physically weak on the trip, thus applying the great law of the survival of the fittest; and further ... the great number were pioneers in the true sense of the word—frontiersmen for generations before—hence were by training and habits eminently fitted to meet the exigencies of the trip and conditions to follow." Much like Lang, Bancroft, and Victor before him, Meeker framed pioneers as heroes.[53]

Thus, those who had been unheroic had not been real pioneers. The Indian war of 1855–56, he wrote, "brought to the front many vicious characters. ... Yet there were genuine pioneer settlements." Meeker had his "unsettled class" and "genuine pioneers," which were analogous to Lang's "rogues and honest men." "A majority of the ... volunteer forces," Meeker wrote, "were sturdy pioneers who went to the war from a sense of duty." The "cruel murders" committed were the work of a few "poltroons" within an otherwise honorable body of "pioneers [who] treated their Indian neighbors justly, and we may say generously." What got Meeker into trouble was that he counted Governor Isaac I. Stevens among the poltroons.[54]

Meeker's accusations that Isaac I. Stevens had been a drunkard raised much more ire than Meeker's assertions that Stevens's deceits had led to the wars. Meeker presented Stevens's supposed drunkenness as backhanded exculpation. If the governor was not a drunkard, Meeker wrote, "we must ... write Stevens down as a *very* bad and dishonest man." In truth, *Pioneer Reminiscences of Puget Sound* painted him as both. Meeker traced failed treaties and the "policy of extermination" alike to Stevens, laying the few atrocities against Native communities mentioned in the text—the James A. Lake killing of "Indian Bob" (Squalli-absch Say-oh-sil) and the Maxon Massacre—ultimately at the feet of the governor. Even in this somewhat critical history, other men who had committed mass killings, such as C. C. Hewitt, Benjamin F. Shaw, and George Wright, were presented as heroic.[55]

The culmination of Meeker's book was his argument that Leschi had been "judicially murdered ... a sacrifice to a principle, a martyr to a cause, and a savior of his people." Meeker's discussion of Leschi has been a vital source for historians since he wrote it, not least because he interviewed multiple Native people (mostly Puyallup and Nisqually people) to make the case that the first Treaty of Medicine Creek defrauded Native communities. He may have been, as historian Alexander Olson put it, "less a historian than an eccentric memorialist," but he at least spoke to Native people, and he sometimes indicated which stories he had gotten from whom. And Meeker drew on his own claimed experience as one of the jurors in Leschi's first trial to argue that the case had been a miscarriage of justice, marred by jurisdictional issues, bias, and perjury. Although Meeker removed some of his material on Leschi on the advice of his editors, what remained has been useful supporting evidence for some Indigenous accounts for more than a century.[56]

Meeker decried the first Treaty of Medicine Creek as "one-sided" and "completely [ignoring] the interests of the Indians," amplifying some of his Indigenous informants. But this was not necessarily sympathy or support. More generally, Meeker despised treaties and "the fiction of Indian Nationalities." He celebrated the 1871 Indian Appropriations Act for ending treaty making and wished that no treaties had been made in the Pacific Northwest at all. Maintaining his view of infantilized Indians, he believed they could have and should have been coaxed off most of their land, if only they had been treated gently and firmly by a paternal and unyielding state. Like Jesse Applegate in the 1850s, Meeker wanted Native land and believed in White supremacy; both men simply preferred not to kill for it.[57]

Edmond S. Meany, a historian, politician, and professor at the University of Washington, led many of the public attacks against Ezra Meeker's 1905 book. In a series of newspaper articles, Meany (with the support of Clarence Bagley and several others) took aim at Meeker's sources and his tone. Many pointed to the contradictions between the evidence Meeker brought forth and the recollections of Hazard Stevens, Isaac I. Stevens's son, who had accompanied his father to many events as a young adolescent. Meany, Bagley, and Huggins all apparently agreed Hazard Stevens's account should carry more weight than some "story Meeker got from an Indian." It was actually several stories from several Native people, versus the story of a man reporting on his own father, who had been at most thirteen years old at the time of events. But for many historians, personal bias is no match for racial bias.[58]

Meany kept his attacks on Meeker mostly civil, praising much of *Pioneer Reminiscences of Puget Sound* while arguing that Meeker had been gravely mistaken on the subject of Stevens. In private letters, Meany was concerned about reputation more than accuracy. In an indicative letter, Meany argued that "Leschi's greatness can be shown without throwing mud at Stevens or anyone else." Meany approved of histories that celebrated a few "Great Men" among the Indians; his own master's work, started under famed Western historian Frederick Jackson Turner, had been a project defending the historical reputation of the Nez Perce/Nimiipuu leader Chief Joseph/Hinmatóoyalahtq'it as uniquely "civilized" in his war conduct. But Meany objected to any project of valorization that might threaten pioneer hagiography.[59]

Other Meeker detractors were more menacing. In a letter to Meany, Hazard Stevens, after insisting on the "remarkable and uniform success of [his father's] management of the Indians and the volunteer forces," suggested: "Would it not be well to look up Meeker's own conduct and attitude during the Indian War? Is it not possible that he nourishes some ancient grudge, or grievance against Gov. Stevens? Did he take any part in defending the settlements? Or did he hang around the post at Steilacoom and spend his efforts in sympathizing with an Indian enemy?" Edward Huggins's anger at the man he dubbed "Misery Meeker" led him to privately attack Meeker's family. Writing in secret to Eva Emery Dye, the often slippery Huggins shared a salacious story about Meeker's son, who, Huggins claimed, had abandoned his wife for a fling with a married woman. Huggins had gotten the story from Meeker himself, who had come to his old friend "with tears in his eyes." "After reading what [Meeker] said" about fellow pioneers, Huggins told Dye, he felt "no hesitancy" about sharing this "cruel" story. This was a warning, intentional or not, about what might happen to those who broke the pioneer code.[60]

Huggins was at least as incensed that Meeker made mention of "Kitty," a Nisqually woman married to Lieutenant Augustus V. Kautz of the U.S. Army in the 1850s. After working to make sure that the children of the union between Kautz and Kitty did not get a claim to their father's estate, Huggins had tried to erase them from public memory entirely—perhaps for the sake of Kautz's second, White family. Huggins's sensitivity may have been acute because his own wife, Anne, was of partially Indigenous descent—a fact he apparently kept close to the vest, and which did not stop him from expressing broad contempt for "half-breeds."[61]

One particularly striking letter to Edmond Meany on Meeker came from pioneer historian George E. Blankenship. He began by noting that Meeker was "evidently biased," then in a few sentences explained that his own "interest in the matters [was] well founded" because his family had been a part of the events Meeker discussed. The historian saying things he did not care for was biased. Blankenship's own bias was, by his lights, simply "well founded" "interest." His main objection was not to facts but to what was said and how, complaining that "Meeker's anecdote often rises to the point of brutality." Readers like Blankenship were much more concerned with rough prose about historical figures than with the literal brutality those figures had inflicted.[62]

Even those willing to grant Meeker's evidence legitimacy might still resent publication. As Edward Huggins's wife, Anne Huggins, wrote to Eva Emery Dye, "Like you I do not especially care for Mr. Meeker's book—Historically it may be of value but he most certainly makes unkind remarks about people to whom he owes nothing but favors." The truth, to this reader, apparently to Dye, and to many others, should not be repeated if "unkind," and "favors" owed should shape historical narrative.[63]

Bagley bore no grudge against Meeker. He was one of the first to praise the "stubborn as a mule" Meeker for the Oregon Trail ox team reenactments that eventually catapulted him to national celebrity. But Bagley did warn others not to repeat the same risks. Eva Emery Dye, one of those so warned, assured him that she would not (in his words) be "unduly influenced." She might be "glad Mr. Meeker has persisted and succeeded." But her own work would remain firmly celebratory.[64]

For Meeker, like Lang before him, bucking the pioneer code had financial consequences. Subscriptions—what might now be called preorders—were a key part of book publishing at the time. After Huggins and others spread the word of Meeker's "spiteful attack[s]" on figures such as Isaac I. Stevens, "the paucity of subscribers" came close to keeping the book from print altogether. Meeker took out personal loans himself to complete publication, finally recouping costs only after the strong sales of his later works, which praised pioneering uncritically. Despite Meeker's eventual celebrity, sales of *Pioneer Reminiscences of Puget Sound* remained slow for years.[65]

By contrast, Edmond Meany's 1909 *History of the State of Washington*, with Isaac I. Stevens as its foremost hero, enjoyed near-immediate success—particularly after it was adopted in schools. For decades, history students in Washington would learn from Meany's lightly sourced book that Isaac I. Stevens had been upright in every way, and that the wars of the 1850s were incited by Indians who "simply endeavored to make one more stand against the wave of civilization." The only White wrongdoer in Meany's discussion of the wars was General John E. Wool, a "weak, evasive ... pitiful spectacle of a man" who should have "used sensible coöperation with the citizen soldiery instead of giving rein to his violent prejudices [against Stevens and the volunteers]." In Meany's telling, Wool's distrust for the volunteers had been the real violence, not, say, the many, many massacres and murders those volunteers had committed. Other leaders, such as Charles Mason and George Wright, Meany occasionally critiqued for "relying on the promises of good behavior on the part of ... plotting savages." But although Meany criticized what he implausibly called George Wright's "surfeit [of] mercy," these men were framed as redeemed because of their later embrace of stern violence. After federal ratification of key treaties from the 1850s in 1859, Native people more or less disappeared from Meany's narrative of the state— and thus, presumably, from many of the state history lessons founded on his text in the first half of the 1900s. Indians came up only indirectly, as when Meany risibly blamed mixed-race marriages for the initial failure of White women's suffrage in Washington Territory.[66]

In the summer of 1911, Clarence Bagley wrote Edmond Meany a letter on the duties of a historian—weighty indeed, for two of the most prominent regional historians of the Pacific Northwest. Much of the letter had to do with contemporary debates over Marcus Whitman— whether Whitman had "saved Oregon" for the United States, and whether the killings of members of the Whitman household were martyrdoms or evidence of folly. In this private letter, at least, Bagley described Marcus Whitman as "a mediocre man, stubborn beyond reason, and very ready to take offense" and blamed the missionary for the deaths in his household. Bagley urged Meany to set aside his inclinations toward the "interesting, romantic, patriotic" interpretation of the Whitman story and instead look to the sources. "We should dump no error into the stream of history," Bagley wrote, "and when we discover the stream has been polluted, it is our duty and should be a pleasure to correct the error."[67]

Bagley was not alone among regional historians in his vexation. Frances Fuller Victor fought the Whitman mythos in the 1880s and 1890s, struggling largely in vain against pioneer antipathy locally and the misogynist elitism of the *American Historical Review* nationally. Frederick V. Holman had expressed similar frustrations about the ever-growing

*Professor Edmond S. Meany posing for an oil painting in the early 1920s.
Courtesy of the Museum of History and Industry, Seattle.*

exaggerations of the Whitman story, writing in 1910: "I suppose it will
be ultimately claimed that [Marcus Whitman] was the cause of the discovery of the North Pole. But I doubt it." Historians, up to a point, knew
better.[68]

But Bagley's paean to the historical method came with a caveat. He
planned to keep the full measure of his historical interpretation of Whitman private. Expanding from his assessment of the missionary as a "mediocre man," Bagley wrote: "He had no right to sacrifice the lives of
innocent people confided to his care. It was little short of murder. I am
willing to 'let the dead bury their dead,' and so I do not give expression to
these sentiments in public. What is the good?" Bagley knew that the various legends swirling around Marcus Whitman were false. But he largely
held his tongue. And Bagley applied this sort of strategic silence liberally:
"I feel about this as I do about some matters nearer home. Sometime I
shall write a history of Seattle, and while what I shall say will be the truth
I shall not give *all* the truth. I shall rake up no old stories of evil."[69]

Clarence Bagley's commitment to "rake up no old stories of evil" was part of his historical work, whether it came to monographs, memorials, or monuments. Flagrant falsehoods of the sort Elwood Evans had embraced were, perhaps, to be avoided. But omission of pioneer evils was standard practice—for him, for Edmond Meany, and for much of the world of historical and heritage societies of which they were a part.[70]

At a 1913 pioneer meeting, George Kuykendall, a doctor and amateur historian, spoke to the softening power of nostalgia: "I do not know how it may be with others of the old pioneers ... but I notice that as time goes by, there is a distinct tendency for the unpleasant memories to fade out, the asperities to soften and mellow, and for the memories of the bright and beaut[iful] incidents to come to the front." This "tendency for the unpleasant memories to fade out" was in many cases deliberate.[71]

The informal "pioneer code" was embraced and sometimes enforced by most of those who created Euro-American history in the late nineteenth and early twentieth centuries. Mellowing the memories of pioneer violence was a choice, not just a tendency. Sometimes it was a choice of which sources to believe and which to ignore. Often it was a choice of which stories historians thought they should tell, and which stories historians thought they could sell.

CHAPTER ELEVEN

Making Monuments and Forging Memories in the Progressive-Era Pacific Northwest

Joseph nathan teal was the picture of a pioneer booster. His father, Joseph Teal, had come to Oregon in 1851, "participated helpfully in a number of early Indian troubles Wars" (as the younger Teal put it), and made fortunes in cattle ranching, shipping, and real estate investment. The elder Teal was a power broker in the Oregon Democratic Party. He was also, very publicly, an enslaver—at one point in the early 1860s yoking an enslaved child named Coleman to a wagon, next to a dog, and compelling him to pull a young Joseph Nathan Teal around the streets of Eugene, Oregon. Slavery was illegal and unremarkable in pioneer Oregon, for the Teals and many others. But this was not the sort of pioneer practice they wanted on plaques or statuary.[1]

Joseph Nathan Teal built on the family's political and economic power, becoming a successful lawyer, making lucrative investments, and taking on a number of civic and government positions. The younger Teal acquired yet more connections and fortune from his father-in-law, David P. Thompson, a successful banker and politician who had patrolled Indian internment camps as a youth in the 1850s. Thompson and the younger Teal wanted to shape a lasting legacy honoring the pioneer generation. They opted for statuary, funding three of the earliest such monuments in

Oregon. Roland Hinton Perry's *Elk*, dedicated in downtown Portland in 1900, was meant to evoke the primeval "wilderness" of the region before the arrival of pioneers. Hermon A. MacNeil's *Coming of the White Man*, unveiled in 1904 and installed in Portland's Washington Park, depicted two elegiac Native figures "bravely facing a fate [they] could not avoid" at the approach of the Lewis and Clark Expedition. And Alexander Phimister Proctor's *The Pioneer*, erected in Eugene in 1919, depicted a rough-and-ready Indian killer in heroic pose. White conquest of Native people and land was central to the memories Teal wanted to engrave on the landscape. And he wasn't alone.[2]

Pacific Northwest settlers strove for monuments in the early 1900s but only occasionally achieved statuary. The broader push to memorialize the Euro-American wars of conquest in the Pacific Northwest took many forms, playing a part in ephemeral parades and pageants as well as more permanent parks and plaques. Created largely by a new generation of Euro-American settlers, in consultation with their pioneer forebears, these monuments tried to engrave a heroic story of White supremacy triumphant on the landscape.

Pioneer memory making in the early decades of the twentieth century was also inflected by rising fascination with often mythic Indianness and debates over the nature of American imperialism. Although virtually all monuments to the wars of the 1850s celebrated American empire, many focused on perceived Native participation in Americanization. Stories of a few "good Indians" supplemented rather than replaced stories of White "civilization" triumphant against Indians generally. Such stories were popular, opening avenues for fund-raising. And in at least a few cases, Native people were able to leverage the pioneer nostalgia for such stories to gain Euro-American audiences for fights against injustices past and present.

There had been calls for monuments even as the War on Illahee was under way. Following the news of the conflicts during which Peo-Peo-Mox-Mox was murdered in 1855, the Washington Territorial Legislature included in their declaration of praise for the perpetrators a call for "a monument to the memory of the fallen patriots of Oregon . . . to perpetuate their names and fame to the latest posterity." Speakers at pioneer events would often stress the need for monuments, including calls to "erect a monument to the pioneer mothers of Oregon" at least as far back as 1883. Some organizations, such as the Pierce County Pioneers Association in Washington, made "rais[ing] monuments" part of their charters.[3]

But monuments cost money. Fund-raising or patronage for controversial or partisan figures could be difficult. Edmond Meany was a major agonist for monuments across the state of Washington, yet his most ambitious plans did not come to fruition. While serving in the 1894 state legislature, Meany attempted to drum up political and financial support to send two statues to the National Statuary Hall in Washington, D.C. His choices for the state's exemplars were Marcus Whitman and Isaac I. Stevens. (Meany also wanted a "large heroic statue of Stevens in the public square of Seattle.") But Meany's statue statute fizzled out, and he was forced into more modest monument making. Around half a century later, in 1953, Avard T. Fairbanks's fantastical statue of Marcus Whitman in fringed buckskin as a "ripped, muscular frontiersman" was installed in the National Statuary Hall, where Supreme Court Justice William O. Douglas praised the missionary for having "showed us a new empire" on the Pacific Coast. Meany's dream of an Isaac I. Stevens statue, on the other hand, never came to be.[4]

Many of the earliest statues celebrating the pioneer era in the Pacific Northwest were representations of Native people. In 1904 Joseph Nathan Teal unveiled Hermon A. MacNeil's *Coming of the White Man* in Portland, Oregon. His deceased father-in-law, David P. Thompson, had a bequest to create a memorial "emblematic of the earliest history of this country." Teal and MacNeil had chosen as their subject "Chief Multnomah" (alongside an unnamed young Native man). Multnomah was a half-mythical Native leader along the Columbia River, made famous in Euro-American author Frederic Homer Balch's influential novel, *The Bridge of the Gods.*[5]

Teal's dedication speech underlined the future bloodshed and elegy the monument implied:

> Imagine, if you can, proud old Multnomah when he first caught a glimpse of the white stranger coming unbidden to his land. . . . Haughty, defiant, as became a mighty chieftain, resentful yet interested, wise with the wisdom of age, feeling forebodings of disaster, he stood sternly on the rock, bravely facing a fate he could not avoid. . . .
>
> As one looks on the bronze figures standing on the rock gazing up Columbia gorge, one cannot but feel for old Multnomah

Hermon Atkins MacNeil's Coming of the White Man *(1904), shown here in 1910. Courtesy of the Field Museum Library.*

and his falling star, and pity the youthful innocence of the boy who did not know that before civilization's march barbarism falls, as disappears the dew before the rising sun.[6]

The mention of dew made disappearance sound like a natural inevitability. Teal's speech made only oblique reference to the wars his father, uncle, and father-in-law had been a part of. The younger figure in the monument makes a welcoming gesture—which Teal pitied, as ignorant of what was to come. To Teal's forebears, and perhaps to him, the march of civilization had been somewhat literal, the tramping boots of irregular pioneers and regular soldiers ready to force Native communities to fall.[7]

Alice Cooper's monumental statue *Sacajawea and Jean-Baptiste* (1905), featuring the famed guide Sacagawea pointing west in a near-salute as she energetically strides forward with her baby Jean-Baptiste on her back, was similarly a celebration of American empire. The statue features a representation of a famous Native woman, was planned and funded largely by suffragists, and was unveiled at the Portland Lewis and Clark Centennial Exposition and World's Fair in 1905. Each of those aspects is a lure for academics, and the monument has thus attracted attention from numerous scholars and artists across multiple disciplines. It is perhaps the most analyzed pioneer statue in the Pacific Northwest.[8]

After the success of Eva Emery Dye's 1902 book, *The Conquest*, there was a broad-based movement, led by suffragists, to erect a statue of the woman they called Sacajawea in time for the 1905 Exposition. Many women's suffrage groups and advocates in the American Pacific Northwest had long drawn on women's part in pioneering to build audiences and advocates for the vote. Abigail Scott Duniway, in her lifetime probably the most famed and prolific Northwest suffragist, used her status as a "pioneer champion" to fight for women's rights. As scholar Tiffany Lewis has argued, suffragists like Duniway portrayed the franchise as an "earned right" for Western women, proven by their shared pioneer struggle. The language of pioneering suffused Duniway's writing—temporary setbacks would not end the fight for suffrage and against the "men's rights microbe," she proclaimed, any more than "the Whitman massacre [marked] the end of progress for the Oregon Pioneers." And Duniway's own status as a pioneer helped her build alliances for women's suffrage among various heritage organizations. Along with the celebrity guest Susan B. Anthony,

Alice Cooper's Sacajawea and Jean-Baptiste (1905), *shortly after it was moved, in* 1906, *to its current home in Portland's Washington Square Park. Courtesy of University of Southern California Libraries and the California Historical Society.*

Duniway was one of several speakers at the *Sacagawea and Jean-Baptiste* unveiling.[9]

Eva Emery Dye, also a suffragist, became president of the Sacajawea Statue Association in 1903. Dye circulated promotional materials framing Sacagawea as "the first pioneer mother to cross the Rocky mountains and carry her baby into the Oregon country." She and other members raised money not only from suffragist gatherings and the Daughters of the American Revolution (DAR), but also from redface heritage groups like the Improved Order of Red Men (IORM), along with their auxiliary group, the Ladies of the Degree of Pocahontas, suggesting the statue could be "a joint memorial of the Red Men and the white women of the country."[10]

In her fund-raising and speeches, Dye Pocahontas-ed Sacagawea, turning her into one of many Native women whose stories were reshaped by imperialists to affirm American land taking and innocence. In her letter to the IORM, Dye described her as "the bravest maiden of the Indian race. Of course this statue can be and is typical of all the Indian women who literally gave their country to America, by aid or succ[o]r like that of Pocahontas and Sacajawea, from the Atlantic Ocean to the Pacific." Dye was unusually successful in boosting her half-fantasy version of Sacagawea. But many similar narratives have been created by colonizers, in the Northwest and well beyond it, and there may have been a heightened hunger for them in the period.[11]

The IORM and similar groups playacted Native ritual as part of their meetings and civic events, dressing in a pastiche of presumed Native costumes (often with face paint) and dropping mannerisms associated with White stereotypes of Native speech into their communication—practices now known, pejoratively, as "redface." Redface speeches in the Northwest included interjections of "ughs" and "hows," as was typical across the United States, but they often also used the simplified "Boston" version of Chinook Jargon. In the Northwest as elsewhere, redface performers often took for themselves Native names for persons, communities, or objects, mixing the regionally specific with the nationally famous. Redface was sometimes a fund-raising activity, as when members in Oregon City raised money for the statue by means of "a pantomime from Fenimore Cooper's 'Last of the Mohicans.' " Membership might or might not denote fascination or sympathy with Native people—LaFayette Mosher, one of the more strident political voices calling for genocide in the 1800s, was also a member of the Improved Order of Red Men. Actual "Indians of any tribe" were explicitly forbidden to join the IORM in 1871. It was an organization for White people to play Indian, only.[12]

Speakers at the dedication of *Sacajawea and Jean-Baptiste* used the language of benevolent conquest. The ceremony was thronged with White "Red Men" and Native children on a field trip from the abusive Chemawa Indian School in Salem, as speaker after speaker turned Sacagawea into a tool of American empire. Susan B. Anthony praised her "patriotic deeds," a representative from the IORM lauded her "efforts" in effecting "the transformation of a wilderness into a marvelous commonwealth of wonderful cities and great commercial enterprises." Duniway at least allowed for inadvertency, saying of the "feminine [A]tlas" (Duniway's term for Sacagawea), "Little did she know or realize that she was helping to upbuild a Pacific empire, whose borders the white man and white woman would unite." Dye went further, suggesting that Sacagawea

had "beckoned the white man on" to Asia as well as America. Pacific empire could include new conquests as well as old.[13]

The speakers did not agree on the subject of Indian wars. Dye more
or less argued that they did not exist, or at least that they were immaterial. "The Indians expected to see an army with banners when the white
man came," she proclaimed, "but no, the mother and the child took Oregon." She had written about the Indian wars only a few years earlier, including a section on how women had helped provide banners to
volunteers in the lead-up to the Cayuse War. But wars were already disappearing from her conception of pioneering. She now praised Joseph
Lane for his chivalry, not his soldiery.[14]

The last speaker of the day, Portland Mayor Harry Lane, did talk
about the Indian wars—and critiqued them, along with wanton White
violence more generally: "The Indians have many sterling traits of character that we do not possess. When they have not been contaminated by
the evils of the white race, they are the personification of tireless energy,
patience and hospitality. All of the wars resulted from the white people
ill-treating the Indians who had befriended them." This was unusual for
a Euro-American leader, shockingly so for the grandson of the notorious
Joseph Lane. But Harry Lane, by the standards of the time an actual Native rights advocate, had already embraced a picture of his grandfather as
a "friend of the Indians," constructed by the Lane family from half-truths
and whole cloth.[15]

As the younger Lane moved from being Portland's mayor to serving
as a U.S. senator in 1912, he acted in support of Native peoples and Native issues while speaking in favor of the pioneers who had ravaged their
communities—and saw no contradiction. He fought against allotment,
supported the continuation of traditional lifeways, and amplified the
concerns of the Native activists he spoke with. But Harry Lane also believed in a false pioneer history of rogues and honest men. Harry Lane
left his rogues largely undefined, and he counted as honest men his
grandfather, the members of the Indian War Veterans of the North Pacific Coast, and any number of other murderers and rapists. The wars
might have "resulted" from the actions of bad White people—typically
left undefined—but for Harry Lane the people who *fought* in the wars
were mostly noble. "Hospitality" justified Euro-American presence, and
conquest was recast as "ill-treatment."[16]

Harry Lane was a believer in a version of Native rights, *and* a believer in the inherent rightness of American ownership of the land. He

departed from many of his fellow citizens in believing Native Americans should continue to own *all* their land that had not yet been taken, under U. S. jurisprudence. As a U.S. senator in the 1910s, this was enough to make him, by comparison to his contemporaries in government, a radical fighter for Native rights. Similarly, the *Sacajawea* monument has not yet come in for the same level of criticism as other pioneer monuments have in the early 2000s. Compared to other statuary of the era, the *Sacajawea* monument at least shows a Native woman in pose of power, despite the celebration of empire it was meant to embody.[17]

As Paul Scolari, Jean O'Brien, Lisa Blee, and others have argued, monumental statues of peacemaking Native figures have been, among other things, a means of dispelling doubts about the rectitude of American empire. In the Pacific Northwest at least as much as elsewhere, they were also a part of a rising fascination with representations of Native people as art objects—and not just as peacemakers. As Norwood Curry, an Oregon art dealer, wrote in 1904, images of "Sacajawea [or of] an Indian scene on the plains attacking an immigrant train ... appeal very strongly to our people in the northwest. More so ... [than] old masters works. Many of our people cannot appreciate old art but many can an Indian scene, of the Northwest." Indian-themed pageantry, variously performed by actual Native people and White folks in redface, was often an analog or accompaniment to these visual arts.[18]

The Seattle monument *Seattle, Chief of the Suquamish* (conceived in 1907, dedicated in 1912) was, like *Sacajawea and Jean-Baptiste*, a representation of a Native person read as handing over land to White people. James A. Wehn, the sculptor, had originally been brought in to "erect a statue ... emblematic of commerce"—but the city officials and architect who had arranged for the project found little agreement on what that might mean. Given free rein to "proceed as [he] though[t] best" and bored with the idea of simply putting up some classical god or other, Wehn lit upon the idea of a sculpture of Sealth/Seattle/Siʔal, a Suquamish and Duwamish leader who had signed the Treaty of Point Elliot with Isaac I. Stevens in 1855, stayed out of the Puget Sound War, and was most famous among colonizers for a valedictory address of murky provenance. With the eager approval of Clarence Bagley (and soon Edmond Meany), Wehn pursued art to cement the leader's place as the face of the city that had taken a garbled version of his name as its own.[19]

Wehn came of age as an artist at a time when artistic representations of Indians were common and marketable. His primary professional mentors

Tututni/Takelma Elder Oscharwasha ("Jennie") in the early 1890s. Courtesy of the Southern Oregon Historical Society.

gained fame from portraiture of Oscharwasha/"Old Jennie," a Tututni/ Takelma woman in southern Oregon who was feted (incorrectly) as the "last representative of the famous Rogue River Indians" in 1892. In this last year before her death, Oscharwasha used her fame to tell stories of wrongs perpetrated by pioneers—including recounting how she had been "captured by the whites, and later rescued by her people," and, as a Jacksonville newspaper reporter put it, "the grievous outrages and nameless wrongs perpetrated upon her people, and their consequent annihilation from the face of the earth, [stories that] would touch the stoutest heart with sympathy, and almost make one wish he could face again the brawny braves who fought and died for this fair heritage."[20]

One might well wonder whether it was the journalist or the speaker who left the "wrongs" "nameless"—and what the journalist wanted to do in the do-over he imagined. This moment of sympathy was short-lived; before the end of the paragraph the journalist was cracking wise about supposed Indian backwardness and lasciviously speculating about what "Old Jennie" would have looked like young and naked. The artists, meanwhile, were most interested in her robe, formal traditional raiment that Oscharwasha had made herself. Rowena Nichols (later Leinss), Wehn's first art teacher, had painted picture of Oscharwasha in this clothing to be displayed alongside a commissioned painting of Table Rock for the 1893 Chicago World's Fair. August Hubert, Wehn's primary mentor as a sculptor, collaborated with Leinss to create a sculpture of "Old Jennie" from that portrait for the Alaska-Yukon-Pacific Exposition of 1909.[21]

From 1907, James Wehn worked with Clarence Bagley and Edmond Meany to create a statue of Chief Sealth to celebrate commerce and the city of Seattle. Bagley was useful politically as well as historically. Deploying the same political acumen with which he had "cleaned up several thousand" dollars of taxpayers' money for his own pocket by vastly overcharging the government as a printer during the pioneer period, Bagley made sure the "open" contest to create the statue was a mere formality: Wehn was always going to win. Wehn modeled the body for his statue first after a local émigré and debauchee who claimed to be a German count, then after a former U.S. soldier who had fought in the Nez Perce War. The face he patterned after an image of the historical Chief Sealth, pictures of Native people he had taken without their knowledge when visiting regional communities, and pilfered skulls he had dug up in Duwamish country.[22]

The redface Euro-American group Tilikums of Elttaes at the dedication of James Wehn's Chief Seattle *(1912); their leader, Edgar L. Webster, stands in the center with his arms crossed. Courtesy of the Seattle Municipal Archives.*

Wehn's grave robbing, as his biographer Fred Poyner IV has shown, made it impossible for him to coax local Native people to model for his artwork. An early model had found out what Wehn had done, and he "passed the word around"—even in ongoing hard times for Native people in Seattle, Wehn's thievery meant no one in the community would accept pay to sit for him. Sculpting continued without live Native models. The statue, which had been renamed *Chief Seattle* after Wehn's preferred spelling of Sealth was rejected by local Euro-American historians, was unveiled in a grand parade and ceremony on Founder's Day, November 13, 1912.[23]

Much of the fund-raising for the statue, and the ceremonies connected to its unveiling, were managed by yet another redface heritage group—the self-titled Tilikums of Elttaes. The Tilikums were a fraternal organization in Washington state dedicated to civic boosterism, economic development, and redface pantomime. Each branch combined the Chinook Jargon word for *friend* with the name of their city spelled backward—a few days after the unveiling of *Chief Seattle*, the Tilikums of Elttaes announced their annual meeting with the Tilikums of Enakops in a press release replete with Chinook Jargon, bonhomie, and racial slurs. Just as the Improved Order of Red Men had raised money for *Sacajawea and Jean-Baptiste* with redface pageantry, the Tilikums of Elttaes raised money for *Chief Seattle* through "stunts." One recorded stunt, in May 1912, involved crowds of White men in redface costume posing in tableaux next to a stolen Tongass Tlingit totem pole at Seattle's Pioneer Place.[24]

Pioneer memorialists often corralled students from Indian schools for monument dedications. In 1899, for the dedication of an ornate pseudo-neoclassical statuary fountain in Tacoma honoring Narcissa Whitman, the Daughters of the American Revolution shipped in an "Indian band of twenty members from the state school," who the DAR falsely claimed were "descendants of those who perpetrated the [Whitman] massacre." And just as Chemawa Indian School students had been brought to witness the dedication of *Sacajawea and Jean-Baptiste*, at least some students from the abusive Tulalip Indian School attended the unveiling of *Chief Seattle*. One such student, identified as Seattle's descendant Myrtle Loughery, did the unveiling. Bagley, Meany, Wehn, and Tilikums of Elttaes leader Edgar L. Webster did the talking. They wanted Indians there for show, but they didn't want to hear from them.[25]

As Euro-American objectification and fascination with Native cultures and caricatures reached new heights from the 1890s through the 1910s, one particularity in the Pacific Northwest was the rise of what might be called "Chinook mania." A simplified version of Chinuk *wawa* suitable for communication with linguistically indexterous White people—Chinook Jargon—had been the primary means of communication between Indigenous and European-descended people in the Northwest from the early 1800s to the 1860s and beyond. By design easy to learn, with a standard syllabary of only a few hundred words, it had been viewed as a badge of pioneer identity from the earliest invasions of American settlers. But among early pioneer history makers, there were many who viewed the trade language as undignified. In 1869, when Wesleyan minister Thomas Derrick wanted to insist that properly manly men would not use slang words, he made his point by labeling all slang—Jargon or not—as "civilized Chinook." When the Indian War Veterans of the North Pacific Coast had floated the idea of a Chinook motto of "Ick Close Tillikum," meaning

"One Good Indian," LaFayette Mosher had shut down the idea of using Chinook because he saw it as unsuited to an organization that wished to be seen as august. William Fraser Tolmie, the Hudson's Bay factor who served as a key informant for many early histories of Washington, derided the trade language as a "vile compound," an unpleasant necessity unsuited to the civilized.[26]

But by the 1900s, Chinook Jargon went from "vile compound" to what Edmond Meany labeled "an elixir" of memory among heritage groups and other Euro-Americans committed to nostalgia. The Indian War Veterans of the North Pacific Coast, the Improved Oregon of Red Men, the Washington Pioneer Association, and the Oregon Pioneer Association all made Chinook Jargon a semiregular feature of their meetings in the first two decades of the twentieth century. Flyers and menus for organizational dinners were often almost entirely in Chinook Jargon—no translation provided.[27]

In a "Camp-Fire" meeting of the 1909 Oregon Pioneer Association— typically a lighter entertainment toward the end of a day—there was a series of five-minute talks, short pieces of music, a poetry reading, and (singled out for special praise) "the conversation in the Chinook jargon language between Cyrus H. Walker, of Albany, Oregon, born December 7, 1838, the oldest native son of white parents now living, and Mrs. Abigail Scott Duniway, a pioneer of 1852, and Dr. [Bethenia] Owens-Adair, a pioneer of 1843." The performance and pioneer identity par excellence of the participants were connected. The ability to converse in Chinook jargon was a marker of pioneer prowess for all three of these formidable figures (Walker by this time the head of the IWV-NPC, Duniway a leading women's rights advocate who connected suffrage to the sufferings of pioneer women, Owens-Adair a doctor and eventually a leading proponent of involuntary sterilization in the Pacific Northwest; all three were amateur historians). Cyrus Walker regularly led the singing of hymns in Chinook Jargon at pioneer gatherings and volunteer veterans' events, building on more generic entertainment of "Indian songs" in the 1900s to include a "Chinook choir" by the 1910s. Heritage organizations like the Native Daughters of Oregon saw no conflict between their insistence on the superior "royal blood" of those of pioneer lineage and their Chinook Jargon motto ("Klose Nesika Illahee," which they translated as "Our country is good, or best").[28]

In 1914 use of Chinook Jargon at the Oregon Pioneer Association Reunion included not just songs and dialogue but whole skits in redface.

White pioneers entertained in redface as members of the "Unimproved Order of Red Men"—a racist play on the all-White Improved Order of Red Men, to which members of many heritage organizations belonged. Ebenezer Barnes McFarland, remembered for attacking Native people in the Rogue River region in the early 1850s, put on a skit giving "an impassioned 'wa-wa,' protesting against the habit of 'Boston men' in poaching upon aboriginal preserves." Later the same day Walker seems to have taken part in a "Chinook Dialogue between representatives of the 'Unimproved Order of Red Men,' led by a kloochman who will scold her lazy man for failing to do his share in digging camas and other household duties." As historian Daniel J. Burge has noted, "burlesque" redface performances were one way Euro-Americans leavened the reality of genocide to soothe themselves.[29]

Walker's and McFarland's Chinook dialogues were again featured in 1915, 1916, and 1917. Pioneers and their descendants in Steilacoom, Washington, dressed in redface and sang "My Country 'Tis of Thee" in Chinook Jargon—with "My Country" replaced by the Chinook Jargon term for homeland, Illahee. In Oregon Pioneer Association programs through the 1920s, alongside the lyrics to "The Battle Hymn of the Republic" and "Dixie" (reflecting a desire to appeal to Unionists and Confederates alike), the remaining pioneers found an enjoinment: "Pioneers, greet each other. Then you will have a 'good time.' You may find an old sweetheart, or an old til-li-kum you have not seen for years." The regular reference to "an old til-li-kum" ceased in 1931, which perhaps reflects a feeling that Chinook Jargon was no longer widely known among the group's members.[30]

The assumption of wide pioneer knowledge of and delight in Chinook Jargon extended to the theater. In a preserved stage version of Dye's *The Conquest*, the speech of most Native characters was rendered as unintelligible grunting, which other characters would then "translate" into English. But in the scenes set in the Pacific Northwest, Native characters spoke in simple Chinook Jargon—sometimes without any translation at all. It is unclear whether this version of *The Conquest* was ever staged; if the logy logorrhea of the text is any indication, the play was unlikely to have run for long. But the presumption that pioneer audiences would appreciate the Chinook Jargon sprinkled into the work was reasonable.[31]

Edmond Meany was fascinated by Chinook Jargon, and by almost any other element of Native culture he could lay his hands on. He interviewed and collected stories from numerous Native people and tried to possess—for himself, and perhaps posterity—Native objects when he could. Fascination did not mean respect. The Suquamish site D'Suq'Wub ("Place of Clear Waters" in Lushootseed), known to Euro-Americans as "Old Man House," was wrested from the Suquamish in 1904. Euro-American artifact hunters did their best to bull past Native objections to get a piece of what remained. Edmond Meany got assistance in his acquisitive pursuit in 1907 from Cyrus B. Pickrell, at the time the Indian agent to the Suquamish. As Pickrell wrote: "About a year ago I received a request . . . to ship you . . . the last remaining post of the famous 'Old Man House' formerly standing at this place. At the time this request came there were some objections made by a few of the old indians to its removal, and I thought it best to wait until these were overcome. I think I can ship it to you now without any trouble if you care for it, as the indian had died who made the strongest objections to the removal."[32]

To Meany and Pickrell, Native objects were prized, Native objections were ignored. Meany was interested in Native people's stories, but not their wishes. He once wrote that "Indian Songs and Legends are the soul-voices of a primitive people who lived closer to nature than any other race of men." Although the tone generally (and the "primitive" specifically) is grating to a modern reader, there was perhaps a note of veneration in this reflection—a note made more discordant by the reason Meany wrote it: as an endorsement for the singer and "impersonator of the North American Indian" Louise Merrill-Cooper. Meany called for a "greater appreciation of Indian ways and days"—and thought redface impersonations were a means of building that appreciation. In Meany's pursuit of Native objects, languages, and cultures, Native people themselves were often brushed aside.[33]

In the Pacific Northwest, the Daughters of the American Revolution were the most prolific organization that raised monuments commemorating the wars of the region—especially so in Washington state, where they had Edmond Meany's help. As historian Simon Wendt has shown, DAR chapters in the West "highlighted primarily the heroic accomplishments of pioneer men whom they regarded as masculine warriors for their violent confrontations with Native Americans." Other heritage organizations shared members and methods with the DAR; many pioneer heritage organizations used the same genealogical forms (with fewer steps). Like other heritage organizations focused on pioneers, the DAR spent plenty of effort on "firsting"—marking the first White house, the first White baby, the first White church. And they funded many of the early Oregon Trail monuments. But the DAR was unusually interested in the battles.[34]

When thousands of people, including Washington Governor Albert E. Mead, gathered in 1908 for the dedication of Steptoe Memorial Park, they were treated to a series of speeches celebrating violent White supremacy. The park was set to play host to one of the earliest projects of the Spokane DAR—the erection of a monument to the May 17, 1858, event known variously among Euro-Americans as Steptoe's Defeat, Steptoe's Retreat, and the Battle of Te-hots-nim-me, when a mixed force of Indigenous fighters had routed a Euro-American expedition that had invaded their territory (see chapter 6). The ceremony was part of a broader push in early 1900s Spokane to appropriate and appreciate a white-washed Native history of the region for Euro-American consumption.[35]

The keynote address came from Colonel Lea Febiger, a veteran of the Philippine-American War and the commanding officer of Fort Wright—itself named after George Wright, who had killed his way across Washington Territory following Steptoe's retreat in 1858. When Febiger's speech touched on the wars at all, he largely praised Wright's scorched-earth invasion rather than talking about the battle the monument was meant to commemorate. And his speech went beyond this specific war, aligning the armed services with the patriotism of pioneering. Mirroring Elwood Evans's proclamation of pioneers-as-soldiers a few decades earlier, Febiger titled his speech "The Value of Soldiers as Pioneers," proclaiming:

> The history of the world shows the soldier always as the advance agent of civilization or conquest, or both, and savage[s] have either had to conform or cease to exist. The centers of civilization of all times have been extended not by the quiet arts, so-called, but by arms, and the so called wars of conquest [for civilizations across all epochs] were all against barbarian tribes[—]eventually extending to them, in spite of the slaughter incident to the process, the ben[e]fits of the highest civilization of their respective days. . . .
>
> We are now approaching a stage in the world's history where there are practically no more barbarous people or uncivilized countries, and the soldier of today will soon cease to act as

a pioneer for lack of raw material and confine himself more and more to his dual duty of national and universal policeman.[36]

Febiger denoted soldiers' conduct against "barbarous people or uncivilized countries"—when they were "act[ing] as . . . pioneer[s]"—as something different from conventional warfare. Indigenous people, presumably whether in the Americas or in the Philippines, were the "raw material" that pioneering acted on and eliminated. Indian warfare, with all of what he called "the slaughter incident to the process," *was* pioneering—to Febiger and many others across the Northwest. Following this talk of beneficent slaughter, Governor Mead thanked the "army which has been such a great factor in compelling peace and maintaining the reign of law in the Indian country." Although there might still be a few grumbling IWV-NPC members, many official events of the early twentieth-century Northwest buried former tensions between local pioneers and troops in service of the national government.[37]

The other major speaker at the Steptoe Memorial Park dedication was Thomas J. Beall, George Wright's former hangman and one of the last living Euro-American survivors of the battle. Beall's insistence on the vital role Nez Perce/Nimiipuu allies played in keeping most of Steptoe's regiment alive shaped the focus of the monument. And this was also the focus of his speech, wherein he remembered that "many of the soldiers" thought the Nez Perce/Nimiipuu poised for betrayal at every step and were instead saved only through their assistance.[38]

Eventgoers in 1908 were already looking ahead to future monuments and markers. They asked Beall for help locating the site where General Wright had ordered him to hang "Qual-Shon" (Ḵwáłchin) and his associates. Beall claimed to have found the spot (where "old Kaintuck trail crosses Hangman Creek," also named for Wright's lynching campaign). He remembered, possibly conflating two different murderous episodes, that "four of the Indians that were hung were of the Umatilla tribe and were hung on general principles. The fifth Indian was of the Yakima tribe and was known as Qual-Shon. He was hung for the murder of Indian Agent Bolon." Official records might unjustly imply guilt on the part of all who were hanged. But Beall could remember no more justification than "general principles" for most of the killings.[39]

By and large, the memorialization of the Battle of Te-hots-nim-me focused at least as much on the lethal campaign by General Wright that followed it. Steptoe's Defeat thus served a role similar to that of the

Whitman Massacre, a tragedy that justified and glorified the violence that followed. In the 1900s and 1910s, there seem to have been attempts in Washington state to put up tragic monuments to nearly every American-aligned soldier known to have died in the wars of the 1850s.[40]

The 1908 Steptoe dedication was meant in part to raise awareness and support for an envisioned marble monument to be placed at the park. This process lasted until 1914. State government support for the monument was not widespread enough to shake loose funds from Congress, and the DAR and affiliated private groups raised the money for the obelisk themselves. The part of the eventual inscription they thought most important reflected Beall's account of the battle and a settler worldview that separated a few "good Indians" from a mass enemy: "Sacred to the memory of the officers and soldiers of the United States Army who lost their lives on this field in desperate conflict with the Indians in the Battle of Te-hots-nim-me, May 17th 1858. In memory of Chief Tam-mu-tsa (Timothy) and the Christian Nez Perce Indians—rescuers of the Steptoe Expedition."[41]

In DAR memory, "the Indians" were the enemy, not any of the semi-specific tribal designations they had at their fingertips, such as Palouse/Palus or Umatilla/Imatalamłáma. Only "the Christian Nez Perce Indians" got a particular identifier. In the Northwest and beyond, the DAR and other groups mixed praise of specific Native allies with general assumptions of Indian perfidy.[42]

Forced internment got monuments too. Fort Yamhill was a blockhouse built on the outskirts of the Grand Ronde Reservation in 1856, what was called "a defense against Indian treachery" as the internment process was reaching its heights. Soldiers went out from it to scour the countryside for Native people, sometimes going house to house in attempts to seize "runaway Indians" for internment. In 1858 it was moved onto the reservation and used as a jail as well as a stronghold. In 1912 the blockhouse that had originally been built to house the regulars and volunteers readying for violence against the Native peoples of Grand Ronde Reservation was moved to Dayton, Oregon, and rededicated as a monument to Indian Superintendent "General" Joel Palmer (who had, perhaps coincidentally, profited from the building of the original blockhouse back in 1856).[43]

Melvin Clarke George, a politician and professor, gave a speech in which he proclaimed that the threat embodied in Palmer's fort had helped keep the residents of the Grand Ronde Reservation from allying with the Yakama in the east. George's dedication glossed over the vigilantes with guns who had played a signature role in that overwatch, focusing instead on the famous military figures who had fought in Oregon's Indian wars before fighting in the Civil War. George ended his oration with a celebration of violence, "civilization," and eventually assimilation:

> Block Houses are symbols of the Pioneer past. They were scattered far and near in Oregon and Washington. They were the outposts of civilization. ... [Now] Indian barbarity and danger [are] extinct. Civilization triumphant and progressing....
>
> Here the old soldiers of our country, and here the Indians of Grand Ronde—now citizens of our common land, may come and dream of the days long ago, when the war clouds hung low, and here Pioneers may recall the times of their early hardships and their struggles to build themselves a home on the soil of Oregon.[44]

The blockhouse had served as a base for soldiers extending force across the reservation, and for patrols that went out hunting for Indians to intern there. But amid the unvarnished colonialist celebration of "Civilization triumphant," there was a call for shared appreciation by "the Indians of Grand Ronde." Professor George celebrated what he called the extinction of "Indian barbarity and danger," but he was at least rhetorically open to the idea of shared citizenship with contemporary Native people. This was the part of the speech that lasted longest; when the park was rededicated decades later, in 1971, "General" Joel Palmer's part in the wars had all but disappeared. He was praised instead as a "friend of the Indian." Much historical writing since has reiterated that view, reading past Palmer's dogged pursuit of dispossession to focus on his distaste for genocide.[45]

The most prolific sculptor of monumental statuary in twentieth-century Oregon began his relationship with the state in a grand celebration of pioneer violence. Alexander Phimister Proctor made a name for himself as a Western sculptor in multiple senses, a man proud of his refined training in art and unrefined habits in nature. In his unexpurgated and unpublished autobiography, "From Buckskins to Paris," he wrote endlessly of his three great loves: family, art, and shooting. In passages mostly struck from the posthumously published version, Proctor reveled in stories of his own (perceived) violent mastery: hunting anecdotes and episodes of animal cruelty, but also stories about pulling a gun on a rude chauffeur, shooting near peddlers on the road he deemed overly ethnic, shooting near a neighbor's guests whom Proctor perceived as drunk, shooting near a hired hand named Jake who Proctor presumed was thinking about getting drunk, shooting (and wounding in the buttocks) a man Proctor perceived as a "tramp" (who had knocked on Proctor's door looking for work), and (when Proctor was a young man) pining for a chance to shoot down hostile Indians—a chance that apparently never came.[46]

Proctor identified as a Westerner as well as a shootist, and like many others so identified linked "hunting, pioneering, and the violent suppression of nonwhite people," as historian Christopher Herbert puts it. Across artistic media, Proctor lionized Indian killers—particularly a man named "Big Frank, a typical frontiersman and Indian Fighter." Proctor met Frank as a teenager, and he venerated him as a masculine ideal for a lifetime. Proctor described Big Frank as tall, broad, bewhiskered, and "sinuous"; his "face was that of a killer, but not the murder type ... [a face] of the kind developed only in the Wild West, where dangers and hardships are the order of the day. ... Killing an occasional Inj_n was all in the day's work with him." And indeed, throughout his life Proctor wrote and rewrote a story of how Big Frank murdered a Ute man named Yellow Moccasin, in 1870s Colorado, when Proctor had come closest to getting a chance to shoot at Indians.[47]

Alone among the seven-plus monumental sculptures Alexander Phimister Proctor eventually designed for Oregon's public spaces, his 1919 work *The Pioneer* was from the beginning his own notion rather than the vision of a sponsor. Carrying his love for "typical frontiersmen" through his arts education in New York and Paris, Proctor came to Oregon to experience the annual Pendleton Round-Up in 1914. He found inspiration and stayed there sketching and sculpting through 1916. The Round-Up, which continues today, had rodeo events, Native arts, parades, and pageants. But the performances differed from those of other Wild West shows, as historian Katrina M. Phillips has shown, in that "organizers wanted to celebrate their history without highlighting hostilities"—which seems to have meant an aversion to war scenes, but not to reenactments of individual violence.[48]

Many of Proctor's celebrated sculptures came out of his time at the Round-Up. He modeled at least three sculptures of Native and White riders and buckaroos during his stay, and more afterward. Another source of inspiration was the winner of an Indian beauty contest at the Round-Up, whom Proctor reimagined naked with a deer in his *Indian Maiden and Fawn* (1917?). And the sculptor met and modeled his "typical frontiersman," a trapper named Jess Cravens who, like Big Frank, was tall, "keen-eyed and taciturn." When Joseph Nathan Teal put out the call for a pioneer sculpture, Proctor was ready. Teal had envisioned something like a pilgrim, akin to the sculptor Augustus Saint-Gaudens's *The Puritan* (1886). Proctor coaxed him into funding something more like Big Frank—a mountain man primed for violence, with a gun and a whip at the ready.[49]

Proctor's *The Pioneer* was unveiled in Eugene, Oregon, before a crowd of reportedly hundreds of students and elderly pioneers in 1919, to general acclaim. Robert Asbury Booth, a lumber baron and accused grafter who supported history education, spoke of how the statue represented pioneer bravery, "unselfish devotion," and the courage of those who had fought to take Oregon. He was impressed enough with *The Pioneer* as an "interpretation of frontier life" that he hired Proctor to sculpt his *Circuit Rider* monument (1924) for the capitol grounds in Salem.[50]

Frederick V. Holman, the keynote speaker for the 1919 unveiling of *The Pioneer*, praised the martial virtues of pioneers—violence he had been celebrating as a historian for the better part of three decades. As he wrote to a fellow history enthusiast after the dedication, the monument reminded Holman of his uncle, who was "a very forceful man, a typical pioneer." But though Holman praised racist violence in his speech, he said little of war: "The instincts and traditions of the Anglo-Saxon race have ever been to move westward. The star it had followed, which showed the westward course of empire, at last stood and shone over Oregon . . . 'the land where dreams come true.' There were great numbers of savage Indians to be encountered and forced to respect the rights and property of these immigrants."[51]

In standard settler colonial rhetoric, Holman posed the pioneers as both imperialists and defenders, the land of Native people immediately and already transformed into pioneer property upon the arrival of White men. Holman praised the Oregon pioneers for having prevented "a long and bloody war" with Great Britain, but he made no mention of the wars of conquest through which so much land had been seized. Joseph Nathan Teal, at the *Circuit Rider* dedication only a few years later, similarly skipped over the wars his fathers had fought in, mentioning only the

The dedication ceremony for Alexander Phimister Proctor's Pioneer *(1919).*
Courtesy of the University of Oregon Special Collections.

Cayuse War before moving swiftly to statehood in 1859. Many in the early twentieth century still valorized Indian fighting, but now as a generic and individual act common to pioneers generally rather than volunteers specifically. *The Pioneer* was a paean to Indian killing, not Indian wars. Those were already starting to disappear.[52]

Pioneer pride was near immutable among the first several generations of Euro-Americans in the Pacific Northwest; Native people fighting against the harms being done to their communities might find more success in channeling it than challenging it. Inscribing memories and histories of peaceful coexistence or honorable battle could serve Euro-American and Native goals. Playing along with a sweetened version of the pioneer past allowed at least some Native people a platform from which to speak to the broader Euro-American world about their communities—and perhaps to shift pioneer history away from the mix of erasure and violence that monuments like *The Pioneer* represented. At times, portraying the wrongs being done to Indians as an aberration from the fantasy of American greatness was effective in recruiting White allies. If pioneer pride was unavoidable, a narrative of rogues and honest men could, at least in the near term, serve some Native communities' interests.[53]

Franklin Pierce Olney, the son of Indian wars volunteer Nathan Hale Olney and Twa-Wy/Annette Hallicola, became a voice for Yakama rights and Native rights generally in local newspapers by the 1880s and

1890s, as scholars Michelle M. Jacob and Wynona M. Peters have found. It was in part through his status as "A Son of Nathan Olney . . . a Prominent Pioneer," as he was termed, that Franklin P. Olney was able to convince newspaper editors to print his invocations of Yakama rights. First, he wrote to defend the pioneer bona fides of his father, who, after "buying" his mother, running a ferry, becoming an Indian agent, and setting up a farm, "fought the Indians, who then broke out" in the 1860s. Franklin P. Olney was of Native descent himself, but even he spoke of "Indians" generally when referencing the war—although he wrote more specifically and positively of the "tribe of the Yakimas" to which he belonged. After proving his pioneer bona fides, "Young Olney" was able to get a more trenchant letter to the editor printed a few months later, in which he denounced attempts to "open" treaty lands generally to White settlement.[54]

In 1917 the Puyallup/Nisqually leader Henry Sicade presented "The Indians' Side of the Story" of the 1850s violence on Puget Sound. This speech condemned the chicanery of Isaac I. Stevens and the horrors of the Maxon Massacre. But, as historian Lisa Blee has argued, this speech was a careful "mix of indictment and flattery," attributing the wrongs done to Native people to dishonorable individuals while reaffirming and appealing to the legitimacy of the American citizenry and United States law. Sicade's aim was to persuade his Euro-American audience that American ideals demanded support for Native American rights. His speech did not call for his pioneer listeners to be held collectively responsible for the wrongs that they were, in fact, collectively responsible for. Such a demand would have been unlikely to serve his ends.[55]

Spokane people, including Nellie Garry, used William S. Lewis's fascination with the pioneer past to nudge him into limited advocacy for Native nations. As a young Euro-American attorney in Spokane with an admiration for mythic pioneers, Lewis stumbled into Native history and eventually activism between the 1900s and the 1920s. His fascination with history led him to cofound the Spokane Historical Society (later the Eastern Washington Historical Society) in 1916. As a historian, he is most famous for his short book *The Case of Spokane Garry*, arguing with evidence and interviews that the scurrilous rumors about Garry in the later nineteenth century were incorrect, and that the leader had fought for Native land rights and peace throughout his life, only to be unjustly robbed. Working with the Garry family, Lewis helped convince the local DAR to co-fund a monumental gravestone honoring Spokane Garry in

1925. Although he never lost his hero-worship of pioneers, Lewis's Native interlocutors pushed him toward actions for Native rights. In the 1920s he took on several cases for Indigenous nations in Washington, sometimes working without pay.[56]

Although Native actions spurred Lewis to support Native goals, he remained a proponent of heroic pioneer history. Lewis was a major figure in multiple historical societies, responsible for a 1926 monument to the Battle of Spokane Plains. Although Lewis's attempt to rehabilitate Spokane Garry in the eyes of Euro-Americans is his most famous publication, most of his works, as the historian Stacy Nation-Knapper has pointed out, celebrated the pioneers and settlers who invaded eastern Washington. In his short history of the "Spokane Invincibles," a small group of local Euro-American volunteers, Lewis portrayed them as heroes fighting enemy "Indians." Lewis was unusual in his willingness to fight for some measure of "justice and fair play" for Native people and nations in eastern Washington. But he was still in thrall to a celebratory vision of colonization. Lewis insisted the wrongs done to Native communities had been the work not of his neighbors, or of the volunteers he lionized, but rather of "principally transient miners passing through"— presumably miners *other* than those he honored in the pages of the *Washington Historical Quarterly*.[57]

Lewis tried to bring together his urge to celebrate pioneering and his yen to support Native personhood in his 1926 article "Oldest Pioneer Laid to Rest." As was typical of a eulogy, Lewis celebrated Mrs. Mary Ann King, "a pioneer of the Colville Valley," who had died at 104 as "Washington's oldest daughter." Somewhat unusually, Lewis extolled King's Native heritage as part of her pioneer story—albeit in terms troubling to the modern ear. "She was an excellent example of the best of Indian character and Indian blood in this country," Lewis wrote. "She was of mixed blood, far above the average, and very few like her inherited the good traits of both her ancestors." Lewis celebrated King's thrift, her devout Catholicism, and her ability to "tan a deer hide, make moccasins, gloves and . . . fancy bead work."[58]

When Lewis described the wider circumstance of King's life amid colonial conquest, his tone revealed the contradictions of his predilections:

After the railroad was built into Colville Valley nearly all the Indian settlers were crowded out and lost their lands and were forced to go onto the reservations, but Mrs. King stayed. Her self pride tempted her to stay with the whites; and her native shrewdness was sufficient to protect her property from the covetous and scheming white men who would have possessed her lands. . . .

The present generation says only: "another old timer gone," but to the old pioneers she is of deeper interest, as she recalls the days when everyone knew everyone else throughout the entire valley, and when all were, so to say, one great family. Very few people were permitted to see as much change take place in a country as she did, from the time when the aborigines held full sway over this entire domain, till this country developed and progressed to its present state.[59]

Blinkered by racial prejudice, Lewis never resolved or perhaps even noticed the contradictions in his historical work. He framed Indians as "settlers" who deserved their lands, the initial pioneers who seized those lands as heroes, and both as part of "one great family." The "covetous and scheming white men," like the "transient miners," could be safely decried as outsiders, something other than pioneers. More prominent historians, such as George Himes and Clarence Bagley, eventually lit upon a similar condemnation of outsiders, in their case bureaucrats—as Himes put it, "The difficulties of the settlers with the Indians of the Pacific Northwest have grown out [of] the fa[i]lure of our own government to keep its treaty promises." Among the desperate fights for Indigenous survivance, rights, land, dignity, and nationhood in the Progressive Era (1890s–1920s), White narratives that praised pioneers but insisted on treaty rights might have been viewed as the best option available.[60]

In 1920 Indian schools around the United States were "directed to observe in some suitable manner . . . the 'Tercentenary of the Landing of the Pilgrims.' " In an address titled "A Prophecy Fulfilled" at the Tulalip Indian School that year, Edmond Meany spoke at length of his vision of a Native and White future, beginning his speech with a *longue durée* view of history:

Three hundred years ago today the Pilgrim Fathers landed at Plymouth Rock. We are assembled to celebrate that event as an epoch in American history. There is a peculiar significance in the fact that Indians should gather here on the shores of the Pacific Ocean in 1920 to celebrate the landing of white men among other Indians in 1620 on that distant Atlantic shore. A cycle has been completed; a continent has been spanned; and two races of men have learned the meaning of clasped hands as together they turn hopeful eyes toward the future.[61]

In keeping with the queasy norms of the day, Meany suggested that the Native students should "celebrate the landing of white men." But he also proposed a present and future of comity between Native and White people. Unlike more ardent assimilationists, he did not dismiss Native culture entirely. But he did consign it to memory:

In that old time which we are honoring your people knew the bays and shores of this beautiful arm of the sea. Those towering snow-crowned peaks they knew and the rivers running through the deep forests of fir and spruce and cedar. Their canoes were swift in war or chase and they sought omens and guidance from forest, sea and sky.

The white man came with iron and gold, with cloth and flour. The old wild life was quickly changed. The legends of bluejay and beaver gave place to the book and the school.

The book speaks of all time and all people. We still love the legends. They are like voices of the forest. But now we are Americans. We salute our flag and we would honor the Pilgrim Fathers on this anniversary day.

Oh my Indian friends, I would share your spirit and join this festival of remembrance with a feeling that mingles reverence and hope.[62]

This speech contained no mention of Indian wars or violence anywhere in the Pacific Northwest—although the "Battle of Little Bighorn" did make a brief appearance. And Meany ended with a benediction to the Indigenous pupils compelled to attend his speech:

What shall we say to those who may assemble here on the next centennial anniversary? We have numerous records of Indians who attain ages greater than a hundred years. So it may be that some of you younger Indians may live that long and bear witness of this meeting to that one. Those who will assemble then are the future. . . .

They will cherish faint echoes of the forests and your fathers' legends of eagle, of beaver and bluejay. They will know that we met here to remember the past and to greet the future.

We lift our voices to you of the future. We ask you to cherish good government, civil and religious freedom, improved education, equality of opportunities for all. We transmit to you all the best legacies of the past. We trust that your century's survey will reveal a progress far greater than our own. We beseech you to send the time-honored American ideals forward to the unnumbered years of our beloved Republic.[63]

This became perhaps Meany's most famous speech, sent to dignitaries, libraries, and the movers and shakers of the Pacific Northwest and broader American history. To the extent that Meany has a reputation as a "friend of the Indians," it stems from speeches like this one. Whatever the many, many faults of the Native-White future he envisioned (not least his support for "means of force" to coerce younger Native children into boarding schools), he did at least presume a continuing Native presence. His call to "remember the past and greet the future" has worn far better than most of the specifics he articulated—especially since Meany's version of "remembering the past" sometimes included treaty rights and other "neglected pledges," even as it excluded wanton pioneer violence. For some descendants of pioneers, a preferred way to remember the past was with fewer wars and more friendship. And that was a narrative some Native people could work with, as they took on the battles of the twentieth century, recruiting even organizations like the DAR into select battles for Native rights through strategic uses of history and culture.[64]

Monuments, as the Oregon Trail Association once put it, are a matter of "sympathy . . . soul and sentiment." They represent history more through powerful feelings than complicated facts. In the Progressive-Era Pacific Northwest, as they had before, Euro-Americans agreed on the general heroism of colonization—but not on the specifics of the stories or Native people's places within them. Although there were still celebrations of violence aplenty, the kinds of violence that they found acceptable—and therefore worthy of repetition and remembrance—shrank. Heightened Euro-American nostalgia for Native life and practice met with these changing boundaries of acceptability to shape a history of the pioneer Pacific Northwest that stressed moments of friendship, real and imagined, and steered away from the bloody details. In pursuit of survivance, some Native people were willing to partially assent to a kinder, gentler, half-true history of the pioneer period—at least publicly—if it served their communities' needs. Those fighting for Indigenous peoples' futures had to be mindful of which truths might be too much for White audiences. As the successful Okanagan writer and activist Christine Quintasket ("Mourning Dove") put it in 1928, one had to make sure not to "roast" the White people "too strong to get their sympathy."[65]

Any accounting of Native uses of White nostalgia and pioneer history for activist ends must consider the difficulties of striving for justice when so many wanton murderers of Native people still captivate the Euro-American public imagination. This was especially true when those killers and their relatives were still living and still shaping history. In the shadow of *The Pioneer*, and the celebrations of murderous violence memorials like it represented, many Native rights activists took a tactical approach to when, how, and to whom one might tell terrible truths.[66]

Conclusion
Erasing Invasion and the War on Illahee

H ARRIET NESMITH MCARTHUR, JAMES W. Nesmith's daughter, shaped how history would be told, especially in her role as a cofounder of the Oregon Historical Society. But rather than embrace her father's enthusiasm for genocide, she came to prefer a sympathetic take on Oregon's Native peoples. When she published her own pioneer memoir, in 1929, she disappeared the wars in the Pacific Northwest. McArthur brought up her father's role as an Indian agent, his part in treaty negotiations through 1853, and his army acquaintances. But she did not breathe a word about any of the regional wars he had participated in, or the central part those wars of conquest had played in his political successes. The passage that came closest to mentioning the wars instead reframed the Oregon Trails of Tears as a story of comity and bonhomie: "In 1856 a great many Indians were placed on the reservations of Grand Ronde and Siletz, with an army post at each reservation. There were many Rogue River and Klickitat Indians, both quite superior people. The men were allowed out on passes issued by the agent, and they did good work in the harvest fields, binding grain by hand. The women gathered berries and hazelnuts, and we children were allowed to visit the women, and in their limited 'Boston talk' and in our limited Chinook, we heard the stories of their tribal homes."[1]

The carceral system that the pioneers had attempted to make with reservations hovered invisibly in the margins of Harriet Nesmith McArthur's account; the word *placed* just barely conceals the Trails of Tears. The murderous assaults that had led to those placements were wholly absent. Even the war acts James Nesmith had been proud of were gone. And neither did McArthur celebrate the killings of Native people or repeat the more vile epithets that frothed in the writings of her father. Historians in previous eras had valorized or downplayed or isolated the violence of the volunteers. Harriet Nesmith McArthur simply cut them out of history altogether.[2]

Among Euro-Americans in the Pacific Northwest, memories of wanton pioneer violence, along with most of the War on Illahee, was slowly, unevenly, and incompletely erased over the course of the 1900s. The biggest changes seem to have been generational. As the pioneers themselves died, the settlers who followed them—including their own children—sometimes pruned away their acts of racist violence and overwrote the crimes against humanity they had committed.

Some of Joseph Lane's descendants who fought for Native rights projected their beliefs onto the family patriarch. The politician and doctor Harry Lane and his daughter, Nina Lane Faubion, a writer and historian, invented a long family history of activism for Native people and even claimed a lineage of attenuated indigeneity for themselves. Nina Lane Faubion proclaimed, but could not prove, that her "branch of the family [had] always been proud of the fact, whether rightfully or not," that her great-great-grandmother was a "full blood Cherokee Indian." Any such pride her family might have felt was kept strictly out of the record in the 1800s, and there was no direct evidence to support her claim.[3]

Besides attempting to claim Native heritage, Faubion expanded even further on her family's generations-long effort to rehabilitate Joseph Lane as a "friend of the Indians," setting him against the "bad whites that lied cheated and stole from the Indians." Before launching into unfortunate racial stereotypes about Black people, assertions of the innate nobility of the Lane bloodline, and wild historical imaginings that defined her late historical work, Nina Lane Faubion opened her celebratory biography of her great-grandfather mournfully: "To the everlasting shame of both Indiana and Oregon, is the spoliation of the Indians of their homelands. Through force and deceit this great northwest was wrested from them, sluiced in [the] blood of the venturesome to the pay-dirt that has been minted by the Yankee speculators. The settlers acted as hosts to the parasites that we have so constantly had with us since."[4]

Joseph Lane, an eager user of violence, rape, and murder in pursuit of land conquest, a man who to the end had blamed most violence on the "treachery, which all Indians are full of," would have been gobsmacked by this gloss from his filial great-granddaughter—who spent her last days trying to fight the seizure of Indigenous lands in Alaska—in his name. Historians might recognize yet another formulation of rogues and honest men, bad "Yankee speculators" now contraposed against good "settlers" *and* "Indians."[5]

In 1938 Leslie M. Scott (a newspaperman, politician, and son of IWV-NPC member Harvey W. Scott) gave the keynote address at the unveiling of the new Oregon State Capitol in Salem. The old building had burned down in 1935, and the new complex—topped with the monumental *Oregon Pioneer*, a twenty-two-foot gold-leafed bronze statue by Ulric Ellerhusen—was meant among other things to portray and celebrate Oregon's "ancient past, its discovery and conquest, and the epic of its pioneer history." But there was hardly a hint of conquest or any other violence in the art selected for the new capitol. The "epic" of Oregon's pioneer history was distorted into one of peaceful White supremacy, including camp meetings, covered wagons, and lots and lots of Lewis and Clark. Everything between 1843 and 1859 was omitted—including all of the wars.[6]

Leslie M. Scott praised Oregon as "a monument to American expansion," a place where American "racial and national energies" reached a fever pitch. But where his father had fought to make veterans of Indian wars central to the history of the state, Leslie M. Scott instead described Oregon as "the one part of the United States obtained by discovery, diplomacy, and peaceful settlement." This was a chosen ignorance—Leslie M. Scott had edited his father's histories, and he thus had to have known about the wars. But in changing times, they no longer made the cut for "Great Events in Oregon History." Instead of older debates about which parts of the wars to seize the Pacific Northwest needed to be celebrated and which erased, settlers like Leslie M. Scott simply ignored the wars, the invasion, and most Native Americans altogether. The 1938 gold-leafed bronze pioneer in Salem was no less a symbol of White supremacy than the half-as-high bronze pioneer unveiled in Eugene back in 1919. But the violence of pioneering was ever more obscured.[7]

And the erasure hasn't ended.

The term *pioneer* is slapped on all sorts of businesses, spaces, and awards across the Northwest, now less a signifier of a settler-soldier than a generic gesture toward durability, innovation, democratic merit, or down-home values. It seems likely that most non-Native people who gather in the Pioneer Squares at the centers of Portland and Seattle are ignorant of the violent origins of the word. The pioneer awards at universities like Washington State University, University of Oregon, Portland State University, and Oregon State University blend the dual meanings of the word, in some cases lauding innovation (one meaning) while using historical pioneer iconography (the other meaning). Ellerhusen's golden pioneer statue, still standing astride the Oregon state capitol, is one of the most looming and inescapable symbolic reminders to Native people in the region of continuing colonial oppression and violence—but there is little indication it is known as such by the non-Native public. Often-oblivious celebrations of murderers who killed Native people and took their lands are everywhere, across and beyond the West.[8]

Most modern histories of the Pacific Northwest acknowledge that there were decades of violence perpetrated against Native people in the region, but some struggle to face the extent to which pioneers in general enacted that violence. Some histories once again narrate a story of rogues and honest men, with murders hidden under phrases like "tragedy" and "decline." Frequently, the perpetrators of anti-Indian violence are artificially localized and anonymized, isolated to unnamed vigilantes or a few especially perfidious persons. Too often, any pioneer who evinced a hint of sympathy for Native people is taken for a friend and ally—even, in some cases, those pioneers who belied their vague sympathetic words with acts of rape and murder. We must treat pioneer invaders' claims of friendliness to the Indigenous people whose land they were taking with a level of skeptical rigor akin to how we have finally begun to treat enslavers' claims of kindness to the people they enslaved. These assertions are typically false, and even when true are not usually exculpatory of the underlying injustice.[9]

One purpose of this book has been to show the ubiquity of support for colonial violence as a tool for expropriation. Clashes over colonial policies are too often narrated with presumptions of heroism on at least one side. There is no question that those pressing for genocide were more noxious than those hoping to seize all Indigenous land without it. But highlighting important differences—between the thieving invaders who saw violence as the first response and the thieving invaders who preferred violence as a last resort—should not obscure the shared goals and perfidy of both.

The tendency to put pioneer violence against Native people in a separate and ignorable category is by no means restricted to the Pacific Northwest. In the subdiscipline of American Western history, debates over violence and its extent have often deliberately excluded the kinds of violence I have detailed here—most strikingly in the 2009 words of the historian Robert Dykstra, denying the prevalence of violence in the West: "The whole thing boils down to whether the incidence of inter-personal killing (a definition that excludes Indian wars and related vio-lence, a conceptually separate topic) was—or was not—as commonplace and large in volume as widely thought."[10]

The troubling conceptual exclusion of Native people from "interper-sonal killing" is telling, and it continues. Dykstra argues that there were actually very few shooting deaths in the West by "excluding firefights with Indians" from his totals. Most killings of Native people he does not count as homicides—presumably because they could always be attributed to one or another "Indian war" or "related violence." Nor is Dykstra the only modern historian to make such violence a "conceptually separate topic." Many other historians engaged in debates over historical Western homicide statistics have framed the issue less risibly, but they have never-theless done their counting in ways that exclude much—perhaps most—settler violence against Native people. A 1999 Western Historical Association roundtable on Western violence—held in Portland—was a particularly surreal instance of this trend, as four out of five participants noted that violence against Native people was real and pervasive, then ar-gued that the West was not particularly violent because famous instances of intraracial White violence had been blown out of proportion—thus first acknowledging violence against Native people, then dismissing it as irrelevant regarding the question of "frontier violence" in the West.[11]

Through and beyond the 1800s, most killings of Native people in the West were not present in the sources we typically use to construct homicide statistics because most Euro-American Westerners did not consider them true homicides—that is, unjust killings of persons. Rather, they saw the killings as justified, the "Indians" as less than people, or both. And too often, killings in wars or in uniform are seen as somehow wholly different from other killings—an assumption always worth ques-tioning, and especially so amid the decades of war and quasi-war against Native polities and people in the United States, and the decades more of wanton violence inflicted by soldiers, citizens, and those of an unclear status in between—before, during, and after those wars. Soldiers can be murderers. Many of those who fought in Indian wars were.

The average pioneer in the Pacific Northwest was complicit in theft and murder. Specific evidence can condemn specific persons—and many of the men and women I discuss here have somehow previously escaped historical censure. Movements to reframe history, topple monuments, or dename colonial namesakes can make potent ammunition out of such specific evidence. But too often, historians have equivocated about the general culpability of pioneers. At a 2021 roundtable on monuments at the Oregon Center for Holocaust Education, a scholar I respect declared, "The pioneers weren't evil, they were human." One could certainly argue that *evil* is not a useful term for analysis and should not be used as a descriptor by serious scholars (though such an argument might also preclude use of terms like *good*). Or one might argue that condemning pioneers as evil might still, as Christine Quintasket once put it, "roast" too many present-day White people "too strong to get their sympathy."[12]

But there is a vast difference between arguing that the term *evil* is an unsuitable descriptor for historical figures and arguing that the pioneers or similar perpetrator groups *weren't* evil. The average Pacific Northwest pioneer in the 1850s supported atrocious acts of violence against Native people and communities, an "evil" opinion by any reasonable definition of the phrase (whether it stemmed from race hatred, material interest, or, more usually, a mix of both). Not every pioneer was a killer, in the Pacific Northwest or in most other sites of broad-based racial violence. Some few resisted norms of White supremacy and genocide, including unknown numbers of people for whom no record of that resistance persists. But the broad guilt of pioneers, on average and as a group, should be difficult to contest—at least once the hangover from the lies of previous generations of historians has cleared. Pioneers were, of course, human. But that does not signify an absence of evil. The perpetrators of the Holocaust, and of every other genocide, were human too.

Scholars, like other people, are vulnerable to a tendency for humanization to turn into exoneration, and they too often let necessary empathy turn into dangerous sympathy. Empathy is a key tool for historians, and I have tried to employ it throughout this book. And sympathy often follows: I felt it keenly, for example, when reading through Loren L. Williams's journal entries on his years of suffering from an infected arrow wound. But just because his very human struggle with pain touched me, this sympathy should in no way dim the monstrousness of his acts as a serial killer of Native people. Too many biographers, especially, are lulled by sympathetic familiarity into unduly absolving the sins of their subjects. One of the barriers to truer history is the assumption that evil is not just inhumane, but inhuman. Evidence that this or that pioneer was human should not lead one to discount the violence they condoned or committed. If anything, the fact that all perpetrators are complex human beings should heighten the horror of their actions.[13]

There is a long-standing tradition among historians of American colonialism to assert reassuring complexity. "Of course not all whites considered Indians 'uncivilized' people, nor were all whites aggressive, land-hungry thieves," as one classic text on colonial invasion in the Northwest put it. Such assertions are invariably true; no large body of people is uniformly anything. Pointing out exceptions to pioneer norms can be a worthy pursuit: both to find those courageous enough to stand against the horrific norms of their present, and to disprove assertions that people within the context of their time couldn't have known any better. And it is vital to find and underline instances and actions of Indigenous power, when Native people bent or broke the colonial scripts they rejected. But an overfocus on exceptional moments or people can warp readers' perceptions of the horrible norms.[14]

Calls for complexity must not become cause for complicity. Nearly all pioneers in the 1800s *were* "aggressive, land-hungry thieves," whether they admitted it to themselves or not. The Euro-Americans who committed, condoned, or at least tolerated mass murder for land *were* people of their time and place. Exceptions were few and far between and often overstated by latter-day apologists. The story of colonial conquest is fiendishly complicated, and it will never be finished—in the Pacific Northwest or elsewhere. But it is also, in key ways, simple. Pioneers came to take Indigenous land, they were willing to kill to get it, and they had (or correctly expected to have) the numbers to force the issue. There are many great histories written, and many more to tell, about the complexities of colonialism in the Pacific Northwest: stories of successful Native resistance and horrific loss, of Indigenous power and Indigenous penury, of accommodation and incarceration, of cultural preservation and forced assimilation, of Indigenous political continuities and American microtechniques of dispossession. But hovering over it all is what one might call a macrotechnique of dispossession: the oft-realized threat of overwhelming violence from the hordes of White invaders bent on making Native land their own. The worthy work of unpacking nuance should not obscure this overarching element.[15]

Euro-American attitudes toward Native people in the Pacific Northwest have shifted in important ways since the 1850s. The structures of settler colonialism are ongoing but not unchanging. The actions of generations of Native people and their allies have altered White norms, attitudes, and even legal customs since. The number of Americans consciously comfortable with new thefts and murders in the region has declined precipitously, and more and more settlers today are willing to reconsider the justice of the crimes perpetrated by their pioneer fore-bears. Racist violence remains endemic, but it is not as ubiquitous, sup-ported, or protected as it was in the mid-1800s United States.

Changes should not be overstated. Native people, communities, and lands still face horrific violence under settler regimes. Law enforcement officers today kill Indigenous people at a rate rivaled only by the rate at which they kill Black people. Colonial sexual violence continues—as scholar Sarah Deer bluntly puts it, "White men are still raping Native women with impunity." A third or more of Indigenous women experience sexual violence in their lifetimes, and few perpetrators face justice. Colo-nial customs continue to harm and destroy. That violence in the 1800s was even more sweeping and annihilatory than the horrors of the present is cold comfort to those still brutalized by settlers and their systems.[16]

But essential continuities of settler violence do not render moot the changes that have been wrought by Native people and their allies. Settler colonial structures are ongoing, but they are neither unassailable nor monolithic. Despite the mutable pervasiveness of settler colonial logics, as historian Jean M. O'Brien notes, "Indigenous resistance to colonial power structured through racial imaginaries continues to override the logic of elimination." Many settlers who struggled over policy, law, and memory had shared goals of subjugation and elimination. Native people and their allies nonetheless found purchase in the cleavages of conflict-ing colonial strategies, and they have changed and challenged them since. As historian J. Kēhaulani Kauanui points out, Indigenous peoples "exist, resist, and persist" within settler colonial structures—*and* those structures adapt and evolve new ways to maintain oppressive power rela-tionships. To frame settler colonialism as an *unchanging* set of structures would be to overwrite generations of Indigenous actions *and* to underes-timate the challenge of dismantling dynamic systems of injustice.[17]

One overarching goal for this work has been to denature settler co-lonial structures and stories in the Pacific Northwest. I have attempted to supplant the myth of pioneer virtue with the reality of pioneer rapac-ity, drawing often on the kinds of evidence those still dedicated to the myth might struggle to disbelieve. And I have also tried to show some of the ways these myths—and the structures of oppression they justified and hid—were created and re-created regionally. Unraveling these myths makes it harder to discount the horrors of colonial conquest. Revealing the evils embraced in pursuit of a White Northwest can, I hope, play some small role in convincing Americans of the need to repudiate and fight the continuities of deceit, injustice, and violence that persist to the present.

Postscript

As I WAS COMPLETING MY initial research into Proctor's *Pioneer* in February 2019, I went to the annual banquet of one of the last surviving heritage organizations from the era of pioneer memorialization. The Sons and Daughters of Oregon Pioneers, founded in 1901 as a successor to the Oregon Pioneer Association, allows full membership only to those who can prove their "ancestors c[a]me to the Oregon country before Oregon statehood." Through my father William's descent from the pioneer farmer and translator James Gibson, we were able to get tickets. At the banquet we attended, pageantry and playacting were a major focus, from middle-aged men dressed as nineteenth-century soldiers and "mountain men" to a young woman in gingham crowned "Miss Pioneer Oregon 2019" and given a college scholarship. The history presentations were mostly genial genealogy, listing family trees and displaying family photographs and artifacts. The old tradition of pioneer meetings as a time for "mutual congratulations" was still, in this hotel conference room at the edge of Portland, going strong.[1]

Native people were largely absent from the stories, but they were all over the merchandise in the room. Hazy portraits of Native women were painted with a purply-pink palette on drums and pseudo-dreamcatchers up for auction. Crude Indian figures with oars were sculpted in plastic on canoes, posed next to the miniature Conestoga wagon centerpieces on many tables. As I wandered among groups between events, I heard one man speak of his pride in a pioneer forebear who had "fought the Indians." The tension at his table was palpable, and after a few excruciating seconds the conversation picked up as if he hadn't spoken. The only official

285

mention of Native people at the event was in the benediction, asking that all members give thanks to their "brave" ancestors who had "forged a trail" across the continent—and to the "people who had been waiting here to greet them." Stories of pioneer violence are no longer explicitly a part of what even this group is trying to celebrate.[2]

The violence is still here—and not just in story or metaphor. A few months after the banquet, I gave my first public talk on Proctor's 1919 *Pioneer* statue. I connected the sculptor's love of Indian killers with the broader history of colonial violence in the Northwest and shared stories from people of color in Eugene, who had reflected on how the statue continued to do them harm. After my talk, a Native woman came up, shook my hand, and shared a story of how her bones were broken by a pack of racist skinheads when she was young, and how she had only just survived. Today as in the pioneer era, there are still people who assault and kill in pursuit of a White Northwest.

I ended up talking about that statue more than I had expected in the year that followed. In part this was because of the surprising richness of the archives I dug through. The *Pioneer* project was a particularly vivid example of violence and cover-up, showing a latter-day instance of how history could be carefully manipulated and erased, and how that erasure could be furthered by unknowing actors working off of malformed stories. And talking about Proctor's *Pioneer* was a way into talking about the broader violence of the seizure of the Pacific Northwest. Many of the predominantly White audiences I talked to were shocked. They had not heard much about the violence, they had not heard anything about the cover-ups, and many had not considered the effects that veneration of pioneers continued to have on Native people. In some ways, the cover-ups worked too well—many, perhaps most, White people in the Northwest are no longer consciously in on the lies. When racist murderers of the past are celebrated today, the killings they committed tend to be ignored or forgotten rather than highlighted by the celebrants.

Proctor's *Pioneer*, along with its colonial counterpart, Proctor's *Pioneer Mother*, was dragged from its pedestal by parties unknown on June 13, 2020—part of a wave of iconoclasm striking at symbols of racial injustice across the United States and the world. Research seems to have played a small role in making sure they didn't go back up again, demonstrating with archival evidence what generations of Native and Black activists had already known and shown: that both statues were, and were meant to be, monuments celebrating violent White supremacy. Nor has anything, so far, gone up in their place to explain the history behind their rise and fall. They have simply been erased from the landscape. A celebration of colonial violence has been replaced with silence—another kind of settler tradition.[3]

This toppling of pioneer statuary was not the only iconoclastic act amid the broader protests against police violence and White supremacy in the Northwest. In October 2020 a monumental statue of Harvey W. Scott in Portland was toppled and vandalized. The statue was a little-known work by sculptor and White supremacist John Gutzon de la Mothe Borglum, most famous for gouging Mount Rushmore into Pahá Sápa/the Black Hills and a panoramic paean to the Confederacy into Stone Mountain, Georgia. Borglum's monumental sculpture *Harvey W. Scott* was unveiled by Leslie M. Scott in July 1933. The monument captured the elder Scott's famous scowl and taste for fine clothing. An epitaph praised Scott as a "pioneer, editor, publisher, and molder of opinion in Oregon and the nation." The particularities of those opinions—Scott's support for brutal colonial wars and vociferous attacks on women's suffrage—went unmentioned.[4]

In a February 20, 2021, act of guerilla art, sculptor Todd McGrain put up in Scott's stead a bust of York, the enslaved Black man who had been a key member of the Lewis and Clark expedition. Among the few statues depicting the long history of Black people in the Pacific Northwest, this statue, like others dedicated to York, commemorated his part in the early stages of colonial conquest—before it, too, was torn down by iconoclasts, this time by "conservative protestors." It makes one long for a monument instead to someone like Hattie Redmond, not least because as a Black woman and Oregon women's suffragist she represents almost the polar opposite of Harvey W. Scott. But the lure of a heroic pioneer past continues to snare even some of those trying to remake history. Participation in pioneering should not be presumptively praiseworthy, for the marginalized or the privileged.[5]

The push to reexamine namesakes and monuments to racists in the Pacific Northwest sometimes achieves changes with official imprimaturs. On April 14, 2021, Washington Governor Jay Inslee signed a bipartisan bill to replace the Marcus Whitman statue that has represented the state in the National Statuary Hall since 1953. Barring disaster, the state will instead be represented by a new statue, of Nisqually fishing rights activist Billy Frank Jr. On June 7, 2021, the Oregon legislature voted to replace racist language in the official Oregon state song. Lyrics celebrating a land "blest by the blood of martyrs" and "conquered and held by free men/fairest and the best" seem increasingly out of step with present-day Oregon tastes. Responding to the wishes of many constituents, Oregon legislators no longer want the state celebrated as the "Land of the Empire Builders," as the first verse of the song used to go. The new lyrics extol the land's mountains, forests, and rivers—among the few things Northwesterners can agree are worth celebrating.[6]

Jettisoning racist statues, names, songs, and even histories is at best a beginning. I have heard from Native friends that the experience of walking through Eugene, Oregon, is different without *Pioneer* looming over them with his whip and gun. I have no doubt that a statue of Billy Frank Jr. will change the experience of visiting the National Statuary Hall, especially for Indigenous people. But changing the monuments, or changing the names, or even changing the history books, does not return land, or make reparations, or forestall ongoing oppressions. What these small changes can do, I hope, is be a part of the much more ephemeral—but necessary—work of changing hearts and minds. And that, perhaps, can lead to more substantive changes in actions, laws, and policies—from the long overdue to the yet unimagined.

Notes

Introduction and Apologia

1. "An Act to Provide for the Relief of Indigent Union and Mexican War Soldiers, Sailors, Mariners, and Indian War Volunteers," February 25, 1889, in William Lair Hill, comp., *The Codes and General Laws of Oregon*, 2 vols., 2nd ed. (San Francisco: Bancroft-Whitney, 1892), 2:1841–43.

2. Alexander York application to Oregon Soldiers' Home, November 24, 1894, folder "Wren—York," box 29, Military Department Records 89-A12, Oregon State Archives, Salem (hereafter cited as Oregon Soldiers Home Applications); Jesse A. Applegate application to Oregon Soldiers' Home, August 18, 1903, folder 6, box 29, Oregon Soldiers Home Applications; W. F. Tolmie claim record, folder 9, box 53, Oregon Soldiers Home Applications; Elijah F. Whisler application to Oregon Soldiers' Home, May 6, 1895, folder "Westall—Whitcomb," box 29, Oregon Soldiers Home Applications. Old soldiers' homes in Washington were officially admitting veterans of Indian Wars by the 1900s, but they required only a listing of the regiment rather than a description of the war. John C. Kohler, "Washington Soldiers Home Application," October 13, 1891, Washington Soldiers Home Records, 1891–1945, Washington State Archives, Olympia, accessed via FamilySearch; Urban E. Hicks, "Washington Soldiers Home Application," September 30, 1901, Washington Soldiers Home Records, 1891–1945. The term *Yakima War* here refers to the war as it was described (and spelled) by those who first named it.

3. Samuel Stewart to T. A. Wood, December 30, 1896, folder 44, box 4, Military Collection, Mss 1514, Oregon Historical Society Special Collections, Portland (hereafter cited as Oregon Military Collection MSS); Antone Minthorn, "Wars, Treaties, and the Beginning of Reservation Life," in *As Days Go By: Our History, Our Land, and Our People: The Cayuse, Umatilla, and Walla Walla*, ed. Jennifer Karson (Pendleton, Ore.: Tamástslikt Cultural Institute, 2006),

289

61–89, esp. 64–65; Patrick Wolfe, "Settler Colonialism and the Elimination of the Native," *Journal of Genocide Research* 8, no. 4 (2006): 387–409, https://doi.org/10.1080/14623520601056240. In 1920 pension legislation, the state of Oregon inscribed the period of 1847 to 1858 as a general "Indian War." Hon. Conrad Patrick Olson, Code Commissioner, *Oregon Laws: Showing All the Laws of a General Nature in Force in the State of Oregon*, 2 vols. (San Francisco: Bancroft-Whitney, 1920), 2:3482–84.

4. Henry Zenk and Tony A. Johnson, "A Northwest Language of Contact, Diplomacy, and Identity: Chinuk Wawa/Chinook Jargon," *Oregon Historical Quarterly* 111, no 4 (Winter 2010): 444–61, https://doi.org/10.5403/oregonhistq.111.4.0444. See also Kylie N. Johnson, " 'As Our Elders Taught Us to Speak It': Chinuk Wawa and the Process of Creating Authenticity" (master's thesis, University of Denver, 2013), esp. 21–36; Lily Hart, "Voices of the River: The Confluence Story Gathering Interview Collection," *Oregon Historical Quarterly* 119, no. 4 (2018): 508–27, esp. 519, https://doi.org/10.5403/oregonhistq.119.4.0508.

5. Katrine Barber, " 'We Were at Our Journey's End': Settler Sovereignty Formation in Oregon," *Oregon Historical Quarterly* 120, no. 4 (2019): 382–413, esp. 391–92 (quotation), https://doi.org/10.5403/oregonhistq.120.4.0382; Anne F. Hyde, *Empires, Nations, and Families: A History of the North American West, 1800–1860* (Lincoln: University of Nebraska Press, 2011), 421.

6. Julius Wilm, "Old Myths Turned on Their Heads: Settler Agency, Federal Authority, and the Colonization of Oregon," *Oregon Historical Quarterly* 123, no. 4 (Winter 2022): 326–57, https://muse.jhu.edu/article/873179; Tom Pessah, "Violent Representations: Hostile Indians and Civilized Wars in Nineteenth-Century USA," *Ethnic and Racial Studies* 37, no. 9 (July 2014): 1628–45, https://doi.org/10.1080/01419870.2013.767918.

7. Alexandra Harmon, *Indians in the Making: Ethnic Relations and Indian Identities around Puget Sound* (Berkeley: University of California Press, 1998); Aeron Teverbaugh, "Tribal Constructs and Kinship Realities: Individual and Family Organization on the Grand Ronde Reservation from 1856" (master's thesis, Portland State University, 2000); Tracy Neal Leavelle, " 'We Will Make It Our Own Place': Agriculture and Adaptation at the Grand Ronde Reservation, 1856–1887," *American Indian Quarterly* 22, no. 4 (1998): 433–56, https://doi.org/10.2307/1184835; Patrick Stephen Lozar, " 'An Anxious Desire of Self Preservation': Colonialism, Transition, and Identity on the Umatilla Indian Reservation, 1860–1910" (master's thesis, University of Oregon, 2013); Andrew H. Fisher, *Shadow Tribe: The Making of Columbia River Indian Identity* (Seattle: University of Washington Press, 2010), esp. chap. 2. The very term *Pacific Northwest*, of course, privileges the spatial and geographic perspective of the United States.

8. Scott Richard Lyons, *X-Marks: Native Signatures of Assent* (Minneapolis: University of Minnesota Press, 2010), 119–21, 139–40.

9. Cora Snelgrove, Rita Kaur Dhamoon, and Jeff Corntassel, "Unsettling Set-
    tler Colonialism: The Discourse and Politics of Settlers, and Solidarity with
    Indigenous Nations," *Decolonization: Indigeneity, Education & Society* 3, no. 2
    (October 2014): 1–32, https://jps.library.utoronto.ca/index.php/des/article/
    view/21166/17970; Lisa Ford, *Settler Sovereignty: Jurisdiction and Indigenous
    People in America and Australia, 1788–1836* (Cambridge: Harvard University
    Press, 2010); James H. Merrell, "Second Thoughts on Colonial Historians
    and American Indians," *William and Mary Quarterly* 69, no. 2 (July 2012):
    451–512, https://doi.org/10.5309/willmaryquar.69.3.0451; Marc James
    Carpenter, "Pioneer Problems: 'Wanton Murder,' Indian War Veterans, and
    Oregon's Violent History," *Oregon Historical Quarterly* 121, no. 2 (2020):
    156–85, https://doi.org/10.5403/oregonhistq.121.2.0156.

10. Gary Clayton Anderson, the most prominent American genocide denier
    among U.S. historians in the 2010s, hung his arguments on risible acts of
    inference, illogical inductions, and an unspecified definition of genocide
    much narrower than that established by the United Nations. Jeffrey Ostler,
    "Denial of Genocide in the California Gold Rush Era: The Case of Gary
    Clayton Anderson," *American Indian Culture and Research Journal* 45, no. 2
    (2022): 81–101, https://doi.org/10.17953/aicrj.45.2.ostler; cf. Gary Clayton
    Anderson, "The Native Peoples of the American West: Genocide or Ethnic
    Cleansing?," *Western Historical Quarterly* 47, no. 4 (Winter 2016): 407–33,
    https://doi.org/10.1093/whq/whw126; United Nations, "Convention on
    the Prevention and Punishment of the Crime of Genocide. Adopted by the
    General Assembly of the United Nations on 9 December 1948," *United Na-
    tions Treaty Series* 78, no. 1021 (1951): 278–322, esp. 280 (quotations).

11. Benjamin Madley, "Reexamining the American Genocide Debate: Meaning,
    Historiography, and New Methods," *American Historical Review* 120, no. 1
    (February 2015): 98–139, esp. 107–8, https://doi.org/10.1093/ahr/120.1.98;
    Alex Alvarez, *Native America and the Question of Genocide* (Lanham, Md.:
    Rowman & Littlefield, 2016), 36–37; Jeffrey Ostler, *Surviving Genocide: Na-
    tive Nations and the United States from the American Revolution to Bleeding
    Kansas* (New Haven: Yale University Press, 2019), esp. appendix 1; Alexan-
    der K. A. Greenawalt, "Rethinking Genocidal Intent: The Case for a
    Knowledge-Based Interpretation," *Columbia Law Review* 99, no. 8 (Decem-
    ber 1999): 2259–94; Jürgen Zimmerer, "Colonialism and the Holocaust:
    Towards an Archeology of Genocide," trans. Andrew H. Beattie, in *Genocide
    and Settler Society: Frontier Violence and Stolen Indigenous Children in Austra-
    lian History*, ed. A. Dirk Moses (New York: Berghahn Books, 2004), 49–76;
    Robert Melson, "Critique of Current Genocide Studies," *Genocide Studies
    and Prevention* 6, no. 3 (December 2011): 279–86, https://utpjournals.press/
    doi/10.3138/gsp.6.3.279.

12. Edward B. Westermann, *Hitler's Ostkrieg and the Indian Wars: Comparing
    Genocide and Conquest* (Norman: University of Oklahoma Press, 2016); Car-
    roll P. Kakel III, "Patterns and Crimes of Empire: Comparative Perspectives

on Fascist and Non-Fascist Extermination," *Journal of Holocaust Research* 33, no. 1 (February 2019): 4–21, https://doi.org/10.1080/23256249.2019.154816 4; Marko Milanović, "State Responsibility for Genocide," *European Journal of International Law* 17, no. 3 (June 2006): 553–604, https://doi.org/10.1093/ejil/chlo19; United Nations, "Convention on the Prevention and Punishment of the Crime of Genocide," 280, 282 (quotations).

13. Shamiran Mako, "Cultural Genocide and Key International Instruments: Framing the Indigenous Experience," *International Journal on Minority and Group Rights* 19, no. 2 (January 2012): 175–94, https://doi.org/10.1163/157181112X639078; Elisa Novic, *The Concept of Cultural Genocide: An International Law Perspective* (New York: Oxford University Press, 2016), esp. chap. 4; Andrew Woolford, "Ontological Destruction: Genocide and Canadian Aboriginal Peoples," *Genocide Studies and Prevention* 4, no. 1 (May 2009): 81–97, https://doi.org/10.1353/gsp.0.0010.

14. Elliott West, "California, Coincidence, and Empire," in *A Global History of Gold Rushes*, ed. Benjamin Mountford and Stephen Tuffnell (Oakland: University of California Press, 2018), 42–64, esp. 45 ("attempted"). Cf. Benjamin Madley, *An American Genocide: The United States and the California Indian Catastrophe* (New Haven: Yale University Press, 2016).

15. George B. Wasson, "The Coquelle Indians and the Cultural 'Black Hole' of the Southern Oregon Coast," in *Worldviews and the American West: The Life of the Place Itself*, ed. Polly Stewart, Steve Siporin, C. W. Sullivan III, and Suzi Jones (Logan: Utah State University Press, 2000), 191–210; Minthorn, "Wars, Treaties, and the Beginning of Reservation Life," 64; Blaine Harden, *Murder at the Mission: A Frontier Killing, Its Legacy of Lies, and the Taking of the American West* (New York: Viking, 2021), 357.

16. Donald Bloxham, *History and Morality* (New York: Oxford University Press, 2020), 91–102.

17. Lorenzo Veracini, *Settler Colonialism: A Theoretical Overview* (New York: Palgrave Macmillan, 2010), 35 (necropolitical ... transfers); Gray H. Whaley, "American Folk Imperialism and Native Genocide in Southwest Oregon, 1851–1859," in *Colonial Genocide in Indigenous North America*, ed. Andrew Woolford, Jeff Benvenuto, and Alexander Laban Hinton (Durham, N.C.: Duke University Press, 2014), 131–48 (folk imperialism); Loren L. Williams to his nephew, July 22, 1876, Loren L. Williams Journals, vol. 4, attached to frontispiece ("than be in any other position"), Graff 4683, Newberry Library Special Collections, Chicago.

18. Gerald Vizenor, "Aesthetics of Survivance: Literary Theory and Practice," in *Survivance: Narratives of Native Presence*, ed. Gerald Vizenor (Lincoln: University of Nebraska Press, 2008), 1–24, esp. 1 ("renunciations"); Lyons, *X-Marks*, 97–98; David A. Chappell, "Active Agents versus Passive Victims: Decolonized Historiography or Problematic Paradigm?," *Contemporary Pacific* 7, no. 2 (Fall 1995): 303–26, https://www.jstor.org/stable/23706930.

19. There were some government-backed bounty systems for killing in the Pacific Northwest. U.S. naval officer Thomas Stowell Phelps claimed to have been an intermediary who collected "several" heads of Native men for the government of the Washington Territory to pay out bounties to Indigenous auxiliaries in 1856, during the Puget Sound War, for example. Thomas Stowell Phelps, *Reminiscences of Seattle, Washington Territory, and the U.S. Sloop-of-War "Decatur" during the Indian War of 1855–1856*, ed. Alice Harriman (1902; repr., New York: Alice Harriman, 1908), 41–42.

20. Cf. Hyde, *Empires, Nations, and Families*, 429; Harwood P. Hinton and Jerry D. Thompson, *Courage above All Things: General John Ellis Wool and the U.S. Military, 1812–1863* (Norman: University of Oklahoma Press, 2020), 265; Gregory Michno, *The Deadliest Indian War in the West: The Snake Conflict, 1864–1868* (Caldwell, Idaho: Caxton Press, 2007), 84.

21. On the problem of the tragic, see among others Boyd Cothran, *Remembering the Modoc War: Redemptive Violence and the Making of American Innocence* (Chapel Hill: University of North Carolina Press, 2014), esp. 109. Cf. Richard Kluger, *The Bitter Waters of Medicine Creek: A Tragic Clash between White and Native America* (New York: Knopf, 2011).

Chapter One. Settler-Soldiers and Folk Imperialism in the Pacific Northwest

1. "Address of Hon. Francis Henry," 1884, Washington Pioneer Association Transactions, 1883–89, 41, box 30, Center for Pacific Northwest Studies, Western Washington University, Bellingham (hereafter cited as WWU Center for Pacific Northwest Studies).

2. Elwood Evans, *Puget Sound: Its Past, Present, and Future* (Olympia, 1869), 12; Patrick Wolfe, "Settler Colonialism and the Elimination of the Native," *Journal of Genocide Research* 8, no. 4 (2006): 387–409, https://doi.org/10.1080/14623520601056240; J. Kēhaulani Kauanui, " 'A Structure Not an Event': Settler Colonialism and Enduring Indigeneity," *Lateral* 5, no. 1 (2016), https://csalateral.org/issue/5-1/forum-alt-humanities-settler-colonialism-enduring-indigeneity-kauanui/; Gray H. Whaley, *Oregon and the Collapse of Illahee: U.S. Empire and the Transformation of an Indigenous World, 1792–1859* (Chapel Hill: University of North Carolina Press, 2010), chap. 7; Katrine Barber, " 'We Were at Our Journey's End': Settler Sovereignty Formation in Oregon," *Oregon Historical Quarterly* 120, no. 4 (2019): 382–413, https://doi.org/10.5403/oregonhistq.120.4.0382.

3. Whaley, *Oregon and the Collapse of Illahee*; Robert T. Boyd, *The Coming of the Spirit of Pestilence: Introduced Infectious Diseases and Population Decline among Northwest Coast Indians, 1774–1874* (Seattle: University of Washington Press, 1999).

4. Whaley, *Oregon and the Collapse of Illahee*, 89–91, 136 (quotations on 90); Gray H. Whaley, "American Folk Imperialism and Native Genocide in

Southwest Oregon, 1851–1859," in *Colonial Genocide in Indigenous North America*, ed. Andrew Woolford, Jeff Benvenuto, and Alexander Laban Hinton (Durham, N.C.: Duke University Press, 2014), 131–48.

5. Nathaniel J. Wyeth to "Friend Weld," April 3, 1835, in *Sources of Oregon History*, ed. F[rederic] G[eorge] Young, 1, no. 3–6 (1899): 149; W. Clement Eaton, "Nathaniel Wyeth's Oregon Expeditions," *Pacific Historical Review* 4, no. 2 (1935): 101–13, https://doi.org/10.2307/3633722; Alexander Spoehr, "Fur Traders in Hawai'i: The Hudson's Bay Company in Honolulu, 1829–1861," *Hawaiian Journal of History* 20 (1986): 27–66; Stacey L. Smith, *Freedom's Frontier: California and the Struggle over Unfree Labor, Emancipation, and Reconstruction* (Chapel Hill: University of North Carolina Press, 2013), 32.

6. Wyeth to "Friend Weld" ("providence"); Kerry R. Oman, "Winter in the Rockies: The Winter Quarters of the Mountain Men," *Montana: The Magazine of Western History* 52, no. 1 (Spring 2002): 34–47; Susanah Shaw Romney, "Settler Colonial Prehistories in Seventeenth-Century North America," *William and Mary Quarterly* 76, no. 3 (July 2019), 375–82, https://www.muse.jhu.edu/article/730606.

7. Rev. Samuel Parker, *Journal of an Exploring Tour beyond the Rocky Mountains*, 4th ed. (Ithaca, N.Y.: Andrus, Woodruff, & Gauntlett, 1844), 269 (quotation); Norbert Finzch, " '[…] Extirpate or Remove That Vermine': Genocide, Biological Warfare, and Settler Imperialism in the Eighteenth and Early Nineteenth Century," *Journal of Genocide Research* 10, no. 2 (June 2008): 215–32, https://doi.org/10.1080/14623520802065446.

8. Parker, *Journal of an Exploring Tour*, 270–71.

9. Whaley, *Oregon and the Collapse of Illahee*, 125–60 (quotation on 136); Jonathan W. Olson, "Apostles of Commerce: The Fur Trade in the Colonial Northwest and the Formation of a Hemispheric Religious Economy, 1807–1859" (PhD diss., Florida State University, 2014), 284–97; cf. Albert Furtwangler, *Bringing Indians to the Book* (Seattle: University of Washington Press, 2005), esp. 4–7. I depart from Whaley's interpretation of Parker by making more of a distinction between what he saw as inevitable and what he deemed desirable. At least on the page, Parker regretted rather than supported the genocide he predicted.

10. Marcus Whitman to Stephen and Clarissa Prentiss, May 16, 1844, in *Mrs. Whitman's Letters, 1843–1847*, ed. George H. Himes (Portland: Oregon Pioneer Association, 1894), 64–65.

11. James V. Walker, " 'Providence will take care of me … I will wear a crown': Frontier Circuit Rider, James O. Rayner, and the Land Laws of Early Oregon," *Oregon Historical Quarterly* 120, no. 3 (Fall 2019): 246–75, https://doi.org/10.1353/ohq.2019.0026.

12. E[lijah] L[afayette] Bristow [Jr.], "E. L. Bristow's Narrative," June 13, 1878, 1–3, folder: E. L. Bristow, box 5, Willamette University and Northwest Collection, WUA014, Willamette University Special Collections; Marc

James Carpenter, "Naming a Killer: Elijah Bristow and Lane County's History of Colonial Violence," in *Lane County Historian Anthology* (Eugene: Lane County Historical Society, 2022), 172–79.

13. Joseph Henry Brown, "Autobiography," 1878, 1, folder 1, box 1, Joseph Henry Brown Papers, Mss 1002, Oregon Historical Society Special Collections.

14. Brown, "Autobiography," 14–15.

15. Jason E. Pierce, *Making the White Man's West: Whiteness and the Creation of the American West* (Boulder: University Press of Colorado, 2016), 130–32; Brown, "Autobiography," 16–17.

16. Antone Minthorn, "Wars, Treaties, and the Beginning of Reservation Life," in *As Days Go By: Our History, Our Land, and Our People: The Cayuse, Umatilla, and Walla Walla*, ed. Jennifer Karson (Pendleton, Ore.: Tamástslikt Cultural Institute, 2006), 61–89; Sarah Koenig, *Providence and the Invention of American History* (New Haven: Yale University Press, 2021), chap. 1; Cassandra Tate, *Unsettled Ground: The Whitman Massacre and Its Shifting Legacy in the American West* (Seattle: Sasquatch Books, 2020), esp. 8. Two of the slain were male teenagers (fifteen and seventeen)—sometimes portrayed as children in Euro-American history, but young adults by Cayuse (and arguably American) norms at the time. Americans in the 1850s Northwest identified all Native males over the age of twelve as dangerous men, and White teenagers with guns did kill people during the War on Illahee.

17. Tate, *Unsettled Ground*, 132–33, 136–37, 151–52; William C. McKay to Eva Emery Dye, February 1, 1892 ("how they have been"), folder 7, box 2, Eva Emery Dye Papers, Mss 1089, Oregon Historical Society Special Collections; Frances Fuller Victor (uncredited) and Hubert Howe Bancroft, *History of Oregon*, 2 vols., ed. Matthew P. Deady (uncredited) and Hubert Howe Bancroft (San Francisco: History Company, 1886–88), 2:651; Nina Lane, "Biography of Joseph Lane," 88, folder 3, box 2, Joseph Lane Papers, Ax 183, University of Oregon Special Collections (hereafter cited as Joseph Lane Papers); Koenig, *Providence and the Invention of American History*, 44.

18. Tate, *Unsettled Ground*, 134, 165, 255n10; Victor and Bancroft, *History of Oregon*, 1:652–53; "An Interview with a Survivor of the Whitman Massacre," *Oregon Native Son* 1, no. 2 (1899): 63–65; Chelsea Kristen Vaughn, "Playing West: Performances of War and Empire in Pacific Northwest Pageantry" (PhD diss., University of California, Riverside, 2016), 178–83.

19. Tate, *Unsettled Ground*, 169; Minthorn, "Wars, Treaties, and the Beginning of Reservation Life," esp. 61–64; Clifford E. Trafzer and Richard D. Scheuerman, *Renegade Tribe: The Palouse Indians and the Invasion of the Inland Pacific Northwest* (Pullman: Washington State University Press, 1986), 26. I use the words *presumed* and *seems to* here to signal the uncertainty of underlying explanations that went through multiple translations by parties that had a stake in the outcome.

20. "A Bill to Authorize the Raising of a Regiment of Volunteers &c," *Oregon Spectator* (Oregon City), January 6, 1848; Warren J. Brier, "Political Censorship in the Oregon Spectator," *Pacific Historical Review* 31, no. 3 (August 1962): 235–40, https://doi.org/10.2307/3637167; Julius Wilm, *Settlers as Conquerors: Free Land Policy in Antebellum America* (Wiesbaden, Germany: Franz Steiner, 2018), 222–23.

21. Joseph Shafer, "Jesse Applegate: Pioneer, Statesman and Philosopher," *Washington Historical Quarterly* 1, no. 4 (July 1907): 217–33, esp. 228 (quotations), https://www.jstor.org/stable/40734418.

22. William D. Stillwell to Conrad C. Walker, January 21, 1915, folder 20, box 1, Oregon Military Collection MSS.

23. Stillwell to Walker, January 21, 1915.

24. Tate, *Unsettled Ground*, 176–82; George Guy Delamarter, *The Career of Robert Newell, Oregon Pioneer* (Saint Paul, Ore.: Newell House Museum, 2005), 78–82.

25. Whaley, *Oregon and the Collapse of Illahee*, 180–81 (quotations); Colonel William Thompson, *Reminiscences of a Pioneer* (San Francisco: Alturas Plain Dealer, 1912), 12; Everett Earle Stanard, "Many Descendants of Indian Fighters Live in Linn County," *Albany Democrat-Herald*, September 7, 1948, 6; Oscar Johnson, "The Molalla: A Nation of Good Hunters," *Smoke Signals* (Grand Ronde), Spring 1999.

26. John Minto, *Rhymes of Early Life in Oregon and Historical and Biological Facts* (Salem, Ore.: Statesman, 1915), 9 ("fiendish"); John Minto to Eva Emery Dye, December 18, 1900, folder 9, box 2, Eva Emery Dye Papers ("Of course"). On recollections of Pacific Northwest pioneers being raised with Indian hating from birth, see T[imothy] W[oodbridge] Davenport, "Recollections of an Indian Agent—IV," *Quarterly of the Oregon Historical Society* 8, no. 1 (December 1907): 1–41, esp. 41, https://www.jstor.org/stable/20609748; W[illiam] J. Trimble, "American and British Treatment of the Indians in the Pacific Northwest," *Washington Historical Quarterly* 5, no. 1 (January 1914): 32–54, esp. 34, https://www.jstor.org/stable/40473722. This norm suggests that historian Brian Rouleau's insights about American children's literature as colonial imperial indoctrination can be fruitfully applied to literature less specifically aimed at children published before the 1860s—and that readings of this literature as "didactic" rather than "avowedly imperial" should be reexamined. Brian Rouleau, *Empire's Nursery: Children's Literature and the Origins of the American Century* (New York: New York University Press, 2021), 11 (quotation); Brian Rouleau, "How the West Was Fun: Children's Literature and Frontier Mythmaking toward the Turn of the Twentieth Century," *Western Historical Quarterly* 51, no. 1 (Spring 2020): 49–74, https://doi.org/10.1093/whq/whz099.

27. Frederick V. Holman, "ADDRESS ... at the Unveiling of the Memorial Stone to Peter Skene Ogden, at Mountain View Cemetery, Oregon City, Oregon, October 28, 1923," in "The Occasion of the Unveiling of the Me-

526–27 ("even to the" and "all sorts")Malcolm Clark Jr., *Eden Seekers: The Settlement of Oregon, 1818–1862* (Boston: Houghton Mifflin, 1981), 225 ("an awesome orgy");; Albert G. Brackett, *General Lane's Brigade in Central Mexico* (Cincinnati: H. W. Derby, 1854), 95 ("gallant conduct"). As Riffel notes, the stock American military response to accusations of atrocity during the U.S.–Mexico War was to deny, deflect, and then claim that the real atrocities were committed by their opponents. Any errors of translation are mine.

35. Joseph Lane to Capt. Samuel Gilmore, April 9, 1849, file 22, container 34, Oregon State Archives, http://truwe.sohs.org/files/jolaneletters.html.

36. Francis Paul Prucha, *The Great Father: The United States Government and the American Indian*, 2 vols. (Lincoln: University of Nebraska Press, 1984), 1:397 ("cause of humanity"). Many of the errors in Prucha's magisterial work, in the section on the Pacific Northwest as elsewhere, stem from Prucha's presumption that colonizers tell the truth.

37. "Letter from General Lane," *Indiana Sentinel*, August 21, 1851, 2; Joseph Lane to "Editor of the Statesman," June 28, 1851, 2 ("war [that] had commenced"), *Oregon Statesman*, https://truwe.sohs.org/files/jolaneletters.html; "Southern Oregon—No. 2," *Oregon Sentinel* (Jacksonville), May 11, 1867, 2, http://truwe.sohs.org/files/scraps.html; E. A. Schwartz, *The Rogue River Indian War and Its Aftermath, 1850–1980* (Norman: University of Oklahoma Press, 1997), esp. 36–37.

38. Joseph Lane to "Editor of the Statesman," June 28, 1851.

39. Joseph Lane to "Editor of the Statesman," June 28, 1851; Schwartz, *Rogue River Indian War and Its Aftermath*, esp. 32–33.

40. Joseph Lane to "Editor of the Statesman," June 28, 1851.

41. Schwartz, *Rogue River Indian War*, 44 ("clashes"). See also Nathan Douthit, *Uncertain Encounters: Indians and Whites at Peace and War in Southern Oregon, 1820s–1860s* (Corvallis: Oregon State University Press, 2002), 159; David G. Lewis, "Causes of the 1853 Rogue River War," *Quartux Journal* (March 30, 2020), https://ndnhistoryresearch.com/2020/03/30/causes-of-the-1853-rogue-river-war/; Ashley Cordes, "Revisiting Stories and Voices of the Rogue River War (1853–1856): A Digital Constellatory Autoethnographic Mode of Indigenous Archaeology," *Cultural Studies ←→ Critical Methodologies* 21, no. 1 (2021): 56–69, https://doi.org/10.1177/1532708620953189; Tveskov, " 'Most Disastrous' Affair," esp. 45.

42. J. M. Kirkpatrick, *Oregon Statesman*, July 15, 1851, 2; Schwartz, *Rogue River Indian War*, 33–36; Adam Fitzhugh, "Battle Rock: Anatomy of a Massacre," research paper for Oregon Heritage Fellowship (Salem: Oregon Parks and Recreation Department, April 2020), https://www.oregon.gov/oprd/OH/Documents/Battle%20Rock,%20Anatomy%20of%20a%20Massacre,%20Adam%20Fitzhugh.pdf; David G. Lewis and Thomas J. Connolly, "White American Violence on Tribal Peoples on the Oregon Coast," *Oregon Historical Quarterly* 120, no. 4 (Winter 2019): 368–81, esp. 370, https://doi.

org/10.1353/ohq.2019.0028; George Bundy Wasson Jr., "Growing Up Indian: An Emic Perspective" (PhD diss., University of Oregon, 2001), 182–85. Although there was a longer text published around 1904 purportedly from Kirkpatrick, doubts have been cast on its authenticity. See Roberta L. Hall and Don Alan Hall, "The Village at the Mouth of the Coquille River: Historical Questions of Who, When, and Where," *Pacific Northwest Quarterly* 82, no. 3 (July 1991): 101–8, esp. 104, https://www.jstor.org/stable/40491202.

43. Loren L. Williams Journals, 1:14–15, 19, Graff 4683, Newberry Library Special Collections, Chicago; George S. Turnbull, *History of Oregon Newspapers* (Portland: Binfords & Mort, 1939), 26, 41–42; Brier, "Political Censorship in the Oregon Spectator"; Jeff LaLande, "'Dixie' of the Pacific Northwest: Southern Oregon's Civil War," *Oregon Historical Quarterly* 100, no. 1 (Spring 1999): 32–81, https://www.jstor.org/stable/20614943.

44. Loren L. Williams Journals, 1:30 (quotations); William T'Vault to Anson Dart, September 19, 1851, in *[Portland] Weekly Oregonian*, October 4, 1851, 2; Charles F. Wilkinson, *The People Are Dancing Again: The History of the Siletz Tribe of Western Oregon* (Seattle: University of Washington Press, 2010), 77. Some scholars and people within the community prefer *Coquille*, others *Coquelle*. I use *Coquelle* here, following pronunciation in the original language.

45. Loren L. Williams Journals, 1:51–52 (quotations).

46. Loren L. Williams Journals, 1:54–55, 59–60 (quotations).

47. Loren L. Williams Journals, 1:68–87; T'Vault to Dart, September 19, 1851; Hall and Hall, "The Village at the Mouth of the Coquille River," esp. 105.

48. Wilkinson, *The People Are Dancing Again*, 77; Robert Marshall Utley, *Frontiersmen in Blue: The United States Army and the Indian, 1848–1865* (Lincoln: University of Nebraska Press, 1967), 36 ("scraped together"); John D. Biles to Michael Albright, May 23, 1852 ("come on the indians"; inconsistent capitalization in the original), folder 7, box 1, Malick Family Papers WA MSS S-1298, Yale Collection of Western Americana, Beinecke Rare Book and Manuscript Library; Loren L. Williams Journals, 1:144 ("fractious miners"); Lewis and Connolly, "White American Violence on Tribal Peoples on the Oregon Coast," 371.

49. David G. Lewis, "Anson Dart's Report on the Tribes and Treaties of Oregon, 1851," *Quartux Journal* (October 8, 2017), https://ndnhistoryresearch.com/2017/10/08/anson-darts-report-on-the-tribes-and-treaties-of-oregon-1851/; David G. Lewis, "Termination of the Confederated Tribes of the Grand Ronde Community of Oregon: Politics, Community, Identity" (PhD diss., University of Oregon, 2009), appendix B.

50. David G. Lewis, "Rogue River Treaty of 1853," *Quartux Journal* (January 17, 2018), https://ndnhistoryresearch.com/2018/01/17/rogue-river-treaty-of-1853-negotiated-september-10-1853-ratified-april-12-1854/; *[Olympia] Pioneer and Democrat*, March 31, 1855, 1.

51. Carol Reardon, *With a Sword in One Hand and Jomini in the Other: The Problem of Military Thought in the Civil War North* (Chapel Hill: University of North Carolina Press, 2012), chap. 1; John Fabian Witt, *Lincoln's Code: The Laws of War in American History* (New York: Simon and Schuster, 2012), chap. 3.

52. Jean S. Pictet et al., eds, *The Geneva Conventions of 12 August 1949* (Geneva: International Committee of the Red Cross, 1952), 32.

53. "Address of Hon. Francis Henry"; Kenneth R. Coleman, " 'We'll All Start Even': White Egalitarianism and the Oregon Donation Land Claim Act," *Oregon Historical Quarterly* 120, no. 4 (Winter 2019): 414–39, https://doi.org/10.5403/oregonhistq.120.4.0414; Paul Frymer, " 'A Rush and Push and the Land Is Ours': Territorial Expansion, Land Policy, and U.S. State Formation," *Perspectives on Politics* 12, no. 1 (March 2014): 119–44, esp. 125, https://www.jstor.org/stable/43281105; Wilm, *Settlers as Conquerors*.

54. Boyd, *The Coming of the Spirit of Pestilence*, esp. chaps. 8, 9; John Sutton Lutz and Keith Thor Carlson, "The Smallpox Chiefs: Bioterrorism and the Exercise of Power in the Pacific Northwest," *Western Historical Quarterly* 55 (Summer 2024): 87–104, esp. 88n4.

55. Jeffrey Ostler, *Surviving Genocide: Native Nations and the United States from the American Revolution to Bleeding Kansas* (New Haven: Yale University Press, 2019), esp. 86, 121, 136; Paige Raibmon, "Unmaking Native Space: A Genealogy of Indian Policy, Settler Practice, and the Microtechniques of Dispossession," in *The Power of Promises: Rethinking Indian Treaties in the Pacific Northwest*, ed. Alexandra Harmon (Seattle: University of Washington Press, 2008), 56–85; M. Susan Van Laere, *Fine Words and Promises: A History of Indian Policy and Its Impact on the Coast Reservation Tribes of Oregon in the Last Half of the Nineteenth Century* (Philomath, Ore.: Serendip Historical Research, 2010), chap. 3; Ronald Spores, "Too Small a Place: The Removal of the Willamette Valley Indians, 1850–1856," *American Indian Quarterly* 17, no. 2 (Spring 1993): 171–91, esp. 176–77 ("If you remain"), https://doi.org/10.2307/1185526.

56. John P. Gaines, "Governor's Message, Executive Department, Oregon City, Dec. 2d, 1850," *Oregonian*, December 4, 1850, 2–3.

57. As David G. Lewis notes, Anson Dart was not initially part of Gaines's Treaty Commission in 1850, and his involvement or absence at various treaty negotiations is less clear than has previously been assumed. David G. Lewis, "Anson Dart and the Willamette Treaty Commission," *Quartux Journal* (January 4, 2018), https://ndnhistoryresearch.com/2018/01/04/anson-dart-and-the-willamette-treaty-commission/; Commissioners Allen, Gaines, and Skinner to Dr. Anson Dart, April 16, 1851 ("the reserve"), frame 00528, reel 3, John Pollard Gaines Papers, 1832–1864, Microfilm collection, in Katherine Louise Huit, "Oregon Territorial Governor John Pollard Gaines: A Whig Appointee in a Democratic Territory" (master's thesis, Portland State University, 1996); Spores, "Too Small a Place"; MacKenzie Katherine

Lee Moore, "Making Place and Nation: Geographic Meaning and the Americanization of Oregon: 1834–1859" (PhD diss., University of California, Berkeley, 2012), 130–32; Daniel L. Boxberger and Herbert C. Taylor Jr., "Treaty or Non-Treaty Status," *Columbia* 5, no. 3 (Fall 1991): 40–45.

58. Joel Palmer to Nathan Olney, September 28, 1854 (quotations; emphasis added), folder 51, box 1, Joel Palmer Papers, Mss 114, Oregon Historical Society Special Collections.

59. Sarah Cullen, " 'Little Difficulties Will Get to Be Great Difficulties': Joel Palmer and the Office of Indian Affairs in the Oregon Territory, 1853–56," *British Association for American Studies Digital Essay Competition* 2 (February 28, 2017) ("Experience has taught"), https://www.amdigital.co.uk/about/blog/item/sarah-cullen-oregon; Jo N. Miles, "Kamiakin's Impact on Early Washington Territory," *Pacific Northwest Quarterly* 99, no. 4 (Fall 2008): 159–72, esp. 165 ("prevent the wind"), https://www.jstor.org/stable/40492173.

60. "Joel Palmer and Isaac I. Stevens Biographies," *Oregon Historical Quarterly* 106, no. 3 (Fall 2005): 356–57, https://www.jstor.org/stable/20615555; *[Olympia] Pioneer and Democrat*, March 31, 1855, 2 (quotations); Mary Ellen Rowe, *Bulwark of the Republic: The American Militia in the Antebellum West* (Westport, Conn.: Praeger, 2003), 144.

61. Charles F. Wilkinson, *Messages from Frank's Landing: A Story of Salmon, Treaties, and the Indian Way* (Seattle: University of Washington Press, 2000), 12.

62. SuAnn M. Reddick and Cary C. Collins, "Medicine Creek Remediated: Isaac Stevens and the Puyallup, Nisqually, and Muckleshoot Land Settlement at Fox Island, August 4, 1856," *Pacific Northwest Quarterly* 104, no. 2 (Spring 2013): 80–98, esp. 81 ("injudicious"), https://www.jstor.org/stable/24631631; *[Olympia] Pioneer and Democrat*, March 31, 1855, 2 ("summarily"); Alexandra Harmon, "Pacific Northwest Treaties in National and International Historical Perspective," in Harmon, *Power of Promises*, 3–31, esp. 6; Joshua L. Reid, *The Sea Is My Country: The Maritime World of the Makahs* (New Haven: Yale University Press, 2015), esp. chap. 4; Arthur Spirling, "U.S. Treaty Making with American Indians: Institutional Change and Relative Power, 1784–1911," *American Journal of Political Science* 56, no. 1 (January 2012): 84–97, https://www.jstor.org/stable/23075145.

63. SuAnn M. Reddick and Cary C. Collins, "Medicine Creek to Fox Island: Cadastral Scams and Contested Domains," *Oregon Historical Quarterly* 106, no. 3 (Fall 2005): 374–97, esp. 380–81 ("solve their trouble"), https://doi.org/10.1353/ohq.2005.0087; Candace Wellman, *Man of Treacherous Charm: Territorial Justice Edmund C. Fitzhugh* (Pullman: Washington State University Press, 2023), 82.

64. Andrew Dominique Pambrun, "Reminiscences of A. D. Pambrun of Athena, Oregon," quoted in Miles, "Kamiakin's Impact on Early Washington Territory," 167; Reddick and Collins, "Medicine Creek to Fox Island"; Miles, "Kamiakin's Impact on Early Washington Territory," 167; Lin Tull Cannell,

"William Craig: Governor Stevens's Conduit to the Nez Perce," *Pacific Northwest Quarterly* 97, no. 1 (Winter 2005–6): 19–30, esp. 21, https://www.jstor.org/stable/40491895.

65. Chris Friday, "Performing Treaties: The Culture and Politics of Treaty Remembrance and Celebration," in Harmon, *Power of Promises*, 157–85; Harmon, "Pacific Northwest Treaties," esp. 26–27; Nancy Shoemaker, *A Strange Likeness: Becoming Red and White in Eighteenth-Century North America* (Oxford: Oxford University Press, 2004), esp. 63–64.

66. Cf. Douthit, *Uncertain Encounters*; Elliott West, "The Nez Perce and Their Trials: Rethinking America's Indian Wars," *Montana: The Magazine of Western History* 60, no. 3 (Autumn 2010): 3–18, 92–93, https://www.jstor.org/stable/27922525.

Chapter Two. Everyday Violence and the Embrace of Genocide in Oregon

1. John Beeson, *A Plea for the Indians; with Facts and Features of the Late War in Oregon* (New York: John Beeson, 1857), 46, 50–51 (quotations); E. A. Schwartz, *The Rogue River Indian War and Its Aftermath, 1850–1980* (Norman: University of Oklahoma Press, 1997), 85–89.

2. Thomas J. Cram, *Topographical Memoir and Report of Captain T. J. Cram, on Territories of Oregon and Washington*, H.R. Exec. Doc. no. 114, 35th Cong., 2nd sess. (1859), 44; Marc James Carpenter, "Pioneer Problems: 'Wanton Murder,' Indian War Veterans, and Oregon's Violent History," *Oregon Historical Quarterly* 121, no. 2 (2020): 156–85, https://doi.org/10.5403/oregonhistq.121.2.0156.

3. George E. Cole, *Early Oregon: Jottings of a Pioneer of 1850* (Spokane: Shaw & Borden, 1905), 52.

4. *Harper's New Monthly Magazine*, December 1855, found in *Harper's New Monthly Magazine* 12 (New York: Harper and Brothers, 1856), 254; "Oregon—Rogue River War," *New York Daily Tribune*, November 14, 1855; Benjamin Madley, "Reexamining the American Genocide Debate: Meaning, Historiography, and New Methods," *American Historical Review* 120, no. 1 (February 2015): 98–139, esp. 112, https://doi.org/10.1093/ahr/120.1.98. On the tendency for the Lupton Massacre to inadequately stand in for the whole, see, for example, Elliott West, *Continental Reckoning: The American West in the Age of Expansion* (Lincoln: University of Nebraska Press, 2024), 63.

5. Gray H. Whaley, *Oregon and the Collapse of* Illahee: *U.S. Empire and the Transformation of an Indigenous World, 1792–1859* (Chapel Hill: University of North Carolina Press, 2010), chap. 7; Katrine Barber, " 'We Were at Our Journey's End': Settler Sovereignty Formation in Oregon," *Oregon Historical Quarterly* 120, no. 4 (2019): 382–413, https://doi.org/10.5403/oregonhistq.120.4.0382. The presumption that *Indians* means *hostile Indians* per-

sists in modern military history particularly. In his fawning biography of General Crook, the historian Charles M. Robinson III claims in the preface that he will be using the terms *friendly Indians* and *hostile Indians*—bad enough—but then proceeds throughout most of the book to simply use the term *Indians* for the latter. Charles M. Robinson III, *General Crook and the Western Frontier* (Norman: University of Oklahoma Press, 2001), xi, 21, 168.

6. Schwartz, *Rogue River Indian War*; Boyd Cothran, *Remembering the Modoc War: Redemptive Violence and the Making of American Innocence* (Chapel Hill: University of North Carolina Press, 2014); Whaley, *Oregon and the Collapse of Illahee*.

7. Beeson, *Plea for the Indians*, 52.

8. Neil M. Howison, "Report of Lieutenant Neil M. Howison on Oregon, 1846: A Reprint," *Quarterly of the Oregon Historical Society* 14, no. 1 (1913): 1–60, esp. 46 (quotation), https://www.jstor.org/stable/20609921.

9. Julius Wilm, *Settlers as Conquerors: Free Land Policy in Antebellum America* (Wiesbaden, Germany: Franz Steiner, 2018), 222; Brad Asher, *Beyond the Reservation: Indians, Settlers, and the Law in Washington Territory, 1853–1889* (Norman: University of Oklahoma Press, 1999), esp. 212–13.

10. Howison, "Report of Lieutenant Neil M. Howison," 46, 24.

11. John Samuel Ferrell, "Indians and Criminal Justice in Early Oregon, 1842–1859" (master's thesis, Portland State University, 1973), 51–52.

12. *[Salem] Oregon Statesman*, June 2, 1855; emphasis in original.

13. Ferrell, "Indians and Criminal Justice in Early Oregon," 49–52; Asher, *Beyond the Reservation*, appendix.

14. Carpenter, "Pioneer Problems," 162; Beeson, *Plea for the Indians*, 28.

15. Laurence M. Hauptman, "General John E. Wool in Cherokee Country, 1836–1837: A Reinterpretation," *Georgia Historical Quarterly* 85, no. 1 (Spring 2001): 1–26, esp. 3 (quotations), https://www.jstor.org/stable/40584373; Jeffrey Ostler, *Surviving Genocide: Native Nations and the United States from the American Revolution to Bleeding Kansas* (New Haven: Yale University Press, 2019), chap. 8.

16. John E. Wool to Col. J. Cooper, March 14, 1854 ("lawless barbarity"), roll 2, Letters sent October 10, 1853, to April 23, 1859, M 2114, War Department Records of the Division and Department of the Pacific, 1847–1873, National Archives and Records Administration (hereafter cited as War Department Records of the Pacific); Harwood P. Hinton and Jerry D. Thompson, *Courage above All Things: General John Ellis Wool and the U.S. Military, 1812–1863* (Norman: University of Oklahoma Press, 2020), 244 ("the lawlessness"); John E. Wool to Inspector Genl Infantry Col. J. Mansfield, May 12, 1854 ("give the best protection"), War Department Records of the Pacific.

17. E. D. Townsend [on behalf of Gen. Wool] to L. Loe[ser], October 10, 1854, War Department Records of the Pacific.

18. Wool to Mansfield, May 12, 1854.

19. Wool to Col. J. Cooper, December 12, 1854, War Department Records of the Pacific.

20. W. W. Stevens, "The Old Oregon Trail as Told by the Trailers," ca. 1913, chaps. 9 ("contracted"), 14 ("a soldier in Florida"), and 15 ("decided"), Baker County Library Archive; Fred Lockley, "Experiences of an Oregon Pioneer," *Overland Monthly* 69, no. 3 (March 1917): 245–46; David G. Lewis, "Ka'hosadi Shasta Peoples of Oregon and California," *Quartux Journal* (November 30, 2019), https://ndnhistoryresearch.com/2019/11/30/kahosadi-shasta-peoples-of-oregon/.

21. Stevens, "Old Oregon Trail as Told by the Trailers," chap. 16. On the Nasomah Massacre, see George B. Wasson, "The Coquelle Indians and the Cultural 'Black Hole' of the Southern Oregon Coast," in *Worldviews and the American West: The Life of the Place Itself*, ed. Polly Stewart, Steve Siporin, C. W. Sullivan III, and Suzi Jones (Logan: Utah State University Press, 2000), 191–210; Bob Zybach, "The 1855–1856 Oregon Indian War in Coos County, Oregon: Eyewitnesses and Storytellers, March 27, 1855–August 21, 1856," Report Prepared for Coquille Indian Tribe Tribal Historic Preservation Office (Cottage Grove, Ore.), May 15, 2012, esp. 118–19; Madonna L. Moss and George B. Wasson Jr., "Intimate Relations with the Past: The Story of an Athapaskan Village on the Southern Northwest Coast of North America," *World Archaeology* 29, no. 3 (February 1998): 317–32, https://www.jstor.org/stable/125033; "Slaughter of Indians by the Vigilantes Recalled," *Oregonian*, January 29, 1928, 8.

22. Stevens, "Old Oregon Trail as Told by the Trailers," chaps. 17, 12; W. A. Pettit, "Constitution Framer Is Last of Sturdy Men," *Oregonian*, November 26, 1911, 13; Lockley, "Experiences of an Oregon Pioneer; William H. Packwood Dies at Age of 85," *Oregonian*, September 22, 1917, 1 ("subjugat[ing]"). William H. Packwood's great-grandson Robert W. Packwood was a six-term U.S. senator from Oregon and a serial sexual harasser. See Mark Kirchmeier, *Packwood: The Public and Private Life from Acclaim to Outrage* (San Francisco: HarperCollinsWest, 1995).

23. Oregon Constitution, Article 2, Section 5, in Charles H. Carey, ed., *The Oregon Constitution and Proceedings and Debates of the Constitutional Convention of 1857* (Salem: State Printing Department, 1926), 401; Cecily N. Zander, *The Army under Fire: The Politics of Antimilitarism in the Civil War Era* (Baton Rouge: Louisiana State University Press, 2024), esp. chap. 2; Matthew Deady to James W. Nesmith, January 21, 1856 ("elevated"), folder 16, box 1, James W. Nesmith Papers, Mss 577, Oregon Historical Society Special Collections; besides the newspapers cited elsewhere in these notes, see *Oregonian*, October 20, 1855.

24. Gaines and Lane were both slaveholders, although Gaines was publicly against the spread of slavery. Frederick Waymire accused (or possibly applauded) both Gaines and Lane of seeking to "obviate the vexatious slave question in Oregon by using *Indians*." Lane is known to have enslaved Na-

morial Stone on the Grave of Peter Skene Ogden," by Henry L. Bates et al., *Quarterly of the Oregon Historical Society* 24, no. 4 (December 1923): 361–85, esp. 377 ("Judge Lynch"), https://www.jstor.org/stable/20610258; Minthorn, "Wars, Treaties, and the Beginning of Reservation Life," esp. 64–65; Ronald B. Lansing, *Juggernaut: The Whitman Massacre Trial, 1850* (San Francisco: Ninth Judicial Circuit Historical Society, 1993).

28. *Yreka Herald*, August 7, 1853 (quotation); James Mason Hutchings Diary (transcript by Gertrude Hutchings Mills), 18–19, box 105a, Peter E. Palmquist Collection of Male Photographers in the American West, WA MSS S-2733, Yale Collection of Western Americana, Beinecke Rare Book and Manuscript Library.

29. Whaley, *Oregon and the Collapse of* Illahee, 195–96; John E. Ross, "Report to Gov. Curry, Nov 10, 1854," in *Protections Afforded by Volunteers of Oregon and Washington Territories to Overland Immigrants in 1854*, ed. Benjamin F. Harding, Misc. Doc no. 47, U.S. House of Representatives, 35th Cong., 2nd sess., 1858; Mark Axel Tveskov, "A 'Most Disastrous' Affair: The Battle of Hungry Hill, Historical Memory, and the Rogue River War," *Oregon Historical Quarterly* 118, no. 1 (Spring 2017): 42–73, https://doi.org/10.5403/oregonhistq.118.1.0042; Benjamin Madley, "California and Oregon's Modoc Indians: How Indigenous Resistance Camouflages Genocide in Colonial Histories," in Woolford, Benvenuto, and Hinton, *Colonial Genocide in Indigenous North America*, 95–148.

30. Jesse Applegate, "Notes upon Oregon History," n.d., 17–18, folder: Jesse A. Applegate, box 5, Willamette University and Northwest Collection.

31. Benjamin Mountford, "The Pacific Gold Rushes and the Struggle for Order," in *A Global History of Gold Rushes*, ed. Benjamin Mountford and Stephen Tuffnell (Oakland: University of California Press, 2018), 88–108, esp. 90–91; cf. Anne F. Hyde, *Empires, Nations, and Families: A History of the North American West, 1800–1860* (Lincoln: University of Nebraska Press, 2011), 425; Rodman Wilson Paul and Elliott West, *Mining Frontiers of the Far West, 1848–1880*, rev. ed. (Albuquerque: University of New Mexico Press, 2001), 230–31.

32. Colonel William Thompson, *Reminiscences of a Pioneer* (San Francisco: Alturas Plain Dealer, 1912), 17.

33. Thompson, *Reminiscences of a Pioneer*, 40–41. By Thompson's own account, the only "suspicious" act the Native man committed was his seeming to be on guard around his White companions—perhaps because he feared, correctly, that they might try to murder him.

34. Richard Bruce Winders, *Mr. Polk's Army: The American Military Experience in the Mexican War* (College Station: Texas A&M University Press, 1997), 43, 47 ("mushroom generals," "anti-guerrilla activity"); Andreas Riffel, "Greasers, Gringos und Gräueltaten im mexikanisch-amerikanischen Krieg 1846–1848" ("Greasers, Gringos, and Atrocities in the U.S.–Mexican War, 1846–1848") (PhD diss. University of Heidelberg, 2016), 521–27, esp.

tive people; Gaines remains understudied. Frederick Waymire to James W. Nesmith, November 4, 1850, folder 32, box 2, James W. Nesmith Papers; Katherine Louise Huit, "Oregon Territorial Governor John Pollard Gaines: A Whig Appointee in a Democratic Territory" (master's thesis, Portland State University, 1996), 147–56, 185–87; R. Gregory Nokes, *Breaking Chains: Slavery on Trial in the Oregon Territory* (Corvallis: Oregon State University Press, 2013), 117; Matthew Deady to James W. Nesmith, April 29, 1855, folder 16, box 1, James W. Nesmith Papers (quotations).

25. Whaley, *Oregon and the Collapse of* Illahee; David G. Lewis, "Acknowledgement Is Long Past Due for Attempts to Exterminate the Tribes of Oregon," *Quartux Journal* (March 28, 2019), https://ndnhistoryresearch. com/2019/03/28/acknowledgement-is-long-past-due-for-attempts-to-exterminate-the-tribes-of-oregon/; George Bundy Wasson Jr., "Growing Up Indian: An Emic Perspective" (PhD diss., University of Oregon, 2001).

26. Charles S. Drew to Quartermaster General, December 30, 1854, in *Protection Afforded by Volunteers of Oregon and Washington Territories to Overland Immigrants in 1854: Papers Transmitted by the Secretary of the Oregon Territory* (Washington, D.C.: House of Representatives, 35th Cong., 2nd sess., Misc. Doc. no. 47, 1859), 25 (quotation). On war crimes against "savage nations" being deemed acceptable by European-descended people internationally, nationally, and locally, see [Emmerich de] Vattel, *The Law of Nations; or, Principles of the Law of Nature Applied to the Conduct and Affairs of Nations and Sovereigns* (1758; repr., Philadelphia: H. Nicklin & T. Johnson, 1829), 92, 414, 432; Ostler, *Surviving Genocide*, 100; Donald L. Cutler, *"Hang Them All": George Wright and the Plateau Indian War* (Norman: University of Oklahoma Press, 2016), 27–29; Karl Jacoby, " 'The Broad Platform of Extermination': Nature and Violence in the Nineteenth Century North American Borderlands," *Journal of Genocide Research* 10, no. 2 (Summer 2008): 249–67, https://doi.org/10.1080/14623520802075205; W. J. Martin, "The Expedition to Fight the Emigrants," *Umpqua Weekly Gazette*, August 9, 1855, 1.

27. Thomas H. Smith, "An Ohioan's Role in Oregon History," *Oregon Historical Quarterly* 66, no. 3 (September 1965): 218–32, esp. 220 ("Every man"), https://www.jstor.org/stable/20612872; George Riddle to R[obert] A[sbury] Booth, August 21, 192[7?] ("who had some grievance," "six bits"), folder 2, box 1, Robert Sawyer Papers, Ax 100, University of Oregon Special Collections. The men were described as "packers" in this account, which may have reflected reality or a broad norm of blaming illegal violence on men of low-class professions; as I discuss in chapter 8, even James Lupton was sometimes changed to "a packer" in critical accounts of his mass killing.

28. George H. Parker, "Short History of Josephine County," March 1922, 6, George R. Riddle Papers, Mss 1388, Oregon Historical Society Special Collections ("an inveterate hatred," "Hang him," "a half-breed"); "Indian War in Rogue River," *Oregon Statesman*, August 23, 1853, 2 ("Angell, from

his own door"); Bill Miller, "The Ambush of Martin Angel," *Medford Mail Tribune*, June 15, 2009 ("a kind husband").

29. Clinton Schieffelin to Jacob and Elizabeth [Berard] Schieffelin, November 27, 1853, folder 68, box 5, Schieffelin Family Papers, WA MSS S-1401, Yale Collection of Western Americana, Beinecke Rare Book and Manuscript Library.

30. Clinton Schieffelin to Jacob Schieffelin, October 23 and November 4, 1855, folder 70, box 5, Schieffelin Family Papers.

31. Laura Ishiguro, *Nothing to Write Home About: British Family Correspondence and the Settler Colonial Everyday in British Columbia* (Vancouver: University of British Columbia Press, 2019).

32. John Beeson to the editors of *True Californian*, ca. 1856, https://truwe.sohs.org/files/beeson.html ("mischief-making," "violence and outrage"); Beeson, *Plea for the Indians* 17, 25, 48–49 ("came to be," "shot whenever").

33. Welborn Beeson Diary, May 23, 1856, folder 5, box 1, Welborn Beeson Papers, Ax 799, University of Oregon Special Collections ("kill him [as] an Indian"); John Beeson, "To My Family and Friends in Rogue River Valley," *Oregon Argus*, June 21, 1856, https://truwe.sohs.org/files/beeson.html; John K. Lamerick to Joseph Lane, September 22, 1856, https://truwe.sohs.org/files/jolaneletters.html; Jan Wright, *Oregon Outcast: John Beeson's Struggle for Justice for the Indians, 1853–1889* (self-published, 2018).

34. James W. Nesmith to Jesse Applegate, January 18, 1859 ("the Inj_ns"), folder 1, box 3, James W. Nesmith Papers; Marc James Carpenter, " 'Justice and Fair Play for the American Indian': Harry Lane, Robert Hamilton, and a Vision of Native American Modernity," *Pacific Historical Review* 87, no. 2 (May 2018): 305–32, esp. 314–15 ("friend of the Indians"), https://doi.org/10.1525/phr.2018.87.2.305; cf. Nathan Douthit, *Uncertain Encounters: Indians and Whites at Peace and War in Southern Oregon, 1820s–1860s* (Corvallis: Oregon State University Press, 2002), esp. 69–77; Nathan Douthit, "Joseph Lane and the Rogue River Indians: Personal Relations across a Cultural Divide," *Oregon Historical Quarterly* 95, no. 4 (Winter 1994–95): 472–515, https://www.jstor.org/stable/20614625.

35. Hiram T. French, *History of Idaho: A Narrative Account of Its Historical Progress, Its People and Its Principal Interests*, 3 vols. (Chicago: Lewis, 1914), 2:770 ("Uncle Jimmy"); James Twogood to Dudley & Michener, November 10, 1897, 11 ("I made"), James Henry Twogood Papers, 1888–1910, Graff 4224, Newberry Library Special Collections; James Twogood, untitled reminiscence, 7 ("on the War path"), James Henry Twogood Papers.

36. Matthew P. Deady, "Southern Oregon Names and Events," in *Transactions of the Eleventh Annual Re-Union of the Oregon Pioneer Association for 1883* (Salem: E. M. Waite, 1884), 23–24; Whaley, *Oregon and the Collapse of Illahee*, 202–3.

37. " 'Reminiscences of the First Settlements of Southern Oregon Early Times in Idaho and a Few of Idaho's Pioneers' The Upbuilders of the Territory

with Brief Reminiscences of a Few Good Friends of Olden Times—First Gold Discoveries North of California—By 'Uncle Jimmy,' Twogood" [broadside], James Henry Twogood Papers.

38. James Twogood to Dudley & Michener, November 10, 1897, 10–11.

39. Mark Axel Tveskov, "A 'Most Disastrous' Affair: The Battle of Hungry Hill, Historical Memory, and the Rogue River War," *Oregon Historical Quarterly* 118, no. 1 (Spring 2017): 42–73, https://doi.org/10.5403/oregonhistq.118.1.0042. On the more general tendency for American incompetence and Native success to obscure the frequency of Euro-American genocidal intent, see Ostler, *Surviving Genocide*, 121–22; Benjamin Madley, "California and Oregon's Modoc Indians: How Indigenous Resistance Camouflages Genocide in Colonial Histories," in Woolford, Benvenuto, and Hinton, *Colonial Genocide in Indigenous North America*, 95–148.

40. James H. Twogood to Joseph Lane, June 20, 1856, https://truwe.sohs.org/files/jolaneletters.html; emphasis in original (the slur represented by "Inj_n" is spelled different ways in different places throughout).

41. John Hamblock to T. A. Wood, May 1, 1896, folder 35, box 4, Oregon Military Collection MSS; Grace Thill, "Tablet in Coast Cemetery Relates Pioneer Family's Role in Settlement," *Oregonian*, January 18, 1967, 16.

42. Hamblock to Wood, May 1, 1896. John Hamblock's focus on the Long family came in part because he married into it following wartime events.

43. Hamblock to Wood, May 1, 1896; Edward Otho Cresap Ord, "Diary of E. O. C. Ord 3rd Art U.S. Army," in Ellen Francis Ord, "The Rogue River Indian Expedition of 1856" (master's thesis, University of California, 1922), 27, 32.

44. Ord, "Diary of E. O. C. Ord," 27.

45. Charles D. Sexton, "Notes from the Life of Caroline Sexton Oregon Pioneer," ca. 1926, George R. Riddle Papers; Charles D. Sexton, "Judge Walton to the Rescue: Notes on the Life of Caroline Sexton, Oregon Pioneer," *Lane County Historian* 24, no. 2 (Fall 1979): 55–57. For the possibility of anxiety as overemphasized in settler memory, see Ishiguro, *Nothing to Write Home About*, 97. On shared devotion to genocide regardless of gender among Euro-American pioneers, see Mark Axel Tveskov, Chelsea Rose, Geoffrey Jones, and David Maki, "Every Rusty Nail Is Sacred, Every Rusty Nail Is Good: Conflict Archaeology, Remote Sensing, and Community Engagement at a Northwest Coast Settler Fort," *American Antiquity* 84, no. 1 (February 2019): 48–67, esp. 54, https://doi.org/10.1017/aaq.2018.80.

46. S. R. Templeton to T. A. Wood, May 26, 1896, folder 44, box 1, Oregon Military Collection MSS.

47. George Law Curry to Judge William D. Kell[e]y, December 2, 1855, quoted in George L. Curry [Jr.] to Eva Emery Dye, January 1, 1927, folder 8, box 1, Eva Emery Dye Papers, Mss 1089, Oregon Historical Society Special Collections.

48. Mary Ellen Rowe, *Bulwark of the Republic: The American Militia in the Antebellum West* (Westport, Conn.: Praeger, 2003), 140–41. Rowe suggests both

broad support for the volunteers (citing contemporary newspapers) and distaste for them in northern Oregon (citing a work of historical fiction written in the 1910s). The former was assuredly the case, the latter more doubtful—though some may have both supported the volunteers *and* found them distasteful.

49. David G. Lewis, "Four Deaths: The Near Destruction of Western Oregon Tribes and Native Lifeways, Removal to the Reservation, and Erasure from History," *Oregon Historical Quarterly* 115, no. 3 (Fall 2014): 414–37, https://doi.org/10.5403/oregonhistq.115.3.0414; Kari Marie Norgaard, *Salmon and Acorns Feed Our People: Colonialism, Nature, and Social Action* (New Brunswick, N.J.: Rutgers University Press, 2019), 57; Benjamin Madley, *An American Genocide: The United States and the California Indian Catastrophe* (New Haven: Yale University Press, 2016); Daniel Marshall, *Claiming the Land: British Columbia and the Making of a New El Dorado* (Vancouver, B.C.: Ronsdale Press, 2018), chap. 5; Rodman Wilson Paul and Elliott West, *Mining Frontiers of the Far West, 1848–1880*, rev. ed. (Albuquerque: University of New Mexico Press, 2001), 202–6.

50. E. D. Townsend to Lieut. W. M. Dye, 4th Infantry, Benicia, Calif., February 14, 1854 ("that there is"), War Department Records of the Pacific; Bion Freeman Kendall to James W. Nesmith, November 12, 1861 ("strong doubts"), folder 10, box 2, James W. Nesmith Papers.

51. Louis Wapato (Colville), interview by Jeff Wilner (part 1), May 15, 1973, folder 9, box 1, NW Tribal Oral History Interviews, WWU Center for Pacific Northwest Studies; Frank Teck, "Indians and Indian Wars," 8 ("stampede"), folder 2, box 1, Frank Teck Papers, WWU Center for Pacific Northwest Studies; Marshall, *Claiming the Land*; Arielle Rose Gorin, "The Battle for the Pacific Northwest Borderlands after the Oregon Treaty" (PhD diss., Yale University, 2018), chap. 2; Jeremy Mouat, "After California: Later Gold Rushes of the Pacific Basin," in *Riches for All: The California Gold Rush and the World*, ed. Kenneth N. Owens (Lincoln: University of Nebraska Press, 2002), 264–95; Christopher Herbert, *Gold Rush Manliness: Race and Gender on the Pacific Slope* (Seattle: University of Washington Press, 2018), 85–93; James Robbins Jewell, *Agents of Empire: The First Oregon Cavalry and the Opening of the Interior Pacific Northwest during the Civil War* (Lincoln: University of Nebraska, 2023), 76; James A. Hardie to James W. Nesmith, January 9, 1861 ("this portion"), folder 7, box 2, James W. Nesmith Papers.

52. Affidavit of Andrew J. Miner, June 23, 1903, folder 25, box 29, Oregon Soldiers Home Applications.

53. Deposition of Lucian B. Lindsey, July 6, 1903, folder 25, box 29, Oregon Soldiers Home Applications.

54. Charles Baum, interview by Shirley Tanzer, August 22, 1977, Oregon Jewish Oral History and Archive Collection, Oregon Jewish Museum and Center for Holocaust Education, Portland; Ellen Eisenberg, "Negotiating

Jewish Identities in Oregon: From White Pioneer to Ethnic Minority," in *Jewish Identities in the American West: Relational Perspectives*, ed. Ellen Eisenberg (Waltham, Mass.: Brandeis University Press, 2022), 56–96; "Administrators Appointed," *Eugene Guard*, May 28, 1898. Cf. David T. Courtwright, *Violent Land: Single Men and Social Disorder from the Frontier to the Inner City* (Cambridge: Harvard University Press, 1996), 37–41.

55. "Ainsworth Statement," 5–7 (quotations), folder: Captain John Commingers Ainsworth, box 5, Willamette University and Northwest Collection; Rowe, *Bulwark of the Republic*, 178.

56. Rowe, *Bulwark of the Republic*, 171; Abigail Malick to Mary and Michael Albright, April 16, 1856, folder 28, box 1, Malick Family Papers; Philip Henry Sheridan, *Personal Memoirs of P. H. Sheridan, General, United States Army*, 2 vols. (New York: C. L. Webster, 1888), 1:81–84; Cutler, *"Hang Them All,"* 101–2; David G. Lewis, "A Startling History of the Cascades Indians, 1855–1862," *Quartux Journal* (July 24, 2016), https://ndnhistoryresearch.com/2016/07/24/forever-terminated-the-cascades/.

57. Robert Hull, quoted in Ronald Spores, "Too Small a Place: The Removal of the Willamette Valley Indians, 1850–1856," *American Indian Quarterly* 17, no. 2 (Spring 1993): 179, https://doi.org/10.2307/1185526.

Chapter Three. Dreams of Genocide and Roads to War in Washington Territory

1. Mrs. Emma Jane Cavanaugh Fulford, "Uncle Henry Van Asselt," ca. 1935, 296–97, vol 5, folder 5, box 1, DAR Family Rec. of Wash. Pioneers, cage 472, Washington State University Special Collections. There were other versions of the story, all involving Van Asselt's gunshot wound purportedly striking fear into the hearts of Native people. Rev. H[arvey] K[imball] Hines, *An Illustrated History of the State of Washington* (Chicago: Lewis, 1893), 522–23; Emily Inez Denny, *Blazing the Way; or, True Stories, Songs and Sketches of Puget Sound and Other Pioneers* (Seattle: Rainier, 1909), 322–23.

2. Cf. Alexandra Harmon, *Indians in the Making: Ethnic Relations and Indian Identities around Puget Sound* (Berkeley: University of California Press, 1998), 87. Frederic James Grant, *History of Seattle, Washington* (New York: American Publishing and Engraving, 1891), 48; E. B. Mapel, "A Short Autobiography of E. B. Maple ... One of the First Settlers of Seattle or Puget Sound Country," unidentified clipping dated November 16, 1902 (quotations), Clarence B. Bagley Scrapbooks, 1:38–39, microfilm reel no. A2254, University of Washington Special Collections; Elwood Evans et al., *History of the Pacific Northwest: Oregon and Washington*, 2 vols. (Portland: North Pacific History, 1889), 1:595; Virgil F. Field, *The Official History of the Washington National Guard*, vol. 2, *Washington Territorial Militia and the Indian Wars of 1855–56* (Tacoma: Washington National Guard State Historical Society, 1961), 91, 84.

3. Lissa K. Wadewitz, "Rethinking the 'Indian War': Northern Indians and Intra-Native Politics in the Western Canada–U.S. Borderlands," *Western Historical Quarterly* 50, no. 4 (Winter 2019): 339–61, https://doi.org/10.1093/
   whq/whz096; Henri M. Chase to James Tilton, July 31, 1856, in Field, *Official History of the Washington National Guard*, 2:57.

4. Coll Thrush, *Native Seattle: Histories from the Crossing-Over Place*, 2nd ed.
   (Seattle: University of Washington Press, 2017), 42; BJ Cummings, *The
   River That Made Seattle: A Human and Natural History of the Duwamish* (Se-
   attle: University of Washington Press, 2020), 29–30; Vera Parham, " 'These
   Indians Are Apparently Well to Do': The Myth of Capitalism and Native
   American Labor," *International Review of Social History* 57, no. 3 (December
   2012): 446–70, esp. 452, https://doi.org/10.1017/S002085901200051X. On
   omissions, see, for example, Megan Asaka, *Seattle from the Margins: Exclusion, Erasure, and the Making of a Pacific Coast City* (Seattle: University of
   Washington Press, 2022), 20–27.

5. Cf. Jo N. Miles, *Kamiakin Country: Washington Territory in Turmoil, 1855–
   1858* (Caldwell, Idaho: Caxton Press, 2016).

6. Arthur A. Denny, "Pioneer Days on Puget Sound," 1888, 15, folder 7, box 1,
   Eloise Thomas Papers, Mss 1717, Oregon Historical Society Special Collections; Michael J. Pfeifer, *The Roots of Rough Justice: Origins of American
   Lynching* (Urbana: University of Illinois Press, 2011), 49–50; David Peterson del Mar, *Beaten Down: A History of Interpersonal Violence in the West* (Se-
   attle: University of Washington Press, 2002), 28–29; John Robert Finger,
   "Henry L. Yesler's Seattle Years, 1852–1892" (PhD diss., University of
   Washington, 1968), 29 ("when an Indian"); Harmon, *Indians in the Making*,
   chap. 2. Of course, marriages between Native people and White settlers
   were a part of Oregon history, too. See, for example, Melinda Marie Jetté,
   *At the Hearth of the Crossed Races: A French-Indian Community in Nineteenth-
   Century Oregon, 1812–1859* (Corvallis: Oregon State University Press,
   2015).

7. Jonathan McCarty, "Hard Times in the Early Fifties," *Tacoma Ledger*, June
   12, 1892 (quotations), in vol. 4, folder 4, box 1, DAR Family Rec. of Wash.
   Pioneers; Mary Ellen Snodgrass, *Settlers of the American West: The Lives of
   231 Notable Pioneers* (Jefferson, N.C.: McFarland, 2015), 110. Jonathan Mc-
   Carty does not seem to be on the official rolls of any Washington volunteer
   company. The records may have been lost, or he may well have "volunteered" in a less official capacity. Field, *Official History of the Washington National Guard*, 2:83. There are other McCartys on the rolls, so the issue may
   be one of transcription.

8. Percival R. Jeffcott, untitled work on the Gischer family, 81–82 ("many
   tales"), 46, folder 26, box 3, Percival R. Jeffcott Papers, WWU Center for
   Pacific Northwest Studies.

9. Roxa S. Shackleford to Eva Emery Dye, September 23, 1906 ("cedar bark,"
   "we children"), enclosed in [Edwin?] Bingham to Eva Emery Dye, October

9, 1906, folder 13, box 2, Eva Emery Dye Papers; *Puget Sound Courier*, April 25, 1856, 3 ("*all* the Indians"; emphasis in original); Lisa Blee, *Framing Chief Leschi: Narrative and the Politics of Historical Justice* (Chapel Hill: University of North Carolina Press, 2014), 96; SuAnn M. Reddick and Cary C. Collins, "Medicine Creek to Fox Island: Cadastral Scams and Contested Domains," *Oregon Historical Quarterly* 106, no. 3 (Fall 2005): 385–86, 391, https://doi.org/10.1353/ohq.2005.0087; Martin Case, *The Relentless Business of Treaties: How Indigenous Land Became U.S. Property* (St. Paul: Minnesota Historical Society Press, 2018), 85–86.

10. Corey L. Larson, "Negotiating Fort Nisqually: Reconfiguring the Social and Environmental Landscapes of the South Salish Sea, 1833–1858" (PhD diss., Simon Fraser University, 2020), 185–86; Evans et al., *History of the Pacific Northwest*, 1:469–71.

11. Denny, "Pioneer Days on Puget Sound," 18. Denny skipped over the wars themselves almost entirely.

12. Jonathan McCarty, "Hard Times in the Early Fifties" (quotations; underscore in original); Mary Ellen Rowe, *Bulwark of the Republic: The American Militia in the Antebellum West* (Westport, Conn.: Praeger, 2003), 167; *Puget Sound Courier*, November 16, 1855, 2; W. A. Katz, "Public Printers of Washington Territory, 1853–1863," *Pacific Northwest Quarterly* 51, no. 3 (July 1960): 103–14, https://www.jstor.org/stable/40487491.

13. Abigail Malick to Mary [Malick] and Michael Albright, January 31, 1850, folder 1, box 1, Malick Family Papers; Rachel Malick to Mary and Michael Albright, May 14, 1852, folder 7, box 1, Malick Family Papers. Spelling, grammar, and punctuation have been edited for clarity in all quotations from Abigail Malick.

14. "Death of Justice J. D. Biles," *Oregonian*, September 14, 1890, 4. Lillian Schlissel's work on the Malicks ignores genocide and geography and uncritically reproduces their racism. Lillian Schlissel, Byrd Gibbens, and Elizabeth Hampsten, *Far from Home: Families of the Western Journey* (Lincoln: University of Nebraska Press, 2002), 13, 11, 24, 31; Lillian Schlissel, " 'They Have No Father and They Will Not Mind Me': Families and the River," in *Great River of the West: Essays on the Columbia River*, ed. William L. Lang and Robert C. Carriker (Seattle: University of Washington Press, 1999), 112–25, esp. 116, 123.

15. John D. Biles to Michael Albright, May 23, 1852, folder 7, box 1, Malick Family Papers.

16. Abigail Malick to Mary and Michael Albright, September 28, 1853; Abigail Malick to Mary and Michael Albright, [April?] 13, 1854, folder 18, box 1, Malick Family Papers.

17. Abigail Malick to Mary and Michael Albright, June 10, 1855, folder 24, box 1, Malick Family Papers. Although Euro-American parlance predominately used the slur *Snake* as a descriptor for Northern Paiute/Numu, Bannock/Nimi, and Shoshone/Newe peoples by the end of the 1850s, Malick here

used it to describe plateau peoples like the Yakama, Palus, and presumably others. Slurs are flexible.

18. Abigail Malick to Mary and Michael Albright, June 10, 1855; Abigail Malick to Mary and Michael Albright, August 12, 1855, folder 25, box 1, Malick Family Papers.

19. John D. Biles to Mary and Michael Albright, November 9, 1855 (quotations), folder 26, box 1, Malick Family Papers; Field, *Official History of the Washington National Guard*, 2:83.

20. John D. Biles to Mary and Michael Albright, May 30, 1856, folder 29, box 1, Malick Family Papers; emphasis in original.

21. Abigail Malick to Michael and Mary Albright, December 8, 1855, folder 26, box 1, Malick Family Papers.

22. Thomas N. Strong, "How Whites Supplanted the Indians at Cathlamet," ca. December 1902, folder 14, box 2, Lulu Donnell Crandall Papers, cage 249, Washington State University Libraries Special Collections, Pullman. Cf. Thomas Nelson Strong, *Cathlamet on the Columbia: Recollections of the Indian People and Short Stories of Early Pioneer Days in the Valley of the Lower Columbia River* (Portland, Ore.: Binfords and Mort, 1906), 144–45.

23. Livestock protection was often the stated reason for dog killings—but cruelty to animals was an amusement favored by many American men in the 1800s. Grant, *History of Seattle, Washington*, 48; William F. Tolmie, "To the Citizens of Washington Territory Dated February 10, 1858," *Oregonian*, August 26, 1900; Ralph Fisk, "Ralph Fisk Relates Some Pioneer History: Came to Canyon with Father in 1864," *Blue Mountain Eagle*, March 17, 1922; Richard Stott, *Jolly Fellows: Male Milieus in Nineteenth-Century America* (Baltimore: Johns Hopkins University Press, 2009), 22–24.

24. Strong, *Cathlamet on the Columbia*, 122; Harry M. Strong, "Adventures of a Pioneer Judge and His Family," *Columbia* 16, no. 4 (2002–3): 18–23.

25. Strong, *Cathlamet on the Columbia*, 124.

26. Strong, *Cathlamet on the Columbia*, 124 (quotation); Terence O'Donnell, *An Arrow in the Earth: General Joel Palmer and the Indians of Oregon* (Portland: Oregon Historical Society Press, 1991), 154–55.

27. Strong, *Cathlamet on the Columbia*, 125–26.

28. Peterson del Mar, *Beaten Down*, 54–57; Gail Bederman, *Manliness and Civilization: A Cultural History of Gender and Race in the United States, 1880–1917* (Chicago: University of Chicago Press, 1996).

29. Abigail Malick to Mary and Michael Albright, March 18, 1856, folder 27, box 1, Malick Family Papers.

30. Thomas J. Cram, *Topographical Memoir and Report of Captain T. J. Cram, on Territories of Oregon and Washington*, H.R. Exec. Doc. no. 114, 35th Cong., 2nd sess. (1859), 98; A[ndrew] J[ackson] Splawn, *Ka-mi-akin: Last Hero of the Yakimas*, ed. Margaret C. Splawn (1917; repr., Portland: Binfords & Mort/Oregon Historical Society, 1944), 287; Susan Sleeper-Smith, *Indigenous Prosperity and American Conquest: Indian Women of the Ohio River Valley*,

1690–1792 (Williamsburg, Va.: Omohundro Institute of Early American History and Culture, 2018), 210–22; Michael John Witgen, *Seeing Red: Indigenous Land, American Expansion, and the Political Economy of Plunder in North America* (Williamsburg, Va.: Omohundro Institute of Early American History and Culture, 2022), 20, 339–43; Alexandra Harmon, *Rich Indians: Native People and the Problem of Wealth in American History* (Chapel Hill: University of North Carolina Press, 2010), esp. 4–5.

31. Abigail Malick to Mary and Michael Albright, April 16, 1856, folder 28, box 1, Malick Family Papers. These killings were separate from the official retaking of the Cascades at Columbia; see Philip Henry Sheridan, *Personal Memoirs of P. H. Sheridan, General, United States Army*, 2 vols. (New York: C. L. Webster, 1888), 1:72–84. Rachel Malick Biles died in 1855.

32. Abigail Malick to Mary and Michael Albright, April 27, 1856 ("no soldier," "very resolute"), folder 28, box 1, Malick Family Papers; Abigail Malick to Mary Albright, October 31, 1860 ("Jane's husband"), folder 38, box 1, Malick Family Papers; Abigail Malick to Mary and Michael Albright, December 17, 1860 ("would be"), folder 38, box 1, Malick Family Papers.

33. Abigail Malick to Mary and Michael Albright, September 1, 1861, folder 39, box 1, Malick Family Papers.

34. "Rapport de R. P. Pandosy," August 30, 1854, folder 14, box 160, Oblates of Mary Immaculate Collection, Record Group 840, Catholic Archdiocese of Seattle Archives (hereafter cited as OMI Collection); Clifford E. Trafzer, *Death Stalks the Yakama: Epidemiological Transitions and Mortality on the Yakama Indian Reservation, 1888–1964* (East Lansing: Michigan State University Press, 1997), 29; Alex Saluskin, "A Historical Account of the Yakima War," ed. Catherine Arquette, comp. Inez R. Strong (1967; repr., Toppenish, Wash.: Yakima Tribal School, 1989), 4; Emily Washines, "War Cry: Will Crossing Historical Boundaries in Indian Wars Help Yakama Women?," in *Enduring Legacies: Native Case Studies Initiative* (Olympia: Evergreen State College, 2020), esp. 6–9, https://nativecases.evergreen.edu/collection/a-z. Ichishkíin name spellings, here and throughout, are adapted from Virginia Beavert and Sharon Hargus, *Ichishkíin Sínwit: Yakama/Yakima Sahaptin Dictionary* (Toppenish, Wash.: Heritage University, 2009); any errors or omissions are mine.

35. Lucullus Virgil McWhorter and Su-el-lil, *Tragedy of the Wahk-Shum: The Death of Andrew J. Bolon, Yakima Indian Agent, as Told by Su-el-lil, Eyewitness*, ed. Donald M. Hines (1937; repr., Issaquah, Wash.: Great Eagle, 1994), 5–32, esp. 26 ("the man who hanged"); Jo N. Miles, "The Life and Death of A. J. Bolon, 1826–1855," *Pacific Northwest Quarterly* 97, no. 1 (Winter 2005–6): 31–37, https://doi.org/10.2307/40491896; Virginia R. Beavert, *The Gift of Knowledge/Ttnúwit Átawish Nch'inch'imamí: Reflections on Sahaptin Ways*, ed. Janne L. Underriner (Seattle: University of Washington Press, 2017), 136 ("Mishíil was").

36. For historians reflexively blaming Native actions for wars, see among many others Francis Paul Prucha, *The Great Father: The United States Government*

and the American Indian, 2 vols. (Lincoln: University of Nebraska Press, 1984), 1:407.

37. Granville O. Haller, "[Auto]Biographical Memoir of Brevet Major Granville Owen Haller, U.S. Army," 4–5, folder 1, box 1, Granville O. Haller Papers, Acc. 3431-001, University of Washington Special Collections; Granville O. Haller, "A Brief Memoranda of the Services and Life of Colonel Granville O. Haller, U.S. Army, Retired," 9–11, folder 1, box 1, Granville O. Haller Papers; Hauptman, "General John E. Wool in Cherokee Country."

38. Gregory R. Campbell, "The Lemhi Shoshoni: Ethnogenesis, Sociological Transformations, and the Construction of a Tribal Nation," *American Indian Quarterly* 25, no. 4 (Autumn 2001): 539–78, esp. 544, https://www.jstor.org/stable/1186016; Herbert O. Lang, *History of the Willamette Valley: Being a Description of the Valley and Its Resources, with an Account of Its Discovery and Settlement by White Men, and Its Subsequent History* (Portland, Ore.: Himes and Lang, 1885), 363; John D. Unruh Jr., *The Plains Across: The Overland Emigrants and the Trans-Mississippi West, 1840–60* (1979; repr., Urbana: University of Illinois Press, 1993), 189–90; Priscilla Knuth, " 'Picturesque' Frontier: The Army's Fort Dalles," *Oregon Historical Quarterly* 67, no. 4 (December 1966): 293–345, esp. 311–12, https://www.jstor.org/stable/20612941; David L. Bigler, *Fort Limhi: The Mormon Adventure in Oregon Territory, 1855–1858* (Norman: University of Oklahoma Press, 2003), 82–83.

39. Granville O. Haller, *The Dismissal of Major Granville O. Haller of the Regular Army . . . and a Few Observations* (Paterson, N.J.: Daily Guardian, 1863), 35.

40. Knuth, " 'Picturesque' Frontier," 312 ("final punishment"); Haller, *Dismissal of Major Granville O. Haller,* 35–36, 42 ("murderers," "hung and killed"). Miles, *Kamiakin Country;* cf. Unruh, *Plains Across,* 215–16.

41. Haller, *Dismissal of Major Granville O. Haller,* 38.

42. Haller, *Dismissal of Major Granville O. Haller,* 38 ("perhaps six hundred"); Granville O. Haller, "Biography," n.d., 4, folder 5, box 2, Granville O. Haller Papers ("2200 fighting men").

43. Roxa Cock Shack[le]ford, "Major Haller in 1855," enclosed in Charlotte Haller McKee to Lulu Crandall, January 22, 1909 ("Donald McKay was"), folder 9, box 2, Lulu Donnell Crandall Papers; "Big Chief's Will: Moses Gets a Yakima Attorney to Write the Legal Document," *Spokane Spokesman-Review,* October 5, 1895, 8 ("dr[i]ve them"); Lisa Philips, "Written Out of the Script: Three Generations of McKays," in *Before and After the State: Politics, Poetics, and People(s) of the Pacific Northwest* (Vancouver: University of British Columbia Press, 2018), 179–206; Anne F. Hyde, *Born of Lakes and Plains: Mixed-Descent Peoples and the Making of the American West* (New York: Norton, 2022), esp. chap. 5, epilogue; Juana Fraser Lyon, "Archie McIntosh, the Scottish Indian Scout," *Journal of Arizona History* 7, no. 3 (Autumn 1966): 103–22, esp. 107–8, https://www.jstor.org/stable/41695368; Ryan Wayne Booth, "Crossed Arrows: The US Indian Scouts, 1866–1947" (PhD diss., Washington State University, 2021), 19.

44. Kamiakin/K'amáyakin et al. to "the soldiers and the Americans," enclosed in P. Ricard to "Grand Vicaire," October 19, 1855, folder 7, box 24, OMI Collection. Translated by Alissa J. Hartig and Marc James Carpenter. Any errors are mine alone.

45. Kamiakin/K'amáyakin et al. to "the soldiers and the Americans."

46. Kamiakin/K'amáyakin et al. to "the soldiers and the Americans." The letter uses the personal *tu* rather than the formal *vous* form when referring to Gov. Stevens, here and elsewhere.

47. Kamiakin/K'amáyakin et al. to "the soldiers and the Americans."

48. Kamiakin/K'amáyakin et al. to "the soldiers and the Americans."

49. W. Davis Waters, " 'Deception Is the Art of War': Gabriel J. Rains, Torpedo Specialist of the Confederacy," *North Carolina Historical Review* 66, no. 1 (January 1989): 29–60, esp. 32–34, https://www.jstor.org/stable/23520746. Rains objected to unprovoked volunteer attempts at genocide during the 1859–60 "Mendocino War"; see Jason E. Pierce, *Making the White Man's West: Whiteness and the Creation of the American West* (Boulder: University Press of Colorado, 2016), 231.

50. G[abriel] J. Rains "to Kam-i-ah-kan," November 13, 1855, Miscellaneous Letters Received August 22, 1853–April 9, 1874, Records of the Washington Superintendency of Indian Affairs, 1853–1874, Records of the Bureau of Indian Affairs, RG 75, National Archives and Records Administration, accessed via microfilm (M5, roll 23). See also Edward J. Kowrach, *Mie. Charles Pandosy O.M.I.: A Missionary of the Northwest* (Fairfield, Wash.: Galleon Press, 1992), 104.

51. Rains "to Kam-i-ah-kan," November 13, 1855.

52. Charles Pandosy to Bishop Mazenod, June 5, 1854, in Kowrach, *Mie. Charles Pandosy O.M.I.*, 78.

53. For periodization as a decolonization tool, see Brenda Child, "Rethinking Environmental Crisis and Global Colonialism—Caribou Time and Indigenous Environmental History" (paper presented at the Native American and Indigenous Studies Association annual conference, June 7, 2024, Bodø, Norway).

54. Frederick E. Hoxie, "Denouncing America's Destiny: Sarah Winnemucca's Assault on US Expansion," *Cultural and Social History* 9, no. 4 (December 2012): 549–67, esp. 551 (quotations), https://doi.org/10.2752/1478004 12X13434063754526; Amy S. Greenberg, *A Wicked War: Polk, Clay, Lincoln, and the 1846 Invasion of Mexico* (New York: Knopf, 2012).

Chapter Four. Extermination, Incarceration, and the War on Illahee at Its Zenith

1. SuAnn M. Reddick and Cary C. Collins, "Medicine Creek Remediated: Isaac Stevens and the Puyallup, Nisqually, and Muckleshoot Land Settlement at Fox Island, August 4, 1856," *Pacific Northwest Quarterly* 104, no. 2 (Spring 2013): 86–87, https://www.jstor.org/stable/24631631.

2. John Nugen to Acting Governor Mason, October 23, 1855, transcribed in Virgil F. Field, *The Official History of the Washington National Guard*, vol. 2, *Washington Territorial Militia and the Indian Wars of 1855–56* (Tacoma: Washington National Guard State Historical Society, 1962), 7. Other army personnel remembered something similar—see Lisa Blee, *Framing Chief Leschi: Narrative and the Politics of Historical Justice* (Chapel Hill: University of North Carolina Press, 2014), 58.

3. Mary Ellen Rowe, *Bulwark of the Republic: The American Militia in the Antebellum West* (Westport, Conn.: Praeger, 2003), 151–52; Shannon Bentley, "Indians' Right to Fish: The Background, Impact, and Legacy of *United States v. Washington*," *American Indian Law Review* 17, no. 1 (1992): 1–36, esp. 35, https://www.jstor.org/stable/20068716.

4. Urban E. Hicks, *Yakima and Clickitat Indian Wars, 1855 and 1856* (Portland, Ore.: Himes, 1886), 5–6; Blee, *Framing Chief Leschi*, 58–59, 162–63; James Longmire, "Narrative of James Longmire, a Pioneer of 1853 (Concluded)," *Washington Historical Quarterly* 23, no. 2 (April 1932): 138–50, esp. 144, https://www.jstor.org/stable/23908658.

5. Blee, *Framing Chief Leschi*, esp. chap. 4. I largely avoid two of the standard sources often used to narrate the Puget Sound War: Richard Kluger, *The Bitter Waters of Medicine Creek: A Tragic Clash between White and Native America* (New York: Knopf, 2011), and J. A. Eckrom, *Remembered Drums: A History of the Puget Sound Indian War* (Walla Walla: Pioneer Press, 1989). Neither book uses thorough notes, and it is thus difficult to tell when either is unknowingly leaning on untrustworthy sources or (in Kluger's case) engaging in unmarked "speculative nonfiction."

6. George B. Wasson, "The Coquelle Indians and the Cultural 'Black Hole' of the Southern Oregon Coast," in *Worldviews and the American West: The Life of the Place Itself*, ed. Polly Stewart, Steve Siporin, C. W. Sullivan III, and Suzi Jones (Logan: Utah State University Press, 2000), 191.

7. Lorraine McConaghy, "The Old Navy in the Pacific West: Naval Discipline in Seattle, 1855–1856," *Pacific Northwest Quarterly* 98, no. 1 (Winter 2006–7): 18–28, https://www.jstor.org/stable/40491995; Cecilia Svinth Carpenter, *Tears of Internment: The Indian History of Fox Island and the Puget Sound War* (Tacoma: Tahoma Research Services, 1996).

8. Isaac I. Stevens to George W. Mannypenny [*sic*], May 31, 1856, No. 72 in United States Bureau of Indian Affairs, *Annual Report of the Commissioner of Indian Affairs to the Secretary of the Interior* (Washington, D.C.: U.S. Government Printing Office, 1856), 735–41, esp. 736 ("submissive," "5,350"); Reddick and Collins, "Medicine Creek Remediated," esp. 87; BJ Cummings, *The River That Made Seattle: A Human and Natural History of the Duwamish* (Seattle: University of Washington Press, 2020), 46–47; Thomas W. Prosch, "Seattle and the Indians of Puget Sound," *Washington Historical Quarterly* 2, no. 4 (July 1908): 303–8, https://www.jstor.org/stable/40473935.

9. Andrew H. Fisher, *Shadow Tribe: The Making of Columbia River Indian Identity* (Seattle: University of Washington Press, 2010), 57; Judith W. Irwin, "The Dispossessed: The Cowlitz Indians in Cowlitz Corridor," *Columbia* 8, no. 2 (1994): 10–15; David G. Lewis and Thomas J. Connolly, "White American Violence on Tribal Peoples on the Oregon Coast," *Oregon Historical Quarterly* 120, no. 4 (Winter 2019): 368–81, https://doi.org/10.1353/ohq.2019.0028; Wasson, "The Coquelle Indians and the Cultural 'Black Hole' of the Southern Oregon Coast"; "Mrs Lottie Bagley" (interview in Memorandum), folder 3, box 86, Edmond S. Meany Papers, 1883–1935, Acc. 106-001, University of Washington Special Collections; Carpenter, *Tears of Internment*, 45, 75; Candace Wellman, *Man of Treacherous Charm: Territorial Justice Edmund C. Fitzhugh* (Pullman: Washington State University Press, 2023), 85. Cf. Alexandra Harmon, *Indians in the Making: Ethnic Relations and Indian Identities around Puget Sound* (Berkeley: University of California Press, 1998), 87 ("camps for non-combatants"); Terence O'Donnell, *An Arrow in the Earth: General Joel Palmer and the Indians of Oregon* (Portland: Oregon Historical Society Press, 1991), 221 ("sanctuaries").

10. Rowe, *Bulwark of the Republic*, 153. It is common to connect Hewitt's patrols to killings at White River because they occurred on the same day: October 28, 1855. But Hewitt's men went on their first patrol before the news reached Seattle. See Charles H. Mason (composed by John Nugen) to G[abriel] J. Rains, October 30, 1855, in Field, *Official History of the Washington National Guard*, 2:8.

11. Samuel Stewart to T. A. Wood, December 30, 1896, folder 44, box 4, Oregon Military Collection MSS.

12. Thomas Stowell Phelps, *Reminiscences of Seattle, Washington Territory, and the U.S. Sloop-of-War "Decatur" during the Indian War of 1855–1856*, ed. Alice Harriman (1902; repr., New York: Alice Harriman, 1908), 43.

13. Field, *Official History of the Washington National Guard*, 2:91. Cf. Harmon, *Indians in the Making*, 87.

14. Joel Palmer, "Regulations for the Guidance of Agents in the Oregon Indian Superintendency Pending Existing Hostilities," October 13, 1855, WA MSS 370, Letters 1855 – 1856 Collection, Beinecke Rare Book and Manuscript Library, https://collections.library.yale.edu/catalog/2054831.

15. In general, Oregon law in the 1800s attempted to reserve firearms for White use. William Lair Hill, comp., *The Codes and General Laws of Oregon*, 2 vols., 2nd ed. (San Francisco: Bancroft-Whitney, 1892), 2:chap. 27, §3171.

16. Palmer, "Regulations"; cf. O'Donnell, *Arrow in the Earth*, 221.

17. Alphons[o] D. Boone [Jr.] to Eva Emery Dye, April 25, 1904, folder 6, box 1, Eva Emery Dye Papers; Ezra Meeker, *Pioneer Reminiscences of Puget Sound: The Tragedy of Leschi* (Seattle: Lowman & Hanford, 1905), 171–72; George Himes Certificate of Participation in the Indian Wars, folder OSC2-2, Indian War Veterans of the North Pacific Coast Records, Mss 364, Oregon Historical Society Special Collections (hereafter cited as

IWV-NPC Records); J[ohn] W[atermelon] Redington to Eva Emery Dye, July 31, 1928 ("Mr. Himes"), folder 12, box 2, Eva Emery Dye Papers; "Records of the Annual Encampments: 1885–1933," 35, 68 ("monkey[ing] with guns"), folder 3, box 1, IWV-NPC Records.

18. William Barnhart, "History of the Yakima Indian War," ca. 1856 ("Palmher"), folder 2, box 1, Thomas J. Hobbs Papers, Mss 977, Oregon Historical Society Special Collections; William Barnhart to James Nesmith, May 9, 1856, folder 6, box 1, James W. Nesmith Papers; Joel Palmer to General John E. Wool, January 27, 1856 (Palmer quotations), in *Message from the President of the United States to the Two Houses of Congress at the Commencement of the Third Section of the Thirty-Fourth Congress* (Washington, D.C.: A. O. P. Nicholson, 1856), 744–45. See also O'Donnell, *Arrow in the Earth*, chap. 12.

19. Rowe, *Bulwark of the Republic*, 146–47, 173.

20. Rowe, *Bulwark of the Republic*, 166. In 1925 (when genocidal violence was less in fashion) editors of the *Washington Historical Quarterly* inserted a long footnote justifying the Peo-Peo-Mox-Mox killings as righteous, and the dismemberment as "sad," into an account of the Yakima War that never mentioned it. Notably, the wantonness involved in the killings the article discussed (and the others it didn't) was, by contrast, entirely omitted. Waman C. Hembree, "Yakima Indian War Diary," *Washington Historical Quarterly* 16, no. 4 (October 1925): 273–83, esp. 279, https://www.jstor.org/stable/40474952.

21. *Puget Sound Courier*, January 4, 1856, 2 (quotations); Elwood Evans, et al., *History of the Pacific Northwest: Oregon and Washington*, 2 vols. (Portland: North Pacific History, 1889), 2:402–3. Specific author credits for this section of Evans's book were not provided.

22. W. W. Stevens, "The Old Oregon Trail as Told by the Trailers," ca. 1913, chap. 7, Baker County Library Archive; Hicks, *Yakima and Clickitat Indian Wars*, 13, 11.

23. Famous as an adolescent survivor of the so-called Ward Massacre (see chap. 3), Newton Ward made no distinction between the Native people (presumed to be Eastern Shoshone/Newe) who had killed his family in 1854 and the Paiute/Numu, Yakama, and other bands he rode against as a teenage soldier in 1855. They were simply "the Indians," in both cases. The only specific descriptor he used was for the one "Nez Perce Boy" whom the volunteers in this case decided not to murder along with the rest of their captives. Newton Ward to T. A. Wood, n.d., folder 46, box 4, Oregon Military Collection MSS.

24. James Sinclair to William Cowan, February 10, 1856, transcribed in William N. Bischoff, introduction to Plympton J. Kelly, *We Were Not Summer Soldiers: The Diary of Plympton J. Kelly*, ed. William N. Bischoff (Tacoma: Washington State Historical Society, 1976), 39. See also Simon Harrison, *Dark Trophies: Hunting and the Enemy Body in Modern War* (New York: Berghahn Books, 2012).

25. Newton Ward to T. A. Wood ("there were"); Kelly, *We Were Not Summer Soldiers*, 70 ("Yesterday," "enough beef entrails"); William Norbert Bischoff, "The Yakima Indian War, 1855–56" (PhD diss., Loyola University, 1950), 223n52.

26. William Barnhart to James Nesmith, April 22, 1856, folder 6, box 1, James W. Nesmith Papers. Scatological humor and racism were both common themes in Barnhart's writing, so the nonstandard "PuPu" spelling may have been intentional.

27. Granville O. Haller to Eva Emery Dye, June 24, 1894, folder 13, box 1, Eva Emery Dye Papers. This kind of trophy taking after executions was famously a part of lynching culture in the American South—see, among many others, Roger C. Hartley, *Monumental Harm: Reckoning with Jim Crow Era Confederate Monuments* (Columbia: University of South Carolina Press, 2021), 64.

28. Ida J. Steele, transcribing a speech by Fred Lockley, Sons + Daughters of the Indian War Veterans of the North Pacific Coast meeting minutes, June 17, 1936 (quotation), folder 9, box 2, IWV-NPC Records; Evans et al., *History of the Pacific Northwest*, 2:402–3.

29. Waman C. Hembree, "Yakima Indian War Diary" (copy), enclosed in Walter L. Embree to Mrs. Lulu Crandall, June 7, 1925, folder 23, box 86, Edmond S. Meany Papers.

30. A. J. Hembree to Joel J. Hembree, April 2, 1856 (copy), folder 23, box 86, Edmond S. Meany Papers; William P. Bonney, "Monument to Captain Hembee [*sic*]," *Washington Historical Quarterly* 11, no. 3 (July 1920): 178–82, https://www.jstor.org/stable/40474591. See also Rowe, *Bulwark of the Republic*, 175.

31. "Account of Wm. D. Stillwell," folder 24, box 16, cage 24, Lucullus Virgil McWhorter Papers, Washington State University Libraries Special Collections.

32. Hicks, *Yakima and Clickitat Indian Wars*, 16.

33. As in the other conflicts of the War on Illahee, looting was endemic. See Kelly R. McAllister and Annabelle Mounts Barnett, "Catherine McLeod Mounts: Growing Up Strong in Tough Times on Puget Sound," *Columbia* 25, no. 2 (2011): 3–8.

34. "Complete Surprise on an Indian Encampment! Eight Hostiles Killed," *[Olympia] Pioneer and Democrat*, April 11, 1856, 2.

35. "Complete Surprise on an Indian Encampment! Eight Hostiles Killed"; Edward Otho Cresap Ord, "Diary of E. O. C. Ord 3rd Art U.S. Army," in Ellen Francis Ord, "The Rogue River Indian Expedition of 1856" (master's thesis, University of California, 1922), 32. Henry Sicade, "The Indians' Side of the Story," address to the Research Club of Tacoma, April 10, 1917, in *Building a State, Washington: 1889–1939*, ed. Charles Miles and O. B. Sperlin (Olympia: Washington State Historical Society, 1940), 490–503, esp. 495 ("quotation).

36. Abbi Wonacott, *Where the Mashel Meets the Nisqually: The Mashel Massacre of 1856* (Spanaway, Wash.: Bellus Uccello, 2008); Blee, *Framing Chief Leschi*,

45–48; Oscar H. Jones, "In a Familiar Yet Foreign Land: The Life and Memories of Henry Sicade, 1866–1938," ed. Cary C. Collins, *Columbia* 19, no. 2 (Summer 2005): 1–11, esp. 2.

37. Tove Hodge, "The Family of Sidney S. Ford, Senior," in *Centralia: The First Fifty Years*, ed. Herndon Smith (Centralia, Wash.: F. H. Cole, 1942), esp. 88. The Chehalis leader Koolah Yuanan claimed to have successfully pressured Ford to accede to Chehalis gun ownership with a bit of theater: he tore his clothes and pretended to have been attacked by "hostile Indians," and he used this as evidence that his men needed to remain armed in order to defend themselves and the Americans.

38. Hodge, "The Family of Sidney S. Ford, Senior," esp. 87; Isaac I. Stevens to Jefferson Davis, Secretary of War, March 21, 1856 ("summarily dispos[ing]"), transcribed in Field, *Official History of the Washington National Guard*, 2:32. Ford's son, also named Sidney S. Ford, oversaw the Fox Island internment camp; see Carpenter, *Tears of Internment*. For the shootings, see "Personal Recollections of Mary Jane Brown," 235, folder 2, box 1, DAR Family Rec. of Pioneers. Cf. Kent D. Richards, *Isaac I. Stevens: Young Man in a Hurry* (Provo, Utah: Brigham Young University Press, 1979), 269.

39. Richards, *Isaac I. Stevens*, 316–21; Roy N. Lokken, "The Martial Law Controversy in Washington Territory, 1856," *Pacific Northwest Quarterly* 43, no. 1 (April 1952): 91–119, https://www.jstor.org/stable/40486984; Rowe, *Bulwark of the Republic*, 145.

40. James Tilton to Col. Hurd, March 2, 1856, folder 22, box 5, Clarence B. Bagley Papers, Acc 0036-001, University of Washington Special Collections; Judy Bentley and Lorraine McConaghy, "Slave Master or Benefactor? James Tilton in Antebellum Washington Territory," *Columbia* 28, no. 2 (2014): 6–11; "Fugitive Slave Case," *[Olympia] Pioneer and Democrat*, September 28, 1860, 2.

41. James Tilton to Col. Hurd, March 2, 1856 ("As they occupy"); "Governor Isaac I. Stevens to the Fourth Annual Session of the [Washington Territory] Legislative Assembly, December 3, 1856" in *Messages of the Governors of the Territory of Washington to the Legislative Assembly, 1854–1889*, ed. Charles M. Gates (Seattle: University of Washington Press, 1940), 28–47, esp. 32 ("There is no such thing").

42. Elwood Evans to Isaac I. Stevens, May 30, 1856 (quotation), folder 22A, box 5, Clarence B. Bagley Papers; Rowe, *Bulwark of the Republic*, 177–80; Isaac I. Stevens to Stephen A. Douglas, May 25, 1856, Pacific Northwest Historical Documents, University of Washington Digital Collection; Lokken, "Martial Law Controversy in Washington Territory."

43. Peter Ruffner to James W. Nesmith, April 18, 185[6], folder 24, box 2, James W. Nesmith Papers. Spelling and punctuation have been corrected for readability in the Ruffner quotations. Word order has been slightly reworked for clarity, but the original intent and implications have been left intact.

44. Ord, "Diary of E. O. C. Ord," 30; George Bundy Wasson Jr., "Growing Up Indian: An Emic Perspective" (PhD diss., University of Oregon, 2001), 217–20.

45. Peter Ruffner to James W. Nesmith, April 18, 185[6] (quotations); Wasson, "Growing Up Indian," 217–20.

46. Wellman, *Man of Treacherous Charm*, 84; Lissa K. Wadewitz, "Rethinking the 'Indian War': Northern Indians and Intra-Native Politics in the Western Canada–U.S. Borderlands," *Western Historical Quarterly* 50, no. 4 (Winter 2019): 355 https://doi.org/10.1093/whq/whz096 (quotation; emphasis in original).

47. Hodge, "Family of Sidney S. Ford, Senior," 94.

48. Hicks, *Yakima and Clickitat Indian Wars*, 17; William Fraser Tolmie to Colonel Silas Casey, May 23, 1856, in Clarence B. Bagley, "Attitude of the Hudson's Bay Company during the Indian War of 1855–1856," *Washington Historical Quarterly* 18, no. 4 (October 1917): 291–307, esp. 304–5, https://www.jstor.org/stable/23908627; Rowe, *Bulwark of the Republic*, 181–82; Corey L. Larson, "Negotiating Fort Nisqually: Reconfiguring the Social and Environmental Landscapes of the South Salish Sea, 1833–1858" (PhD diss., Simon Fraser University, 2020), 200–201. "Bob" claimed he needed to leave the internment camp because of his fear of his former enslaver.

49. Hicks, *Yakima and Clickitat Indian Wars*, 17.

50. Hicks, *Yakima and Clickitat Indian Wars*, 17–18.

51. Blee, *Framing Chief Leschi*, 173; Larson, "Negotiating Fort Nisqually," 201; Meeker, *Pioneer Reminiscences of Puget Sound*, 365–67. On the long-standing norm of Euro-American militiamen supporting their fellows no matter the heinousness of their crimes, see Rob Harper, "Looking the Other Way: The Gnadenhutten Massacre and the Contextual Interpretation of Violence," *William and Mary Quarterly* 64, no. 3 (July 2007): 621–44, https://www.jstor.org/stable/25096733.

52. Brad Asher, *Beyond the Reservation: Indians, Settlers, and the Law in Washington Territory, 1853–1889* (Norman: University of Oklahoma Press, 1999), 112; David Douglas Robertson, "Native Ad from Mawich Man," January 22, 2016, *Chinook Jargon* (blog), https://chinookjargon.com/2016/01/22/native-ad-from-mawich-man/.

53. Blee, *Framing Chief Leschi*, 172; Field, *Official History of the Washington National Guard*, 2:50; Leslie M. Scott, comp., *History of the Oregon Country by Harvey W. Scott, Fifty Years the Editor of the Morning Oregonian*, 6 vols. (Cambridge, Mass.: Riverside Press, 1924), 2:41.

54. Rowe, *Bulwark of the Republic*, 170 ("more demonstration"). Rowe's assertions about the Battle of Seattle are based in large part on later Native testimony. On the framing of the Puget Sound War, see Wadewitz, "Rethinking the 'Indian War' "; Mike Vouri, "Raiders from the North: The Northern Indians and Northwest Washington in the 1850s," *Columbia* 11, no. 3 (1997): 24–35; J. Overton, "The Battle of Port Gamble," *Columbia* 29, no. 1 (2015): 23–27;

John Lutz, "Inventing an Indian War: Canadian Indians and American Settlers in the Pacific West, 1854–1864," *Journal of the West* 38, no. 3 (July 1998): 7–13; Blee, *Framing Chief Leschi*; David M. Buerge, *Chief Seattle and the Town That Took His Name: The Change of Worlds for the Native People and Settlers on Puget Sound* (Seattle: Sasquatch Books, 2017), chaps. 6, 7.

55. Grand Ronde Valley should not be confused with the similarly named Grand Ronde Reservation, located much farther to the west. Walter Washington De Lacy, "Diary of the Yakima Indian War Kept by W. W. De Lacy, Captain, Engineers and Acting Adjutant, W. T. V. Covering Period June 12th to August 29, 1856," in Field, *Official History of the Washington National Guard*, 2:60–71; Clifford E. Trafzer and Richard D. Scheuerman, *Renegade Tribe: The Palouse Indians and the Invasion of the Inland Pacific Northwest* (Pullman: Washington State University Press, 1986), 72–74; Richards, *Isaac I. Stevens*, 297–98; William L. Lang, " 'Ambition Has Always Been My God': William Winlock Miller and Opportunity in Washington Territory," *Pacific Northwest Quarterly* 83, no. 3 (July 1992): 101–9, esp. 105, https://www.jstor.org/stable/40491291; Thomas J. Cram, *Topographical Memoir and Report of Captain T. J. Cram, on Territories of Oregon and Washington*, H.R. Exec. Doc. no. 114, 35th Cong., 2nd sess. (1859), 115; F. Shaw to James Tilton, July 1, 1856, quoted in *Message of the Governor of the Washington Territory* (Olympia: Edward Furste, 1857), 258–59; Benjamin F. Shaw to Isaac I. Stevens, May 22, 1856 ("make a fight"), quoted in *Message of the Governor of the Washington Territory*, 245.

56. De Lacy, "Diary of the Yakima Indian War."

57. James R. Masterson, "The Records of the Washington Superintendency of Indian Affairs, 1853–1874," *Pacific Northwest Quarterly* 37, no. 1 (January 1946): 31–57, https://www.jstor.org/stable/40486736; Isaac I. Stevens, "Governor's Message," in *Message of the Governor of the Washington Territory*, 1–23, esp. 9 (quotation). Cf. Mark Spence, " 'Soyaapo' and the Making of Lewis and Clark," *Oregon Historical Quarterly* 105, no. 3 (Fall 2004): 482–99, esp. 484–85, https://www.jstor.org/stable/20615452.

58. Stevens, "Governor's Message," 13 (quotations); "Substance of the Remarks of Gov. Stevens at the Dinner Given to Col. Shaw and the Volunteers," *[Olympia] Pioneer and Democrat*, November 7, 1856, 2.

59. Isaac I. Stevens, *Speech of Hon. Isaac I. Stevens, Delegate from Washington Territory, on the Washington and Oregon War Claims, Delivered in the House of Representatives of the United States, May 31, 1858* (Washington, D.C.: Lemuel Towers, 1858); Benjamin J. Klebaner, "Poor Relief and Public Works during the Depression of 1857," *Historian* 22, no. 3 (May 1960): 264–67.

60. Stevens, *Speech of Hon. Isaac I. Stevens*. Word order has been slightly reworked for clarity, but the original intent and implications have been left intact.

61. Stevens, *Speech of Hon. Isaac I. Stevens* (quotation); SuAnn M. Reddick and Cary C. Collins, "Medicine Creek to Fox Island: Cadastral Scams and Contested Domains," *Oregon Historical Quarterly* 106, no. 3 (Fall 2005): 374–97,

https://doi.org/10.1353/ohq.2005.0087; Jo N. Miles, "Kamiakin's Impact on Early Washington Territory," *Pacific Northwest Quarterly* 99, no. 4 (Fall 2008): 167, https://www.jstor.org/stable/40492173; Richards, *Isaac I. Stevens*, 342, 436n48.

62. Feliks Banel, "Remembering Washington's Complicated First Governor Isaac Stevens," *My Northwest* (Seattle), September 1, 2023, orig. August 31, 2016, https://mynorthwest.com/381266/remembering-first-governor-stevens/; Richards, *Isaac I. Stevens*, 336, 435n38 (quotation).

63. Wasson, "Growing Up Indian," 98, 34 ("Oregon Holocaust"; "the terrible years"); Wasson, "The Coquelle Indians and the Cultural 'Black Hole' of the Southern Oregon Coast."

Chapter Five. Theft, Murder, Complicity, and the Oregon Trails of Tears

1. Matthew P. Deady, "Southern Oregon Names and Events," in *Transactions of the Eleventh Annual Re-Union of the Oregon Pioneer Association for 1883* (Salem: E. M. Waite, 1884), 23–24; Nathan Douthit, "Between Indian and White Worlds on the Oregon-California Border, 1851–1857: Benjamin Wright and Enos," *Oregon Historical Quarterly* 100, no. 4 (1999): 402–33, esp. 432n54, https://www.jstor.org/stable/20615005; John K. Lamerick to E. M. Barnum, December 13, 1855 ("the quantity of men"; emphasis in original), Yakima and Rogue River War, Document File B, reel 2, document 522, Oregon State Archives; John K. Lamerick to Joseph Lane, September 22, 1856 ("citizens," "few scattering"); Peter Laufer, "All We Ask Is to Be Left Alone," *Humboldt Journal of Social Relations* 36 (2014): 17–33, esp. 19, https://www.jstor.org/stable/humjsocrel.36.17.

2. Robert W. Johannsen, "The Secession Crisis and the Frontier: Washington Territory, 1860–1861," *Journal of American History* 39, no. 3 (December 1952): 415–40, esp. 419, https://doi.org/10.2307/1895003; James Robbins Jewell, *Agents of Empire: The First Oregon Cavalry and the Opening of the Interior Pacific Northwest during the Civil War* (Lincoln: University of Nebraska, 2023).

3. Brook Colley, *Power in the Telling: Grand Ronde, Warm Springs, and Intertribal Relations in the Casino Era* (Seattle: University of Washington Press, 2018), 33–36, esp. 33 ("concentration camps"); Tracy Neal Leavelle, " 'We Will Make It Our Own Place': Agriculture and Adaptation at the Grand Ronde Reservation, 1856–1887," *American Indian Quarterly* 22, no. 4 (1998): 433–56, https://doi.org/10.2307/1184835; Alexandra Harmon, *Reclaiming the Reservation: Histories of Indian Sovereignty Suppressed and Renewed* (Seattle: University of Washington Press, 2019).

4. Stephen Dow Beckham, ed., "Trail of Tears: 1856 Diary of Indian Agent George Ambrose," *Southern Oregon Heritage* 2, no. 1 (Summer 1996): 16–21; David G. Lewis, "We Are Willing to Remove Anywhere, Where We Can

Obtain Peace: Removal of the Rogue River Tribes to the Grand Ronde Reservation," *Quartux Journal* (September 16, 2017) ("some declaring"), https://ndnhistoryresearch.com/2017/09/16/we-are-willing-to-remove-anywhere-where-we-can-obtain-peace-removal-of-the-rogue-river-tribes-to-the-grand-ronde-reservation/. See also MacKenzie Katherine Lee Moore, "Making Place and Nation: Geographic Meaning and the Americanization of Oregon: 1834–1859" (PhD diss., University of California, Berkeley, 2012), 136–43.

5. Gray H. Whaley, *Oregon and the Collapse of* Illahee: *U.S. Empire and the Transformation of an Indigenous World, 1792–1859* (Chapel Hill: University of North Carolina Press, 2010), 201–2 (quotations); Mark Tveskov and Chelsea Rose, "The Ordeal and Redemption of Betsy Brown, Christina Geisel, and Mary Harris: Historical Memory, Placemaking, and the Archaeology of Oregon's Rogue River War," in *The Archaeology of Place and Space in the West*, ed. Emily Dale and Carolyn L. White (Salt Lake City: University of Utah Press, 2022), 91–100, esp. 100.

6. David G. Lewis, "Umpqua Journal of Removal to the Grand Ronde Encampment, 1856," *Quartux Journal* (October 29, 2016), https://ndnhistoryresearch.com/2016/10/26/umpqua-journal-of-removal-to-grand-ronde-encampment-1856/; Thomas J. Cram, *Topographical Memoir and Report of Captain T. J. Cram, on Territories of Oregon and Washington*, H.R. Exec. Doc. no. 114, 35th Cong., 2nd sess. (1859), 44–45.

7. Charles F. Wilkinson, *The People Are Dancing Again: The History of the Siletz Tribe of Western Oregon* (Seattle: University of Washington Press, 2010), 155–67; E. A. Schwartz, "Sick Hearts: Indian Removal on the Oregon Coast, 1875–1881," *Oregon Historical Quarterly* 92, no. 3 (Fall 1991): 229–64, https://www.jstor.org/stable/20614395; Sarah Deer, *Beginning and End of Rape: Confronting Sexual Violence in Native America* (Minneapolis: University of Minnesota Press, 2015), chap. 5.

8. Rosella White Hammer reminiscences, April 6, 1927, 7–8, vol. 1, folder 1, box 1, DAR Family Rec. of Wash. Pioneers.

9. Cram, *Topographical Memoir and Report*, 110.

10. C. H. Mott Report, September 22, 1858, in David G. Lewis, "Mott's Special Report on Grand Ronde and Siletz in 1858," *Quartux Journal* (January 4, 2017), https://ndnhistoryresearch.com/2017/01/04/motts-special-report-on-grand-ronde-and-siletz-in1858/. Mott had been sent by Congress to investigate conditions in the Oregon territory, following disagreements between Gen. John E. Wool and several figures in territorial government. Kent D. Richards, *Isaac I. Stevens: Young Man in a Hurry* (Provo, Utah: Brigham Young University Press, 1979), 331.

11. The soldiers who kept armed guard over Native people at the Coastal Reservation, meanwhile, also plundered local Euro-American farms to such a great extent that in 1858 they were banned from carrying their guns outside the fort when not on duty—implying not only thievery but armed robbery.

See Julie M. Schablitsky, "Duty and Vice: The Daily Life of a Fort Hoskins Soldier" (master's thesis, Oregon State University, 1996), 77.

12. James R. Masterson, "The Records of the Washington Superintendency of Indian Affairs, 1853–1874," *Pacific Northwest Quarterly* 37, no. 1 (January 1946): 31–57, https://www.jstor.org/stable/40486736; George Bundy Wasson Jr., "Growing Up Indian: An Emic Perspective" (PhD diss., University of Oregon, 2001), 176–77; Albert J. Partoll, "Frank L. Worden, Pioneer Merchant, 1830–1887," *Pacific Northwest Quarterly* 40, no. 3 (July 1946): 189–202, https://www.jstor.org/stable/40486839.

13. James W. Nesmith to James O'Meara, June 3, 1873 ("commanded troops"), folder 6, box 3, James W. Nesmith Papers; Stafford Hazelett, " 'To the World!!': The Story behind the Vitriol," *Oregon Historical Quarterly* 116, no. 2 (Summer 2015): 196–219, https://doi.org/10.5403/oregonhistq.116.2.0196; James W. Nesmith to Asahel Bush, October 22, 1855, folder 2, box 3, James W. Nesmith Papers; Mary Ellen Rowe, *Bulwark of the Republic: The American Militia in the Antebellum West* (Westport, Conn.: Praeger, 2003), 163; Plympton J. Kelly, *We Were Not Summer Soldiers: The Diary of Plympton J. Kelly*, ed. William N. Bischoff (Tacoma: Washington State Historical Society, 1976), 34–36; Cram, *Topographical Memoir and Report*, 113 ("outrages"); David G. Lewis, "Curry's Volunteers," *Quartux Journal* (October 25, 2020), https://ndnhistoryresearch.com/2020/10/25/currys-volunteers/.

14. Sydney Teiser, "Life of George H. Williams: Almost Chief-Justice," *Oregon Historical Quarterly* 47, no. 3 (September 1946): 255–80, esp. 266, https://www.jstor.org/stable/20611694; Harry Kelsey, "The Doolittle Report of 1867: Its Preparation and Shortcomings," *Arizona and the West* 17, no. 2 (Summer 1975): 107–20, https://www.jstor.org/stable/40168425; Merle W. Wells, "Caleb Lyon's Indian Policy," *Pacific Northwest Quarterly* 61, no. 4 (October 1970): 193–200, https://www.jstor.org/stable/40488834; James W. Nesmith, "Speech of Hon. J. W. Nesmith of Oregon, on Reconstruction, Delivered in the Senate of the United States, January 18, 1866" (Washington, D.C.: Congressional Globe Office, 1866).

15. James W. Nesmith to Asahel Bush, October 14, 1855 ("would rather die"), folder 2, box 3, James W. Nesmith Papers; James W. Nesmith to Charles E. May, November 19, 1859 ("the rights of the Indians"), folder 19, box 3, James W. Nesmith Papers; James W. Nesmith, "Remarks of Hon. J. W. Nesmith of Oregon upon the Indian Appropriation Bill, May 13 + 14 1862" ("the farce"), folder 19, box 3, James W. Nesmith Papers; James W. Nesmith to Isaac Ingalls Stevens, November 17[?], 1858 ("clean[ing] out"), folder 6, box 3, James W. Nesmith Papers.

16. James W. Nesmith, "1875 Address to the Oregon Pioneer Society," 30 ("Indian sympathizers," "exaggerated accounts"), folder 13, box 3, James W. Nesmith Papers; Nesmith to O'Meara, June 3, 1873 ("hypocritical scoundrels," "understand the proper policy").

17. Cf. David G. Lewis and Thomas J. Connolly, "White American Violence on Tribal Peoples on the Oregon Coast," *Oregon Historical Quarterly* 120, no. 4 (Winter 2019): 368–81, esp. 376, https://doi.org/10.1353/ohq.2019.0028.

18. C. H. Mott Report, September 22, 1858.

19. T[imothy] W[oodbridge] Davenport, "Recollections of an Indian Agent—IV," *Quarterly of the Oregon Historical Society* 8, no. 1 (December 1907): 4–5, https://www.jstor.org/stable/20609748. Davenport leaves out James W. Nesmith's name in the text, but he is far and away the most likely person to fit all the descriptors Davenport includes about the person whom he was quoting.

20. On Nesmith's corruptions, see John H. Mitchell to J[ohn] W[atermelon] Redington, January 30, 1905, folder 2, box 21, Edmond S. Meany Papers; Kelsey, "The Doolittle Report of 1867."

21. Harriet Nesmith McArthur, "Recollections of the Rickreall," *Oregon Historical Quarterly* 30, no. 4 (December 1929): 362–83, esp. 377 ("allowed out," "good work"), https://www.jstor.org/stable/20610502; Louis Kenoyer, *Reminiscences of a Grand Ronde Reservation Childhood*, trans. Jedd Schrock and Henry Zenk (Corvallis: Oregon State University Press and the Confederated Tribes of Grand Ronde, 2017), 86–87.

22. Davenport, "Recollections of an Indian Agent," 7; Robert E. Ficken, "After the Treaties: Administering Pacific Northwest Indian Reservations," *Oregon Historical Quarterly* 106, no. 3 (Fall 2005): 442–61, esp. 444, https://www.jstor.org/stable/20615560; Michael John Witgen, *Seeing Red: Indigenous Land, American Expansion, and the Political Economy of Plunder in North America* (Williamsburg, Va.: Omohundro Institute of Early American History and Culture, 2022); Ryan Hall, "Patterns of Plunder: Corruption and the Failure of the Indian Reservation System, 1851–1887," *Western Historical Quarterly* 55, no. 1 (Spring 2024): 21–38, https://doi.org/10.1093/whq/whad124.

23. William H. Barnhart, Umatilla Indian Agency, to William H. Rector, August 5, 1862, U.S. Office of the Commissioner of Indian Affairs, Report no. 62, 270 ("small band," "their own master"), https://digitalcollections.lib.washington.edu/digital/collection/lctext/id/2378; George B. Currey to Justus Steinberger, August 23, 1862, in *The War of the Rebellion: A Compilation of the Official Records of the Union and Confederate Armies*, serial 105, ed. George W. Davis, Leslie J. Perry, and Joseph W. Kirkley (Washington, D.C.: Government Printing Office, 1897), 164 ("California volunteers"); James Robbins Jewell, ed., *On Duty in the Pacific Northwest during the Civil War: Correspondence and Reminiscences of the First Oregon Cavalry Regiment* (Knoxville: University of Tennessee Press, 2018), 187–97, esp. 190; David Peterson del Mar, *Beaten Down: A History of Interpersonal Violence in the West* (Seattle: University of Washington Press, 2002), chap. 1.

24. Justus Steinberger to Fort Walla Walla, August 23, 1862, in Davis, Perry, and Kirkley, *The War of the Rebellion*, 163–64.

25. Jewell, *Agents of Empire*, 81 ("attackers"); Scott McArthur, *The Enemy Never Came: The Civil War in the Pacific Northwest* (Caldwell, Idaho: Caxton Press, 2012), 109 ("true terrorist[s]"). See also Henry McCann, Fort Walla Walla, Order no. 110, June 13, 1862, transcribed in Davis, Perry, and Kirkley, *War of the Rebellion*, 1140.

26. Davenport, "Recollections of an Indian Agent," 12, 14–15 ("very few").

27. Robert H. Milroy to Janus J. Berry, July 18, 1877 (quotations), "United States Bureau of Indian Affairs Agency for the Puyallup, Nisqually and other Indian Tribes correspondence, 1877–1878," Acc. 4933-001, University of Washington Special Collections; C. Joseph Genetin-Pilawa, " 'Friends' and Fistfights: Federal Indian Policy Debates and Late Nineteenth-Century State Development," *Journal of the Gilded Age and Progressive Era* 14, no. 4 (October 2015): 512–20, esp. 514, https://www.jstor.org/stable/43903531; Ficken, "After the Treaties," 444; Michael C. Blumm and James Brunberg, " 'Not Much Less Necessary ... Than the Atmosphere They Breathed': Salmon, Indian Treaties, and the Supreme Court—A Centennial Remembrance of *United States v. Winans* and Its Enduring Significance," *Natural Resources Journal* 46, no. 2 (Spring 2006): 489–546, esp. 511–19, https://www.jstor.org/stable/24889047.

28. Davenport, "Recollections of an Indian Agent," esp. 31–33 ("Damn the Indians"; "want[ing] to kill"); Donald L. Cutler, *"Hang Them All": George Wright and the Plateau Indian War* (Norman: University of Oklahoma Press, 2016), 259 ("hanging a few").

29. Davenport, "Recollections of an Indian Agent," 35 (quotation).

30. "Soger Boy," "Letter from Fort Lapwai," April 5, 1863, in Jewell, *On Duty in the Pacific Northwest*, 51–52; William Barnhart, "The Oregon Squibobs' Farewell to His Indians," *Oregonian*, September 27, 1869, 1.

31. Andrew H. Fisher, *Shadow Tribe: The Making of Columbia River Indian Identity* (Seattle: University of Washington Press, 2010).

32. David G. Lewis, "Umpqua Valley Settlers Murder Klikitat Farmers: Dick Johnson's Family Story, by Sallie Applegate Long," *Quartux Journal* (May 29, 2019), https://ndnhistoryresearch.com/2019/05/29/umpqua-valley-settlers-murder-klikitat-farmers-dick-johnsons-family-story-by-sallie-applegate-long; Leta Lovelace Neiderheiser, *Jesse Applegate: A Dialogue with Destiny* (Mustang, Okla.: Tate, 2010), 175–95; Moore, "Making Place and Nation," 143–58; and especially John Samuel Ferrell, "Indians and Criminal Justice in Early Oregon, 1842–1859" (master's thesis, Portland State University, 1973), chap. 10.

33. Jesse Applegate to James W. Nesmith, September 18, 1856 ("by the advice," "many warm friends," "efforts to throw"), folder 3, box 1, James W. Nesmith Papers; Ferrell, "Indians and Criminal Justice in Early Oregon," 66; Jesse Applegate to Frances Fuller Victor [?], October 15, 1865 ("treacherous and rapacious," "taught"), folder 1, box 1, Frances Fuller Victor Papers, Mss 1199, Oregon Historical Society Special Collections.

34. Ferrell, "Indians and Criminal Justice in Early Oregon," 66; Les McConnell, "The Treaty Rights of the Confederated Tribes of Warm Springs," *Pacific Northwest Quarterly* 97, no. 4 (Fall 2006): 190–201, esp. 191–92, https://www.jstor.org/stable/40491973; Genealogical Forum of Portland, Oregon, comp., *Genealogical Material in Oregon Donation Land Claims*, 5 vols. (Portland: Genealogical Forum of Portland, Oregon, 1957–75), 3:23–24, 69.
35. Applegate to Nesmith, September 18, 1856; Lewis, "Umpqua Valley Settlers Murder Klikitat Farmers" ("because he was an 'Inj_n' ").
36. Jesse Applegate to James W. Nesmith (private), December 3, 1858, folder 3, box 1, James W. Nesmith Papers; Ferrell, "Indians and Criminal Justice in Early Oregon," 67.
37. William J. Martin to Joseph Lane, August 19, 1856 ("red devils"), https://truwe.sohs.org/files/jolaneletters.html; Jesse Applegate to James W. Nesmith, December 26, 1858 ("with neglect"), folder 3, box 1, James W. Nesmith Papers; Jesse Applegate to James W. Nesmith, September 26, 1856 ("very anxious"); Ferrell, "Indians and Criminal Justice in Early Oregon," 67–70.
38. J. Applegate to Nesmith (private), December 3, 1858 ("atrocious"); Jesse Applegate to James W. Nesmith, October 19, 1858 ("paltry present"), folder 3, box 1, James W. Nesmith Papers.
39. Jesse Applegate to James W. Nesmith, September 18, 1858 (quotation), folder 3, box 1, James W. Nesmith Papers; Ferrell, "Indians and Criminal Justice in Early Oregon," 71. Purportedly the intervention of Judge Matthew Deady helped overturn the arson charge.
40. Stewart E. Tolnay and E. M. Beck, *A Festival of Violence: An Analysis of Southern Lynchings, 1882–1930* (Urbana: University of Illinois Press, 1995); Stephen Kantrowitz, *Ben Tillman and the Reconstruction of White Supremacy* (Chapel Hill: University of North Carolina Press, 2000).
41. Applegate to Nesmith (private), December 3, 1858.
42. Applegate to Nesmith (private), December 3, 1858. "Jim" was probably a moniker bequeathed by White neighbors.
43. Applegate to Nesmith (private), December 3, 1858; [Jesse Applegate?], "Umpqua, *Oregon Statesman*, December 14, 1858, 1.
44. Ferrell, "Indians and Criminal Justice in Early Oregon," 76; Applegate to Nesmith (private), December 3, 1858. All quotations in this section come from the same paragraph and retain their original meaning, but they have been rearranged for tense and flow.
45. Lewis, "Umpqua Valley Settlers Murder Klikitat Farmers" (quotation); Ferrell, "Indians and Criminal Justice in Early Oregon," 76–78. Strikingly, the murderers were (mis?)remembered as miners by some of those who quietly objected to the murders. See McConnell, "The Treaty Rights of the Confederated Tribes of Warm Springs," 191–92.
46. Lewis, "Umpqua Valley Settlers Murder Klikitat Farmers" ("attempt to bring"); Neiderheiser, *Jesse Applegate*, 194–95 ("resist or use arms"). The

main investigator in the records seems to have restricted himself or been restricted to issues of property. Stephen Fowler Chadwick to James W. Nesmith, December 28, 1858, folder 10, box 1, James W. Nesmith Papers.

47. Applegate to Nesmith (private), December 3, 1858 (quotations).
48. George H. Parker, "Short History of Josephine County," March 1922, George R. Riddle Papers, Mss 1388, Oregon Historical Society Special Collections. One might also contrast Jesse Applegate's insistence that the rule of law should protect Dick Johnson's murderers with his 1864 opinion (of unknown seriousness) that George McClellan should be shot as an incompetent traitor. Jesse Applegate to James W. Nesmith, April 3, 1864, folder 3, box 1, James W. Nesmith Papers.
49. Jesse Applegate to James W. Nesmith, December 3, 1858; Applegate to Nesmith (private), December 3, 1858.
50. Jesse Applegate to James W. Nesmith, December 26, 1858 ("keep from the public eye," "aimed to give"), folder 3, box 1, James W. Nesmith Papers; Jesse Applegate to James W. Nesmith January 12, 1859 ("merely for your amusement"), folder 3, box 1, James W. Nesmith Papers; Roland L. De Lorme, "Westward the Bureaucrats: Government Officials on the Washington and Oregon Frontiers," *Arizona and the West* 22, no. 3 (Autumn 1980): 223–36, https://www.jstor.org/stable/40168946; Jesse Applegate to Joseph Lane, July 18, 1878, folder 6, box 1, Joseph Lane Papers.
51. Joseph Lane to Dr. Joseph Drew, March 2, 1856 (quotation; emphasis in original), folder 2, box 1, Joseph Lane Papers.
52. Cf. Boyd Cothran, "Melancholia and the Infinite Debate," *Western Historical Quarterly* 47, no. 4 (Winter 2016): 435–38, https://doi.org/10.1093/whq/whw091.

Chapter Six. Lynchings Legal and Extralegal in the Pacific Northwest

1. John E. Smith, "A Pioneer of the Spokane Country," *Washington Historical Quarterly* 7, no. 4 (October 1916): 267–77, https://www.jstor.org/stable/40474448.
2. Smith, "A Pioneer of the Spokane Country," 270.
3. Christian G. Fritz, "Popular Sovereignty, Vigilantism, and the Constitutional Right of Revolution," *Pacific Historical Review* 63, no. 1 (February 1994): 39–66, https://doi.org/10.2307/3640668. Under more expansive definitions of the term, many of the killings discussed in earlier chapters would count as lynchings; see Helen McLure, " 'Who Dares to Style This Female a Woman?' Lynching, Gender, and Culture in the Nineteenth-Century U.S. West," in *Lynching beyond Dixie: American Mob Violence outside the South*, ed. Michael J. Pfeifer (Urbana: University of Illinois Press, 2013), 21–53. There has never been a broadly agreed-upon definition of the parameters of lynching, even among the leaders of antilynching movements. See Christopher

Waldrep, *The Many Faces of Judge Lynch: Extralegal Violence and Punishment in America* (New York: Palgrave Macmillan, 2004), 127–50.

4. Michael J. Pfeifer, *The Roots of Rough Justice: Origins of American Lynching* (Urbana: University of Illinois Press, 2011), 49–50, appendix; David Peterson del Mar, *Beaten Down: A History of Interpersonal Violence in the West* (Seattle: University of Washington Press, 2002), esp. 11–12, 185n14; Nicholas K. Geranios, "Asotin: Discovery of Old Documents Casts New Light on Lynchings," *Kitsap Sun*, April 14, 2002 ("tended to be white"); Paul Dorpat, "The Dark Days of Mob Rule and Lynching as Sport in Seattle," *Seattle Times*, July 18, 2014; Kristian Foden-Vencil, "Coos Bay Remembers Alonzo Tucker and Oregon's Only Documented Lynching," Oregon Public Broadcasting, March 5, 2020; Larry Cebula, "More on the 1884 Cheney Lynching," *Northwest History* (blog) April 22, 2015, http://northwesthistory.blogspot.com/2015/04/more-on-1884-cheney-lynching.html; Riva Dean, "A Peaceable Mob: The Lynching of Frank Viles and Community Identity in Asotin, Washington, 1896" (master's thesis, Central Washington University, 2005); Jean F. Hankins, "Whitman County Grit: Palouse Vigilantes and the Press," *Columbia* 6, no. 1 (1992): 20–26; Howard D. Baumgart and Michael Honey (uncredited), "The Ellensburg Tree of Justice," *Columbia* 15, no. 4 (2001–2): 6–15; Terrell D. Gottschall, "Let the Law Take Its Course: Vigilante Justice and Due Process in Walla Walla," *Columbia* 26, no. 1 (2012): 20–28.

5. Vincent P. Mikkelsen, "Fighting for Sergeant Caldwell: The NAACP Campaign against 'Legal' Lynching after World War I," *Journal of African American History* 94, no. 4 (Fall 2009): 464–86, https://www.jstor.org/stable/25653974; Melanie S. Morrison, *Murder on Shades Mountain: The Legal Lynching of Willie Peterson and the Struggle for Justice in Jim Crow Birmingham* (Durham, N.C.: Duke University Press, 2018); Margaret A. Burnham, *By Hands Now Known: Jim Crow's Legal Executioners* (New York: Norton, 2022), esp. chap. 5; Michael J. Klarman, "The Racial Origins of Modern Criminal Procedure," *Michigan Law Review* 99, no. 1 (October 2000): 48–97, https://doi.org/10.2307/1290325; Kamiakin/K'amáyakin et al. to "the soldiers and the Americans," enclosed in P. Ricard to "Grand Vicaire," October 19, 1855 ("They hang us"), folder 7, box 24, OMI Collection.

6. Lisa Blee, *Framing Chief Leschi: Narrative and the Politics of Historical Justice* (Chapel Hill: University of North Carolina Press, 2014), 108–9; Cecilia Svinth Carpenter, *Tears of Internment: The Indian History of Fox Island and the Puget Sound War* (Tacoma: Tahoma Research Services, 1996), 57–62; SuAnn M. Reddick and Cary C. Collins, "Medicine Creek to Fox Island: Cadastral Scams and Contested Domains," *Oregon Historical Quarterly* 106, no. 3 (Fall 2005): 374–97, esp. 393, https://doi.org/10.1353/ohq.2005.0087; Ezra Meeker, *Pioneer Reminiscences of Puget Sound: The Tragedy of Leschi* (Seattle: Lowman & Hanford, 1905), 273.

7. "Substance of the Remarks of Gov. Stevens at the Dinner Given to Col. Shaw and the Volunteers," *[Olympia] Pioneer and Democrat*, November 7, 1856, 2.

8. Blee, *Framing Chief Leschi*, 60 ("familiarly"); Isaac I. Stevens to George Wright, June 18, 1856, in Virgil F. Field, *The Official History of the Washington National Guard*, vol. 2, *Washington Territorial Militia and the Indian Wars of 1855–56* (Tacoma: Washington National Guard State Historical Society, 1962), 52 ("I presume"); George Wright to Isaac I. Stevens, October 4, 1856, in Field, *Official History of the Washington National Guard*, 2:72 ("suspended"); Isaac I. Stevens to George Wright, October 14, 1856, in Field, *Official History of the Washington National Guard*, 2:50 ("If this demand").

9. Blee, *Framing Chief Leschi*, 60–65. Ironically, Washington Territory laws barring Indian testimony in court scuttled a few of the cases.

10. Blee, *Framing Chief Leschi*, 163–65, 178; James Longmire, "Narrative of James Longmire, a Pioneer of 1853 (Concluded)," *Washington Historical Quarterly* 23, no. 2 (April 1932): 138–50, https://www.jstor.org/stable/23908658; Tove Hodge, "The Family of Sidney S. Ford, Senior," in *Centralia: The First Fifty Years*, ed. Herndon Smith (Centralia, Wash.: F. H. Cole, 1942), 92–93 ("[Stevens] said").

11. Blee, *Framing Chief Leschi*, 65–67; "Trial and Conviction of Leschi," *[Olympia] Pioneer and Democrat*, March 20, 1857, 2.

12. "Leschi, Quiemuth, etc.," *[Olympia] Pioneer and Democrat*, November 28, 1856, 2; Martin Schmitt, "The Execution of Chief Leschi and the 'Truth Teller,'" *Oregon Historical Quarterly* 50, no. 1 (March 1949): 30–39, https://www.jstor.org/stable/20611895.

13. Blee, *Framing Chief Leschi*, 68 ("the [Washington] territory's"), 4; [Charles H. Prosch?], "How to Serve a Writ," *Puget Sound Herald*, April 22, 1859, 2.

14. [Prosch?], "How to Serve a Writ."

15. [Prosch?], "How to Serve a Writ." The presumption that the killing of Quiemuth was an act of vengeance should be treated with the same skepticism as all such claims. Hodge, "The Family of Sidney S. Ford, Senior," 92–93.

16. Blee, *Framing Chief Leschi*, 72–73; Sidney Berland, "Yelm Jim v. Washington Territory: An Enigma," *Portage* (1984): 4–7; Marian W. Smith, *The Puyallup-Nisqually* (1940; repr., New York: AMS Press, 1969), 64 (quotation). One tradition has it that Yelm Jim used his Thunder power to make an escape. See Jay Miller, "Chehalis Area Traditions, a Summary of Thelma Anderson's 1927 Ethnographic Notes," *Northwest Anthropological Research Notes* 33, no. 1 (Spring 1999): 1–72, esp. 46.

17. Brad Asher, *Beyond the Reservation: Indians, Settlers, and the Law in Washington Territory, 1853–1889* (Norman: University of Oklahoma Press, 1999), 133–37, 212–13; Mark D. Walters, "Review: Histories of Colonialism, Legality, and Aboriginality," *University of Toronto Law Journal* 57, no. 4 (Fall 2007): 819–32, esp. 830–31, https://www.jstor.org/stable/20109829; cf. Paul G. McHugh, *Aboriginal Societies and the Common Law: A History of Sovereignty, Status, and Self-Determination* (New York: Oxford University Press, 2004), 21–26.

18. Asher, *Beyond the Reservation*; Blee, *Framing Chief Leschi*, 97, 171–72, quotations on 181–82.

19. "Halo," *[Olympia] Pioneer and Democrat*, November 14, 1856, 2.
20. Field, *Official History of the Washington National Guard*, 2:50.
21. Blee, *Framing Chief Leschi*, 50–51, 66 ("summary mode").
22. Donald L. Cutler, *"Hang Them All": George Wright and the Plateau Indian War* (Norman: University of Oklahoma Press, 2016), 259, 251, 38 (quotations); George Rollie Adams, *General William S. Harney: Prince of Dragoons* (Lincoln: University of Nebraska Press, 2001), 184–86, 193.
23. Cutler, *"Hang Them All,"* 101–2.
24. Joseph Seltice, *Saga of the Coeur d'Alene Indians: An Account of Chief Joseph Seltice*, ed. Edward J. Kowrach and Thomas E. Connolly (Fairfield:, Wash. Galleon Press, 1990), 98–99; Cutler, *"Hang Them All,"* chap. 8; Elizabeth F. Tannatt, comp., *Indian Battles of the Inland Empire in 1858* (Spokane: Daughters of the American Revolution, 1914); Mahlon E. Kriebel, "Battle of To-Hots-Nim-Me: The U.S. Army vs. the Coeur d'Alene Indians," *Bunchgrass Historian* 34, nos. 2 & 3 (2008), 3–46, esp. 45n1.
25. George Crook, *General George Crook, His Autobiography*, ed. Martin F. Schmitt (Norman: University of Oklahoma Press, 1946), 59–60 ("ascertained"); cf. Thomas W. Prosch, "The Indian War of 1858," *Washington Historical Quarterly* 2, no. 3 (April 1908): 237–40 ("gallant"), https://www.jstor.org/stable/40473913; Frances Fuller Victor (uncredited) and Hubert Howe Bancroft, *History of Washington, Idaho, and Montana* (San Francisco: History Company, 1890), 196 ("surprised").
26. Crook, *General George Crook, His Autobiography*, 61–64; Cutler, *"Hang Them All,"* 177. On Crook's complicated legacy, see Ryan Wayne Booth, "Crossed Arrows: The US Indian Scouts, 1866–1947" (PhD diss., Washington State University, 2021), esp. 7–9, 176. Crook's principal modern biographer tended to presume the best and ignore the worst; see Charles M. Robinson III, *General Crook and the Western Frontier* (Norman: University of Oklahoma Press, 2001), esp. chaps. 2, 8, 15.
27. Robinson, *General Crook and the Western Frontier*, 178–83.
28. Stephen W. Henderson and Michael M. Hamilton, "The Influence of Geology and Geography on the Indian Wars in Eastern Washington Territory," in *Military Geosciences and Desert Warfare*, ed. Eric V. McDonald and Thomas Bullard (New York: Springer, 2016), 67–82; "Value of the New Fire-Arms in Indian Warfare," *New York Times*, November 2, 1858, 8. The cannon in the 1851 clash at Battle Rock, near Port Orford, made a difference in the battle, but ultimately the goals of the Native community (getting the Euro-American invaders to leave) were still achieved. The warship *Decatur* could be considered decisive technology in the 1856 Battle of Seattle, depending on one's interpretation of the aims of the attackers.
29. Dan Webster, "Monumental Struggle: Craig Bickerton's Dying Wish? To Set Record Straight on Battle of Four Lakes," *Spokane Spokesman-Review*, August 13, 2006; Cutler, *"Hang Them All,"* 196.

30. Cutler, *"Hang Them All,"* 192–94; Spokane Tribe and Jim Sijohn, " 'Whist-alks Way—Woman Warriors—Then and Now' sncmsci (woman who goes into battle)," in "Renaming of Ft. George Wright Drive to Whistalks Way," Spokane City Council Agenda packet, December 14, 2020, https://static. spokanecity.org/documents/projects/renaming-fort-george-wright-drive/ renaming-ft-george-wright-drive-whist-alks-way-women-warriors-then-now.pdf.

31. Cutler, *"Hang Them All,"* 202–12, esp. 210, 208 ("human quality," "exult"); David G. Lewis, "Starving the Deschutes Tribe into Submission, 1856," *Quartux Journal* (March 16, 2021), https://ndnhistoryresearch.com/2021/03/ 16/starving-the-deschutes-tribe-into-submission-1856/; Sleeper-Smith, *Indigenous Prosperity and American Conquest;* James Daschuk, *Clearing the Plains: Disease, Politics of Starvation, and the Loss of Aboriginal Life* (Regina, Sask.: University of Regina Press, 2013).

32. Cutler, *"Hang Them All,"* 204. See also Lin Tull Cannell, "William Craig: Governor Stevens's Conduit to the Nez Perce," *Pacific Northwest Quarterly* 97, no. 1 (Winter 2005–6): 19–30, esp. 26–29, https://www.jstor.org/ stable/40491895.

33. Cutler, *"Hang Them All,"* 225–26.

34. Thomas Beall to L. V. McWhorter, December 13, 1916, folder 434, box 45, cage 24, Lucullus Virgil McWhorter Papers.

35. Multiple witnesses recall Whist-alks defiantly driving a beaded lance into the ground, but they disagree about whether this was before Qualchan/ Kwálchin's arrival or just after he was betrayed. The "lance" was probably a medicine eagle feather staff. Cutler, *"Hang Them All,"* chap. 11; Beall to McWhorter, December 13, 1916; Smith, "A Pioneer of the Spokane Country," 272. In a modern-day coda to the story, in December 2020 the city of Spokane changed the name of Fort George Wright Drive to Whist-alks Way. Margo Hill, "No Honor in Genocide: A Case Study of Street Renaming and Community Organizing in the Wake of National Decolonization Efforts," *Journal of Hate Studies* 7, no. 1 (2021): 85–107, esp. 85, https://doi. org/10.33972/jhs.200.

36. Lawrence Kip, *Army Life on the Pacific: A Journal of the Expedition against the Northern Indians, the Tribes of the Coeur d'Alenes, Spokans, and Pelouzes, in the Summer of 1858* (New York: Redfield, 1859), 116–17; cf. Cutler, *"Hang Them All,"* 231–33; Netta W. Phelps, "Dedication of Steptoe Memorial Park," *Washington Historical Quarterly* 2, no. 4 (July 1908): 344–51, https:// www.jstor.org/stable/40473938.

37. [Joseph Henry Brown], 1879 note, folder 8, box 1, Joseph Henry Brown Papers

38. A[ndrew] J[ackson] Splawn, *Ka-mi-akin: Last Hero of the Yakimas,* ed. Margaret C. Splawn (1917; repr., Portland: Binfords & Mort/Oregon Historical Society, 1944) viii, 218, 219, 205 (quotations); Talea Alise Anderson, "A Conflicted History: Margaret Splawn, Yakama Indians, and Native

American Policy Reform, 1910s–1940s" (master's thesis, Central Washington University, 2013), 13–14.

39. William Sidney Shiach and Harrison B. Averill (uncredited), eds., *An Illustrated History of Klickitat, Yakima and Kittitas Counties, with an Outline of the Early History of the State of Washington* ([Chicago]: Interstate, 1904), 565 ("in all the Indian troubles"); Splawn, *Ka-mi-akin*, 272–75 (" 'Old Nick' ").

40. David K. Beine, *Whodunnit? The Continuing Case of Chief Spokane Garry* ([Sacramento]: I Street Press, 2021), 69; Jeffrey Ostler, " 'To Extirpate the Indians': An Indigenous Consciousness of Genocide in the Ohio Valley and the Lower Great Lakes," *William and Mary Quarterly* 72, no. 4 (October 2015): 587–622, esp. 607–8; John Harris, "Hiding the Bodies: The Myth of Humane Colonisation of Aboriginal Australia," *Aboriginal History* 27 (2003): 73–104.

41. Splawn, *Ka-mi-akin*, 278, 272–73; Anderson, "A Conflicted History," 23–25; Ann Fulton, "The Restoration of an Iłkák'mana: A Chief Called Multnomah," *American Indian Quarterly* 31, no. 1 (Winter 2007): 110–28, esp. 116, https://www.jstor.org/stable/4138897.

42. Keith Thor Carlson, "The Lynching of Louie Sam," *BC Studies* 109 (Spring 1996): 63–79, https://doi.org/10.14288/bcs.v0i109.1309.

43. Susan Osterman Alverson, "Wm. H. Osterman," 74, folder 3, box 1, DAR Family Rec. of Wash. Pioneers.

44. Carlson, "The Lynching of Louie Sam," 74 ("I would kill"); Johnnie Kilcup, "First White Settlers in Lynden District," folder 20, box 8, Percival R. Jeffcott Papers; Percival R. Jeffcott, "Billy Clark Stories," 6, folder 23, box 7, Percival R. Jeffcott Papers.

45. Kilcup, "First White Settlers in Lynden District."

46. Pfeifer, *Roots of Rough Justice*, appendix; Michael J. Pfeifer, *Rough Justice: Lynching and American Society, 1874–1947* (Chicago: University of Illinois Press, 2004), 19. On lynching as public spectacle in the South, see Amy Louise Wood, *Lynching and Spectacle: Witnessing Racial Violence in America, 1890–1940* (Chapel Hill: University of North Carolina Press, 2009); Grace Elizabeth Hale, *Making Whiteness: The Culture of Segregation in the South* (New York: Pantheon, 1998), chap. 5.

47. *Oregonian*, August 14, 1852, 2; Elizabeth Laughlin Lord, *Reminiscences of Eastern Oregon* (Portland: Irwin-Hodson, 1903), 163–64, 195; E. L. Bristow [Jr.], E[lijah] L[afayette] Bristow [Jr.], "E. L. Bristow's Narrative," June 13, 1878, 4, folder: E. L. Bristow, box 5, Willamette University and Northwest Collection, WUA014, Willamette University Special Collections; Emma Holm Davis of southeastern Washington state implied something similar in her childhood recollections. See "Paper by Mrs. Emma Holm Davis, Given June 12, 1946," folder 7, box 1, Eloise Thomas Papers.

48. Kurt Kim Schaefer, "The Promise and Price of Contact: Puyallup Indian Acculturation, Federal Indian Policy and the City of Tacoma, 1832–1909" (PhD diss., University of Washington, 2016), esp. 286–94, 289n13; Nathan

Roberts, "The Death of Peter Stanup," *Columbia* 22, no. 3 (2008): 24–31. Cf. George P. Castile, "Edwin Eells, U.S. Indian Agent, 1871–1895," *Pacific Northwest Quarterly* 72, no. 2 (April 1981): 61–68, https://www.jstor.org/stable/40490672.

49. Mattie Gallaway reminiscence, 88, folder 2, box 1, DAR Family Rec. of Pioneers; Julius Charles (Lummi), interview by Howard E. Buswell, April 13, 1943, folder 16, box 5, Howard E. Buswell Papers and Photographs, WWU Center for Pacific Northwest Studies.

50. David Martínez, "Remembering the Thirty-Eight: Abraham Lincoln, the Dakota, and the U.S. War on Barbarism," *Wicazo Sa Review* 28, no. 2 (2013): 5–29, https://doi.org/10.5749/wicazosareview.28.2.0005; Waziyatawin, "Colonial Calibrations: The Expendability of Minnesota's Original People," *William Mitchell Law Review* 39, no. 2 (2013): 450–85; Linda M. Clemmons, *Dakota in Exile: The Untold Stories of Captives in the Aftermath of the U.S.–Dakota War* (Iowa City: University of Iowa Press, 2019).

51. Louie Wapato (Colville), interview by Jeff Wilner (part 2), May 15, 1973, folder 10, box 1, Northwest Tribal Oral History Interviews, WWU Center for Pacific Northwest Studies.

Chapter Seven. The Snake War as a Continuation of the War on Illahee

1. E[lisha] L[indsay] Applegate to James W. Nesmith, October 29, 1861, folder 2, box 1, James W. Nesmith Papers; emphasis in original. Letters proclaiming bounteous land and demanding military intervention (without obvious cause) were not uncommon, nor were they relegated to remote areas. The historian Kurt Kim Schaefer has unpacked an almost identical 1860 letter from Pierce County settlers in the Puyallup region of Washington. Kurt Kim Schaefer, "The Promise and Price of Contact: Puyallup Indian Acculturation, Federal Indian Policy and the City of Tacoma, 1832–1909" (PhD diss., University of Washington, 2016), 147–48.

2. Theodore Stern, "The Klamath Indians and the Treaty of 1864," *Oregon Historical Quarterly* 57, no. 3 (September 1956): 229–73, esp. 247–48, https://www.jstor.org/stable/20612272.

3. Applegate to Nesmith, October 29, 1861.

4. Stern, "The Klamath Indians and the Treaty of 1864," esp. 246; Patience Collier, "The Failure of Reservation Policy in Oregon" (master's thesis, University of Oregon, 2018), 1, 5; Jeff LaLande, " 'Dixie' of the Pacific Northwest: Southern Oregon's Civil War," *Oregon Historical Quarterly* 100, no. 1 (Spring 1999): 32–81, esp. 61, https://www.jstor.org/stable/20614943; K. Keith Richard, "Unwelcome Settlers: Black and Mulatto Oregon Pioneers, Part II," *Oregon Historical Quarterly* 84, no. 2 (Summer 1983): 173–205, esp. 184, https://www.jstor.org/stable/20613905.

5. Applegate to Nesmith, October 29, 1861.

6. Stern, "The Klamath Indians and the Treaty of 1864," 257–58; Collier, "The Failure of Reservation Policy in Oregon."

7. Stern, "The Klamath Indians and the Treaty of 1864," 258 ("given up to the soldiers"); Charles S. Drew, *Official Report of the Owyhee Reconnoissance* (Jacksonville: Oregon Sentinel, 1865), 3–6, 17 ("he and his"); Scott McArthur, *The Enemy Never Came: The Civil War in the Pacific Northwest* (Caldwell, Idaho: Caxton Press, 2012), 126.

8 Frances Fuller Victor (uncredited) and Hubert Howe Bancroft, *History of Oregon*, 2 vols., ed. Matthew P. Deady (uncredited) and Hubert Howe Bancroft (San Francisco: History Company, 1886–88)2:508n35; Merle W. Wells, "Caleb Lyon's Indian Policy," *Pacific Northwest Quarterly* 61, no. 4 (October 1970): 193–200, https://www.jstor.org/stable/40488834; Ralph M. Shane, "Early Explorations through Warm Springs Reservation Area," *Oregon Historical Quarterly* 51, no. 4 (December 1950): 273–309, esp. 290–98, https://www.jstor.org/stable/20611996; David H. Wilson Jr., *Northern Paiutes of the Malheur: High Desert Reckoning in Oregon Country* (Lincoln: University of Nebraska Press, 2022), 33–34; Donna Clark and Keith Clark, "William McKay's Journal, 1866–67: Indian Scouts, Part I," *Oregon Historical Quarterly* 79, no. 2 (Summer 1978): 121–71, esp. 128–31; Simone Smith, "Governor George L. Woods: 'The Exterminator' Governor," in "Northern Paiute History Project Paper Collection 2014," by Soo Hwang et al. (Eugene: University of Oregon Honors College, 2014), 96–118. One way historians might resolve disagreements about the beginnings and endings of the Snake War would be to divide the conflict into multiple Snake Wars.

9. Gregory Michno, *The Deadliest Indian War in the West: The Snake Conflict, 1864–1868* (Caldwell, Idaho: Caxton Press, 2007); Wilson, *Northern Paiutes of the Malheur*, chap. 7; James Robbins Jewell, *Agents of Empire: The First Oregon Cavalry and the Opening of the Interior Pacific Northwest during the Civil War* (Lincoln: University of Nebraska, 2023), xxii, xxiv, 271 (quotations).

10. Kass Fleisher, *Bear River Massacre and the Making of History* (New York: SUNY Press, 2012), esp. 59–64; Harold Schindler, "The Bear River Massacre: New Historical Evidence," *Utah Historical Quarterly* 67, no. 4 (Fall 1999): 300–308, https://doi.org/10.2307/45062576; and esp. Darren Parry, *The Bear River Massacre: A Shoshone History* (Salt Lake City: By Common Consent Press, 2019), chaps. 3, 4.

11. Michno, *Deadliest Indian War in the West*, chap. 3; Jewell, *Agents of Empire*, 104.

12. J[ohn] W. Hopkins to John M. Drake, May 22, 1863 (the *"Bloody Snakes"*), folder 1, box 1, John Miller Drake Papers, Mss 80, Oregon Historical Society Special Collections; "Snake Hunter," "Letter from Fort Hall," August 23 1863, in *On Duty in the Pacific Northwest during the Civil War: Correspondence and Reminiscences of the First Oregon Cavalry Regiment*, ed. James Robbins Jewell (Knoxville: University of Tennessee Press, 2018), 71–73 ("If the boys").

13. Susan Gregg Walton (Mrs. C. W. Walton), "Wagon Days with Mother Walton," ca. 1931, 325–26, folder 7, box 1, DAR Family Rec. of Wash. Pioneers; John D. Unruh Jr., *The Plains Across: The Overland Emigrants and the Trans-Mississippi West, 1840–60* (1979; repr., Urbana: University of Illinois Press, 1993), 186–89.

14. Walton, "Wagon Days with Mother Walton," 325–26.

15. Walton, "Wagon Days with Mother Walton," 325–26.

16. Cf. Unruh, *Plains Across*, 187, 458n160; Justin Smith, "The Massacre That Never Happened," *Idaho State Journal*, February 7, 2020; Donald H. Shannon, *Massacre Rocks and City of Rocks: 1862 Attacks on Emigrant Trains* (Caldwell, Idaho: Snake Country, 2008), esp. chap. 7.

17. W. W. Stevens, "The Old Oregon Trail as Told by the Trailers" ca. 1913, chap. 6, Baker County Library Archive; Benjamin Madley, *An American Genocide: The United States and the California Indian Catastrophe* (New Haven: Yale University Press, 2016), esp. 139.

18. Stevens, "Old Oregon Trail as Told by the Trailers." George Freeman's descendants reported that he had also been involved in the Rogue River conflicts—it remains unclear whether this was the case. Pearl Jones, "George Freeman," *Baker City Herald*, April 24, 2006 (updated October 2, 2019).

19. Michno, *Deadliest Indian War in the West*, 34–38; Captain John M. Drake, "Private Journal," Priscilla K. Knuth, annotator, 17, folder 4, box 1, John Miller Drake Papers. The version of John M. Drake's journal annotated by Priscilla K. Knuth includes accurate transcriptions of both the original and the edited 1905 versions.

20. "John M. Drake Called," *Oregonian*, December 14, 1913, 10; Drake, "Private Journal," Knuth, annotator, I; "Accessions," *Oregon Historical Quarterly* 45, no. 4 (December 1944): 386, https://www.jstor.org/stable/20611589.

21. Drake, "Private Journal," Knuth, annotator, 66–67 (quotation); Jewell, *Agents of Empire*, xxii–xxiii.

22. Drake, "Private Journal," Knuth, annotator, 6 ("the citizen volunteers"); J. M. Drake (age eleven), "Composition for Stroudsburg, Pa. Academy," 1841 ("his hunt"), folder 10, box 1, John Miller Drake Papers.

23. Drake, "Private Journal," Knuth, annotator, 15; Jewell, *On Duty in the Pacific Northwest*, 89; George W. Aguilar Sr., *When the River Ran Wild! Indian Traditions on the Mid-Columbia and the Warm Springs Reservation* (Portland: Oregon Historical Society Press, 2005), 194–96, 209–11; Colonel William Thompson, *Reminiscences of a Pioneer* (San Francisco: Alturas Plain Dealer, 1912), 52; Carson C. Masiker, "Stock Whitley and Kloshe Nesika Illahee," *Oregon Native Son*, 2 vols. (Portland, Ore.: Native Son, 1899–1901), 2:427; John W. Hopkins to John M. Drake, March 24, 1864 ("bright red scarfs"), folder 6, box 1, John Miller Drake Papers; Lewis A. McArthur, "Reminiscences of John Y. Todd," *Oregon Historical Quarterly* 30, no. 1 (March 1929): 70–73, https://www.jstor.org/stable/20610451; J. W. Reese, "OMV's Fort Henrietta: On Winter Duty, 1855–1856," *Oregon Historical Quarterly*

66, no. 2 (June 1965): 132–60, https://www.jstor.org/stable/20612857; Kimi Lerner, "A History of Racism and Prejudice: The Untold Story of the Northern Paiute," in "Northern Paiute History Project Paper Collection 2014," by Soo Hwang et al., 31–60, esp. 43 ("the substitution"); Clara Gorman, "Inter-Tribal Dynamics of the Warm Springs and Grand Ronde Reservations: A Historical Legacy of Discrimination, Prejudice, and Settler-Colonialism" (undergraduate honor's thesis, University of Oregon, 2018), esp. 76.

24. Drake, "Private Journal," Knuth, annotator, 7; Ron McFarland, "Frontier Soldier," *Columbia* 31, no. 2 (2017): 20–27; Lulu Crandall, "Autobiography," n.d., folder 5, box 1, Lulu Donnell Crandall Papers.

25. Drake, "Private Journal," Knuth, annotator, 16, 23.

26. Drake, "Private Journal," Knuth, annotator, 28. On "little thing" vs. "little creature," see L. T. Meade [Elizabeth Thomasina Meade Smith], *Deb and the Duchess: A Story for Boys and Girls* (New York: W. L. Allison, [189?]), 31, 379; Elizabeth Stuart Phelps, *Loveliness: A Story* (Boston: Houghton, Mifflin, 1900), 27, 3; Mary Hazelton Wade, *Our Little Brown Cousin* (Boston: L. C. Page, 1901), 26–27; Pansy [Mrs. G. R. Alden], *Mag & Margaret: A Story for Girls* (Boston: Lothrop, 1901), 50, 140.

27. Drake, "Private Journal," Knuth, annotator, 29; Donald H. Clark, "Remember the Winter of ___? Weather and Pioneers," *Oregon Historical Quarterly* 54, no. 2 (June 1953): 140–48, esp. 145, https://www.jstor.org/stable/20612100; Rosemary Stremlau, "Rape Narratives on the Northern Paiute Frontier: Sarah Winnemucca, Sexual Sovereignty, and Economic Autonomy, 1844–1891," in *Portraits of Women in the American West*, ed. Dee Garceau-Hagen (New York: Routledge, 2005), 37–62; Frederick E. Hoxie, *This Indian Country: American Indian Political Activists and the Place They Made* (New York: Penguin, 2012), chap. 4; Jennifer Bailey, "Voicing Oppositional Conformity: Sarah Winnemucca and the Politics of Rape, Colonialism, and 'Citizenship': 1870–1890" (master's thesis, Portland State University, 2012), esp. chap 3. Some records suggest that the Warm Springs scouts attempted to moderate the Euro-American soldiers' behavior, worried that attacks on noncombatants would spur reciprocal violence. See Clark and Clark, "William McKay's Journal, 1866–67," esp. 130. Others suggest that the Warm Springs fighters, like many of the Euro-American volunteers, "went out there to kill babies, old people, women." Quotation from Myra Johnson-Orange, in Lerner, "A History of Racism and Prejudice," 44. Both reticence and determination in the killing of noncombatants may well be true, reflecting different people or periods of the wars.

28. Drake, "Private Journal," Knuth, annotator, 45 ("[Nathan] Olney"); R. F. Maury to John M. Drake, April 23, 1864 ("the citizens"), folder 6, box 1, John Miller Drake Papers; R. F. Maury to John W. Hopkins, ca. April 1864 ("to remedy both evils"), folder 6, box 1, John Miller Drake Papers.

29. Capt. John Mullan, *Report on the Construction of a Military Road from Fort Walla-Walla to Fort Benton* (Washington, D.C.: Government Printing Office, 1863), 52.

30. Ralph Fisk, "Ralph Fisk Relates Some Pioneer History: Came to Canyon with Father in 1864," *Blue Mountain Eagle*, March 17, 1922; Sarah Winnemucca Hopkins, *Life among the Piutes: Their Wrongs and Claims*, ed. Mrs. Horace [Mary Tyler Peabody] Mann (Boston: Cupples, Upham, 1883), 177.

31. *Oregon Sentinel*, September 17, 1879; George N. Belknap, "Oregon Miscellany," *Papers of the Bibliographical Society of America* 57, no. 2 (1963): 191–200, esp. 199–200, https://www.jstor.org/stable/24300879; Benjamin Franklin Dowell to Nathan Olney, February 21, 1865, folder 1, box 1, Benjamin Franklin Dowell Papers, Ax 031, University of Oregon Special Collections; Nathan Olney to George Curry, October 12, 1855, in Roscoe Sheller, *The Name Was Olney* (1965; repr., Astoria, Ore.: S Dot S, 1993), 79–80 (quotations).

32. Cutler, *"Hang Them All,"* 77–81.

33. Carson C. Masiker, "Reminescences [*sic*] [of] Early Settlers on Fifteen Mile Creek," 1911, 4 (*"the more the flag"*; emphasis in original), folder 23, box 4, Lulu Donnell Crandall Papers; Cyrus A. Reed, "Adjutant's Report for 1868," in *Biennial Report of the Secretary of State of the State of Oregon* (Salem: William A. McPherson, 1870), 20; Sidney Teiser, "Cyrus Olney, Associate Justice of Oregon Territory Supreme Court," *Oregon Historical Quarterly* 64, no. 4 (December 1963): 308–22, esp. 317, https://www.jstor.org/stable/20612764; Ronald Todd, "Reader's Scrapbook," *Pacific Northwest Quarterly* 47, no. 3 (July 1956): 95–96, https://www.jstor.org/stable/40487200.

34. Loren L. Williams, "General Orders No 7: Troops to Be Ready to Pursue Hostile Indians +c +c +c," Camp Wright Oregon, October 5, 1865, Loren L. Williams Journals, vol. 3, between 85 ½ and 86. Other military men of the period also killed despite "certificates of good character." See Ari Kelman, *A Misplaced Massacre: Struggling over the Memory of Sand Creek* (Cambridge: Harvard University Press, 2013), esp. 35–36.

35. Williams, "General Orders No. 7: Troops to Be Ready to Pursue Hostile Indians" ("exhaust every means"; emphasis mine); Loren L. Williams Journals, 3:60 ("mistaken policy"). His use of the term (and, typically, slur) *digger* was meant to encompass nearly all Native people in the far West.

36. Capt. George B. Currey had killed at least four Native fishermen (probably Northern Paiute/Numu) along the Malheur River the previous summer, in 1864. Jewell, *On Duty in the Pacific Northwest*, 92; Loren L. Williams Journals, 3:83 ½; Loren L. Williams to his nephew, July 22, 1876, Loren L. Williams Journals, vol. 4, attached to frontispiece.

37. Victor and Bancroft, *History of Oregon*, 2:514; Michno, *Deadliest Indian War in the West*, chap. 12.

38. Loren L. Williams Journals, 3:71 ½.

39. Loren L. Williams Journals, 3:71 ½.

40. Loren L. Williams Journals, 3:71 ½.

41. Loren L. Williams Journals, 3:70 ½, 78–78 ½; Loren L. Williams Journals, 1:75.
42. William D. Stillwell to Conrad C. Walker, January 21, 1915 ("My gun"), folder 20, box 1, Oregon Military Collection MSS; Harvey Robbins, "Journal of Rogue River War, 1855," *Oregon Historical Quarterly* 34, no. 4 (December 1933): 345–58, esp. 353 ("certain they killed some"), https://www.jstor.org/stable/20610833; T. C. Elliott, "Steptoe Butte and Steptoe Battle-Field," *Washington Historical Quarterly* 18, no. 4 (October 1927): 243–53, esp. 252 ("twelve dead"), https://www.jstor.org/stable/40475154.
43. Loren L. Williams to "C<u>mdg</u> Officer, Dept of Columbia, Ft Vancouver," November 13, 1865 (emphases in original), Loren L. Williams Journals, vol. 3, between 94 ½ and 95.
44. Michno, *Deadliest Indian War in the West*, chap. 13; Wilson, *Northern Paiutes of the Malheur*, chap. 8.
45. Frances Fuller Victor, "The First Oregon Cavalry," *Quarterly of the Oregon Historical Society* 3, no. 2 (June 1902): 123–63, https://www.jstor.org/stable/20609527; Jewell, *On Duty in the Pacific Northwest*, xv—xx; "Veterans Association First Oregon Cavalry and Infantry Volunteers, Roster 1907," folder 7, box 42, Associations Collection, Mss 1511, Oregon Historical Society Special Collections (hereafter cited as Associations Collection MSS); Stacey L. Smith, "Oregon's Civil War: The Troubled Legacy of Emancipation in the Pacific Northwest," *Oregon Historical Quarterly* 115, no. 2 (Summer 2014): 154–73, https://doi.org/10.5403/oregonhistq.115.2.0154; Scott McArthur titled his book on the early 1860s Northwest *The Enemy Never Came*, to reflect the perceived lack of a Confederate enemy rather than the brutal war on Native peoples that typified military actions in the Far West during the Civil War. Like Michno, McArthur mirrors the focus as well as the racism of many of the sources he uncritically draws on. McArthur, *The Enemy Never Came*, esp. 133.

Chapter Eight. Settler Colonial Sin-Eaters and the Isolation of Atrocity

1. Thomas J. Cram, *Topographical Memoir and Report of Captain T. J. Cram, on Territories of Oregon and Washington*, H.R. Exec. Doc. no. 114, 35th Cong., 2nd sess. (1859), 2–3, 40 (quotations); Donald L. Cutler, *"Hang Them All": George Wright and the Plateau Indian War* (Norman: University of Oklahoma Press, 2016), 73–77; Judkin Browning and Timothy Silver, "Nature and Human Nature: Environmental Influences on the Union's Failed Peninsula Campaign, 1862," *Journal of the Civil War Era* 8, no. 3 (September 2018): 388–415, https://www.jstor.org/stable/26483633; John W. Larson, *Those Army Engineers: A History of the Chicago District U.S. Army Corps of Engineers* (Chicago: U.S. Army Corps of Engineers, 1979), 49–53.

2. Cram, *Topographical Memoir and Report*, 86. Cf. Kent D. Richards, *Isaac I. Stevens: Young Man in a Hurry* (Provo, Utah: Brigham Young University Press, 1979), 336.

3. Cram, *Topographical Memoir and Report*, 34–46, esp. 34 ("smart successful"), 40 ("infernal acts"), 43 ("gallant general," "notorious," "just retribution"), 98 ("sends an armed force").

4. Cram, *Topographical Memoir and Report*, 36 ("another less fortunate"), 64 (cannibalism), 123 ("the practice"), 122 ("bad citizens"), 63 ("orderly"); Thomas J. Cram, *Memoir Upon the Northern Inter-Oceanic Route of Commercial Transit, between the Tide Water of Puget Sound of the Pacific, and, Tide Water on the St. Lawrence Gulf of the Atlantic Ocean* (Detroit: Detroit Board of Trade, [1869?]), 7 ("cupidity"), 5 ("Northwest," "at least twenty millions").

5. Cram, *Topographical Memoir and Report*, 2–3, 1 (quotations); William P. MacKinnon, "Epilogue to the Utah War: Impact and Legacy," *Journal of Mormon History* 29, no. 2 (2003): 186–248, esp. 193–94; Edwin C. Bearss, "Unconditional Surrender: The Fall of Fort Donelson, Part I," *Tennessee Historical Quarterly* 21, no. 2 (1962): 47–65.

6. Elwood Evans to Col. Haller, May 6, 1893, folder 11, box 1, Granville O. Haller Papers. See also James Belich, *Replenishing the Earth: The Settler Revolution and the Rise of the Anglo-World, 1783–1939* (New York: Oxford University Press, 2009).

7. Jane Levi, "Melancholy and Mourning: Black Banquets and Funerary Feasts," *Gastronomica* 12, no. 4 (Winter 2012): 96–103, https://doi.org/10.1525/GFC.2012.12.4.96; Candi K. Cann, "Starters: The Role of Food in Bereavement and Memorialization," in *Dying to Eat: Cross-Cultural Perspectives on Food, Death, and the Afterlife*, ed. Candi K. Cann (Lexington: University Press of Kentucky, 2018), 3; August Grove Bell, *Circling Windrock Mountain: Two Hundred Years in Appalachia* (Knoxville: University of Tennessee Press, 1998), 176; Marc James Carpenter, "Settler Colonial Sin-Eaters: Disavowal of Atrocity and Its Uses, In and Beyond the Late 1800s American Pacific Northwest," *Settler Colonial Studies* (December 2024): 1–14, https://doi.org/10.1080/2201473X.2024.2447152.

8. On the uses and transformations of settler memory and settler guilt, see among many others Rebecca Weaver-Hightower, *Frontier Fictions: Settler Sagas and Postcolonial Guilt* (New York: Palgrave Macmillan, 2018); Lorenzo Veracini, "Settler Collective, Founding Violence and Disavowal: The Settler Colonial Situation," *Journal of Intercultural Studies* 29, no. 4 (Fall 2008): 363–79, esp. 370, https://doi.org/10.1080/07256860802372246; Eve Tuck and K. Wayne Yang, "Decolonization Is Not a Metaphor," *Decolonization: Indigeneity, Education & Society* 1, no. 1 (Fall 2012): 1–40, https://jps.library.utoronto.ca/index.php/des/article/view/18630; Kelly Lytle Hernández, *City of Inmates: Conquest, Rebellion, and the Rise of Human Caging in Los Angeles, 1771–1965* (Chapel Hill: University of North Carolina Press, 2017), 177–180.

9. George H. Ambrose to Joseph Lane, June 3, 1856, https://truwe.sohs.org/files/jolaneletters.html.

10. William Lair Hill, "Annual Address of Hon. W. Lair Hill," in *Transactions of the Eleventh Annual Re-Union of the Oregon Pioneer Association* (Salem: E. M. Waite, 1884), 10–21, quotation on 14.

11. Herbert O. Lang, *History of the Willamette Valley: Being a Description of the Valley and Its Resources, with an Account of Its Discovery and Settlement by White Men, and Its Subsequent History* (Portland, Ore.: Himes and Lang, 1885), i (quotations); Minnie Roof Dee, *From Oxcart to Airplane: A Biography of George H. Himes* (Portland: Binfords and Mort, 1939), 107; Herbert O. Lang [uncredited] and A.G. Walling, *History of Southern Oregon, Comprising Jackson, Josephine, Douglas, Curry and Coos Counties* (Portland: Walling, 1884), esp. 242.

12. Lang, *History of the Willamette Valley,* 366–67.

13. Lang, *History of the Willamette Valley,* 188, 229, 139 (quotations). The "rogues and honest men" Lang adopted from British Hudson's Bay Company factor John McLoughlin.

14. Lang, *History of the Willamette Valley,* 266, 231, 306–8, 367–68.

15. Lang, *History of the Willamette Valley,* 456.

16. Lang, *History of the Willamette Valley,* 372–73.

17. Lang, *History of the Willamette Valley,* 373.

18. Lang, *History of the Willamette Valley,* 373–74.

19. Lang, *History of the Willamette Valley,* esp. 375.

20. Dee, *From Oxcart to Airplane.*

21. Ricardo D. Salvatore, "Progress and Backwardness in Book Accumulation: Bancroft, Basadre, and Their Libraries," *Comparative Studies in Society and History* 56, no. 4 (October 2014): 995–1026, esp. 1009–10, https://www.jstor.org/stable/43908322; Harry Clark, *A Venture in History: The Production, Publication, and Sale of the* Works of Hubert Howe Bancroft (Berkeley: University of California Press, 1973), chap. 3; Victor and Bancroft, *History of Oregon,* 2:379, 373 ("The fate"); Frances Fuller Victor, "The Oregon Indians, Part I," *Overland Monthly* 7, no. 4 (October 1871): 344–52, esp. 348 ("Decidedly," "savage wars").

22. Victor and Bancroft, *History of Oregon,* 2:385, 372.

23. Richard White, "The Gold Rush: Consequences and Contingencies," *California History* 77, no. 1 (Spring 1998): 42–55, esp. 44 ("was a man"), https://doi.org/10.2307/25462461; Albert L. Hurtado, "Professors and Tycoons: The Creation of Great Research Libraries in the American West," *Western Historical Quarterly* 41, no. 2 (Summer 2010): 149–69, https://doi.org/10.2307/westhistquar.41.2.0149; Homer Jenne to "Leno at Home," n.d. ("subscription part"), folder 1, box 1, Homer Jenne Papers, cage 4961, Washington State University Libraries Special Collections (hereafter cited as Homer Jenne Letters); Clark, *Venture in History,* 61–68.

24. John C. Ainsworth, "Autobiography," October 20, 1889, 125–27 ("large sum," "determination"), folder 4, box 1, John C. Ainsworth Papers, Coll.

250, University of Oregon Special Collections; Clark, *Venture in History;* Jesse Applegate to Elwood Evans, October 18, 1867, folder 1, Elwood Evans Papers, Mss 603, Oregon Historical Society; Alice Bay Moloney, "The Distressingly Virtuous Isaac: Biographical Notes on Isaac Cox, Author of 'The Annals of Trinity County,' " *California Historical Quarterly* 21, no. 2 (June 1942): 127–40.

25. R. E. Gosnell to Eva Emery Dye, October 31, 1903 ("remain closed"), folder 12, box 1, Eva Emery Dye Papers; Clark, *Venture in History,* 16 ("as safe as possible"), 121–42.

26. Victor and Bancroft, *History of Oregon,* 2:636.

27. W. J. Martin, "The Expedition to Fight the Emigrants," *Umpqua Weekly Gazette,* August 9, 1855, 1; Franklyn Daniel Mahar, "Benjamin Franklin Dowell, 1826–1897: Claims Attorney and Newspaper Publisher in Southern Oregon" (master's thesis, University of Oregon, 1964), 5–6, 58–64.

28. "Benjamin Franklin Dowell Narrative: Jacksonville, Oregon, 1878" (quotations), BANC MSS P-A 26, Hubert Howe Bancroft Collection, Bancroft Library Special Collections, University of California, Berkeley. Cf. George H. Parker, "Short History of Josephine County," March 1922, George R. Riddle Papers; Benjamin Franklin Dowell to Samuel F. Dowell, January 31, 1856, folder 1, box 1, Benjamin Franklin Dowell Papers; Gray H. Whaley, *Oregon and the Collapse of* Illahee*: U.S. Empire and the Transformation of an Indigenous World, 1792–1859* (Chapel Hill: University of North Carolina Press, 2010), 200–201.

29. Benjamin Franklin Dowell, "Letter from B. F. Dowell," *Oregon Sentinel,* December 5, 1868, 1 ("not only free in name"); Benjamin Franklin Dowell, "Letter from B. F. Dowell," *Oregon Sentinel,* February 20, 1869, 1 ("savages").

30. Jesse Applegate, "A Day with the Cow Column in 1843," *Quarterly of the Oregon Historical Society* 1, no. 4 (December 1900): 371–83, esp. 377 (quotations), https://www.jstor.org/stable/20609477.

31. Jesse Applegate, "Notes upon Oregon History," 18, folder: Jesse A. Applegate, box 5, Willamette University and Northwest Collection.

32. Jesse Applegate to Joseph Henry Brown, ca. late 1870s ("Oregon"), folder 3, box 1, Joseph Henry Brown Papers; Applegate, "A Day with the Cow Column in 1843," esp. 377; Unruh, *Plains Across,* 5.

33. Granville O. Haller, *The Dismissal of Major Granville O. Haller of the Regular Army . . . and a Few Observations* (Paterson, N.J.: Daily Guardian, 1863); Austin Mires, "Remarks on the Constitution of the State of Washington," *Washington Historical Quarterly* 22, no. 4 (October 1931): 276–88, esp. 278, https://www.jstor.org/stable/40475451.

34. Granville O. Haller, "The Indian War of 1855–6, in Washington and Oregon," n.d., folder 5, box 2, Granville O. Haller Papers.

35. Haller, "The Indian War of 1855–6."

36. Haller, "The Indian War of 1855–6."

37. Granville O. Haller to Eva Emery Dye, September 19, 1893, folder 13, box 1, Eva Emery Dye Papers. The passage on the "baneful presence of the whites" came from Haller's description of Kamiakin/K'amáyak̲ịn, but it could reasonably be extended to the broader sweep of his work.

38. Haller, *The Dismissal of Granville O. Haller*; Granville O. Haller, *Granville O. Haller, San Juan and Secession: Possible Relation to the War of the Rebellion* (Tacoma: R. L. McCormick, [1896?]); Granville O. Haller to Eva Emery Dye, June 24, 1894 ("yielded up"), folder 13, box 1, Eva Emery Dye Papers.

39. Haller to Dye, June 24, 1894; emphasis in original.

Chapter Nine. Indian War Veterans and the Battle for Northwest History

1. "Address of Hon. Francis Henry," 1884, 31, Washington Pioneer Association Transactions, 1883–89, box 30, Center for Pacific Northwest Studies, WWU Center for Pacific Northwest Studies; emphasis mine. Elements of this chapter appeared in an earlier form in Marc James Carpenter, "Pioneer Problems: 'Wanton Murder,' Indian War Veterans, and Oregon's Violent History," *Oregon Historical Quarterly* 121, no. 2 (2020): 156–85, https://doi.org/10.5403/oregonhistq.121.2.0156.

2. "Address of Hon. Francis Henry," 31; "Address of Hon. Elwood Evans," 1885," Washington Pioneer Association Transactions, 1883–89, 50; Kerwin Lee Klein, *Frontiers of Historical Imagination: Narrating the European Conquest of Native America* (Berkeley: University of California Press, 1997), 78–88.

3. Edmond S. Meany, "The Pioneer Association of the State of Washington," *Washington Historical Quarterly* 8, no. 1 (January 1917): 3–6, https://www.jstor.org/stable/40474417.

4. [Address of Orange Jacobs], Washington Pioneer Association Transactions, 1883–89, 118. On the use of wolf metaphors to justify genocide, see Karl Jacoby, "'The Broad Platform of Extermination': Nature and Violence in the Nineteenth Century North American Borderlands," *Journal of Genocide Research* 10, no. 2 (Summer 2008): 249–67, https://doi.org/10.1080/1462 3520802075205.

5. [Address of Orange Jacobs], 118.

6. James W. Nesmith, "The Occasional Address of Hon. J. W. Nesmith," *Transactions of the Third Annual Re-Union of the Oregon Pioneer Association* (Salem: E. M. Waite, 1876), 42–62, esp. 51, 55 (quotations). Before it was related metaphorically to discovery or innovation, the word *pioneer* was derived from French and had the meaning of "a soldier going in advance of an army," as Elwood Evans claimed. C. T. Onions, ed., *The Oxford Dictionary of English Etymology* (1966; repr., Oxford: Oxford University Press, 1994), 682.

7. John D. Unruh Jr., *The Plains Across: The Overland Emigrants and the Trans-Mississippi West, 1840–60* (1979; repr., Urbana: University of Illinois Press,

1993),383–85, esp. 383 (quotation); Lindsey Peterson, "The Expansionist Cause: Union Civil War Commemorations as Weapons of Colonization in the American West" (PhD diss., University of Southern Mississippi, 2022), esp. 60–61, 101, 160.

8. William Lair Hill, "Annual Address of Hon. W. Lair Hill," in *Transactions of the Eleventh Annual Re-Union of the Oregon Pioneer Association* (Salem: E. M. Waite, 1884).

9. *Constitution and By-Laws of the Indian War Veterans of the North Pacific Coast,* 1885, folder 2, box 1, IWV-NPC Records.

10. Richard Slotkin, *Regeneration through Violence: The Mythology of the American Frontier, 1600–1860* (Norman: University of Oklahoma Press, 1973), 76–77; C[harles] S[tewart] Drew, "Communication from C. S. Drew, Late Adjutant of the Second Regiment of Oregon Mounted Volunteers, Giving an Account of the Origin and Early Prosecution of the Indian War in Oregon" (Washington, D.C.: Government Printing Office, 1860), 17, 20 (quotations); cf. Charles S. Drew to Quartermaster General, December 30, 1854, in *Protection Afforded by Volunteers of Oregon and Washington Territories to Overland Immigrants in 1854: Papers Transmitted by the Secretary of the Oregon Territory* (Washington, D.C.: House of Representatives, 35th Cong., 2nd sess., Misc. Doc. no. 47, 1859).

11. Drew, "Communication from C. S. Drew," 29, 7.

12. Drew, "Communication from C. S. Drew," 36.

13. Drew, "Communication from C. S. Drew," 48. See also "Resolution," May 31, 1856, folder 36, box 1, series 2, Oregon Methodist Episcopal Church Administrative Records, 1851–1945, WUA035, Willamette University Special Collections.

14. *Constitution and By-Laws of the Indian War Veterans of the North Pacific Coast,* 1885 ("true history"); "Records of the Annual Encampments: 1885–1933," 282, folder 3, box 1, IWV-NPC Records.

15. "Records of the Annual Encampments: 1885–1933," 5, 76; Peter Boag, *Pioneering Death: The Violence of Boyhood in Turn-of-the-Century Oregon* (Seattle: University of Washington Press, 2022), chap. 8.

16. "Records of the Annual Encampments: 1885–1933," 5, 12–13, 219; John F. Winters application to the Oregon Soldiers' Home, January 29, 1899, folder: "Oregon Soldiers Home Applications: 1898–1933; Wilson—Withrow," box 29, Oregon Soldiers Home Applications; "Records of the Annual Encampments: 1937–1941," 11–12, folder 4, box 1, IWV-NPC Records; Harvey Kimball Hines, *An Illustrated History of the State of Oregon* (Chicago: Lewis, 1893), 768–69, 909–11; Leslie M. Scott, comp., *History of the Oregon Country by Harvey W. Scott, Fifty Years the Editor of the Morning Oregonian,* 6 vols. (Cambridge, Mass.: Riverside Press, 1924), 38–43.

17. "Records of the Annual Encampments: 1885–1933," 7, 11; Lang, *History of the Willamette Valley,* 231.

18. "Records of the Annual Encampments: 1885–1933," 97 ("loose and incorrect"), 109; "Umpqua Camp Minutes, 1885–1896," 13 ("true history"), IWV-NPC Records.

19. "Records of the Annual Encampments: 1885–1933," esp. 94 ("dreaded," "demons"), 7 ("extreme statements"), 6, 25, 27. Many of the supporters and perpetrators of horrific violence discussed elsewhere in this book (including John D. Biles, William Stillwell, and Waman C. Hembree) were also members—as was Dr. William McKay.

20. "Sons + Daughters of Indian War Veterans of the North Pacific Coast Minutes, 1908–1936," June 17, 1936, folder 9, box 2, IWV-NPC Records; Thomas B. Wait to LaFayette Mosher, July 9, 1886, folder 5, box 2, IWV-NPC Records; LaFayette Mosher to U[rban] E. Hicks and Jennings [?] Smith, July 16, 1886, folder 5, box 2, IWV-NPC Records; Wolfgang Mieder, " 'The Only Good Indian Is a Dead Indian': History and Meaning of a Proverbial Stereotype," *Journal of American Folklore* 106, no. 419 (Winter 1993): 38–60, https://doi.org/10.2307/541345.

21. "Records of the Annual Encampments: 1885–1933," 22; Virgil F. Field, *The Official History of the Washington National Guard*, vol. 2, *Washington Territorial Militia and the Indian Wars of 1855–56* (Tacoma: Washington National Guard State Historical Society, 1962), 88; Oliver Cromwell Applegate to Eva Emery Day, April 8, 1927, folder 4, box 1, Eva Emery Dye Papers; Elwood Evans et al., *History of the Pacific Northwest: Oregon and Washington*, 2 vols. (Portland: North Pacific History, 1889), 1:434 (quotations); cf. John MacEachern, "Elwood Evans, Lawyer-Historian," *Pacific Northwest Quarterly* 52, no. 1 (January 1961): 15–23, https://www.jstor.org/stable/40487548.

22. Evans et al., *History of the Pacific Northwest*, 1:529, 446, 405.

23. Evans et al., *History of the Pacific Northwest*, 1:528.

24. Evans et al., *History of the Pacific Northwest*, 1:529; Elwood Evans, "Puget Sound: Its Past Present and Future" (address at Port Townsend, W.T.) (Olympia, 1869), 17.

25. "Benjamin Franklin Dowell Narrative: Jacksonville, Oregon, 1878," BANC MSS P-A 26, Hubert Howe Bancroft Collection, Bancroft Library Special Collections, University of California, Berkeley. Cf. George H. Parker, "Short History of Josephine County," March 1922, George R. Riddle Papers; Benjamin Franklin Dowell to Samuel F. Dowell, January 31, 1856, folder 1, box 1, Benjamin Franklin Dowell Papers; Evans et al., *History of the Pacific Northwest*, 2:frontispiece, 306 (quotations).

26. Evans to Haller, May 6, 1893.

27. Evans to Haller, May 6, 1893.

28. Evans to Haller, May 6, 1893; emphasis in original.

29. Abbi Wonacott, *Where the Mashel Meets the Nisqually: The Mashel Massacre of 1856* (Spanaway, Wash.: Bellus Uccello, 2008); Richard Kluger, *The Bitter Waters of Medicine Creek: A Tragic Clash between White and Native America*

(New York: Knopf, 2011), 160–65; Elwood Evans, "Response to John Wickersham's 'The Indian Side of the Puget Sound Indian War,' Address Given to the Washington State Historical Society" (Washington State Historical Society, October 9 1893); Henry Sicade, "The Indians' Side of the Story," address to the Research Club of Tacoma, April 10, 1917, in *Building a State, Washington: 1889–1939*, ed. Charles Miles and O. B. Sperlin (Olympia: Washington State Historical Society, 1940): 490–503; Clarence Bagley to A. N. Brown, August 2, 1906 ("the terror"), folder 15, box 13, Clarence B. Bagley Papers; Elwood Evans to "Dearest Colonel" [Granville O. Haller], May 7, 1893 ("the *people*"; emphasis in original), folder 11, box 1, Granville O. Haller Papers; Evans sometimes posed as a supporter of Native rights to achieve his goals; see Kurt Kim Schaefer, "The Promise and Price of Contact: Puyallup Indian Acculturation, Federal Indian Policy and the City of Tacoma, 1832–1909" (PhD diss., University of Washington, 2016), 257.

30. *Oregon Laws: Showing All the Laws of a General Nature in Force in the State of Oregon*, 2 vols., ed. Conrad Patrick Olson (San Francisco: Bancroft-Whitney, 1920), 2:3482–83. By 1903, the muster rolls in Victor's book had become the de facto standard to prove eligibility for state monies set aside for veterans of Indian wars, although the law had not changed; see Andrew J. Miner Indian War Claim, June 23, 1903, folder 25, box 29, Oregon Soldiers Home Applications.

31. Frances Fuller Victor, *The Early Indian Wars of Oregon* (Salem: Frank C. Baker, 1894), 343 ("went out"; "savages"), iv; Margaret D. Jacobs, "Getting Out of a Rut: Decolonizing Western Women's History," *Pacific Historical Review* 79, no. 4 (November 2010): 585–604, esp. 585 ("triumphalist"), https://doi.org/10.1525/phr.2010.79.4.585. Cf. Sheri Bartlett Browne, " 'What Shall Be Done with Her?' Frances Fuller Victor Analyzes 'The Woman Question' in Oregon," *Oregon Historical Quarterly* 113, no. 3 (Fall 2012): 286–311, esp. 286, 294, 310n16, https://doi.org/10.5403/oregonhistq.113.3.0286; Jim Martin, *A Bit of a Blue: The Life and Work of Frances Fuller Victor* (Salem, Ore.: Deep Well, 1992), 183–84; Janet Floyd, " 'Our Present Work Will Be All Doors': Writers and Periodical Culture in 1860s San Francisco," *Journal of American Studies* 47, no. 3 (August 2013): 659–72, esp. 671, https://www.jstor.org/stable/24485834; Blaine Harden, *Murder at the Mission: A Frontier Killing, Its Legacy of Lies, and the Taking of the American West* (New York: Viking, 2021), 121.

32. Laura Jensen, *Patriots, Settlers, and the Origins of American Social Policy* (New York: Cambridge University Press, 2003); Theda Skocpol, *Protecting Soldiers and Mothers: The Political Origins of Social Policy in the United States* (Cambridge: Harvard University Press, 1992), chap. 2; "An Act to Extend the Provisions, Limitations, and Benefits of an Act Entitled 'An Act Granting Pensions to the Survivors of Indian Wars,' " Public Law no. 174, 57th Cong., 1st sess., *Congressional Record* (June 27, 1902), 399–400 (quotations).

33. "An Act to Provide for the Relief of Indigent Union and Mexican War Soldiers, Sailors, Mariners, and Indian War Volunteers," in Olson, ed., *Oregon Laws*, 2:3482–84.

34. *The General Laws . . . Adopted by the Twenty-Second Regular Session of the [Oregon] Legislative Assembly* (Salem: J. R. Whitney, 1903), 228–29; Olson, ed., *Oregon Laws*, 2:3482–84; "Records of the Annual Encampments: 1885–1933," 69–70; Gray H. Whaley, *Oregon and the Collapse of* Illahee*: U.S. Empire and the Transformation of an Indigenous World, 1792–1859* (Chapel Hill: University of North Carolina Press, 2010), chap. 8; Boyd Cothran, *Remembering the Modoc War: Redemptive Violence and the Making of American Innocence* (Chapel Hill: University of North Carolina Press, 2014), chap. 5; Julius Wilm, "Old Myths Turned on Their Heads: Settler Agency, Federal Authority, and the Colonization of Oregon," *Oregon Historical Quarterly* 123, no. 4 (Winter 2022): 326–57, https://muse.jhu.edu/article/873179; Adam H. Domby, *The False Cause: Fraud, Fabrication, and White Supremacy in Confederate Memory* (Charlottesville: University of Virginia Press, 2020), chaps. 3, 4.

35. Frederick van Voorhies Holman to Clarence B. Bagley, November 20, 1908, folder 6, box 10, Clarence B. Bagley Papers.

36. Ann Laura Stoler, *Along the Archival Grain: Epistemic Anxieties and Colonial Common Sense* (Princeton: Princeton University Press, 2009).

Chapter Ten. Settlers, Scholars, and the Silencing of Pioneer Violence

1. William Lair Hill, "Annual Address of Hon. W. Lair Hill," in *Transactions of the Eleventh Annual Re-Union of the Oregon Pioneer Association* (Salem: E. M. Waite, 1884).

2. Jesse Applegate to John Minto, December 12, 1883, folder 7, box 1, John Minto Papers, Mss 752, Oregon Historical Society Special Collections. See also Abner S. Baker III, "Experience, Personality, and Memory: Jesse Applegate and John Minto Recall Pioneer Days," *Oregon Historical Quarterly* 81, no. 3 (Fall 1980): 228–51, 253–59, https://www.jstor.org/stable/20613739.

3. Jesse Applegate to Elwood Evans, July 26, 1867 (quotation), folder 1, Elwood Evans Papers; Applegate to Evans, October 18, 1867, folder 1, Elwood Evans Papers, Mss 603, Oregon Historical Society.

4. "D. J. Holmes' Address to the Pioneers of Oregon, at their Annual Reunion Held in Dallas, Polk County, Oregon, June 22, 1901," 1, Mss 2236, Oregon Historical Society Special Collections.

5. John Minto to Eva Emery Dye, June 9, 1899, folder 10, box 2, Eva Emery Dye Papers; J. Orin Oliphant to Dr. C. M. Drury, October 24, 1937, folder 33, box 16, J. Orin Oliphant Papers, cage 232, Washington State University Libraries Special Collections.

6. Matthew P. Deady, "Southern Oregon Names and Events," in *Transactions of the Eleventh Annual Re-Union of the Oregon Pioneer Association*, 23–24, 26 ("the sword"); David M. Wrobel, *Promised Lands: Promotion, Memory, and the Creation of the American West* (Lawrence: University Press of Kansas, 2002), 124–26.

7. Ambrose may also have been complaining about Euro-Americans in consenting relationships with Indigenous women. George Ambrose to Col. Ford, January 7, 1856 ("transient, reckless"), in David G. Lewis, "We Are Willing to Remove Anywhere, Where We Can Obtain Peace: Removal of the Rogue River Tribes to the Grand Ronde Reservation," *Quartux Journal* (September 16, 2017), https://ndnhistoryresearch.com/2017/09/16/we-are-willing-to-remove-anywhere-where-we-can-obtain-peace-removal-of-the-rogue-river-tribes-to-the-grand-ronde-reservation/; George Crook, *General George Crook, His Autobiography*, ed. Martin F. Schmitt (Norman: University of Oklahoma Press, 1946), 16; Sarah Deer, *Beginning and End of Rape: Confronting Sexual Violence in Native America* (Minneapolis: University of Minnesota Press, 2015), 33–34.

8. Charles Pandosy to Granville O. Haller, n.d., in Granville O. Haller, *The Dismissal of Major Granville O. Haller of the Regular Army . . . and a Few Observations* (Paterson, N.J.: Daily Guardian, 1863), 40.

9. Kamiakin/K'amáyak̲in et al. to "the soldiers and the Americans," enclosed in P. Ricard to "Grand Vicaire," October 19, 1855 ("into the hands"), folder 7, box 24, OMI Collection; Deer, *Beginning and End of Rape*, esp. 24; Rosemary Stremlau, "Rape Narratives on the Northern Paiute Frontier: Sarah Winnemucca, Sexual Sovereignty, and Economic Autonomy, 1844–1891," in *Portraits of Women in the American West*, ed. Dee Garceau-Hagen (New York: Routledge, 2005), 37–62, esp. 49 ("sexual violence").

10. Albert L. Hurtado, *Indian Survival on the California Frontier* (New Haven: Yale University Press, 1988), chap. 9; Rodman Wilson Paul and Elliott West, *Mining Frontiers of the Far West, 1848–1880*, rev. ed. (Albuquerque: University of New Mexico Press, 2001), 205; Clifford E. Trafzer and Joel R. Hyer, *Exterminate Them: Written Accounts of the Murder, Rape, and Enslavement of Native Americans during the California Gold Rush* (East Lansing: Michigan State University Press, 1999); Brian Roberts, *American Alchemy: The California Gold Rush and Middle-Class Culture* (Chapel Hill: University of North Carolina Press, 2000), 192, 240–42; Alexandra Harmon, *Indians in the Making: Ethnic Relations and Indian Identities around Puget Sound* (Berkeley: University of California Press, 1998), 99.

11. Sarah Deer, Bonnie Clairmont, Carrie A. Martell, and Maureen L. White Eagle, eds., *Sharing Our Stories of Survival: Native Women Surviving Violence* (Lanham, Md.: AltaMira Press, 2007); Roxanne Chinook, "My Spirit Lives," *Social Justice* 31, no. 4 (2004): 31–39, https://www.jstor.org/stable/29768272; Karen Dubinsky, *Improper Advances: Rape and Heterosexual Conflict in Ontario, 1880–1929* (Chicago: University of Chicago Press, 1993), 83–84;

Katrina Jagodinsky, *Legal Codes and Talking Trees: Indigenous Women's Sovereignty in the Sonoran and Puget Sound Borderlands, 1854–1946* (New Haven: Yale University Press, 2016), chap. 3; Adele Perry, *On the Edge of Empire: Gender, Race, and the Making of British Columbia, 1849–1871* (Toronto: University of Toronto Press, 2001), chap. 2.

12. Matthew Deady to James W. Nesmith, April 29, 1855.

13. J. G. Rowton to Lucullus Virgil McWhorter, August 15, 1930, folder 263, box 29, Lucullus Virgil McWhorter Papers.

14. Rowton to McWhorter, August 15, 1930.

15. On settlers lassoing and raping Native women, see Antonia I. Castañeda, "Sexual Violence in the Politics and Policies of Conquest: Amerindian Women and the Spanish Conquest of Alta California," in *Sexual Violence in Conflict Zones: From the Ancient World to the Era of Human Rights*, ed. Elizabeth D. Heineman (Philadelphia: University of Pennsylvania Press, 2011), 39–55; Sarah Winnemucca Hopkins, *Life among the Piutes: Their Wrongs and Claims*, ed. Mrs. Horace [Mary Tyler Peabody] Mann (Boston: Cupples, Upham, 1883), 229; Stremlau, "Rape Narratives on the Northern Paiute Frontier."

16. Christina Williams to Eva Emery Dye, March 28, 1904 (quotation), folder 15, box 2, Eva Emery Dye Papers; Winnemucca Hopkins, *Life among the Piutes;* Stremlau, "Rape Narratives on the Northern Paiute Frontier"; Carolyn Sorisio, " 'I Nailed Those Lies': Sarah Winnemucca Hopkins, Print Culture, and Collaboration," *J19: The Journal of Nineteenth-Century Americanists* 5, no. 1 (Spring 2017): 79–106, https://doi.org/10.1353/jnc.2017.0005.

17. Christina McDonald McKenzie Williams with William S. Lewis [uncredited], "The Daughter of Angus McDonald," *Washington Historical Quarterly* 13, no. 2 (April 1922): 107–17, https://www.jstor.org/stable/40428379.

18. David T. Courtwright, *Violent Land: Single Men and Social Disorder from the Frontier to the Inner City* (Cambridge: Harvard University Press, 1996), 279–80; Roberts, *American Alchemy*, 240–42.

19. John Lutz, "Inventing an Indian War: Canadian Indians and American Settlers in the Pacific West, 1854–1864," *Journal of the West* 38, no. 3 (July 1998): 7–13, esp. 12; Emma Milliken, "Choosing between Corsets and Freedom: Native, Mixed-Blood, and White Wives of Laborers at Fort Nisqually, 1833–1860," *Pacific Northwest Quarterly* 96, no. 2 (Spring 2005): 95–101, https://www.jstor.org/stable/40491837; Chelsea Rose, "Lonely Men, Loose Women: Rethinking the Demographics of a Multiethnic Mining Camp, Kanaka Flat, Oregon," *Historical Archaeology* 47, no. 3 (2013): 23–35, https://www.jstor.org/stable/43491334; Anne F. Hyde, *Born of Lakes and Plains: Mixed-Descent Peoples and the Making of the American West* (New York: Norton, 2022), esp. xiv. Cf. Deer, *Beginning and End of Rape*, 65–67; Dubinsky, *Improper Advances*, chap. 2.

20. Bill Miller, "The Ambush of Martin Angel," *Medford Mail Tribune*, June 15, 2009; Franklin Pierce Olney to the editor, *Yakima Herald*, October 18, 1889,

printed as "A Prominent Pioneer: A Son of Nathan Olney Denies Some Statements Made by the Correspondent of an Eastern Journal," *Yakima Herald,* October 24, 1889, 3; Elizabeth Laughlin Lord, *Reminiscences of Eastern Oregon* (Portland: Irwin-Hodson, 1903), 155–57; Michelle M. Jacob and Wynona M. Peters, " 'The Proper Way to Advance the Indian': Race and Gender Hierarchies in Early Yakima Newspapers," *Wicazo Sa Review* 26, no. 2 (Fall 2011): 39–55, esp. 43, https://doi.org/10.5749/wicazosareview.26. 2.0039.

21. Ruth and Harriette Shelton to P[ercival] R. Jeffcott, November 18, 1953, folder 7, box 1, Percival R. Jeffcott Papers. Unusual Snohomish Lushootseed orthography from the originals.

22. Edmund Clare Fitzhugh to Isaac I. Stevens, April 5, 1857, in "Letters of Isaac I. Stevens, 1857–1858," ed. Ronald Todd, *Pacific Northwest Quarterly* 31, no. 4 (October 1940): 403–59, https://www.jstor.org/stable/40486416; Daniel L. Boxberger, "In and Out of the Labor Force: The Lummi Indians and the Development of the Commercial Salmon Fishery of North Puget Sound, 1880–1900," *Ethnohistory* 35, no. 2 (Spring 1988): 161–90, esp. 165, https://doi.org/10.2307/482701; George Gibbs, "Physical Geography of the North-Western Boundary of the United States," *Journal of the American Geographical Society of New York* 4 (1873): 298–392, esp. 315, https://doi. org/10.2307/196401; Ruth and Harriette Shelton to Jeffcott, November 18, 1953 ("Chief's daughter"); Ruth and Harriette Shelton to P[ercival] R. Jeffcott, November 18, 1953 ("E-yam-alth"), folder 7, box 1, Percival R. Jeffcott Papers; David Peterson del Mar, *Beaten Down: A History of Interpersonal Violence in the West* (Seattle: University of Washington Press, 2002), 37 ("more episodic"); Candace Wellman, *Man of Treacherous Charm: Territorial Justice Edmund C. Fitzhugh* (Pullman: Washington State University Press, 2023), 62–64.

23. Sidney Teiser, "Obadiah B. McFadden, Oregon and Washington Territorial Judge," *Oregon Historical Quarterly* 66, no. 1 (March 1965): 25–37, esp. 34n31, https://www.jstor.org/stable/20612832; James F. Tulloch, *The James Francis Tulloch Diary, 1875–1910,* ed. Gordon Keith (Portland: Binfords & Mort, 1978), 16; Mrs. Hallie Lyle Campbell, interview by Howard E. Buswell, February 23, 1944, folder 16, box 5, Howard E. Buswell Papers and Photographs.

24. Edmund Clare Fitzhugh to Isaac I. Stevens, June 20, 1856, in Virgil F. Field, *The Official History of the Washington National Guard,* vol. 2, *Washington Territorial Militia and the Indian Wars of 1855–56* (Tacoma: Washington National Guard State Historical Society, 1962), 52–53.

25. Ruth and Harriette Shelton to P[ercival] R. Jeffcott, February 5, 1954, folder 7, box 1, Percival R. Jeffcott Papers.

26. Virginia Historical Society, "The Fitzhugh Family (Concluded)," *Virginia Magazine of History and Biography* 9, no. 1 (July 1901): 99–104, https://www. jstor.org/stable/4242410; Ruth and Harriette Shelton to Jeffcott, February 5,

1954; Harriette Shelton Dover, *Tulalip from My Heart: An Autobiographical Account of a Reservation Community*, ed. Darleen Fitzpatrick (Seattle: University of Washington Press, 2013), 73–74 (quotation); Wellman, *Man of Treacherous Charm*, 116, 162, 184–86, 260–64.

27. Dover, *Tulalip from My Heart*, 71–74; Percival R. Jeffcott, "Romance and Intrigue on Bellingham Bay: A Story of Old Sehome," 1955, 30–37, folder 13, box 4, Percival R. Jeffcott Papers; Coll-Peter Thrush and Robert H. Keller Jr., "'I See What I Have Done': The Life and Murder Trial of Xwelas, a S'Klallam Woman," *Western Historical Quarterly* 26, no. 2 (Summer 1995): 168–83, https://doi.org/10.2307/970187.

28. Percival R. Jeffcott, "Billy Clark Stories," 7, folder 23, box 7, Percival R. Jeffcott Papers; emphasis mine.

29. Mrs. E. Graham, interview by Howard E. Buswell, January 6, 1958, folder 13, box 5, Howard E. Buswell Papers and Photographs; P. R. Jeffcott and wife, interview by Howard E. Buswell, n.d., folder 40, box 5, Howard E. Buswell Papers and Photographs.

30. del Mar, *Beaten Down*, 4; Jagodinsky, *Legal Codes and Talking Trees*, esp. 84; Oliver C. Applegate, "The Applegate Report," April 1, 1905, Confederated Tribes of Grand Ronde Tribal Library Collections, Chachalu Museum and Cultural Center; Ruth and Harriette Shelton to Jeffcott, February 5, 1954; Wellman, *Man of Treacherous Charm*, 162, 259–60.

31. James Twogood to Dudley & Michener, November 10, 1897, 10–11 ("Nits breed lice"), James Henry Twogood Papers; Wolfgang Mieder, "'The Only Good Indian Is a Dead Indian': History and Meaning of a Proverbial Stereotype," *Journal of American Folklore* 106, no. 419 (Winter 1993): 38–60, https://doi.org/10.2307/541345; Katie Kane, "Nits Make Lice:Drogheda, Sand Creek, and the Poetics of Colonial Extermination," *Cultural Critique* 42 (Spring 1999): 81–103; G[abriel] J.Rains "to Kam-i-ah-kan," November 13, 1855, Miscellaneous Letters Received August 22, 1853–April 9, 1874, Records of the Washington Superintendency of Indian Affairs, 1853–1874, Records of the Bureau of Indian Affairs, RG 75, National Archives and Records Administration; Loren L. Williams, "Troops to Be Ready to Pursue Hostile Indians" ("mercilessly"); Abigail Malick to Mary and Michael Albright, September 1, 1861, folder 39, box 1, Malick Family Papers; Donna Clark and Keith Clark, "William McKay's Journal, 1866–67: Indian Scouts, Part I," *Oregon Historical Quarterly* 79, no. 2 (Summer 1978): 121–71, esp. 129.

32. Clifford E. Trafzer and Richard D. Scheuerman, *Renegade Tribe: The Palouse Indians and the Invasion of the Inland Pacific Northwest* (Pullman: Washington State University Press, 1986), 72–74; Edward Otho Cresap Ord, "Diary of E. O. C. Ord 3rd Art U.S. Army," in Ellen Francis Ord, "The Rogue River Indian Expedition of 1856" (master's thesis, University of California, 1922), 27 ("8 Indians"), 43; "Complete Surprise on an Indian Encampment! Eight Hostiles Killed," *[Olympia] Pioneer and Democrat*, April 11, 1856, 2.

33. Mark Axel Tveskov, "A 'Most Disastrous' Affair: The Battle of Hungry Hill, Historical Memory, and the Rogue River War," *Oregon Historical Quarterly* 118, no. 1 (Spring 2017): 42–73, https://doi.org/10.5403/oregon-histq.118.1.004; Lisa Blee, *Framing Chief Leschi: Narrative and the Politics of Historical Justice* (Chapel Hill: University of North Carolina Press, 2014); Daniel R. Maher, *Mythic Frontier: Remembering, Forgetting, and Profiting with Cultural Heritage Tourism* (Gainesville: University Press of Florida, 2016); Boyd Cothran, *Remembering the Modoc War: Redemptive Violence and the Making of American Innocence* (Chapel Hill: University of North Carolina Press, 2014).

34. Frances Fuller Victor, "Review of *McLoughlin and Old Oregon: A Chronicle* by Eva Emery Dye," *American Historical Review* 6, no. 1 (October 1900): 148–50, https://doi.org/10.2307/1834712; W[illiam] A. Mowry to Eva Emery Dye, October 10, 1900, folder 3, box 2, Eva Emery Dye Papers.

35. Eva Emery Dye, *The Conquest: The True Story of Lewis and Clark* (Chicago: A. C. McClurg, 1902), 404 ("weaker race"), 443 ("fighting new battles"); Sheri Bartlett Browne, *Eva Emery Dye: Romance with the West* (Corvallis: Oregon State University Press, 2004), esp. 98–99; Richard W. Etulain, "Telling Lewis and Clark Stories: Historical Novelists as Storytellers," *South Dakota History* 34, no. 1 (2004): 62–84, esp. 63–66; Vera J. Maxwell to Eva Emery Dye, May 24, 1917, folder 3, box 2, Eva Emery Dye Papers; Sean McEnroe, "Painting the Philippines with an American Brush: Visions of Race and National Mission among the Oregon Volunteers in the Philippine Wars of 1898 and 1899," *Oregon Historical Quarterly* 104, no. 1 (Spring 2003): 24–61.

36. Rev. Plutarch Stewart Knight, "The Pioneer as an Epoch Maker," 1898, Mss 2250, Oregon Historical Society Special Collections.

37. Knight, "The Pioneer as an Epoch Maker."

38. "Fight Sham Battle: Veterans and Militia Present Realistic Spectacle," *Oregonian*, May 30, 1903, 11; "James H. McMillen," in *Portrait and Biographical Record of Portland and Vicinity, Oregon* (Chicago: Chapman, 1903), 107–9, esp. 109; Peter Boag, "As Silent as Two Graves: Linking Genocide and Parricide in Gilded Age Oregon," *Pacific Northwest Quarterly* 113, no. 2 (Spring 2022): 73–91, esp. 87; Katharine Bjork, *Prairie Imperialists: The Indian Country Origins of American Empire* (Philadelphia: University of Pennsylvania Press, 2019), esp. chap. 6; Stefan Aune, "Indian Fighters in the Philippines: Imperial Culture and Military Violence in the Philippine-American War," *Pacific Historical Review* 90, no. 4 (November 2021): 419–47, esp. 435–36, https://doi.org/10.1525/phr.2021.90.4.419.

39. Eva Emery Dye, "A Paper for the Future Historian of Oregon," n.d. ("loose and lawless," "impartial"), folder 7, box 5, Eva Emery Dye Papers; Williams to Dye, March 28, 1904; John Minto to Frederick G. Young, October 21, 1901 ("the Sentiment"), folder 6, box 1, John Minto Papers; Browne, *Eva Emery Dye*, 90 ("living histories"). Eva Emery Dye popularized the spelling

of *Sacagawea* as *Sacajawea*, accidentally establishing a widespread norm of mispronunciation.

40. Lisa Blee, "Completing Lewis and Clark's Westward March: Exhibiting a History of Empire at the 1905 Portland World's Fair," *Oregon Historical Quarterly* 106, no. 2 (Summer 2005): 232–53, https://www.jstor.org/stable/20615528; Donna J. Kessler, *The Making of Sacagawea: A Euro-American Legend* (Tuscaloosa: University of Alabama Press, 1996), 81–88, esp. 88; Tirzah (Trask) Garnier to Eva Emery Dye, February 11, 1902, folder 12, box 1, Eva Emery Dye Papers; Robert Moulton Gatke to Eva Emery Dye, May 20, 1921, folder 12, box 1, Eva Emery Dye Papers; Eva Emery Dye, *Stories of Oregon* (San Francisco: Whitaker and Ray, 1900), esp. 176 ("massacre followed massacre"), 181 ("must give up").

41. John Minto to Frederick G. Young, October 27, 1902 ("were largely"), folder 6, box 1, John Minto Papers; John Minto to Frederick G. Young, August 12, 1903 ("spiritual"), folder 6, box 1, John Minto Papers.

42. John Minto to Frederick G. Young, October 30, 1903 ("the native race," "the race prejudice"), folder 6, box 1, John Minto Papers; John Minto, "Motives of Oregon Pioneers," 5–6 ("diverse," "whose general," "massacre"), folder 10, box 2, John Minto Papers; John Minto to Frederick G. Young, June 7, 1901, folder 6, box 1, John Minto Papers.

43. Hiram Chittenden, "Pioneer Way," ca. 1911–1915, series 2, vertical file 1, accession no. 4632-001, University of Washington Special Collections (hereafter cited as Chittenden MSS).

44. Hiram Chittenden, " 'He Kept Us Out of the War': A Plea for a More Virile Americanism," ca. 1917, Chittenden MSS.

45. Chittenden, " 'He Kept Us Out of the War' " ("Virile Americanism"); Gordon B. Dodds, *Hiram Martin Chittenden: His Public Career* (Lexington: University Press of Kentucky, 1973), 97–99 ("that evolutionary process"); Ann Marie Wilson, "In the Name of God, Civilization, and Humanity: The United States and the Armenian Massacres of the 1890s," *Le Mouvement Social* 227 (April–June 2009): 27–44.

46. James Wehn, "Clarence B. Bagley at Grave of Chief Seattle, 1931" ("first and preeminent"), POR0045, Clarence Bagley Collection, PH Coll 160, University of Washington Special Collections; Edmond S. Meany, "Clarence Booth Bagley," *Washington Historical Quarterly* 23, no. 2 (April 1932): 131–32, https://www.jstor.org/stable/23908656; George A. Frykman, "Development of the 'Washington Historical Quarterly,' 1906–1935: The Work of Edmond S. Meany and Charles W. Smith," *Pacific Northwest Quarterly* 70, no. 3 (July 1979): 121–30, https://www.jstor.org/stable/40489856.

47. Clarence B. Bagley, "Our First Indian War," *Washington Historical Quarterly* 1, no. 1 (October 1906): 34–49, esp. 34–35, https://www.jstor.org/stable/40481697.

48. Bagley, "Our First Indian War," 36 ("land greed"); Philip Sheridan to William Tecumseh Sherman, February 28, 1870, in "The Piegan Indians," 9–10,

Executive Documents Printed by Order of the House of Representatives during the Second Session of the Forty-First Congress, 1869—'70 (Washington, D.C.: Government Printing Office, 1870); Rodger C. Henderson, "The Piikuni and the U.S. Army's Piegan Expedition: Competing Narratives of the 1870 Massacre on the Marias River," *Montana: The Magazine of Western History* 68, no. 1 (Spring 2018): 48–70, 93–96, https://www.jstor.org/stable/45200742; Clarence B. Bagley, "Pioneer Seattle and Its Founders," 1925, 15 ("Indian fighting"), Pacific Northwest Historical Documents, University of Washington Digital Collection; Clarence B. Bagley, " 'The Mercer Immigration': Two Cargoes of Maidens for the Sound Country," *Quarterly of the Oregon Historical Society* 5, no. 1 (March 1904): 1–24, esp. 5 ("the mixture"), https://www.jstor.org/stable/20609599; John M. Findlay, "Pioneers and Pandemonium: Stability and Change in Seattle History," *Pacific Northwest Quarterly* 107, no. 1 (Winter 2015–16): 4–23, esp. 11–13, https://www.jstor.org/stable/44790738; Clarence B. Bagley, *Indian Myths of the Northwest* (1930; repr., Seattle: Shorey Books, 1971), esp. 11–12.

49. Peter Boag, *Pioneering Death: The Violence of Boyhood in Turn-of-the-Century Oregon* (Seattle: University of Washington Press, 2022), 130–33; Records of the Annual Encampments: 1885–1933," 87, folder 3, box 1, IWV-NPC Records; [Nellie G. Day?], "Notes on the Walla [Walla] Pioneer Association," July 1909, folder 4, box 1, Eloise Thomas Papers; Oregon Pioneer Association Reunion Program, 1917, folder 2, box 29, Associations Collection MSS (hereafter cited as Oregon Pioneer Programs); George A. Frykman, *Seattle's Historian and Promoter: The Life of Edmond Stephen Meany* (Pullman: Washington State University Press, 1998), chap. 5; Edmond Meany to Mary Sheldon Barnes, August 10, 1895, letterpress book, 422 ("life work"), box 4, Edmond S. Meany Papers; Edmond Meany to Hon. Elwood Evans, ca. 1895, letterpress book, 119 ("lock of"), box 3, Edmond S. Meany Papers; Cassandra Tate, *Unsettled Ground: The Whitman Massacre and Its Shifting Legacy in the American West* (Seattle: Sasquatch Books, 2020), 179–80.

50. Dennis Larsen, *Hop King: Ezra Meeker's Boom Years* (Pullman: Washington State University Press, 2016); Peter A. Kopp, *Hoptopia: A World of Agriculture and Beer in Oregon's Willamette Valley* (Oakland: University of California Press, 2016), 36–46; Ezra Meeker, *Pioneer Reminiscences of Puget Sound: The Tragedy of Leschi* (Seattle: Lowman & Hanford, 1905); Edward Huggins to Eva Emery Dye, February 1, 1904 ("there was," "*Venom* and *bitterness*"; emphasis in original), folder 15, box 1, Eva Emery Dye Papers.

51. Meeker, *Pioneer Reminiscences of Puget Sound*, 47–48, 53, 272.

52. Jonathan McCarty, "Hard Times in the Early Fifties," *Tacoma Ledger,* June 12, 1892, folder 4, box 1, DAR Family Rec. of Wash. Pioneers; Meeker, *Pioneer Reminiscences of Puget Sound*, 221, 224, 226 (quotations); Paige Raibmon, *Authentic Indians: Episodes of Encounter from the Late Nineteenth-Century Northwest Coast* (Durham, N.C.: Duke University Press, 2005), chap. 4; Megan Asaka,

Seattle from the Margins: Exclusion, Erasure, and the Making of a Pacific Coast City (Seattle: University of Washington Press, 2022), 62.

53. Meeker, *Pioneer Reminiscences of Puget Sound,* 103.

54. Meeker, *Pioneer Reminiscences of Puget Sound,* 154, 163, 315–16, 343, 224 (quotations); Blee, *Framing Chief Leschi,* 69.

55. Meeker, *Pioneer Reminiscences of Puget Sound,* 258–62, 342–48, 365–70, 403–5, 260 ("we must"; emphasis in original), 343 ("policy of extermination").

56. Meeker, *Pioneer Reminiscences of Puget Sound,* 212 ("judicially"), 242–46, 418–19; Alexander Olson, "Our Leschi: The Making of a Martyr," *Pacific Northwest Quarterly* 95, no. 1 (Winter 2003–4): 26–36, https://www.jstor.org/stable/40491707; Blee, *Framing Chief Leschi.*

57. Meeker, *Pioneer Reminiscences of Puget Sound,* 256–57 ("one-sided," "completely [ignoring]"), xi ("the fiction"), 224–28.

58. Clarence Bagley to Edward Huggins, August 2, 1905 (quotation), folder 14, box 13, Clarence B. Bagley Papers; Frykman, *Seattle's Historian and Promoter,* esp. 73.

59. Frykman, *Seattle's Historian and Promoter,* 93–94, 99, 100 ("Leschi's greatness"); John M. Findlay, "Brides, Brains, and Partisan Politics: Edmond S. Meany, the University of Washington, and State Government, 1889–1939," *Pacific Northwest Quarterly* 99, no. 4 (Fall 2008): 181–93, https://www.jstor.org/stable/40492175; Edmond Stephen Meany, "Chief Joseph, the Nez Perce" (master's thesis, University of Wisconsin, 1901), 32, 40 ("civilized"); Chelsea Kristen Vaughn, "Playing West: Performances of War and Empire in Pacific Northwest Pageantry" (PhD diss., University of California, Riverside, 2016), 161.

60. Hazard Stevens to Professor Meany, April 4, 1905, folder 21-6, box 21, Edmond S. Meany Papers; Edward Huggins to Eva Emery Dye, June 18, 1905 (quotations), folder 15, box 1, Eva Emery Dye Papers; E. L. Huggins to Whom It May Concern, May 18, 1885, folder 90, box 3, Cull A. White Papers, cage 203, Washington State University Libraries Special Collections; Hazard Stevens's denigration of works that seemed less than worshipful of Isaac I. Stevens or sympathetic to Native people continued for decades. See Hazard Stevens to Margaret C. [Larsen] Splawn, July 25, 1918, folder 15, box 2, Homer B. Splawn Papers, MS 10, Central Washington University Special Collections.

61. Huggins to Dye, February 1, 1904; Cecelia Svinth Carpenter, Maria Victoria Pascualy, and Trisha Hunter, *Nisqually Indian Tribe* (Charleston, S.C.: Arcadia, 2008), 14; Nicole Ann Kindle, "The Many Wives of General August V. Kautz: Colonization in the Pacific Northwest, 1853–1895" (master's thesis, Portland State University, 2019), esp. 20–21; Edward Huggins to Eva Emery Dye, February 8, 1904 ("half-breeds"), folder 15, box 1, Eva Emery Dye Papers.

62. George E. Blankenship to Prof. E. J. Meany, May 9, 1905, folder 21-6, box 21, Edmond S. Meany Papers.

63. Anne Huggins to Eva Emery Dye, June 2, 1905, folder 15, box 1, Eva Emery Dye Papers.

64. Clarence Bagley to Edward Huggins, December 31, 1906 ("stubborn"), folder 14, box 13, Clarence B. Bagley Papers; Dennis M. Larsen, *Saving the Oregon Trail: Ezra Meeker's Last Grand Quest* (Pullman: Washington State University Press, 2020); Eva Emery Dye to C[larence] B. Bagley, February 13, 1905 ("unduly," "glad"), folder 24, box 9, Clarence B. Bagley Papers.

65. Edward Huggins to Eva Emery Dye, July 10, 1904 ("spiteful attack[s]"), folder 15, box 1, Eva Emery Dye Papers; Edward Huggins to Eva Emery Dye, September 12, 1904 ("the paucity"), folder 15, box 1, Eva Emery Dye Papers; Edward Huggins to Eva Emery Dye, October 18, 1906, folder 15, box 1, Eva Emery Dye Papers; Larsen, *Saving the Oregon Trail*, 9–15.

66. Frykman, *Seattle's Historian and Promoter*, 134–37; Edmond S. Meany, *History of the State of Washington* (New York: Macmillan, 1909), 187–88, 218–19, 168 ("simply endeavored"), 187 ("weak, evasive"), 216 ("used sensible"), 181 ("relying on"), 198, 212 ("surfeit"), 163.

67. Clarence Bagley to Edmond Meany, June 12, 1911, folder 26-24, box 26, Edmond S. Meany Papers.

68. Blaine Harden, *Murder at the Mission: A Frontier Killing, Its Legacy of Lies, and the Taking of the American West* (New York: Viking, 2021), 279–80; Sarah Koenig, *Providence and the Invention of American History* (New Haven: Yale University Press, 2021), 118–20; Frederick van Voorhies Holman to Clarence B. Bagley, October 31, 1910, folder 6, box 10, Clarence B. Bagley Papers; Sarah Koenig, "The Legend of Marcus Whitman and the Transformation of the American Historical Profession," *Church History* 87, no. 1 (March 2018): 99–121, esp. 118, https://doi.org/10.1017/S0009640718000070.

69. Bagley to Meany, June 12, 1911 (quotations); Bagley, "Our First Indian War," 39; Clarence Bagley to Edmond Meany, June 12, 1911 ("I feel"). . It is unclear whether the "good" here refers to the uselessness of trying to change pioneer minds, a lack of potential profit, or both. See W. A. Katz, "Public Printers of Washington Territory, 1853–1863," *Pacific Northwest Quarterly* 51, no. 3 (July 1960): 103–14, https://www.jstor.org/stable/40487491; Bagley did find an indirect way of amplifying doubt about the Whitmans. He edited (with an unknown and denied amount of input) a critical historical work about the Whitmans written by a man who was by this time dead, and he solicited enough money to get it published. The critique was out there, but under a different man's name and with Bagley's fingerprints only faintly visible. See William I. Marshall, *Acquisition of Oregon and the Long Suppressed Evidence about Marcus Whitman*, part 1 (Seattle: Lowman & Hanford, 1911), foreword.

70. Frykman, *Seattle's Historian and Promoter*, esp. chap. 8.

71. George Kuykendall, "Written for the Pioneer Meeting June 7th, 1913," folder: "Addresses to the Garfield County Pioneer Association 1911–1920," box 5, cage 60, Washington State University Libraries Special Collections.

Chapter Eleven. Making Monuments and Forging Memories in the Progressive-Era Pacific Northwest

1. "Teal Family History," folder 1, box 1, Thompson and Teal Family Papers, Coll 168, Oregon Historical Society Special Collections; Joseph Nathan Teal, "Autobiography," ca. 1929, 38 ("quotation), 62, 1, folder 1, box 3, Thompson and Teal Family Papers; Kenneth R. Coleman, *Dangerous Subjects: James D. Saules and the Rise of Black Exclusion* (Corvallis: Oregon State University Press, 2017); Quintard Taylor, "Slaves and Free Men: Blacks in the Oregon Country, 1840–1860," *Oregon Historical Quarterly* 83, no. 2 (Summer 1982): 153–70, https://www.jstor.org/stable/20613841; cf. R. Gregory Nokes, *Breaking Chains: Slavery on Trial in the Oregon Territory* (Corvallis: Oregon State University Press, 2013).

2. Teal, "Autobiography," 55, 61, 70, 93, 77, 54; Terence O'Donnell and Thomas Vaughan, *Portland: A Historical Sketch and Guide* (Portland: Oregon Historical Society, 1976), 80–82; David P. Thompson Will, December 17 1901, folder 2, box 1, Thompson and Teal Family Papers; Joseph Nathan Teal, "*Coming of the White Man* Presentation Address" (quotation), folder 12, box 10, Marshall Newport Dana Papers, Mss 1798, Oregon Historical Society Special Collections; Marc James Carpenter, "Reconsidering *The Pioneer,* One Hundred Years Later," report submitted to the Oregon Parks and Recreation Department, June 27, 2019, https://www.oregon.gov/oprd/OH/Documents/Fellow2019MarcCarpenterReconsideringThe%20Pioneer.pdf; Jeffry Uecker, " 'The Coming of the White Man,' Onetime Oregon White Supremacist Icon," *Oregon Historical Quarterly* 123, no. 1 (Spring 2022): 6–39, https://doi.org/10.1353/ohq.2022.0000.

3. Mary Ellen Rowe, *Bulwark of the Republic: The American Militia in the Antebellum West* (Westport, Conn.: Praeger, 2003), 166 ("a monument"); William Lair Hill, "Annual Address of Hon. W. Lair Hill," in *Transactions of the Eleventh Annual Re-Union of the Oregon Pioneer Association* (Salem: E. M. Waite, 1884), 21 ("erect a monument"); Pioneer Association Form: Pierce County Pioneers Assn., 1914–16 ("rais[ing] monuments"), folder 2, box 78, Edmond S. Meany Papers.

4. Meany to Henry H. Kitson [November 1894], letterpress book, 94 ("large heroic statue"), box 3, Edmond S. Meany Papers; C[ornelius] H. Hanford to Prof. Edmond S. Meany, January 27, 1905, folder 21-2, box 21, Edmond S. Meany Papers; Cassandra Tate, "Reckoning with Marcus Whitman and the Memorialization of Conquest," History News Network, November 15, 2020 ("ripped, muscular") https://historynewsnetwork.org/article/178222; W. L. Davis, "These Men We Recognize," *Pacific Northwest Quarterly* 44, no. 3 (July 1953): 129–34, esp. 134 ("showed us") https://www.jstor.org/stable/41442096; Blaine Harden, *Murder at the Mission: A Frontier Killing, Its Legacy of Lies, and the Taking of the American West* (New York: Viking, 2021), 279–80.

5. David P. Thompson Will, December 17 1901; Teal, "*Coming of the White Man* Presentation Address" (quotation); "Gleanings from American Art Centers," *Brush and Pencil* 11, no. 5 (February 1903): 388–93, esp. 393, https://www.jstor.org/stable/25505861; Ann Fulton, "The Restoration of an Iłkák'mana: A Chief Called Multnomah," *American Indian Quarterly* 31, no. 1 (Winter 2007): 110–28, https://www.jstor.org/stable/4138897; Chelsea Kristen Vaughn, "Playing West: Performances of War and Empire in Pacific Northwest Pageantry" (PhD diss., University of California, Riverside, 2016), chap. 1; Richard W. Etulain, "Frederic Homer Balch (1861–1891): Romancer and Historian," *Oregon Historical Quarterly* 117, no. 4 (Winter 2016): 604–35, https://doi.org/10.5403/oregonhistq.117.4.0604.

6. Teal, "*Coming of the White Man* Presentation Address"; Uecker, " 'The Coming of the White Man.' " Like Alexander Phimister Proctor and many other successful creators of Western monuments in the early 1900s, MacNeil sculpted both mostly nude depictions of Indians like this one and heroically posed Indian killers—in MacNeil's case, an Indiana statue of the genocidal George Rogers Clark (1934).

7. Mrs. George T. Gerlinger [Irene Strang Hazard Gerlinger], "A Tribute to Mr. and Mrs. Joseph N. Teal," 1944, box 9, UA Ref 2, University Archives Biographical Files, University of Oregon Special Collections.

8. Donna J. Kessler, *The Making of Sacagawea: A Euro-American Legend* (Tuscaloosa: University of Alabama Press, 1996), 81–88; Cindy Koenig Richards, "Inventing Sacagawea: Public Women and the Transformative Potential of Epideictic Rhetoric," *Western Journal of Communication* 73, no. 1 (February 2009): 1–22, https://doi.org/10.1080/10570310802635013; Gail H. Landsman, "The 'Other' as Political Symbol: Images of Indians in the Woman Suffrage Movement," *Ethnohistory* 39, no. 3 (Summer 1992): 247–84, https://doi.org/10.2307/482299; Cynthia Culver Prescott, *Pioneer Mother Monuments: Constructing Cultural Memory* (Norman: University of Oklahoma Press, 2019), 32–35; Michael Heffernan and Carol Medlicot, "A Feminine Atlas? Sacagawea, Suffragettes and the Commemorative Landscape in the American West, 1904–1910," *Gender, Place and Culture* 9, no. 2 (June 2002): 109–31.

9. Tiffany Lewis, "Winning Woman Suffrage in the Masculine West: Abigail Scott Duniway's Frontier Myth," *Western Journal of Communication* 75, no. 2 (March 2011): 127–47, https://doi.org/10.1080/10570314.2011.553877; Abigail Scott Duniway to the editor, *Post Express*, July 30, 1906 ("men's rights microbe," "the Whitman massacre"), folder 1, box 1, Abigail Scott Duniway Papers, Coll 232B, University of Oregon Special Collections; Vaughn, "Playing West," chap. 3; Abigail Scott Duniway, "A Pioneer Incident," esp. 4, enclosed in Abigail Scott Duniway to Dr. Annice F. Jeffreys, December 21, ca. 1902, folder 8, box 1, Abigail Scott Duniway Papers; Albert Furtwangler, "Reclaiming Jefferson's Ideals: Abigail Scott Duniway's

Ode to Lewis and Clark," *Pacific Northwest Quarterly* 98, no. 4 (Fall 2007): 159–68, https://www.jstor.org/stable/40492190.

10. Jan C. Dawson, "Sacagawea: Pilot or Pioneer Mother?," *Pacific Northwest Quarterly* 83, no. 1 (January 1992): 22–28, https://www.jstor.org/stable/40491247; Eva Emery Dye to Sarah Evans, October 19, 1903 ("the first pioneer"), folder 6, box 4, Eva Emery Dye Papers; Deborah M. Olsen, "Fair Connections: Women's Separatism and the Lewis and Clark Expedition," *Oregon Historical Quarterly* 109, no. 2 (Summer 2008): 174–203, https://www.jstor.org/stable/20615848; Lisa Blee, "Completing Lewis and Clark's Westward March: Exhibiting a History of Empire at the 1905 Portland World's Fair," *Oregon Historical Quarterly* 106, no. 2 (Summer 2005): 232–53, https://www.jstor.org/stable/20615528; David Glassberg, *American Historical Pageantry: The Uses of Tradition in the Early Twentieth Century* (Chapel Hill: University of North Carolina Press, 1990), 114; Philip J. Deloria, *Playing Indian* (New Haven: Yale University Press, 1998), 60–68; Madeline Bourque Kearin, "The Many Lives of Chief Kisco: Strategies of Solidarity and Division in the Mythology of an American Monument," *Public Historian* 39, no. 3 (August 2017): 40–61, https://www.jstor.org/stable/26504363; Lucy Maddox, "Politics, Performance and Indian Identity," *American Studies International* 40, no. 2 (June 2002): 7–36, https://www.jstor.org/stable/41279890; Robert E. Davis, *History of the Improved Order of Red Men and Degree of Pocahontas, 1765–1988* (Waco, Tex.: Davis Brothers, 1990), 689–716; Eva Emery Dye to "Great Sachem" [William M. Risley], July 17, 1904 ("a joint memorial"), folder 6, box 4, Eva Emery Dye Papers.

11. Dye to "Great Sachem," July 17, 1904 ("the bravest maiden"); Charles E. Rankin, "A Western Pocahontas: Myth, Reality, and Memorialization for Spotted Tail's Daughter, Mni-Akuwin," *Western Historical Quarterly* 55, no. 2 (Summer 2024): 105–26, https://doi.org/10.1093/whq/whae020; Rebecca Kay Jager, *Malinche, Pocahontas, and Sacagawea: Indian Women as Cultural Intermediaries and National Symbols* (Norman: University of Oklahoma Press, 2015); M. Elise Marubbio, *Killing the Indian Maiden: Images of Native American Women in Film* (Lexington: University Press of Kentucky, 2006), chap. 1; Dan Blumlo, "Pocahontas, Uleleh, and Hononegah: The Archetype of the American Indian Princess," *Journal of the Illinois State Historical Society* 110, no. 2 (Summer 2017): https://doi.org/10.5406/jillistathistsoc.110.2.0129; Boyd Cothran, *Remembering the Modoc War: Redemptive Violence and the Making of American Innocence* (Chapel Hill: University of North Carolina Press, 2014), chap. 3. As Cothran points out, some Indigenous people have played along with Pocahontas-style narratives when it appeared the best option for their or their community's goals.

12. Great Council of Oregon Improved Order of Red Men, "Record of the Great Council of Oregon Improved Order of Red Men," ca. 1913, 56–57, folder 17, box 1, Associations Collection; Eva Emery Dye to Whom It May Concern, March 8, 1904 ("a pantomime"), folder 6, box 4, Eva Emery Dye

Papers; J. W. Todd, Notes on Mosher from Theodore Phillips, folder: Genealogy, box 1, Mosher Family Records, 1853–98, Acc. 0136.001, University of Washington Special Collections; Davis, *History of the Improved Order of Red Men*, 233 ("Indians of any tribe"), 330, 498–99.

13. Cary C. Collins, "The Broken Crucible of Assimilation: Forest Grove Indian School and the Origins of Off-Reservation Boarding-School Education in the West," *Oregon Historical Quarterly* 101, no. 4 (Winter 2000): 466–507, https://www.jstor.org/stable/20615095; Denise Lajimodiere, "A Healing Journey," *Wicazo Sa Review* 27, no. 2 (Fall 2012): 5–19, https://doi.org/10.5749/wicazosareview.27.2.0005; Preston S. McBridge, "A Lethal Education: Institutionalized Negligence, Epidemiology, and Death in Native American Boarding Schools, 1879–1934 (PhD diss., University of California, Los Angeles, 2020), 128–32, 165–73, 253, 329, 519–635; Prescott, *Pioneer Mother Monuments*; "Statue of Bird Woman Unveiled," *Oregonian*, July 7, 1905, 10–11 ("patriotic deeds"; "feminine [A]tlas"; "beckoned"); "Red Men March through Streets," *Oregonian*, July 7, 1905, 10 ("the transformation"); Kat Cleland, "Disruptions in the Dream City: Unsettled Ideologies at the 1905 World's Fair in Portland, Oregon" (master's thesis, Portland State University, 2013), chap. 1. Perhaps coincidentally, Dye's call for American imperialism in Asia was printed just beneath a racist political cartoon about boycotts of American goods in China.

14. "Statue of Bird Woman Unveiled"; Dye, *Stories of Oregon*, 128–29; Amy Kaplan, *The Anarchy of Empire in the Making of U.S. Culture* (Cambridge: Harvard University Press, 2002), chap. 1.

15. Marc James Carpenter, " 'Justice and Fair Play for the American Indian': Harry Lane, Robert Hamilton, and a Vision of Native American Modernity," *Pacific Historical Review* 87, no. 2 (May 2018): 305–32, https://doi.org/10.1525/phr.2018.87.2.305.

16. "Records of the Annual Encampments: 1885–1933," 219, folder 3, box 1, IWV-NPC Records; Harry Lane to Nina Lane, June 22, 1907, folder: Harry Lane Correspondence, box 1, Nina Lane Faubion Papers, Ax 185, University of Oregon Special Collections; Carpenter, " 'Justice and Fair Play' "; Robert D. Johnston, *The Radical Middle Class: Populist Democracy and the Question of Capitalism in Progressive Era Portland, Oregon* (Princeton: Princeton University Press, 2006), chap. 3.

17. Carpenter, " 'Justice and Fair Play' "; Robert D. Johnston, *The Radical Middle Class: Populist Democracy and the Question of Capitalism in Progressive Era Portland, Oregon* (Princeton: Princeton University Press, 2006), chap. 3.

18. Paul Scolari, "Indian Warriors and Pioneer Mothers: American Identity and Closing of the Frontier in Public Monuments, 1890–1930" (PhD diss., University of Pittsburgh, 2005), esp. chap. 2; Jean M. O'Brien and Lisa Blee, *Monumental Mobility: The Memory Work of Massasoit* (Chapel Hill: University of North Carolina Press, 2019); Alexander I. Olson, "Heritage Schemes: The Curtis Brothers and the Indian Moment of Northwest

Boosterism," *Western Historical Quarterly* 40, no. 2 (Summer 2009): 159–78, https://doi.org/10.1093/whq/40.2.159; Norwood Curry to Eva Emery Dye, June 20, 1904 (quotations), folder 8, box 1, Eva Emery Dye Papers; Vaughn, "Playing West"; Sec. Walla Walla Committee to Spokane Betterment Organization, ca. 1924, folder 13, box 5, T. C. Elliott Papers, Mss 231, Oregon Historical Society Special Collections; Katrina M. Phillips, *Staging Indigeneity: Salvage Tourism and the Performance of Native American History* (Chapel Hill: University of North Carolina Press, 2021).

19. Scolari, "Indian Warriors and Pioneer Mothers," esp. chap. 2; James Wehn to Clarence B. Bagley, October 7, 1930 (quotations), folder 27, box 12, Clarence B. Bagley Papers; Robert Spalding, *Monumental Seattle: The Stories behind the City's Statues, Memorials, and Markers* (Pullman: Washington State University Press, 2018), chap. 3; Arnold Krupat, "Chief Seattle's Speech Revisited," *American Indian Quarterly* 35, no. 2 (Spring 2011): 192–214, https://doi.org/10.5250/amerindiquar.35.2.0192.

20. "Last of the Mohicans," *Jacksonville Democratic Times*, May 20, 1892, 3 (quotations), https://truwe.sohs.org/files/takelma.html; "Last of Her Tribe," *Jacksonville Democratic Times*, May 19, 1893, 3, https://truwe.sohs.org/files/takelma.html. See, more broadly, Jean M. O'Brien, *Firsting and Lasting: Writing Indians Out of Existence in New England* (Minneapolis: University of Minnesota Press, 2010). There have been claims for Oscharwasha as both Takelma and Tututni; in choosing to list both, I mean no disrespect to alternative interpretations of her heritage.

21. Fred Poyner IV, *The First Sculptor of Seattle: The Life and Art of James A. Wehn* (North Charleston, S.C.: CreateSpace, 2014), chaps. 4, 6; "Last of the Mohicans," *Jacksonville Democratic Times*, May 20, 1892; " 'Old Jennie' in Marble: Statue of Last Survivor of Rogue River Indians to Be in Exhibit," *Spokane Spokesman-Review*, December 27, 1908, C2, https://truwe.sohs.org/files/rowenanichols.html; "Trade Names and Personals," *Pacific Coast Architect* 3, no. 3 (1912): 433, https://archive.org/details/sim_arts-architecture_1912-06_3_3.

22. Katz, "Public Printers of Washington Territory, 1853–1863, 103 ("cleaned up"); Poyner, *First Sculptor of Seattle*, 63–71.

23. Poyner, *First Sculptor of Seattle*, 68 ("passed the word"); Wehn to Bagley, October 7, 1930; Thomas W. Prosch, "Seattle and the Indians of Puget Sound," *Washington Historical Quarterly* 2, no. 4 (July 1908): 303–8, https://www.jstor.org/stable/40473935; Clarence B. Bagley, "Chief Seattle and Angeline," *Washington Historical Quarterly* 22, no. 4 (October 1931): 243–75, https://www.jstor.org/stable/40475450.

24. Eva Emery Dye to Mr. Freeman, April 26, 1909, enclosed in Jos[i]ah Collins to Edmond Meany, May 5, 1909, folder 24-14, box 24, Edmond S. Meany Papers; Don Sherwood, "Tilikum Place," January 24, 1974, 2, Don Sherwood Parks History Collection, ID 5801-01, Seattle Municipal Archives, http://clerk.seattle.gov/~F_archives/sherwood/TilikumPl.pdf; "Tili-

kums to Unveil Statue of Seattle," *Seattle Daily Times*, November 10, 1912, 20; "Celebrate Seattle's Birthday," *Seattle Star*, November 14, 1912, 7; "Tilikums Off for Spokane Pow Wow," *Seattle Star*, November 15, 1912, 8; "Tilikums of Elttaes Invitation," April 27, 1912, ID 2018.3.3.43, Seattle Museum of History and Industry Digital Collection; "Tilikums of Elttaes Touch Off Potlatch Enthusiasm in City," *Seattle Times*, May 12, 1912, 1; Spalding, *Monumental Seattle*, chap. 1; Daniel Monteith, "Tongass, the Prolific Name, the Forgotten Tribe: An Ethnohistory of the Taantakwaan Tongass People" (PhD diss., Michigan State University, 1998), 183–86.

25. *Third Report of the National Society of the Daughters of the American Revolution: October 11, 1898–October 11, 1900* (Washington, D.C.: Government Printing Office, 1901), 267–68, plate 83 (quotations); Harriette Shelton Dover, *Tulalip from My Heart: An Autobiographical Account of a Reservation Community*, ed. Darleen Fitzpatrick (Seattle: University of Washington Press, 2013), chap. 6; Patrick Stephen Lozar, " 'An Anxious Desire of Self Preservation': Colonialism, Transition, and Identity on the Umatilla Indian Reservation, 1860–1910" (master's thesis, University of Oregon, 2013), 152–69; "Hard Lessons in America: Henry Sicade's History of Puyallup Indian School, 1860 to 1920," ed. Cary C. Collins, *Columbia* 14, no. 4 (Winter 2000–2001): 6–11; John R. Gram, "Acting Out Assimilation: Playing Indian and Becoming American in the Federal Indian Boarding Schools," *American Indian Quarterly* 40, no. 3 (Summer 2016): 251–73, https://doi.org/10.5250/amerindiquar.40.3.0251; Poyner, *First Sculptor of Seattle*, chap. 10; "Statue Dedicated to Chieftain Who Guarded Pioneers," *Seattle Post-Intelligencer*, November 13, 1912, 1; "Seattle's Birthday, Sixty-One Years Old," *Seattle Star*, November 13, 1912, 6; "Celebrate Seattle's Birthday," *Seattle Star*, November 14, 1912, 7.

26. Rev. T[homas] Derrick, *Cariboo Sentinel*, August 21, 1869, 3; Christopher Herbert, *Gold Rush Manliness: Race and Gender on the Pacific Slope* (Seattle: University of Washington Press, 2018), 133; John Sutton Lutz, *Makúk: A New History of Aboriginal-White Relations* (Vancouver: University of British Columbia Press, 2008), x ("vile compound").

27. Edmond Meany, "Last Survivor of the Oregon Mission of 1840," 7 ("an elixir"), folder 1, box 60, Edmond S. Meany Papers; invitation to "St. James Muckamuck Wikiup, Washington D.C., Feb., 1901," folder 3, box 17, Associations Collections MSS; Edgar Bryan to "Sir and Madam" [Clarence and Alice Mercer Bagley], May 9, 1903, folder 25, box 11, Clarence B. Bagley Papers; flyer for "The Stillaguamish Valley Association of Washington Pioneers of Snohomish County Sixth Annual Reunion and Picnic," Pioneer Association Form: Yakima Pioneer Association, ca. 1914–16, folder 2, box 78, Edmond S. Meany Papers.

28. "Oregon Pioneer Association Thirty-Seventh Annual Session [1909]," in *Transactions of the Oregon Pioneer Association*, 1906–12 (Portland: Chausse Prudhomme, 1915), 294 ("the conversation"). On Bethenia Owens-Adair, see

Alexandra Minna Stern, *Eugenic Nation: Faults and Frontiers of Better Breeding in Modern America* (Berkeley: University of California Press, 2005), esp. 23; Mark A. Largent, " 'The Greatest Curse of the Race': Eugenic Sterilization in Oregon, 1909–1983," *Oregon Historical Quarterly* 103, no. 2 (Summer 2002): 188–209, https://www.jstor.org/stable/20615229; Oregon Pioneer Association Reunion Program, June 16, 1897, Oregon Pioneer Programs; Pioneers Programme, Dallas, July 2, 1904 ("Indian song"), Oregon Pioneer Programs; Oregon Pioneer Association Reunion Program, 1911, Oregon Pioneer Programs; Oregon Pioneer Association Reunion Program, 1912, Oregon Pioneer Programs; "Records of the Annual Encampments: 1885–1933," 143; Oregon Pioneer Association Reunion Program, 1913, Oregon Pioneer Programs ("Chinook choir"); Michael V. Pisani, *Imagining Native America in Music* (New Haven: Yale University Press, 2005), chap. 8; Paige Clark Lush, "The All American Other: Native American Music and Musicians on the Circuit Chautauqua," *Americana: The Journal of Popular Culture* 7, no. 2 (Fall 2008), https://www.proquest.com/docview/1519971388; Philip J. Deloria, *Indians in Unexpected Places* (Lawrence: University Press of Kansas, 2004), 236–89; Native Daughters of Oregon pamphlet, 23 ("royal blood"), 21 ("Klose Nesika Illahee"), folder 18, box 23, Associations Collection.

29. Oregon Pioneer Association Program, June 18, 1914 ("an impassioned 'wawa,' " "Chinook dialogue"), Oregon Pioneers Programs; Delia Coon, "Klickitat County: Indians of and Settlement by Whites," *Washington Historical Quarterly* 14, no. 4 (October 1923): 248–61, https://www.jstor.org/stable/40474726; Daniel J. Burge, "Genocidal Jesting: The 'Comic Indian' in U.S. Popular Culture, 1850–1900," *Pacific Historical Review* 91, no. 2 (2022): 163–89, esp. 163 ("burlesque"), https://doi.org/10.1525/phr.2022.91.2.163.

30. Oregon Pioneer Association Program, 1915, Oregon Pioneers Programs; Oregon Pioneer Association Program, 1916, Oregon Pioneers Programs; Oregon Pioneer Association Program, 1917, Oregon Pioneers Programs; Nancy Covert, "Laura Belle Downey Bartlett: Stalwart Steilacoom Settler and Woman of Many Talents," *Columbia* 27, no. 1 (2013): 5–7 ("my country"); Oregon Pioneer Association Program, 1922 ("Pioneers"), Oregon Pioneers Programs; Oregon Pioneer Association Program, 1931, Oregon Pioneers Programs.

31. [Eva Emery Dye?], "The Conquest" (stage play script), n.d., folder 15, box 5, Eva Emery Dye Papers.

32. C[yrus] B. Pickrell to Edmond Meany, December 5, 1907, folder 23-3, box 23, Edmond S. Meany Papers; Leonard Forsman, "We Continue to Build on Chief Seattle's Legacy," *Seattle Times*, August 22, 2019.

33. Flyer for "Indian Lecture-Musicale featuring Louise Merrill Cooper," May 28, 1915 ("Indian Songs," "impersonator"), folder 32, box 86, Edmond S. Meany Papers; George A. Frykman, *Seattle's Historian and Promoter: The Life of Edmond Stephen Meany* (Pullman: Washington State University Press, 1998), 83–84 ("greater appreciation").

34. Folder 86 (entire), box 5, Edmond S. Meany Papers; Simon Wendt, *The Daughters of the American Revolution and Patriotic Memory in the Twentieth Century* (Gainesville: University Press of Florida, 2020), 59 ("highlighted"), 94–126; Woden Sorrow Teachout, "Forging Memory: Hereditary Societies, Patriotism and the American Past, 1876–1898" (PhD diss., Harvard University, 2003), 118–19; Michael S. Sweeney, "Ancestors, Avotaynu, Roots: An Inquiry into American Genealogy Discourse" (PhD diss., University of Kansas, 2010), 50–54; Mary A. O'Neil, "Henry Francis," History of Thurston County Pioneers before 1870 [form], February 1918, manuscript 134, Washington State Library—Historical Department, Pullman; O'Brien, *Firsting and Lasting*; Dennis M. Larsen, *The Missing Chapters: The Untold Story of Ezra Meeker's Old Oregon Trail Monument Expedition* (Puyallup, Wash.: Ezra Meeker Historical Society, 2006), 20–21.

35. John W. W. Mann, "Slough-Keetcha: Spokane Garry in History and Memory," *Pacific Northwest Quarterly* 104, no. 1 (Winter 2012–13): 3–20, esp. 11–12, https://www.jstor.org/stable/24628757.

36. Netta W. Phelps, "Dedication of Steptoe Memorial Park," *Washington Historical Quarterly* 2, no. 4 (July 1908): 344–51, esp. 346 (quotation), https://www.jstor.org/stable/40473938; Elizabeth F. Tannatt, comp., *Indian Battles of the Inland Empire in 1858* (Spokane: Daughters of the American Revolution, 1914), 2; "Garrison Gossip," *Army and Navy Life* 12, no. 4 (1908): 508; "Report Commanding Officer, Cotabato, June 4 1902," *Annual Reports of the War Department for the Fiscal Year Ended June 30, 1902* (Washington, D.C.: Government Printing Office, 1902), 9:522–29; Robert A. Fulton, *Moroland: The History of Uncle Sam and the Moros, 1899–1920*, rev. ed. (Bend, Ore.: Tumalo Creek Press, 2016), chaps. 14, 15; Oliver Charbonneau, "Civilizational Imperatives: American Colonial Culture in the Islamic Philippines, 1899–1942" (PhD diss., University of Western Ontario, 2016), 216–23.

37. Phelps, "Dedication of Steptoe Memorial Park," 348 ("army which has been"); Joseph N. Teal, "Columbia River," speech given at a banquet to the secretary of war, August 2, 1913, folder: Speeches, box 1, Joseph Nathan Teal Papers, Ax 171, University of Oregon Special Collections.

38. Phelps, "Dedication of Steptoe Memorial Park," 349 ("many of the soldiers"); Tannatt, *Indian Battles of the Inland Empire in 1858*, 7–8.

39. Phelps, "Dedication of Steptoe Memorial Park," 350 (quotation).

40. Monuments contributor list, folder 216, box 25, cage 55, Lucullus Virgil McWhorter Papers; Hembree monument correspondence, folder 217, box 25, Lucullus Virgil McWhorter Papers; Bolon Monument Map, folder 535, box 51, Lucullus Virgil McWhorter Papers; Slaughter memorial program, folder 25, box 86, Edmond S. Meany Papers; "Battle of Pa Ho Ti Cute—Two Buttes" (monument description), folder 6, box 24, Edmond S. Meany Papers; Tow-Tow-Nah-Hee monument description, folder 6, box 24, Edmond S. Meany Papers.

41. Tannatt, *Indian Battles of the Inland Empire in 1858*, 16.

42. Wendt, *The Daughters of the American Revolution and Patriotic Memory*, 100–104; "Will Give Fountain," *Seattle Star*, June 1, 1916, 2; "Tablet Shows City's Advance," *Seattle Star*, August 16, 1916, 6.

43. George Bundy Wasson Jr., "Growing Up Indian: An Emic Perspective" (PhD diss., University of Oregon, 2001), 217–20 ("runaway Indians"); "Dayton Historic Resource Inventory: Courthouse Square Park," November 10, 1984, National Register of Historic Places no. 87000336, National Park Service, https://npgallery.nps.gov/NRHP/GetAsset/NRHP/87000336_text; Helen Delight Stone, "The Archaeology of the Smith House (ORYA3), Dayton, Oregon" (master's thesis, Oregon State University, 1997), 9.

44. M[elvin] C[larke] George, "Address Delivered at Dedication of Grand Ronde Military Block House at Dayton City Park, Oregon, Aug. 23, 1912," *Quarterly of the Oregon Historical Society* 15, no. 1 (March 1914): 64–70, https://www.jstor.org/stable/20609950.

45. "Dayton Historic Resource Inventory: Courthouse Square Park" ("friend of the Indian"); Tom McCall, "Remarks by Governor Tom McCall, Dayton Historical Plaque Dedication," August 21, 1971, folder 46, box 1, Joel Palmer Papers; Terence O'Donnell, *An Arrow in the Earth: General Joel Palmer and the Indians of Oregon* (Portland: Oregon Historical Society Press, 1991).

46. Carpenter, "Reconsidering *The Pioneer*"; cf. Alexander Phimister Proctor, *Sculptor in Buckskin: The Autobiography of Alexander Phimister Proctor*, 2nd ed., ed. Katharine C. Ebner (Norman: University of Oklahoma Press, 2009); Peter H. Hassrick with Katharine C. Ebner and Phimister Proctor Church, *Wildlife and Western Heroes: Alexander Phimister Proctor, Sculptor* (Fort Worth: Amon Carter Museum, 2003); Alexander Phimister Proctor, "Lassoing Dog," folder: Early Denver Days, box 1, Alexander Phimister Proctor Papers, Mss. 5352, Oregon Historical Society Special Collections (hereafter cited as OHS Proctor MSS); Proctor, "The Fawn and the Panther," folder: The Fawn and the Panther, box 1, OHS Proctor MSS; Proctor, "Little Wolf: Adventures with Indians in Custer Country, Wyoming, 1914," folder: Little Wolf, box 1, OHS Proctor MSS; Proctor, "Stokes Peddler," folder: Short Stories by APP—#1, box 1, OHS Proctor MSS; Proctor, "Typescript Autobiography" (draft), chap. 4, folder: Typescript + Autobiography Ch 24–34, box 1, OHS Proctor MSS; Proctor, "Hired Hand," folder: Alexander Phimister Proctor—Experiences on Farm in Westchester County, box 1, OHS Proctor MSS; Proctor, "Shooting Up Tramp," folder: Alexander Phimister Proctor—Experiences on Farm in Westchester County, box 1, OHS Proctor MSS; Proctor, "Biog. of A.P.P.," 1931, 2, folder: Birth and Childhood Reminiscences, box 1, OHS Proctor MSS; Proctor, "Indian Outbreak—Bill Cousins," esp. 4–7, folder: Indians 1877, box 1, OHS Proctor MSS.

47. Herbert, *Gold Rush Manliness*, 30 ("hunting"; Proctor, untitled manuscript, folder: Indians, box 1, OHS Proctor MSS ("Big Frank").

48. The major sculptural monuments Alexander Phimister Proctor crafted for Oregon include *The Pioneer* (1919), *Theodore Roosevelt, Rough Rider* (1922),

Circuit Rider (1924), *Til Taylor* (1929), and *The Pioneer Mother* (1932), as well as (designed by Alexander Phimister Proctor, completed after his death by his son Gifford Proctor) *Reverend Jason Lee* (1953) and *Dr. John M. McLoughlin* (1953). Identical statues of Jason Lee and John McLoughlin made from the same casts represent Oregon in the National Statuary Hall. Peter H. Hassrick, "The Oregon Art of Alexander Phimister Proctor," *Oregon Historical Quarterly* 104, no. 3 (Fall 2003): 394–413, https://www.jstor.org/stable/20615346; Renée M. Laegreid, "Rodeo Queens at the Pendleton Round-Up: The First Go-Round, 1910–1917," *Oregon Historical Quarterly* 104, no. 1 (Spring 2003): 6–23, https://www.jstor.org/stable/20615296; Phillips, *Staging Indigeneity*, 26–49, esp. 30 ("organizers").

49. Proctor, *Sculptor in Buckskin*, chap. 22; Hassrick with Ebner and Church, *Wildlife and Western Heroes*, 75, 170–73, 208–9; Rowena L. Alcorn and Gordon D. Alcorn, "Jackson Sundown, Nez Perce Horseman," *Montana: The Magazine of Western History* 33, no. 4 (Autumn 1983): 46–51, https://www.jstor.org/stable/4518779; Prescott, *Pioneer Mother Monuments*, 42–45; Alexander Phimister Proctor, untitled manuscript, 4–5 ("keen-eyed and taciturn"), folder: A Close Call Mayo Clinic to Denver + Idaho, 1916–1917, box 1, OHS Proctor MSS; Erika Doss, "Augustus Saint-Gaudens's *The Puritan:* Founders' Statues, Indian Wars, Contested Public Spaces, and Anger's Memory in Springfield, Massachusetts," *Winterthur Portfolio* 46, no. 4 (Winter 2012): 237–70, https://doi.org/10.1086/669736; Patrick McCarthy, " 'Living History' as the 'Real Thing': A Comparative Analysis of the Modern Mountain Man Rendezvous, Renaissance Fairs, and Civil War Reenactments," *ETC: A Review of General Semantics* 71, no. 2 (April 2014): 106–23, https://www.jstor.org/stable/24761920.

50. Robert A. Booth, "The Outlook from the End of the Trail," in *Dedication of the Pioneer: An Heroic Statue in Bronze Erected on the Campus of the University of Oregon by Hon. Joseph N. Teal of Portland, May 22 1919* (Eugene: University of Oregon, 1919), 13 ("unselfish"); R[obert] A. Booth to Gov. Ben W. Olcott, January 6, 1921, in "Exercises on the Occasion of the Dedication and Unveiling of the Equestrian Statue: 'The Circuit Rider,' Salem, Oregon, April 19, 1924," *Quarterly of the Oregon Historical Society* 25, no. 2 (June 1924): 79–100, esp. 82 ("frontier life"), https://www.jstor.org/stable/20610272; Proctor, *Sculptor in Buckskin*, 190. Robert A. Booth was a beneficiary of the illicit land schemes made famous in the Oregon Land Fraud cases, although he was never criminally convicted. Joan M. Kelley, "Booth-Kelly Lumber Company: An Empire in the Douglas Fir Country," *Lane County Historian* 35, no. 3 (1990): 55–58; John Messing, "Public Lands, Politics, and Progressives: The Oregon Land Fraud Trials, 1903–1910," *Pacific Historical Review* 35, no. 1 (February 1966): 35–66, https://doi.org/10.2307/3636627.

51. Frederick V. Holman to T. C. Elliott, December 29, 1919 ("a very forceful man"), folder 15, box 5, T. C. Elliott Papers; Frederick V. Holman,

"Qualities of Oregon Pioneers," in *Dedication of the Pioneer,* 23–24 ("the instincts"). See also Frederick V. Holman, "Qualities of the Oregon Pioneers: An Address at the Unveiling of 'The Pioneer,' " *Quarterly of the Oregon Historical Society* 20, no. 3 (September 1919): 235–42, https://www.jstor.org/stable/20610139; Lisa Philips, "Later Revisions: (Re)constructing the Cast of US and Canadian Pioneers," *Before and After the State: Politics, Poetics, and People(s) of the Pacific Northwest* (Vancouver: University of British Columbia Press, 2018), 207–32, esp. 211–14.

52. Holman, "Qualities of the Oregon Pioneers," 238 ("a long and bloody"; Joseph N. Teal, "The American Pioneer," in "Exercises on the Occasion of the Dedication and Unveiling of the Equestrian Statue," esp. 93–100.

53. Alexandra Harmon, *Indians in the Making: Ethnic Relations and Indian Identities around Puget Sound* (Berkeley: University of California Press, 1998), 63; Sherry L. Smith, "Reconciliation and Restitution in the American West," *Western Historical Quarterly* 41, no. 1 (Spring 2010): 4–25, esp. 5–6, https://doi.org/10.2307/westhistquar.41.1.0004; Cothran, *Remembering the Modoc War;* Phillips, *Staging Indigeneity;* Paige Raibmon, *Authentic Indians: Episodes of Encounter from the Late Nineteenth-Century Northwest Coast* (Durham, N.C.: Duke University Press, 2005), esp. chaps. 6, 7.

54. Michelle M. Jacob and Wynona M. Peters, " 'The Proper Way to Advance the Indian': Race and Gender Hierarchies in Early Yakima Newspapers," *Wicazo Sa Review* 26, no. 2 (Fall 2011): 39–55, https://doi.org/10.5749/wicazosareview.26.2.0039; Franklin Pierce Olney to the editor, *Yakima Herald,* October 18, 1889, printed as "A Prominent Pioneer: A Son of Nathan Olney Denies Some Statements Made by the Correspondent of an Eastern Journal," *Yakima Herald,* October 24, 1889 ("buying," "fought"); Ronald Todd, "Reader's Scrapbook," *Pacific Northwest Quarterly* 47, no. 3 (July 1956): 95–96, https://www.jstor.org/stable/40487200; Franklin Pierce Olney, "Young Olney's Views," *Yakima Herald,* December 19, 1889 ("open").

55. Henry Sicade, "The Indians' Side of the Story," address to the Research Club of Tacoma, April 10, 1917, in *Building a State, Washington: 1889–1939,* ed. Charles Miles and O. B. Sperlin (Olympia: Washington State Historical Society, 1940): 490–503; Lisa Blee, *Framing Chief Leschi: Narrative and the Politics of Historical Justice* (Chapel Hill: University of North Carolina Press, 2014), 46–49.

56. William S. Lewis, *The Case of Spokane Garry* (1917; repr., Fairfield, Wash.: Galleon Press, 1987), chaps. 5, 4, frontispiece; John Fahey, "The Case of William Lewis," *Pacific Northwest Quarterly* 91, no. 2 (Spring 2000): 86–93, https://www.jstor.org/stable/40492554; David K. Beine, *Whodunnit? The Continuing Case of Chief Spokane Garry* ([Sacramento]: I Street Press, 2021), 47–48, 124–26. It is unclear what mix of altruism and a hope of a future payday (which never came) guided Lewis's uncompensated legal work for Native communities.

57. Fahey, "The Case of William Lewis," esp. 90; William S. Lewis, "The First Militia Companies in Eastern Washington Territory," *Washington Historical*

Quarterly 11, no. 4 (October 1920): 243–49, esp. 244 ("Spokane Invincibles"), https://www.jstor.org/stable/40473837; Donald L. Cutler, *"Hang Them All": George Wright and the Plateau Indian War* (Norman: University of Oklahoma Press, 2016), xv ("justice and fair play"); Stacy Nation-Knapper, " 'Like Putting Birds in a Cage': Territory and the Troubled Life of a Spokane Oral History," *Pacific Northwest Quarterly* 106, no. 3 (Summer 2015): 120–38, esp. 129 ("principally transient"), https://www.jstor.org/stable/44790703; William S. Lewis and Joseph H. Boyd, "Reminiscence of Joseph H. Boyd: An Argonaut of 1857," *Washington Historical Quarterly* 15, no. 4 (October 1924): 243–62, https://www.jstor.org/stable/40474836. See also Carpenter, " 'Justice and Fair Play.' "

58. William S. Lewis, "Oldest Pioneer Laid to Rest," *Washington Historical Quarterly* 17, no. 1 (January 1926): 39–42, esp. 41 (quotations), https://www.jstor.org/stable/40474977; Jean Barman and Bruce M. Watson, "Fort Colvile's Fur Trade Families and the Dynamics of Race in the Pacific Northwest," *Pacific Northwest Quarterly* 90, no. 3 (Summer 1999): 140–53, https://www.jstor.org/stable/40492495.

59. Lewis, "Oldest Pioneer Laid to Rest," 41.

60. George Himes to Clarence Bagley, December 18, 1931, folder 4, box 10, Clarence B. Bagley Papers; Carpenter, " 'Justice and Fair Play' "; Sherry L. Smith, "Reimagining the Indian: Charles Erskine Scott Wood and Frank Linderman," *Pacific Northwest Quarterly* 87, no. 3 (Summer 1996): 149–58, https://www.jstor.org/stable/40491642; Gunlög Fur, "Indian and Immigrants—Entangled Histories," *Journal of American Ethnic History* 33, no. 3 (Spring 2014): 55–76, esp. 61, https://doi.org/10.5406/jamerethnhist.33.3.0055; Nicole Tonkovich, "Parallax, Transit, Transmotion: Reading Race in the Allotment Photographs of E. Jane Gay," *Melus* 39, no. 2 (Summer 2014): 66–92, https://www.jstor.org/stable/44392737; Jennifer Bailey, "Voicing Oppositional Conformity: Sarah Winnemucca and the Politics of Rape, Colonialism, and 'Citizenship': 1870–1890" (master's thesis, Portland State University, 2012), esp. chap. 2; Elias William Nelson, "Making Native Science: Indigenous Epistemologies and Settler Sciences in the United States Empire" (PhD diss., Harvard University, 2018), esp. 58–63.

61. W. J. Dickens to Prof. Ed[mond] S. Meany, October 25, 1920 ("directed to observe), folder 27, box 60, Edmond S. Meany Papers; Gram, "Acting Out Assimilation"; Edmond S. Meany, "A Prophecy Fulfilled," December 21, 1920, 1 ("three hundred"), folder 26, box 60, Edmond S. Meany Papers.

62. Meany, "A Prophecy Fulfilled," 1.

63. Meany, "A Prophecy Fulfilled," 8.

64. Edmond S. Meany, "Indians at School at Fort Spokane," *Seattle Post-Intelligencer*, July 9, 1905 ("means of force"); Edmond S. Meany, "Contracts between Indian Tribes," *Seattle Post-Intelligencer*, July 5 [?], 1905 ("neglected pledges"); Wendt, *The Daughters of the American Revolution and Patriotic Memory*, chap. 3; Pisani, *Imagining Native America in Music*, chap. 8; John

W. Troutman, *Indian Blues: American Indians and the Politics of Music, 1834–1934* (Norman: University of Oklahoma Press, 2009), 233–44; K. Tsianina Lomawaima, "A Principle of Relativity through Indigenous Biography," *Biography* 39, no. 3 (Summer 2016): 248–69, https://www.jstor.org/stable/26405098; Geo[rge] H. Himes to Edmond S. Meany, February 19, 1921, folder 27, box 60, Edmond S. Meany Papers; Katrine Barber, *In Defense of Wyam: Native-White Alliances and the Struggle for Celilo Village* (Seattle: University of Washington Press, 2018); Andrew H. Fisher, "Speaking for the First Americans: Nipo Strongheart and the Campaign for Indian Citizenship," *Oregon Historical Quarterly* 114, no. 4 (Winter 2013): 441–52, https://doi.org/10.5403/oregonhistq.114.4.0441.

65. William Jasper Gilstrap, untitled address, in "Typescripts of addresses to the Pioneer Association, relative to markers on the Oregon Trail," 19 ("sympathy"), vol. 2, box 21, Clarence B. Bagley Papers; William Jasper Gilstrap, *The Memoirs of William Jasper Gilstrap* (copyright 1985; self-published by family 2010), 11–12; Erika Doss, *Memorial Mania: Public Feeling in America* (Chicago: University of Chicago Press, 2010); Robert Strong, "The Uncooperative Primary Source: Literary Recovery versus Historical Fact in the Strange Production of *Cogewea*," in *Building New Bridges: Sources, Methods and Interdisciplinarity*, ed. Jeff Keshen and Sylvie Perrier (Ottawa: University of Ottawa Press, 2005), 63–72, esp. 65 ("too strong"). See also Dolores E. Janiewski, " 'Confusion of Mind': Colonial and Post-Colonial Discourses about Frontier Encounters," *Journal of American Studies* 32, no. 1 (April 1998): 81–103, https://www.jstor.org/stable/27556325; Laurie Arnold, "More Than Mourning Dove: Christine Quintasket—Activist, Leader, Public Intellectual," *Montana: The Magazine of Western History* 67, no. 1 (Spring 2017): 27–45, https://www.jstor.org/stable/26322854.

66. Chelsea K. Vaughn, " 'The Road That Won an Empire': Commemoration, Commercialization, and the Promise of Auto Tourism at the 'Top o' Blue Mountains,' " *Oregon Historical Quarterly* 115, no. 1 (Spring 2014): 6–37, https://doi.org/10.5403/oregonhistq.115.1.0006; Cassandra Tate, *Unsettled Ground: The Whitman Massacre and Its Shifting Legacy in the American West* (Seattle: Sasquatch Books, 2020), 195–96; Talea Anderson, "I Want My Agency Moved Back . . ., My Dear White Sisters": Discourses on Yakama Reservation Reform, 1920s–1930s," *Pacific Northwest Quarterly* 104, no. 4 (Fall 2013): 178–87, https://www.jstor.org/stable/24628811; Maximilian C. Forte, "Seeing beyond the State and Thinking beyond the State of Sight," in *Who Is an Indian? Race, Place, and the Politics of Indigeneity in the Americas*, ed. Forte (Toronto: University of Toronto Press, 2013), 234–41.

Conclusion

1. Harriet Nesmith McArthur, "Recollections of the Rickreall," *Oregon Historical Quarterly* 30, no. 4 (December 1929): 362–83, esp. 377.

2. Omar C. Spencer, "Lewis Ankeny McArthur, 1883–1951," *Oregon Historical Quarterly* 56, no. 1 (March 1955): 4–11, https://www.jstor.org/stable/20612163; Sarah Keyes, "From Stories to Salt Cairns: Uncovering Indigenous Influence in the Formative Years of the Oregon Historical Society, 1898–1905," *Oregon Historical Quarterly* 121, no. 2 (Summer 2020): 186–211, https://doi.org/10.1353/ohq.2020.0050.

3. Claims of long-lost Native heritage must be treated with caution, but it is noteworthy that genealogical records about one Lane ancestor, Col. James Street, tend to note that he was married, but they leave out to whom—which might well indicate some reticence about racial identity. Nina Lane Faubion to J. E. Swain, April 29, 1941 (quotations), folder 1, box 3, Joseph Lane Papers; J. E. Swain to Nina Lane Faubion, May 5, 1941, folder 1, box 3, Joseph Lane Papers; Harry Lane to Nina Lane, April 20, 1904, folder: Harry Lane Correspondence, box 1, Nina Lane Faubion Papers.

4. Nina Lane, "Biography of Joseph Lane" (incomplete draft), 88 ("friend of the Indians," "bad whites"), 1 ("To the everlasting shame"), folder 3, box 2, Joseph Lane Papers,.

5. Joseph Lane to Col. W. M. Cockrum, June 21, 1878 ("treachery"), folder 4, box 2, Joseph Lane Papers; cf. Harriet Lane, "General Joseph Lane and His Relation to the History of Oregon between the Years 1849 and 1853" (bachelor's thesis, University of Oregon, 1909).

6. "Oregon State Capitol," June 13, 1988, National Register of Historic Places no. 10240018, National Park Service, https://npgallery.nps.gov/GetAsset/8e641710-c5bd-4d9e-b66f-192046307e45, 12 ("ancient past"); Barry Faulkner, "Three Murals in the Capitol," in "Creative Historical Research in Fiction, Drama, Art: A Symposium," *Oregon Historical Quarterly* 41, no. 2 (June 1940): 125–36, esp. 132–34, https://www.jstor.org/stable/20611250. See also Ricardo Leon Castro, "The New Oregon State Capitol Building: Events, Sources, and Controversies about Its Design" (master's thesis, University of Oregon, 1976).

7. Leslie M. Scott, "Great Events in Oregon History," in "Addresses Delivered at the Dedication of the State Capitol, October 1, 1938," *Oregon Historical Quarterly* 39, no. 4 (December 1938): 341–51, esp. 341–42 (quotations), https://www.jstor.org/stable/20611146; Frank H. Schwarz, "Three Murals in the Capitol," in "Creative Historical Research in Fiction, Drama, Art," 134–36.

8. Among many other debts owed to scholar and Grand Ronde Nation tribal member David G. Lewis, I am grateful for his insights on the geographical reach and symbolic ubiquity of the golden *Oregon Pioneer*.

9. Cf. William G. Robbins, *Oregon: This Storied Land* (Portland: Oregon Historical Society Press, 2005), esp. chap. 3 (quotations); Nathan Douthit, *Uncertain Encounters: Indians and Whites at Peace and War in Southern Oregon, 1820s–1860s* (Corvallis: Oregon State University Press, 2002).

10. Robert R. Dykstra, "Quantifying the Wild West: The Problematic Statistics of Frontier Violence," *Western Historical Quarterly* 40, no. 3 (Autumn 2009):

321–47, esp. 321 ("conceptually separate"), https://www.jstor.org/stable/40505651.

11. Dykstra, "Quantifying the Wild West," 346 ("excluding firefights"); Randolph Roth, Michael D. Maltz, and Douglas L. Eckberg, "Homicide Rates in the Old West," *Western Historical Quarterly* 42, no. 2 (Summer 2011): 173–95, https://doi.org/10.2307/westhistquar.42.2.0173; Thomas J. DiLorenzo, "The Culture of Violence in the American West: Myth versus Reality," *Independent Review* 15, no. 2 (Fall 2010): 227–39, https://www.jstor.org/stable/24562364; Stewart L. Udall et al., "How the West Got Wild: American Media and Frontier Violence," *Western Historical Quarterly* 31, no. 3 (2000): 277–95, https://doi.org/10.2307/969961. Paula Mitchell Marks, notably, *did* discuss violence against Native people as relevant to the question in this roundtable.

12. Ellen Eisenberg, David Lewis, and April Slabosheski, "History, Place, and the Reckoning with Pioneer Monuments and Memorials," roundtable, Oregon Jewish Museum and Center for Holocaust Education, February 18, 2021; Donald Bloxham, *History and Morality* (New York: Oxford University Press, 2020); Robert Strong, "The Uncooperative Primary Source: Literary Recovery versus Historical Fact in the Strange Production of *Cogewea*," in *Building New Bridges: Sources, Methods and Interdisciplinarity*, ed. Jeff Keshen and Sylvie Perrier (Ottawa: University of Ottawa Press, 2005), 63–72, esp. 65 ("too strong").

13. Loren L. Williams Journals, 1:153–64, Graff 4683, Newberry Library Special Collections, Chicago.

14. Clifford E. Trafzer and Richard D. Scheuerman, *Renegade Tribe: The Palouse Indians and the Invasion of the Inland Pacific Northwest* (Pullman: Washington State University Press, 1986), x ("Of course").

15. On microtechniques of dispossession, see Paige Raibmon, "Unmaking Native Space: A Genealogy of Indian Policy, Settler Practice, and the Microtechniques of Dispossession," in *The Power of Promises: Rethinking Indian Treaties in the Pacific Northwest*, ed. Alexandra Harmon (Seattle: University of Washington Press, 2008), 56–85. On the importance of paying heed to the centrality of force in stories of conquest entangled in paperwork or memory, see, among others, Nancy Shoemaker, *A Strange Likeness: Becoming Red and White in Eighteenth-Century North America* (Oxford: Oxford University Press, 2004), esp. 63–64.

16. Sarah Deer, *Beginning and End of Rape: Confronting Sexual Violence in Native America* (Minneapolis: University of Minnesota Press, 2015), 7 ("White men"); Kevin Bruyneel, *Settler Memory: The Disavowal of Indigeneity and the Politics of Race in the United States* (Chapel Hill: University of North Carolina Press, 2021), 167–68; Sherene H. Razack, *Dying from Improvement: Inquests and Inquiries into Indigenous Deaths in Custody* (Toronto: University of Toronto Press, 2015).

17. Jean M. O'Brien, "Tracing Settler Colonialism's Eliminatory Logic in *Traces of History*," *American Quarterly* 69, no. 2 (June 2017): 249–55, esp. 254 ("Indigenous resistance"), https://www.jstor.org/stable/26360844; Kevin Bruyneel, *The Third Space of Sovereignty: The Postcolonial Politics of U.S.–Indigenous Relations* (Minneapolis: University of Minnesota Press, 2007), esp. xviii; J. Kēhaulani Kauanui, " 'A Structure Not an Event': Settler Colonialism and Enduring Indigeneity," *Lateral* 5, no. 1 (2016), https://csalateral.org/issue/5-1/forum-alt-humanities-settler-colonialism-enduring-indigeneity-kauanui/; Areej Sabbagh-Khoury, "Memory for Forgetfulness: Conceptualizing a Memory Practice of Settler Colonial Disavowal," *Theory and Society* 52 (2023): 263–92, esp. 288–89, https://doi.org/10.1007/s11186-022-09486-0.

Postscript

1. James Gibson remembered himself as a "friend to the Indians," particularly to the Kalapuya at Siletz. Many of his anecdotes involved his own mastery of Chinook Jargon being used to quiet disputes between Native people and White settlers, and he used the language to get land for bargain prices. He turned down a well-paying job as an interpreter in 1852, he claimed, because "to stand between the Indians and the Government is more than I care to undertake." Every pioneer was a hero of their own story (except maybe Jesse Applegate). James Gibson, "From Missouri to Oregon in 1847," transcribed by Minnie Richards, July 23, 1914 (in author's possession); William A. Carpenter, *The Ransom Family Plot: Four Generations in One Cemetery Plot at Forest Grove, Oregon* (Portland: Ransom Family Press, 2017), 19–24; Lillian Gertrude Applegate to Eva Emery Dye, August 5, 1904, folder 3, box 1, Eva Emery Dye Papers.

2. *Sons and Daughters of Oregon Pioneers News* 48, no. 4b (March 2019), https://oregonsdop.org/wp-content/uploads/2019/03/SDOP48-4b.pdf. I did not consent to the faintly eugenic caption that appears beneath a picture that includes me in this newsletter. The organization now welcomes those claiming pioneer status through assertions of Native heritage—one new attendee at the same meeting traced his descent to "Lisette Walla Walla." The July 2024 meeting of this organization featured Shoshone-Bannock performer Ed Edmo, who was celebrated for sharing "fascinating Indian stories." *Sons and Daughters of Oregon Pioneers News* 54, no. 1 (July 2024).

3. K. Rambo, "Pioneer Statues Toppled amid Protests at the University of Oregon," *Oregonian*, June 14, 2020; Brian Klopotek et al., "Why They Had to Go: Statement on the Fall of the Pioneer Statues," *Eugene Weekly*, June 25, 2020; Marc James Carpenter, " 'Two Sides of the Same Story': Colonial Violence and Erasure in the University of Oregon's (Fallen) Pioneer Statues," *Center for the Study of Women and Society Annual Review* 11 (2020): 30–33, https://csws.uoregon.edu/node/3034.

4. Laurel Reed Pavic, "Another One Bites the Dust," *Oregon Artswatch*, October 26, 2020; Albert Boime, "Patriarchy Fixed in Stone: Gutzon Borglum's 'Mount Rushmore,' " *American Art* 5, no. 1–2 (Winter–Spring 1991): 142–67, https://www.jstor.org/stable/3109035; John Taliaferro, *Great White Fathers: The Story of the Obsessive Quest to Create Mount Rushmore* (New York: PublicAffairs, 2002), esp. chap. 8; "News and Comment," *Oregon Historical Quarterly* 34, no. 3 (September 1933): 280–86, esp. 281–82, https://www.jstor.org/stable/20610821.

5. Erika Bolstad, "In Replacing Monuments, Communities Reconsider How the West Was Won," *Stateline*, May 23, 2022 ("conservative protestors"); Elizabeth McLagan, *A Peculiar Paradise: A History of Blacks in Oregon, 1788–1940* (Portland: Georgian Press, 1980), 120; Quinn Spencer, "Hattie Redmond: Suffragist and Founder of Portland's Black Community," *Portland Metro News*, February 17, 2021.

6. Tom Banse, "It's Official: Whitman Statue Being Replaced by One of Tribal-Rights Activist Billy Frank Jr.," Oregon Public Broadcasting, April 14, 2021; Johnny Diaz, "Oregon Removes Lyrics about 'Empire Builders' from State Song," *New York Times*, June 9, 2021.

Acknowledgments

Like anything created in the Americas, this work was researched and written on Indigenous land, some of it unceded, nearly all of it taken unjustly. The bulk of the writing was done on traditional homelands of, among others, Multnomah, Kathlamet, Clackamas, Tumwater, Watlala bands of the Chinook, and Tualatin Kalapuya peoples, and also Chifin, Winefelly, Pee-u (Mohawk), and Chelamela Kalapuya peoples. Much of the editing was done on traditional homelands of Yanktonai and Sisseton-Wahpeton Očeti Šakówiŋ peoples, homelands of Nu'eta (Mandan) and Hidatsa peoples, and homelands of Turtle Mountain Chippewa Ojibwe/Anishinaabe peoples. I hope that there are elements of this book that can be useful to Native people, communities, and nations.

Jeff Ostler has fostered numerous scholars who have reappraised and re-formed the history of the American West, and it an honor to be among their ranks. Excellent scholars are not always excellent mentors, but Jeff is very much both. I couldn't ask for more. Patience Collier is an irreplaceable friend and colleague who has made this book and my life much better—I am grateful to be one of many lives so enriched. I am thankful to Jennifer O'Neal for both counsel and comradery, to Peter Boag for inspiration and encouragement, to Brett Rushforth for never letting up until the point is truly proven, to Brian Klopotek for helping me explore scholarship well outside my comfort zone, to Ari Kelman for revisions and revivification, to Katy Barber for starting me down paths to unexpected places, to Coll Thrush for deep conversations of the historical and personal, to Josh Reid for sage advice on scary subjects, to Marin Aurand for complementary inclinations toward piquant prose, to Curtis Austin for helping me figure out how to be useful, and to Lindsay Braun, Bryna Goodman, Marsha Weisiger, Jack Maddex, James Mohr, Lisa Wolverton, Annelise Heinz, Ryan Jones, Myra Johnson-Orange, Julie Weise, Priscilla Yamin, David Alan Johnson, Tim Garrison, Donna Sinclair, Greg Shine, Tony Johnson, the late Tony Kaye, Matthew Restall, Maia Ramnath, Carol Reardon, Russ Lohse, Jon Brockopp, Ellen Eisenberg, Patricia Schechter, Nichelle Frank, Jack Evans, Moeko Yamazaki, Hayley Brazier,

Spencer Abbe, Preetham Sridharan, Rebecca Hastings, Ian Urrea, Ian Halter, Tyler Sperrazza, Megan J. McDonie, Sara Kern, Kenneth R. Coleman, Corey Larson, Lily Hart, Lindsey Peterson, Akim Reinhardt, John R. Gram, Patrick Lozar, John R. Legg, Raymond Sun, Larry Cebula, Lissa Wadewitz, Sunu Kodumthara, Brian Leech, Kate Stevenson, John Weinzierl, Lisa Lang, Tuya Dutton, Amanda Walch, Brenda Fischer, Esther Wright, Kierra Crago-Schneider, Ed Westermann, Elise Boxer, Adina Popescu, Eva Skewes, Margaret Otzel, Sonia Shannon, Katie Golden, Amanda Cordero, Ann Twombly, Cindy Prescott, Boyd Cothran, Robert D. Johnston, Liza Black, Michael Holloman, Ray Sun, David Lewis, Ruth Steele, Elerina Aldamar, Scott Daniels, and Eliza Canty-Jones for their expertise and assistance.

No scholar ever really works alone, and I owe a litany of debts to all these people and many, many more. My gratitude exceeds my capacity to express it. To all these people, to my loved ones, and to anyone absent from this list who should be present: thank you, thank you, thank you.

Index

Northern Paiute people. *See* Paiute people

Nugen, John, 100

O'Brien, Jean M., 255, 283

Ogden, Peter Skene, 22

"Old Jennie." *See* Oscharwasha

Old Man House. *See* D'Suq'Wub

"Old Sam" (Rogue River leader), 63

Oliphant, James Orin, 222

Olney, Annette. *See* Hallicola, Twa-Wy "Annette"

Olney, Franklin Pierce, 269–70

Olney, Nathan Hale, 43, 176, 178–9, 227–8, 269–70

Olson, Alexander, 241

Olympia (Washington), 116, 119

Ord, Edward Otho Cresap, 70, 231

Oregon Argus (newspaper), 56, 60

Oregon City, 32, 211, 253

Oregon Conference of Missionary Bishops, 208–9

Oregon Constitutional Convention (1857), 60

Oregon Historical Society, 219, 276–7

Oregon Pioneer (Ulric Ellerhusen statue), 278–9

Oregon Pioneer Association, 210, 220–2, 233, 238, 260–1, 285

Oregon Soldiers' Home, 1, 210

Oregon Spectator (newspaper), 60

Oregon State University, 279

Oregon Statesman (newspaper), 36–37, 60

Oregon Trail Association, 274

Oregon Trails of Tears, 8, 55, 64, 127–9, 276–7

Oregonian (newspaper), 60, 218

Oscharwasha, 256–7, 362n20

Osterman, Susan. *See* Alverson, Susan Osterman

Osterman, William Henry, 161–2

Owens-Adair, Bethenia, 260

Owhi, 156–8

packers, colonialism and, 146, 155–7, 197–9, 214, 264, 305n27

Packwood, Robert William, 304n22

Packwood, William Henderson, 58–60, 72, 110, 304n22

Paiute people, 9, 168–9, 173–4, 176, 179–84, 311n17, 318n23

Palmer, Joel, 43–45, 75, 105–7, 127, 131, 139, 208, 265–6

Palouse people. *See* Palus people

Palus people, 30, 92, 146, 153–7, 168, 265, 312n17

Pambrun, Andrew Dominique, 47

Pandosy, Félix Jean Charles, 93, 98, 116, 223–4

"paper fictions." *See* plundering

Parker, Samuel, 24–25, 47, 294n9

Parrish, Josiah, 39

Paulina, 174

Pearson, Henry, 89

Pendleton Round-Up, 267–8

Peo-Peo-Mox-Mox: historical interpretations of, 5–6 109–10, 191, 198, 201, 211–4, 248, 318n20, 319n26; murder and mutilation of, 102, 108–11, 115, 158, 178

Perry, Roland Hinton, 248

Peters, Wynona M., 270

Peterson, Lindsey, 205

Pfeifer, Michael J., 147, 162

Phelps, Thomas Stowell, 105, 293n19

Philippine-American War, 233, 263–4

Pickrell, Cyrus Beede, 262

Pierce County Pioneers Association, 249

Pig War, 202

Pi-li-ni. *See* Paulina

Pioneer, The (Alexander P. Proctor statue), 248, 267–9, 275, 285–7

Pioneer and Democrat (Washington newspaper), 82, 152

pioneer code, 10, 194, 199, 220–3, 226, 238–43, 246

pioneer, definitions of, 13, 21–22, 203–5

Salem (Oregon), 25, 36, 210, 235, 253, 268, 278

Saluskin, Charlie, 161

salvage theology, 25

Sam, Louie, 161

San Francisco (California), 38, 40, 228

Santiam Kalapuya people. *See* Kalapuya people

Sauvie's Island, 23

scalping. *See* body trophies

Schaefer, Kurt Kim, 335n1

Schieffelin, Clinton, 62–63.

Schieffelin, Joseph, 62–63.

Schitsu'umsh. *See* Coeur d'Alene people

Scolari, Paul, 255

Scott, Abigail. *See* Duniway, Abigail Scott

Scott, Harvey Whitefield, 121, 210, 218, 278, 287

Scott, Leslie McChesney, 278, 287

Scott River, 73

Sealth (Suquamish/Duwamish), 78, 255, 257–9

Seattle, Battle of, 121

Seattle, Chief. *See* Sealth

Seattle, Chief of the Suquamish (James A. Wehn statue), 255, 257–9

Seattle (Washington): city of, 79, 81, 93, 103, 120–1, 229; commemoration in, 245, 249, 255, 257–9, 279

Sehome, Julia, 228–30

Seminole Wars, 3, 30, 58, 90, 95, 153

settler colonialism: scripts of, 2–4, 25, 28, 41, 52, 199–201, 204–6, 212, 240–1, 268, 280–2; theories of, 21–2, 166–7, 177, 200–5, 214–5, 282–4

settler colonial sin-eaters, 10, 33, 72, 113, 186–9, 190, 202, 223, 226, 305n27

Sexton, David, 71

sexual assault: and cover-ups, 124, 131, 188, 224–7, 232, 283; as a part of pioneer culture, 51–52, 61, 94, 188, 223,

230, 279, 283; by pioneers, 51–52, 55, 60–61, 89–90, 127, 131, 186–8, 223–8, 254, 257, 277, 279, 350n15; by U.S. soldiers 35, 37, 129, 169, 226, 254.

Shackleford, Roxa S., 81

Shaw, Benjamin Franklin, 46, 117, 119, 121–2, 148, 204, 231, 240

Shaw, Mack, 109–110

Shaw Massacre, 46, 51, 121–2, 148, 204, 231

Shelton, Harriette. *See* Dover, Harriette Shelton

Shelton, Ruth, 228–30

She-nah-nam, Treaty of. *See* Medicine Creek, 1854 Treaty of

Sheridan, Philip Henry, 75, 237, 313n31

Shoshone: attacks on, 2, 4, 91, 169, 171–2; expressions of hatred against, 9, 22, 168–9, 318n23

Sh-yas-tenoe. *See* Shelton, Ruth

Si?al. *See* Sealth (Suquamish/Duwamish)

Sicade, Henry, 115, 270

Siletz Reservation, 59, 130, 134, 146, 276, 373n1

Silverton (Oregon), 31

Silvies River, 179

Silvies River Battle, 181–3

Simmons, Michael Troutman, 46, 81, 103

Sinclair, James, 109

Sixes River Band. *See* Tututni people

Skimarwaw, 154

Skinner, Eugene F., 74

slavery: family legacies of, 58, 159, 197; in the Pacific Northwest, 23, 60–61, 116, 175, 247, 287, 304n24, 321n48; as a political cause, 38, 116, 183–4, 200, 279

Sleeper-Smith, Susan, 88

Slough-Keetcha. *See* Garry, Spokane

Smith, John E., 146, 156

Smith, William C., 30

"Snake" as a slur, 9, 22, 168, 311n17

Snake River, 22